NATIONAL CLEANSING

National Cleansing examines the prosecution of more than one hundred thousand suspected war criminals and collaborators by Czech courts and tribunals after the Second World War. This comprehensive history of postwar Czech retribution provides a new perspective on Czechoslovakia's transition from Nazi occupation to Stalinist rule in the turbulent decade from the Munich Pact of September 1938 to the Communist coup d'état of February 1948. Based on archival sources that remained inaccessible during the Cold War, *National Cleansing* demonstrates the central role of retribution in the postwar power struggle and the expulsion of the Sudeten Germans. In contrast to general histories of postwar Czechoslovakia, which have traditionally portrayed retribution as little more than Communist-inspired political justice, this book illustrates that the prosecution of collaborators and war criminals represented a genuine, if deeply flawed, attempt to confront the crimes of the past, including those committed by the Czechs themselves.

Benjamin Frommer is Assistant Professor of History at Northwestern University.

Studies in the Social and Cultural History of Modern Warfare

General Editor
Jay Winter *Yale University*

Advisory Editors
Omer Bartov *Brown University*
Carol Gluck *Columbia University*
David M. Kennedy *Stanford University*
Paul Kennedy *Yale University*
Antoine Prost *Université de Paris-Sorbonne*
Emmanuel Sivan *Hebrew University of Jerusalem*
Robert Wohl *University of California, Los Angeles*

In recent years the field of modern history has been enriched by the exploration of two parallel histories. These are the social and cultural history of armed conflict, and the impact of military events on social and cultural history.

Studies in the Social and Cultural History of Modern Warfare presents the fruits of this growing area of research, reflecting both the colonization of military history by cultural historians and the reciprocal interest of military historians in social and cultural history, to the benefit of both. The series offers the latest scholarship in European and non-European events from the 1850s to the present day.

For a list of titles in the series, please see end of book.

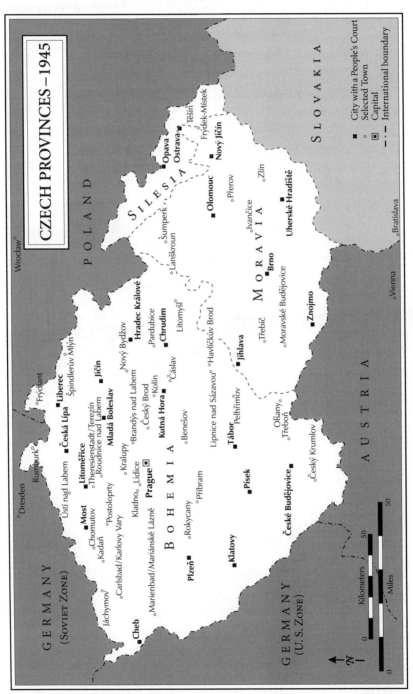

CZECH PROVINCES – 1945

GERMANY
(SOVIET ZONE)

POLAND

SLOVAKIA

AUSTRIA

GERMANY
(U.S. ZONE)

BOHEMIA

MORAVIA

SILESIA

°Dresden

Wrocław°

°Rumburk

°Frýdlant

■ Liberec
■ Česká Lípa
Špindlerův Mlýn°

°Jáchymov

Cheb ■

°Carlsbad/Karlovy Vary

°Marienbad/Mariánské Lázně

Ústí nad Labem ■
Litoměřice ■
°Theresienstadt/Terezín
°Roudnice nad Labem
Mladá Boleslav ■
Jičín ■
°Nový Bydžov

■ Most
°Chomutov
°Kadaň
°Postoloprty
Kladno° °Lidice
Prague ▣
Brandýs nad Labem
°Český Brod
Kolín°
Kutná Hora ■
°Čáslav

°Kralupy

Hradec Králové ■
Pardubice°
Chrudim ■
°Litomyšl
°Lanškroun
Šumperk°

Opava °
Ostrava ■
Těšín°
Frýdek-Místek°
Nový Jičín ■

Olomouc ■
°Přerov
Zlín°

■ Plzeň
°Rokycany
°Příbram

Písek ■

Klatovy ■

České Budějovice ■

°Český Krumlov

Benešov°
Lipnice nad Sázavou°
°Havlíčkův Brod
Tábor ■
Pelhřimov°
Jihlava ■
Olšany°
°Třeboň

Třebíč°
Moravské Budějovice°
Znojmo ■
Ivančice°
Brno ■
Uherské Hradiště ■

°Vienna

°Bratislava

N

Kilometers
Miles

0   50
0   50

■ City with a People's Court
○ Selected Town
▣ Capital
∙–∙– International boundary

Map of the Czech provinces, 1945

NATIONAL CLEANSING

Retribution against Nazi Collaborators in Postwar Czechoslovakia

BENJAMIN FROMMER
Northwestern University

CAMBRIDGE
UNIVERSITY PRESS

PUBLISHED BY THE PRESS SYNDICATE OF THE UNIVERSITY OF CAMBRIDGE
The Pitt Building, Trumpington Street, Cambridge, United Kingdom

CAMBRIDGE UNIVERSITY PRESS
The Edinburgh Building, Cambridge CB2 2RU, UK
40 West 20th Street, New York, NY 10011-4211, USA
477 Williamstown Road, Port Melbourne, VIC 3207, Australia
Ruiz de Alarcón 13, 28014 Madrid, Spain
Dock House, The Waterfront, Cape Town 8001, South Africa

http://www.cambridge.org

First published 2005

Printed in the United States of America

Typeface Sabon 10.25/14 pt.   *System* LaTeX 2_ε [TB]

A catalog record for this book is available from the British Library.

Library of Congress Cataloging in Publication Data
Frommer, Benjamin, 1969–
National cleansing : retribution against Nazi collaborators
in postwar Czechoslovakia / Benjamin Frommer.
p.   cm. – (Studies in the social and cultural history of modern warfare; 20)
Includes bibliographical references and index.
ISBN 0-521-81067-1 – ISBN 0-521-00896-4 (pbk.)
1. War crime trials – Czechoslovakia.   2. War criminals – Czechoslovakia.
3. World War, 1939–1945 – Collaborationists – Czechoslovakia.
I. Title.   II. Series.
KJP43.F76   2004
341.6′9 – dc22   2004041848

ISBN 0 521 81067 1 hardback
ISBN 0 521 00896 4 paperback

To my parents

CONTENTS

ACKNOWLEDGMENTS

As a young scholar, I have been extraordinarily fortunate to have had two mentors: István Deák, who first inspired me to study Central Europe and to pursue an academic career, and Roman Szporluk, whose sage counsel, stimulating ideas, and indefatigable encouragement were instrumental in this accomplishment. Several other scholars deserve special acknowledgment for the important roles they have played in my development as a historian: David Blackbourn, John Bushnell, Jan Gross, Peter Hayes, Tony Judt, Igor Lukes, Charles Maier, Edward Muir, and Norman Naimark. Many other friends and colleagues have provided invaluable support of various sorts along the way. I express my fondest appreciation to Brad Abrams, John Baick, David Brandenburger, Chad Bryant, Noel Calhoun, Peter Carroll, Abby Collins, John Connelly, Patrice Dabrowski, Lisa Eschenbach, Melissa Feinberg, Brodie Fisher, Eagle Glassheim, John Glenn, Anna Grzymala-Busse, Padraic Kenney, Jeremy King, Katerina P. King, Alexandra Kirilcuk, Eric Klinenberg, Rita Krueger, Jen Light, Eric Lohr, Michal Musil, Ethan Shagan, Ana Siljak, Tim Snyder, Corinna Treitel, and Milada Vachudova. To my friends outside of academia, from Wellesley, New York, Prague, Boston, and Chicago, I express my heartfelt thanks for their continued support and understanding. Finally, I owe an immense debt to Darina Jirotková, Vladimír Vavrečka, Honza, and Míša for their generous friendship.

A number of institutions at home and abroad have generously aided my research, first among them, the Minda de Gunzburg Center for European Studies at Harvard University and the Department of History at Northwestern University. I thank the scholars of the Ústav pro soudobé dějiny (especially Karel Jech, Jiří Jindra, Karel Kaplan, Vilém Prečan, František Svátek, and Oldřich Tůma) for their insights and assistance when I was in Prague. Several librarians and archivists have extended help far beyond what could have been reasonably expected: Zuzana Nagy and Heda Margolius Kovaly at Harvard University and Jana Nováková and Dalibor Státník in the Czech Republic. I also thank Mečislav Borák and Dušan Janák of the Slezský ústav in Opava and Slavomír Michálek and Michal Barnovský of the Historický ústav in Bratislava. I further wish to express my gratitude to Gary Cohen, Martin Conway, Gabriella Etmektsoglou, Pieter Judson, Peter Romijn, Marsha Rozenblit, Philipp Ther, Jindřich Toman, Nancy Wingfield, and Larry Wolff for having given me the opportunity to present and publish my work in various forums. In addition to the Center for European Studies, several foundations deserve great appreciation for the financial support they have provided to this project: the American Council of Learned Societies (ACLS), the Jacob K. Javits Fellowship for the Humanities, the Fulbright–Hays Doctoral Dissertation Research Abroad (DDRA) Program, and the International Research and Exchanges Board (IREX).

As for my family, especially my wife Martina, parents Alan and Judy, and sister Michèle, my gratitude is immeasurable. Without them, this project and everything else I have accomplished would have been impossible.

ABBREVIATIONS IN TEXT
AND NOTES

AKPR   Archiv Kanceláře prezidenta republiky (Archive of the President's Office)

AMV   Archiv Ministerstva vnitra (Archive of the Interior Ministry)

ar.j., aj.   archivní jednotka (archive unit number)

ČNR   Česká národní rada (Czech National Council)

ČSD   Československá sociální demokracie (Social Democratic Party)

ČSL   Československá strana lidová (People's Party)

ČSNS   Československá strana národně socialistická (National Socialist Party)

CU   Columbia University Rare Books and Manuscript Library, New York

DS   Demokratická strana (Democratic Party)

f.   fond (archival file)

IMT   International Military Tribunal

k.   karton (archival carton)

KPR   Kancelář prezidenta republiky (Office of the President of the Republic)

KSČ   Komunistická strana Československa (Communist Party of Czechoslovakia)

KSS   Komunistická strana Slovenska (Communist Party of Slovakia)

ABBREVIATIONS IN TEXT AND NOTES

MLS   Mimořádný lidový soud (Extraordinary People's Court)

BR	Brno	KH	Kutná Hora	OP	Opava
CB	České Budějovice	KL	Klatovy	OS	Ostrava
CH	Cheb ·	LB	Liberec	PI	Písek
CL	Česká Lípa	LT	Litoměřice	PL	Plzeň (Pilsen)
CR	Chrudim	MB	Mladá Boleslav	PR	Praha (Prague)
HK	Hradec Králové	MO	Most	TA	Tábor
JC	Jičín	NJ	Nový Jičín	UH	Uherské Hradiště
JH	Jihlava	OL	Olomouc	ZN	Znojmo

MNO   Ministerstvo národní obrany (Ministry of National Defense)

MNV   Místní národní výbor (Local National Committee)

MS   Ministerstvo spravedlnosti (Ministry of Justice)

MS-L   Ministerstvo spravedlnosti-Londýn (Ministry of Justice in London)

MV   Ministerstvo vnitra (Ministry of Interior)

MZV   Ministerstvo zahraničních věcí (Ministry of Foreign Affairs)

MZV-VA   Výstřižkový archiv (Ministry of Foreign Affairs' newspaper cuttings archive)

NKVD   People's Commissariat of Internal Affairs

NOF   Národní obec fašistická (National Fascist Community)

NOÚZ   Národní odborová ústředna zaměstnanecká (National Union of Employees)

NS   Národní soud (National Court)

NSDAP   Nationalsozialistische Deutsche Arbeiterpartei (National Socialist German Worker's Party)

ONV   Okresní národní výbor (District National Committee)

PNS   Prozatímní národní shromáždění (Provisional National Assembly)

SA   Sturmabteilung (Storm Troopers)

SD   Sicherheitsdienst (Nazi Security Service)

SdP   Sudetendeutsche Partei (Sudeten German Party)

sign.   signatura (archival identification label)

SNB   Sbor národní bezpečnosti (National Security Corps)

SNR   Slovenská národna rada (Slovak National Council)

SOA   Státní oblastní archiv (State Regional Archive)

SOkA   Státní okresní archiv (State District Archive)

SOPV	Svaz osvobozených politických vězňů (Union of Liberated Political Prisoners)
SS	Schutzstaffeln (Protective Corps)
SÚA	Státní ústřední archiv (State Central Archive)
sv.	svazek (archival sheaf/volume)
TNK	Trestní nalézací komise (Penal Adjudication Commission)
ÚNS	Ústavodárné národní shromáždění (Constitutive National Assembly)
ÚNV	Ústřední národní výbor (Central National Committee)
UNWCC	United Nations War Crimes Commission
ÚPV	Úřad předsednictva vlády (Office of the Government Presidium)
ÚRO	Ústřední rada odborů (Central Council of Unions)
ÚV	Ústřední výbor (Central Committee)
VHA	Vojenský historický archiv (Military History Archive)
VK	Vyšetřovací komise (Investigative commission)
ZNV	Zemský národní výbor (Provincial National Committee)

NATIONAL CLEANSING

INTRODUCTION

In December 1945 Czechoslovak President Edvard Beneš triumphantly accepted an honorary doctorate of law from Prague's Charles University. Nearly seven years after the Nazis had destroyed his country, Beneš publicly reflected on the principles that had guided his struggle to reestablish the Czechoslovak state and ensure its future security and prosperity. In his commencement address the President emphasized the need for his compatriots "to open the gates of change to the social and economic structure of our national society." First, however, the country had to reckon with its past: postwar Czechoslovakia's primary objectives, he explained, must include "punishment for the guilt and mistakes of the previous regime . . . [for] Nazism and fascism."[1] In linking revolutionary change to retributive justice, Beneš echoed the sentiments of political leaders across Europe. In his classic account of postwar French retribution, Peter Novick noted, "the purge was considered the necessary prerequisite for . . . the removal of impediments to the renovation and reconstruction of the nation."[2] Throughout the newly liberated continent governments committed themselves to punish Nazis, war criminals, and those who had collaborated with them. The French prosecuted Pétain, the Norwegians tried Quisling, and the Allied Powers established the International Military Tribunal at Nuremberg to hold Germany's leaders accountable for "crimes against peace" and "humanity." Amid a wave of popular anger, retribution was not limited to the foremost Nazis

---

[1] Edvard Beneš, *Světová krise, kontinuita práva a nové právo revoluční: Projev na právnické fakultě Karlovy university při slavnostní promoci na doktora práv h.c.* (Prague: V. Linhart, 1946), 33–35.

[2] Peter Novick, *The Resistance versus Vichy: The Purge of Collaborators in Liberated France* (New York: Columbia University Press, 1968), vii.

and the political elite of countries that had been occupied by or allied with Germany; ordinary men and women who had betrayed their acquaintances, neighbors, and relatives were put on trial, convicted, and sentenced to lengthy prison terms, even death. Thus, in the wake of the Second World War, a remarkable phenomenon occurred: As István Deák wrote, "For the first time in history, a whole continent made an attempt to settle accounts with its own political crimes and criminals."[3]

When it came to punishing its own citizens few states in postwar Europe were as thorough as Czechoslovakia. Beginning in the spring of 1945 the country's multiparty government implemented a comprehensive program of "national cleansing" [*národní očista*] designed to right past wrongs and deter future crimes. "In both Slavic and German usages, 'cleansing' has a dual meaning," Norman Naimark explained, "one purges the native community of foreign bodies, and one purges one's own people of alien elements."[4] In the Czech case the "foreign bodies" were the Sudeten Germans, nearly three million of whom were expelled from the country after the war. The "national cleansing," however, also targeted "alien elements" from the Czechs' own ranks. The regime led by Edvard Beneš banned political parties considered responsible for the German occupation, expropriated and redistributed the property of suspected traitors, and purged alleged collaborators from the civil service, the academy, and the arts. Most significantly, the country's postwar leaders created a massive system of summary courts and administrative tribunals designed to "cleanse" society of anyone who had betrayed the Czechoslovak state or oppressed its citizens. In the wake of the Nazi occupation, Czech "People's Courts" tried more than 32,000 alleged collaborators and war criminals. Local tribunals vetted approximately 135,000 cases of so-called "offenses against national honor."[5] Tens of thousands more were arrested, incarcerated for months, then summarily

---

[3] István Deák, "Resistance, Collaboration, and Retribution during World War II and Its Aftermath," *Hungarian Quarterly* 35:134 (1994), 74.

[4] Norman Naimark, *Fires of Hatred: Ethnic Cleansing in Twentieth-Century Europe* (Cambridge, MA: Harvard University Press, 2001), 4–5.

[5] Prokop Drtina, *Na soudu národa: Tři projevy ministra spravedlnosti dr. Prokopa Drtiny o činnosti Mimořádných lidových soudů a Národního soudu* (Prague: Min. spravedlnosti, 1947), 11–12; "Výsledky retribuce," appendix to no. 142.028/48-Pres-7, Vojenský historický archiv (VHA), Prague, f. Čepička, sv. 23, aj. 168; *L'ud* (6 February 1949), Státní ústřední archiv (SÚA), Prague, f. MZV-VA II, k. 218; "Informace pro pana ministra vnitra: Výsledek činnosti národních výborů podle dekretu č. 138/45 sb.," MV no. B-2220-12/8-47-I/2, SÚA, f. MV-NR (B2220), k. 2017, sv. 2.

released without ever being prosecuted. Prior to the Communist coup d'état of February 1948, the Czechs legally executed nearly 700 defendants – more than in the subsequent four decades of Communist rule combined.[6]

This book focuses on "retribution" in the provinces of Bohemia, Moravia, and Silesia – the territory of today's Czech Republic. Developments in neighboring Slovakia, the eastern half of the former Czechoslovakia, are not examined in depth here for the primary reason that in 1945 Slovak resistance leaders successfully demanded the right to punish their nation's collaborators and oppressors themselves. Consequently, Czechoslovakia came to have a dualistic system of retribution, with one set of laws and courts for Slovakia, another for the Czech provinces.[7] Contemporary Czechs employed the foreign term "retribution" [retribuce] to refer specifically to the formal prosecution of Nazi war criminals and collaborators by legally sanctioned state organs. Postwar Czech retribution encompassed the institutions and processes resulting from three presidential decrees: the "Great Decree" (no. 16/1945), which established twenty-four Extraordinary People's Courts for the prosecution of "Nazi criminals, traitors, and their accomplices"; Decree no. 17/1945, which created a National Court in Prague to try the most prominent Czech collaborators; and the "Small Decree" (no. 138/1945), which granted local authorities the power to punish Czechs for "offenses against national honor." Vojta Beneš, the highly respected older brother of the country's president, estimated in June 1947 that the three decrees had affected approximately 1.5 million

---

[6] According to the most recent and extensive tally, the Czechoslovak state officially executed 450 convicts from the time President Edvard Beneš resigned in June 1948 until the fall of the Communist regime in November 1989. (Between February and June 1948 only a handful of defendants were put to death by reestablished retribution courts.) Karel Kaplan, "Zemřeli ve věznicích a tresty smrti 1948–1956," in Dokumenty o perzekuci a odporu, sv. 1 (Prague: Ústav pro soudobé dějiny, 1992), 73–80; Hobza, Těsnopisecké zprávy Ústavodárného národního shromáždění Republiky československé (ÚNS) 56 (10 June 1947), 46; Otakar Liška et al., Vykonané tresty smrti Československo 1918–1989 (Prague: Úřad dokumentace a vyšetřování zločinů komunismu, 2000), 154.

[7] The term "Czech provinces" is a neologism in English, intended as the counterpart to "Slovakia." The author aims thus to convey the contemporary understanding of the term České země as the "Czech" part of "Czechoslovakia" without provoking a fruitless (and, in the postwar period, anachronistic) debate over whether the modifier české should, in fact, be translated as the English word "Bohemian." Although historically České země referred to the "Bohemian lands" of the Crown of St. Wenceslas, by the Second World War the term was popularly associated with the Czech nation, not the long-defunct Bohemian Kingdom.

individuals (counting suspects and their dependents) in the Czech provinces alone.[8]

In the same speech the elder Beneš told the Czechoslovak National Assembly, "For fifty years we will study retribution and all that provoked it."[9] The punishment of collaborators and war criminals generated more controversy than perhaps any other topic in contemporary Czechoslovakia – the parliamentary debate at which the president's sibling uttered his prediction was the longest of the period.[10] Today, however, it is clear that he was mistaken. For decades Czech retribution was not studied; in fact, despite its enormous size and scope, until recently it had been all but forgotten. The Czechoslovak Communist regime dissuaded scholars at home from investigating the postwar period.[11] Researchers from abroad were also unable to access the necessary archives. As a result, during the Cold War the Czechs' prosecution of collaborators and war criminals earned at most cursory, polemical mention in general histories of the country, whether published in the West or in Czechoslovakia.[12] In the past decade Czech scholars have begun to investigate the People's Courts, but their studies have been primarily limited to analyses of selected regions, trials, or topics.[13] Only in the last few years has research even started on the punishment of "offenses

[8] V. Beneš, 56 ÚNS (10 June 1947), 69.

[9] V. Beneš, 56 ÚNS (10 June 1947), 63.

[10] Prokop Drtina, *Československo můj osud* (Toronto: Sixty-Eight Publishers, 1982), II:310–11.

[11] Under Communist rule only one article was published in Czech about the "national cleansing," and it was devoted solely to a recital of the retribution laws. See Radim Foustka, "Národní očista v letech 1945 až 1946," *Československý časopis historický* 3 (1955), 626–42. Two former participants in the trial of Jozef Tiso, Slovakia's wartime president, published studies of Slovak retribution. See Igor Daxner, *L'udactvo pred národným súdom 1945–1947* (Bratislava: SAV, 1961); Anton Rašla, *L'udové súdy v Československu po II. svetovej vojne ako forma mimoriadneho súdnictva* (Bratislava: SAV, 1969).

[12] The one notable exception is the memoirs of former Justice Minister Prokop Drtina. See Prokop Drtina, *Československo můj osud* (Toronto: Sixty-Eight Publishers, 1982).

[13] Mečislav Borák's in-depth analysis of the Ostrava People's Court begins with a summary of Czech retribution as a whole. Mečislav Borák, *Spravedlnost podle dekretu: Retribuční soudnictví v ČSR a Mimořádný lidový soud v Ostravě (1945–1948)* (Ostrava: Tilia, 1998); Mečislav Borák, ed., *Retribuce v ČSR a národní podoby antisemitismu: Židovská problematika a antisemitismus ve spisech mimořádných lidových soudů a trestních komisí ONV v letech 1945–1948* (Prague: Ústav pro soudobé dějiny, 2002); Václav Jiřík, *Nedaleko od Norimberku. Z dějin Mimořádného lidového soudu v Chebu v letech 1946 až 1948* (Cheb: Svět křídel, 2000); Dušan Janák, "Činnost Mimořádného lidového soudu Opava v letech 1945–1948," *Časopis Slezského zemského muzea* B43 (1994), 245–83; Michal Musil, "Příběh Háchova politického

INTRODUCTION

against national honor."[14] Although there is now a rich historiography on retribution in Western European countries after the Second World War,[15] recent international compilations on the topic have not included chapters on the Czech "national cleansing."[16] The following pages, thus, aim to fill in one of the blankest of Czech history's many "blank spaces."[17]

The paucity of literature on postwar retribution has necessitated that this study be based primarily on archival sources. Until the Velvet Revolution of 1989, most of these materials were off limits even to those scholars approved by the Communist regime. The opening of Czech archives in the 1990s cast new light on a range of historical issues concerning retribution. Court records, including interrogation reports, witness depositions, and trial transcripts, help to reorient the study of the Nazi occupation from isolated instances of resistance to the everyday experience of collaboration. Correspondence between local officials and

sekretáře: Josef Kliment před Národním soudem roku 1947," *Soudobé dějiny* 4 (1995), 530–44.

[14] From the Communist coup of February 1948 until the Velvet Revolution of 1989, not a single scholarly piece, not to mention a monograph, was written on the punishment of "offenses against national honor" either in Czechoslovakia or in the West. Over the past decade several authors have briefly commented on the Small Decree, but only recently have the first articles on the topic emerged, and these only consider the prosecution of anti-Semitic acts. See the articles by Marie Crhová, Miroslav Kružík, Andrea Lněníčková, and Jan Ryba in Borák, ed., *Retribuce v ČSR a národní podoby antisemitismu*.

[15] For example, Martin Conway, "Justice in Postwar Belgium: Popular Passions and Political Realities," *Cahiers d'Histoire du Temps Présent* 2 (1997), 7–34; Luc Huyse and Steven Dhondt, *La répression des collaborations 1942–1952: Un passé toujours présent* (Brussels: Crisp, 1993); Alice Kaplan, *The Collaborator: The Trial and Execution of Robert Brasillach* (Chicago: University of Chicago Press, 2000); Fred Kupferman, *Le Procès de Vichy: Pucheu, Pétain, Laval* (Brussels: Editions Complexe, 1980); Henry Lloyd Mason, *The Purge of the Dutch Quislings* (The Hague: Nijhoff, 1952); Herbert Lottman, *The People's Anger: Justice and Revenge in Post-Liberation France* (London: Hutchinson, 1986); Peter Novick, *The Resistance versus Vichy: The Purge of Collaborators in Liberated France* (New York: Columbia University Press, 1968).

[16] István Deák, Jan T. Gross, and Tony Judt, eds., *The Politics of Retribution in Europe: World War II and its Aftermath* (Princeton, NJ: Princeton University Press, 2000), includes a chapter about the Tiso trial in Slovakia (Bradley Abrams, "The Politics of Retribution: The Trial of Jozef Tiso in the Czechoslovak Environment," pp. 252–89). See also Klaus-Dietmar Henke and Hans Wollar, eds., *Politische Säuberung in Europa* (Munich: Deutscher Taschenbuch Verlag, 1991); Claudia Kuretsidis-Haider and Winfried R. Garscha, eds., *Keine "Abrechnung." NS-Verbrechen, Justiz und Gesellschaft in Europa nach 1945* (Leipzig: Akademische Verlagsanstalt, 1998); Neil Kritsch, ed., *Transitional Justice: How Emerging Democracies Reckon with Former Regimes*, 3 vols. (Washington, DC: United States Institute of Peace Press, 1995).

[17] Jan Křen, *Bílá místa v našich dějinách?* (Prague: Lidové noviny, 1990), 48 and *passim*.

5

the Ministries of Interior and Justice illustrate the problems that arose in the quest to punish hundreds of thousands of alleged collaborators. Personal appeals and anonymous denunciations to the Czechoslovak president expose aspects of postwar life that did not necessarily leave a trace in official government records. The political competition that marked the period before February 1948 created considerable space for the press to criticize inconsistencies and injustices, including those caused and revealed by retribution. Together these and other archival sources illustrate the contingent nature of the postwar power struggle and the complexity of contemporary views of allegiance.

To the limited extent that historians have considered postwar retribution, they have traditionally dismissed trials of collaborators as little more than a partisan purge. This dominant frame for understanding retribution was established before the courts even tried their first defendants. In early April 1945 Klement Gottwald, the leader of the Czechoslovak Communist Party, explained the potential value of "national cleansing" to a gathering of party cadres:

[A] tool, which we have today in the fight for leadership of the nation, is the struggle against traitors and collaborators – that is, against the physical leaders of the compromised Slovak and Czech bourgeoisie. . . . [The] law for the prosecution of traitors and collaborators is a very sharp weapon, with which we can cut so many limbs away from the bourgeoisie that only its trunk will remain. This is a matter of the class struggle against the bourgeoisie – a struggle waged under the banner of the state and the nation, under the banner of the republic. Not to use this weapon is to let it rust. With this weapon we can strike our enemy directly, physically.[18]

Taking their cue from Gottwald, during the Cold War non-Communist scholars regularly condemned the trials as political, contentious, and, above all, unjust. When these authors mentioned retribution at all, they argued that the attempt "to eradicate . . . the Nazi and fascist evil," to quote the Great Decree's preamble, created the conditions for another form of totalitarianism, Stalinism, to succeed. Indiscriminate arrests contributed to an atmosphere of legal uncertainty, while the Communist Party, through its operatives in the administrative apparatus and security forces, abused the charge of collaboration for political gain.

---

[18] SÚA, f. 1 (ZÚV KSČ), sv. 1, aj. 1, str. 14; *Komunistická strana Slovenska: Dokumenty z konferencií a plén 1944–1948* (Bratislava: Pravda, 1971), 144.

According to one prominent Czech émigré, after the Second World War the Communists "controlled the Revolutionary Tribunals, the People's Courts, the Police, the Ministry of the Interior [and] the Committees for trying a citizen for offenses against the nation's honor."[19] Even those trials that clearly had no connection to the postwar political struggle have been dismissed en masse as motivated by little more than personal vengeance and greed. In retrospect, Ladislav Feierabend, a conservative opponent of the Party, wrote that retribution "belongs among the saddest pages of Czech history." Pavel Tigrid, one of country's foremost liberals at home and in exile, dismissed postwar trials as "perverted justice." Similar opinions long dominated more detached analyses of the period: For example, historian Vilém Hejl wrote, "Retribution did not strive for justice; its goal was retaliation, in other words, revenge."[20]

The losers of Czechoslovakia's postwar power struggle were not the only ones dissatisfied with retribution. Despite Gottwald's high hopes, after the war Communist leaders bitterly complained in public and private about the People's Courts' allegedly partisan bias and overall leniency. After the 1948 Communist coup d'état the newly installed Justice Minister, Alexej Čepička, commented,

Retribution [before 1948] was carried out according to class such that full, almost draconian penalties were handed down to minor transgressors from the weakest social classes. At the same time, thanks to sabotage by judicial officials, many members of the wealthy classes, particularly the haute-bourgeoisie, either entirely escaped punishment or the punishment meted out to them was laughably small in comparison to their guilt.[21]

Čepička's claims were likely designed in part to justify a purge of judges and the "haute-bourgeoisie." Nevertheless, public criticism of courts' allegedly lenient treatment of prominent defendants – whose guilt had been trumpeted throughout their trials by the Communist press – cannot be discarded as mere propaganda. Internal documents reveal that the Communist leadership was disappointed, and ordinary cadres disoriented, by the failure of the Party to enforce its interpretation of wartime

---

[19] Jan Stransky, *East Wind over Prague* (New York: Random House, 1951), 83.
[20] Ladislav Feierabend, *Politické vzpomínky*, 3 vols. (Brno: Atlantis, 1994–1996), III:349; Pavel Tigrid, *Kapesní průvodce inteligentní ženy po vlastním osudu* (Toronto: Sixty-Eight Publishers, 1988), 373–74; Vilém Hejl, *Zpráva o organizovaném násilí* (Prague: Univerzum, 1990), 21–23.
[21] Alexej Čepička, *Zlidovění soudnictví* (Prague: Min. informací a osvěty, 1949), 21.

collaboration on the courts. Contrary to Gottwald's prediction, the documentary evidence demonstrates that prosecutors and judges prevented the more extreme forms of retribution desired by the leaders of the Communist Party. Largely independent courts helped to mitigate abuses perpetrated by the partisan police and thus proved a surprising buttress to postwar democracy.

In recent years Czech historians Mečislav Borák and Václav Jiřík have written admirable studies of individual People's Courts that have moved scholarship beyond its traditional focus on the Communist Party's manipulation of postwar justice.[22] Nonetheless, the year 1948 continues to exert a hegemony over postwar Czechoslovak historiography in much the same way that 1933 has dominated scholarship on Weimar Germany. Retribution, however, was more than a derivative and determinant of the contemporary power struggle that culminated in the Communist coup d'état. The trials and the controversies they engendered were central to a national debate about the conduct and values of the Czechs both during the occupation and after liberation. The country's postwar Justice Minister, Prokop Drtina, explained,

As long as it was a matter of judging the guilt of Germans, on the whole there was not, in principle, unfavorable criticism in our press or among the public. By contrast, when it came to judging the guilt of individuals prosecuted from the Czechs' ranks, it was very often apparent that... there was not a unified perspective among the public or even the people's judges.[23]

The Czechs' disunity was not unusual in Europe. "Everywhere, the courts struggled with a definition of collaboration," Deák wrote. "Since no consensus existed, every national assembly, in fact nearly every court, arrived at its own definition."[24] In the Czech provinces, political elites, the general public, and, most importantly, the courts developed various definitions of what constituted "collaboration" and what, in contrast, was justifiable accommodation necessary to survive the occupation. The answer was not merely academic – it was a matter of a defendant's liberty or even life.

---

[22] Mečislav Borák, *Spravedlnost podle dekretu: Retribuční soudnictví v ČSR a Mimořádný lidový soud v Ostravě (1945–1948)* (Ostrava: Tilia, 1998); Václav Jiřík, *Nedaleko od Norimberku: Z dějin Mimořádného lidového soudu v Chebu v letech 1946 až 1948* (Cheb: Svět křídel, 2000).

[23] Drtina, *Na soudu národa*, 16.

[24] Deák, "Introduction," in Deák et al., eds., *Politics of Retribution*, 10.

Throughout Europe, postwar retribution failed to satisfy most everyone. As memory of wartime atrocities faded, many complained that the punishment of collaborators was merely a cover for the elimination of political opponents and personal enemies. Others claimed that war criminals and collaborators escaped unscathed or with minimal punishment. In Czechoslovakia the Communist takeover of February 1948 has tended to make all that came before seem a cause or at least a precondition of democracy's demise. Retribution's impact on Czech politics and society was, however, more complex. Trials of collaborators were a battleground between clashing forces intent on imposing their own interpretations of the past in order to determine the country's future. This book aims to restore retribution to its central place in postwar Czech history, not only as an integral part of the struggle for political mastery, but also as a genuine, though inherently flawed, attempt to come to terms with the legacy of the Nazi occupation.

ORGANIZATION OF THE BOOK

The following study is organized thematically and placed within a larger chronological framework, which begins with the origins of Czech retribution during the Second World War and concludes with the consolidation of Communist rule after the 1948 coup. The latter half of this introduction sets the context for postwar trials by reviewing critical wartime developments and briefly exploring the nature of collaboration in the occupied Czech provinces. Chapter 1, Wild Retribution, analyzes the causes and nature of vigilantism against suspected collaborators in the spring of 1945. Although the violence may appear to have been the inevitable result of a brutal foreign occupation, the bloody anarchy that ravaged the Czech provinces for months was the consequence of decisions taken, and not taken, by the country's leaders during the war and afterward. Chapter 2, The Great Decree, traces the development of the main statute that governed trials of collaborators and war criminals. The law's framers – President Edvard Beneš's followers in London, not Communists in Moscow – accepted measures that permitted, even encouraged, gross abuses to be perpetrated later. The combination of the draconian law and the failure to rein in "wild retribution" established a precarious foundation for postwar justice.

Chapters 3 and 4 focus on the twenty-four Czech People's Courts, which the Beneš regime established to try "Nazi criminals, traitors, and their accomplices." Chapter 3, People's Courts and Popular Justice, examines the role of the police, prosecutors, "people's judges," and professional jurists in the punishment of alleged collaborators and war criminals. Over time these "extraordinary" courts evolved from severe executors of revolutionary justice to become a bulwark against police abuse, personal vengeance, and partisan justice. Based on court records, Chapter 4, Denunciation: "The Disease of Our Time," investigates the practice of denunciation during the occupation and its punishment thereafter. Through in-depth analysis of the 1947 trial of Václav Píša, the regional editor of the anti-Semitic weekly *Aryan Struggle*, this chapter reveals how ordinary Czechs contributed to the Holocaust by denouncing compatriots who failed to respect Nazi prohibitions on contacts with Jews and intermarried Gentiles.

Chapters 5 and 6 consider the role of nationality in retribution by examining two specific aspects of the postwar "national cleansing." Chapter 5, Offenses against National Honor, investigates the prosecution of Czechs for everyday collaboration with the occupation regime. Dissatisfied with the People's Courts' inability to convict lesser collaborators, the government empowered local authorities to punish "unbecoming behavior insulting to the national sentiment of the Czech ... people." In punishing economic, professional, and social – especially "amorous" – relations with Germans, the postwar regime conflated civic and national allegiance and retroactively criminalized interethnic relations. Chapter 6, Retribution and the "Transfer," argues that, whereas retribution trials underpinned the postwar expulsion of nearly three million Sudeten Germans from Czechoslovakia, the expulsion, in turn, undermined the prosecution of war criminals and collaborators. Trials of individual Germans served to justify the collective punishment of the Sudeten minority, but the postwar regime ultimately chose to expel thousands of suspected German criminals rather than risk that they might remain in the country after their convictions.

Chapter 7, The National Court, focuses on trials of prominent Czech collaborators and examines the relationship between politics and justice in the postwar republic. Although Communist leaders first pushed for the creation of the National Court, this institution rejected their and their fellow (non-Communist) exiles' stringent interpretation of wartime collaboration. Instead, adopting the home front's more forgiving view, the court's judges repeatedly emphasized that life under foreign occupation necessitated accommodation and that the Czech "bourgeois" elite had not betrayed its country. Finally, Chapter 8, The Road to February and Beyond, examines the months before and after the 1948 Communist coup d'état. The relief with which many Czechs greeted the abolition of the People's Courts and national honor tribunals in May 1947 was tempered by Communist threats that the "national cleansing" was not over. After the February coup, the new regime reinstated the retribution courts and restarted the prosecution of alleged wartime collaborators, many of whom had been previously acquitted. Though this second round of trials arguably helped the Communists to consolidate their hold on power, even in 1948 retribution proved to be a burdensome, potentially divisive, and often unpredictable task.

HISTORICAL CONTEXT

Established in 1918 on the ruins of Habsburg Austria-Hungary, the First Czechoslovak Republic was a multinational state, in which Czechs and Slovaks together amounted to barely two-thirds of the country's nearly fifteen million inhabitants. In addition to considerable numbers of Magyars (Hungarians), Ruthenians (Ukrainians), Poles, Jews, and Roma (Gypsies), the largest national minority was the 3.2 million Germans who primarily inhabited the highlands bordering on Austria and Germany (the area historically known as the Sudetenland).[25] Thanks to the provinces of Bohemia, Moravia, and Silesia, the industrial engine of the former Habsburg Monarchy, interwar Czechoslovakia ranked among the most economically advanced countries in the world.[26]

---

[25] The 1930 Czechoslovak census recorded 14.7 million inhabitants. A question that asked for "mother tongue" yielded approximately 9.69 million "Czechoslovaks," 3.23 million Germans, 692,000 Magyars (Hungarians), 549,000 Ruthenians (Ukrainians), 82,000 Poles, and 187,000 speakers of Hebrew and Yiddish. When counted by religion, 357,000 persons identified with Judaism. Almost all of the Magyars and Ruthenians lived in the eastern provinces of Slovakia and Subcarpathian Rus; the Poles mainly inhabited Silesia; Jews and the uncounted Roma (Gypsies) were scattered throughout the country. Joseph Rothschild, *East Central Europe between the Two World Wars* (Seattle: University of Washington Press, 1974), 89–90.

[26] Scholars of the First Czechoslovak Republic have traditionally noted that the country's production ranked among the top ten advanced industrial economies. E. Kubů and J. Pátek have argued, to the contrary, that weighted indices place interwar Czechoslovakia in the second dozen of "medium advanced" countries like Austria, Finland, and

Under the guidance of its founder, liberal philosopher Tomáš G. Masaryk, and his protégé, renowned diplomat Edvard Beneš, for two decades the country remained a parliamentary democracy, which guaranteed individual rights to its citizens.[27] Nonetheless, throughout the interwar period Czechoslovakia was in thought and deed a "nationalizing state," committed to promoting the interest of its titular nation(s).[28] "The Czech landlord was friendly and tolerant," Igor Lukes commented, "but he made sure his Sudeten [German] tenants knew who owned the house."[29]

Although German representatives initially rejected the new state, in the 1925 elections the vast majority of Sudeten Germans voted for parties that had resolved to work within the system. Afterward these parties even assumed control over powerful ministries in the government. Amid the economic distress of the Great Depression, however, the 1933 Nazi takeover of neighboring Germany fueled a radical nationalist movement, the Sudeten German Party [Sudetendeutsche Partei (SdP)], headed by Konrad Henlein. With a popular demand for regional autonomy (and clandestine financial support from Berlin), the SdP gained more than 60 percent of the German vote in 1935, a result that Henlein's party markedly bettered in 1938 communal elections, when it received eighty-five percent.[30] By then the SdP had forcibly absorbed most other ethnic

Norway. If one were to leave aside relatively unindustrialized Slovakia and fully agrarian Subcarpathian Rus, the interwar Czech provinces, which alone accounted for more than 90 percent of the country's industrial production and 75 percent of its agricultural production, surely ranked near the top in world economic indicators per capita. Zora P. Pryor, "Czechoslovak Economic Development in the Interwar Period," in Victor S. Mamatey and Radomír Luža, eds., *A History of the Czechoslovak Republic, 1918–1948* (Princeton: Princeton University Press, 1973), 190; E. Kubů and J. Pátek, *Mýtus a realita hospodářské vyspělosti Československa mezi světovými válkami* (Prague: Karolinum, 2000), 16, 279, 369–67.

[27] For more on these giants of Czechoslovak history, see Roman Szporluk, *The Political Thought of Thomas G. Masaryk* (Boulder, CO: East European Monographs, 1981); Zbyněk Zeman and Antonín Klimek, *The Life of Edvard Beneš: Czechoslovakia in Peace and War* (Oxford: Clarendon Press, 1997).

[28] The interwar republic officially recognized a "Czechoslovak nation." This language was reflected in the constitution and censuses, but was eventually rejected by most Slovaks and discarded after the war even by Czechs in favor of two separate but theoretically equal nations. Regarding interwar "nationalizing states," see Rogers Brubaker, *Nationalism Reframed: Nationhood and the National Question in the New Europe* (New York: Cambridge University Press, 1996), 83–84.

[29] Igor Lukes, *Czechoslovakia between Stalin and Hitler: The Diplomacy of Edvard Beneš in the 1930s* (New York: Oxford University Press, 1996), 51.

[30] Rothschild, *East Central Europe*, 129.

German parties and Henlein openly espoused the tenets of Nazism. In the wake of Germany's annexation of Austria in March 1938, the SdP racheted up its demands for autonomy and Hitler called for an end to supposed Czech oppression of the Sudeten minority. When, under international pressure, Czechoslovak President Edvard Beneš belatedly offered autonomy to the Sudeten Germans, Berlin demanded the complete transfer of sovereignty over the borderlands to Nazi Germany. British Prime Minister Neville Chamberlain's ill-fated attempts to satisfy the Fuehrer's appetite through appeasement ended in the Munich Pact of 30 September 1938. Without consulting Beneš, the leaders of the United Kingdom, France, Germany, and Italy collectively ordered Czechoslovakia to surrender its borderlands. Over the next weeks, as Nazi Germany occupied the Sudetenland, more than 200,000 persons, mainly Czechs, but also German antifascists and German-speaking Jews, fled to the interior of Czechoslovakia – the first of many forced migrations that tragically marked the Second World War and its aftermath.[31]

In the months after Germany annexed the Sudetenland, the Axis Powers granted Hungary southern Slovakia, and Poland claimed the Teschen (Těšín) region, thereby depriving Czechoslovakia of nearly one-third of its territory and population.[32] Under German pressure Beneš resigned and left for uncertain exile abroad. In his place the Czechoslovak parliament elected the sixty-six-year-old chief justice of the country's supreme court, Emil Hácha, an avuncular but indecisive and increasingly feeble figurehead. Guided by Agrarian Party chief Rudolf Beran, who became Prime Minister of the so-called Second Republic at the beginning of December 1938, Czech conservatives purged followers of Beneš, introduced censorship, banned the Communists, and reduced the political system to only two legal parties.[33] In the meantime, Slovak nationalists, led by the Catholic priest Jozef Tiso, successfully pressed Prague to grant Bratislava wide-ranging autonomy, which they promptly

---

[31] Tomáš Staněk, "Vyhnání a vysídlení Němců," in Ivona Řezanková and Václav Kural, eds., *Cesta do katastrofy: Československo-německé vztahy 1938–1947* (Vrútky, Czech Republic: NADAS – AFGH, c. 1992), 126.

[32] Theodore Procházka, Sr., *The Second Republic: The Disintegration of Post-Munich Czechoslovakia* (Boulder, CO: East European Monographs, 1981), 53.

[33] Procházka, *Second Republic*, 36–37, 107–10; Tigrid, *Kapesní průvodce*, 171–80; Vojtech Mastny, *The Czechs under Nazi Rule: The Failure of National Resistance* (New York: Columbia University Press, 1971), 20–23; Vilém Hejl, *Rozvrat: Mnichov a náš osud* (Toronto: Sixty-Eight Publishers, 1989), 53–63.

exploited to institute a one-party regime in Slovakia. Despite the Beran government's best attempts to meet Nazi demands, the Second Republic survived less than six months.[34] In March 1939 the Germans used a manufactured crisis in Bratislava to offer Tiso the choice between occupation by Hungary or independence under Nazi tutelage. On 14 March the Slovak parliament voted to secede from what remained of Czechoslovakia. That evening, Hácha traveled to Berlin to ascertain Hitler's plans, but by the time he arrived there German troops had already begun their occupation of Czech Silesia. When Hermann Goering threatened to unleash the Luftwaffe on Prague, Hácha succumbed to the Nazis' demands. Early in the morning of 15 March 1939 the Czech President signed a declaration that "he confidently placed the fate of the Czech people and country in the hands of the Fuehrer of the German Reich."[35]

On 16 March 1939, a day after completing their occupation of the Czech provinces, the Germans announced the creation of a "Protectorate of Bohemia and Moravia." Although the Protectorate ostensibly permitted the Czechs the autonomy to run their internal affairs, the Germans viewed the arrangement as a temporary means to exploit the region for the economic and military needs of the Third Reich.[36] Thanks to Hácha's Berlin capitulation, which allowed the Germans to claim that the takeover was legal, the elderly jurist stayed on as State-President of the Protectorate. His government also remained in office, although the occupiers demanded some changes in top personnel and eliminated the now useless Ministries of Defense and Foreign Affairs. In April respected General Alois Eliáš became prime minister, replacing Beran, who went into permanent retirement (only to be later arrested by the Nazis). Above this Czech administration stood the so-called Protector, Konstantin von Neurath, a conservative German nobleman who had served as Foreign Minister in Weimar Germany and under Hitler. Karl Hermann Frank, a prominent member of the Sudeten German Party,

---

[34] The new regime agreed to cut its army in half and to permit transfer of German troops across its soil and even amended the Law for the Protection of the Republic, previously used against German separatists, to outlaw slander of foreign heads of state and their representatives. Procházka, *Second Republic*, 107–10.

[35] Mastny, *Czechs under Nazi Rule*, 41.

[36] Detlef Brandes, *Die Tschechen unter deutschem Protektorat*, 2 vols. (Munich: R. Oldenbourg, 1969 and 1975), I:38.

became Neurath's deputy. Frank's former party boss, Konrad Henlein, found himself sidelined in the Sudetenland, which remained administratively separate from the Protectorate throughout the war. As State-Secretary, Frank directed the Schutzstaffeln (SS) in the Protectorate and quickly became infamous as a proponent of harsh repression of Czech opposition. Although the Czech bureaucracy remained more or less intact, the Germans claimed jurisdiction over matters pertaining to Jews, the investigation and adjudication of political crimes, and the direction of the economy.

In the first few months the Germans established an occupation policy that remained remarkably consistent (and frighteningly effective) throughout the following years irrespective of the fortunes of war and changes in the local Nazi leadership. First and foremost, the occupiers sought to exploit the Protectorate economically. In particular, they placed great value on the region's arms factories and steel foundries, which had made Czechoslovakia a major industrial force before the war and now were harnessed to the Nazi war machine.[37] To promote compliance, the Germans offered Czech workers the old dictatorial standard of "bread and circuses," including free lunches in factories, vocational classes, organized sporting events, concerts, films, theater, and vacations in local resorts. In time, the occupiers even extended existing insurance programs for personal injury, health, and old age.[38] Though the Germans demanded that their subjects perform compulsory labor (mainly at home, but, for a minority, in Germany), they spared Czechs the burden of serving in the Reich's armed forces. In 1942 Frank summed up Nazi policy in the Protectorate: "He who works for the Reich – and the great majority of the population does so – has nothing to fear; his material existence and future are assured. He who stands aside, holds back or secretly sabotages, belongs to the camp of the enemy and will be cut down according to the law of war."[39]

Hitler explained in late 1939 that, in contrast to the approach favored in occupied Poland, in the Protectorate "the German authorities are to

[37] Miroslav Kárný, "Konečné řešení": Genocida českých Židů v německé protektorátní politice (Prague: Academia, 1991), 10; Mastny, Czechs under Nazi Rule, 68.
[38] Mastny, Czechs under Nazi Rule, 195; Brandes, Die Tschechen, I:231.
[39] Brandes, Die Tschechen, II:19.

avoid anything that is likely to provoke...mass actions."[40] During the first years of the occupation, when Czechs signaled their opposition to foreign rule through mass pilgrimages, public displays of national symbols, and boycotts of public transportation and the press, the Nazi authorities reacted with targeted repression. In response to antioccupation demonstrations in October and November 1939, the Germans summarily shot 9 student leaders, sent more than 1,000 of their classmates to concentration camps, and shut down all Czech universities.[41] Historians have traditionally viewed Hitler's September 1941 decision to replace Neurath with Reinhard Heydrich as a radical change of course.[42] Although the SS leader immediately implemented a crackdown, he actually intensified and refined the approach laid down over the previous two years. To break the Czechs' will to oppose Nazi rule, Heydrich declared martial law and ordered the arrest of Protectorate Prime Minister Alois Eliáš, who had unsuccessfully hidden his contacts with the Czechoslovak government-in-exile in London. By the end of November special courts had sentenced 400 Czechs to death. Having instilled terror, Heydrich then offered concessions designed to encourage compliance: The Germans suspended martial law after two months and granted workers larger rations.[43] In January 1942 Heydrich also signaled an end to the Hácha government's limited autonomy by appointing a trusted German to the post of Protectorate Labor Minister and the most zealous Czech collaborator, Emanuel Moravec, to head the Education Ministry.

Targeted represssion and limited economic concessions were merely short-term policies and, moreover, applied only to Gentiles. From the outset the Nazis anticipated the long-term Germanization of the region; hence the decisions to annex the Protectorate to the Reich and to shut Czech institutions of higher education.[44] Remarkably, Nazi authorities

[40] Mastny, *Czechs under Nazi Rule*, 121.
[41] In theory the closure of the universities was for three years, but Czech institutions of higher education were not reopened until after the war. Mastny, *Czechs under Nazi Rule*, 115–17.
[42] Technically, Neurath was recalled for health reasons and only temporarily replaced by Heydrich, who thus functioned as "acting Protector." Gotthold Rhode, "The Protectorate of Bohemia and Moravia, 1939–1945," in Victor S. Mamatey and Radomír Luža, eds., *A History of the Czechoslovak Republic, 1918–1948* (Princeton, NJ: Princeton University Press, 1973), 311.
[43] Rhode, "The Protectorate," 312.
[44] Brandes, *Die Tschechen*, I:250; Kárný, *"Konečné řešení"*, 10.

considered many Protectorate subjects suitable for Germanization, though the percentage of "Aryan" types within the Czech nation was continually a matter of dispute among the so-called experts. Frank once claimed, for example, that one-half of all Czechs could be assimilated into the German nation.[45] For those deemed unsuitable for Germanization, Hitler recommended "special treatment," while Heydrich ominously commented, "Those people I must get rid of. There's plenty of space [for them] in the East."[46] Until victory was achieved, however, the economic mobilization of Czech workers remained the occupiers' first priority. By contrast, the Protectorate's 118,000 Jews did not have to await the end of the war to learn their fate in the new Europe. After the March 1939 invasion the Hácha government immediately issued anti-Semitic professional measures, but the German occupiers soon took the persecution of Jews out of Czech hands. Over the next two years the Nazis applied the Nuremberg Laws to the Protectorate, expropriated Jews' property, and forced them to obey curfews, wear yellow stars, and perform mandatory labor. In 1941 the Nazis created a ghetto in the eighteenth-century military town of Theresienstadt (Terezín) to concentrate the Protectorate's Jews (along with elderly and "privileged" Jews from other countries) before deporting them east to the death camps. More than 73,000 Protectorate Jews passed through Theresienstadt's gates on their way to Nazi killing centers in occupied Poland; fewer than 10,000 of them survived the war.[47]

Although the liquidation of Czech nationhood was relegated to the postwar period, the Nazis did promote limited Germanization during the occupation, especially for intermarried Czech–German families and the remaining Czech minority in the Sudetenland. Individual Czechs could apply for German citizenship and the advantages that such a designation entailed, but the Nazis were not always willing to accept converts, many of whom were determined to be little more than ordinary criminals or rank opportunists whose knowledge of the German language was

---

[45] Under the guise of tuberculosis exams, the German authorities even sent around teams to examine the racial fitness of Czech youths. Brandes, *Die Tschechen*, I:133, 238; Mastny, *Czechs under Nazi Rule*, 129; John Connelly, "Nazis and Slavs: From Racial Theory to Racist Practice," *Central European History* 32:1 (1999), 14.

[46] Mastny, *Czechs under Nazi Rule*, 128; Brandes, *Die Tschechen*, I:210.

[47] Kárný, *"Konečné řešení"*, 9; Miroslav Kárný, "Genocida českých Židů," in Miroslav Kárný, ed., *Terezínská pamětní kniha: Židovské oběti nacistických deportací z Čech a Moravy, 1941–1945*, 2 vols. (Prague: Melantrich, 1995), I:23–33.

limited. Others failed to meet so-called racial standards. Czechs who volunteered for the Wehrmacht (German armed forces) could also gain Reich citizenship as a reward for their military service. Scholars have yet to conclusively determine the number of Czechs who became German during the war, a task greatly complicated by the prevalence of bilingualism and intermarriage among the region's inhabitants, not to mention the contingent nature of national identity in general. Czech historians have estimated that 70,000 Protectorate subjects voluntarily became German, but other sources indicate a substantially higher total of so-called national "renegades." In 1946 the Czechoslovak Interior Minister Václav Nosek told parliament that at least 300,000 Czechs in the borderlands had become German under compulsion, but he did not reveal how many Czechs had voluntarily opted to declare themselves German during the occupation.[48] Regardless of the actual number, or quality, during the war Czech leaders were concerned about the prevalence of "renegades." The underground forwarded lists of German converts to London and called on the Czechoslovak government-in-exile to "broadcast that once all is put in order, all those Czechs who have adopted German nationality will bear all the consequences of that decision."[49]

The unusually pragmatic policies that the Nazis employed proved successful in preventing the growth of an armed resistance movement in the Protectorate. Instead, the various groups that made up the Czech underground mainly restricted their activities to gathering information for use abroad and planning for the end of the war.[50] Thanks to the

---

[48] In government meetings Nosek apparently repeated this figure several times without reference to compulsion. V. Nosek, *Těsnopisecké zprávy Prozatímního národního shromáždění Republiky československé* (PNS) 27 (31 January 1946), 7; 36th meeting, 2nd government (1 March 1946), SÚA, f.100/24 (aj.1494), k. 140; "Tři sta tisíc odrodilců," *Svobodné noviny* (10 November 1945), 2; Mastny, *Czechs under Nazi Rule*, 137; Milan Kučera, *Populace České republiky 1918–1991* (Prague: Česká demografická společnost, 1994), 36; Tomáš Staněk, *Odsun Němců z Československa 1945–1947* (Prague: Naše vojsko, 1991), 434, n. 18; Jeremy King, *Budweisers into Czechs and Germans: A Local History of Bohemian Politics, 1848–1948* (Princeton, NJ: Princeton University Press, 2003), 185; Chad Bryant, "Either German or Czech: Fixing Nationality in Bohemia and Moravia, 1939–1946," *Slavic Review* 61:4 (Winter 2002), 685–91.

[49] "Zprávy z domova" (10 February 1941), no. 146/41/dův., no. 230/41/dův, Columbia University Rare Books and Manuscripts Library, New York, Jaromír Smutný papers, box 11, folder 1.

[50] In addition to the Communists, the Czech underground comprised three main groups. On the left, Social Democrats and union leaders organized the Committee of the Petition "We Remain Faithful" (Petiční výbor "Věrní zůstaneme"). The Political Center (Politické

failure of Czechoslovakia's leaders to defend the country in September 1938 or March 1939, Czechs were neither militarily nor psychologically prepared to resist the occupation violently. As an anonymous letter complained after the war, "First they led us to Munich, without a fight they gave the Germans nearly half of Bohemia, the army laid down its weapons and in March it gave them to the Germans without a shot, and then they wanted us to make a revolution with sticks."[51] The decisions of Beneš and Hácha to sacrifice sovereignty for national survival demoralized Czechs and left a clear lesson that armed resistance was counterproductive, even disloyal. Throughout the occupation the Protectorate government repeatedly reinforced the message that resistance threatened the nation's existence.[52] From abroad, Beneš also called on the public not to "provoke" the Nazis into retaliating. Instead, he counseled, "Observe with secure equanimity everything that our enemy undertakes and the immoral plans to destroy our national position he prepares. And forget nothing."[53]

In time, however, Beneš and members of his government-in-exile grew concerned that the Hácha administration's pragmatic compromises and the Czech people's overall passivity threatened the nation's international reputation and its future position in postwar negotiations. To rectify this situation, the exiles sent Czechoslovak agents from abroad to the Protectorate with the assignment of assassinating Heydrich. On 27 May 1942 two men ambushed and mortally wounded the acting Protector as he was returning by automobile to Prague. After Heydrich succumbed to his wounds, the German authorities singled out the village of Lidice, which had allegedly aided the assassins, for exemplary retaliation. On the morning of 10 June 1942 the SS shot Lidice's entire male population and burned the village to the ground. Lidice's women and those of its children who failed to meet "racial" criteria were

ústředí) brought together members of the Czech political elite, including supporters of Beneš (for example, Prokop Drtina). Demobilized officers of the Czechoslovak Army formed Defense of the Nation (Obrana národu) as the nucleus of a future military force. Mastny, *Czechs under Nazi Rule*, 145–46.
[51] Anonymous letter to the president, KPR no. R-14799/46 (6 November 1946), Archiv Kanceláře prezidenta republiky (AKPR), Prague, f. D-11169/47 (Anonymy).
[52] Verdict, SÚA, f. NS, Ns 10/46, 80–102, 209–53.
[53] "President Beneš československému národu," *Čechoslovák* III:41 (10 October 1941), 1; Libuše Otáhalová and Milada Červinková, eds., *Dokumenty z historie československé politiky 1939–1943* (Prague: Academia, 1966), doc. 374, 490; Brandes, *Die Tschechen*, I:49.

deported to concentration camps. A small minority of "Aryan" boys and girls was delivered to German homes for adoption. Two weeks later, the SS murdered all twenty-four adults in the village of Ležáky and similarly divided its children. In the wave of terror that followed Heydrich's assassination, the Germans arrested 3,188 Czechs, sentenced 1,357 to death, and executed 679, most for having "approved the assassination." Hitler had initially called for 10,000 Czechs to be summarily shot, but Frank warned the Fuehrer of the consequences of overreacting to the assassination: "we would voluntarily deprive ourselves of very valuable political forces and we would paralyze or leave unused collaboration with those who today offer us positive work." Hitler agreed, apparently because he believed "the Czechs to be industrious and intelligent workers." Martial law, implemented immediately after the assassination, was repealed after only seven weeks.[54] By then, the Nazi crackdown had devastated the small Czech underground and convinced the population at large that armed resistance was suicidal.[55]

Although the Czechs as a whole did not vigorously resist the occupiers, their collaboration also lacked fervency. The men who comprised the Protectorate government obeyed the Nazis' directives, but as a group they showed little initiative of their own after the first months of the occupation. In large part, the Protectorate ministers' passivity stemmed from what Jan Gross termed the "occupier-driven" nature of collaboration – the Germans invariably rejected the Hácha administration's attempts to gain concessions in exchange for greater collaboration.[56] As for the Czech fascists, the Nazi Security Service [Sicherheitsdienst (SD)] contemptuously dismissed their leaders as "officers without troops."[57] Even amid the Great Depression, when fascism metastasized throughout Europe, the catchall party of the extreme Czech right, the National Fascist Community [Národní obec fašistická (NOF)], earned only two

---

[54] Brandes, *Die Tschechen*, I:256–57, 265–66; Rhode, "The Protectorate," 311–15; Mastny, *Czechs under Nazi Rule*, 207–17; Dušan Tomášek and Robert Kvaček, *Obžalována je vláda* (Prague: Themis, 1999), 77.

[55] Mastny, *Czechs under Nazi Rule*, 221.

[56] Jan Gross explained, "Whatever takes place as collaboration must have the explicit consent of the occupier." Jan T. Gross, "Themes for a Social History of War Experience and Collaboration," in István Deák, Jan T. Gross, and Tony Judt, eds., *The Politics of Retribution in Europe: World War II and Its Aftermath* (Princeton, NJ: Princeton University Press, 2000), 25.

[57] Brandes, *Die Tschechen*, I:45.

percent of the popular vote in the 1935 general elections.[58] The Banner (Vlajka) movement, which proved far more significant during the occupation, peaked at 13,000 members in 1939 (in a Czech population of more than seven million).[59] In a pattern that repeated itself several times, in March 1939 Czech fascists attempted a putsch only to find that the Nazis had little interest in working with men who clearly had no popular support.[60] When fascists demonstrated on Prague's Wenceslas Square several months later, they managed to mobilize fewer than 300 followers. Within weeks, General Rudolf Gajda, the father of the Czech fascist movement, disbanded the NOF.[61] The leaders of Banner, for their part, repeatedly failed to heed Frank's demand that they cease their vitriolic condemnation of other Czech collaborators. Eventually, the Nazi State-Secretary lost patience and outlawed the movement's newspaper, ordered the deportation of several hundred of its members to work in Germany, and even interned its leaders in Dachau.[62]

The so-called activists were more to the liking of the Nazis. Unlike the fascists, the "activists" did not propagate their own ideology, did not head any movement, and did not seek an equal partnership with the Germans. Instead, they aimed to secure a place for the Czechs in the new Europe as loyal servants of the Third Reich. Among a smattering of journalists, the most prominent activist was the so-called Czech Quisling, Colonel Emanuel Moravec. Despite his Mussolini-like visage – proud, muscular, and bald – Moravec was known in the interwar Republic as a loyal democrat. A decorated veteran, he led the military procession at the funeral of the country's founder and first president, Tomáš G. Masaryk. In September 1938 he outspokenly argued against concessions and even left his military post to plead personally with Beneš not to surrender. After Munich the Beran regime purged Moravec and forbade him to publish, but the Nazis who ran the Protectorate offered him a deal: In exchange for support, they would let him write publicly again. In the

---

[58] Tomáš Pasák, *Český fašismus (1922–1945) a kolaborace (1939–1945)* (Prague: Práh, 1999), 115.

[59] Pasák, *Český fašismus*, 300.

[60] The Nazis, moreover, had good reason to doubt the loyalty of the Czech fascists, who were among the most vehemently outspoken anti-German nationalists in the country before the occupation. Mastny, *Czechs under Nazi Rule*, 57–59.

[61] Interrogation of Walter Jacobi, Sicherheitsdienst Chief Prague, Archiv Ministerstva vnitra (AMV), Prague, 325-166-3, 18–19.

[62] Pasák, *Český fašismus*, 343–48.

new atmosphere, he concluded that only obedience to the Nazis could save the Czechs. Thanks to a slew of procollaboration articles, books, and speeches, Moravec soon became, according to his biographer, the "most hated man in the Protectorate. He became the symbol of treachery."[63] Against Hácha's wishes, in January 1942 Heydrich made Moravec Protectorate Minister of Education, a position from which he pressed the other members of the government to obey the Germans with greater zeal. The Czech Quisling also became chief of the new Office for Public Enlightenment, under whose aegis he founded the Board for Youth Education [Kuratorium pro výchovu mládeže] to propagate the virtues of Nazism to the new generation.[64]

Nothing so well illustrates the symbiosis between calculated German restraint and the limits of collaboration than the question of Czech military contribution to the Nazi war effort. In a concession to the appearance of autonomy, the Germans allowed the Protectorate to maintain a Government Militia of 7,000 men, but Czechs were not drafted to fight for Germany. On the few occasions when leading Czech collaborators offered their countrymen as cannon fodder, the Nazis repeatedly refused the gesture.[65] In response to one such proposal from Moravec, Frank explained, "[The] Fuehrer's position is that the Czech nation should not fight in this war with weapons in hand against the enemies of the Reich, that is, it should not sacrifice any blood for the Reich, but instead should fulfill its contribution to the victory of the Reich through compulsory labor to the end."[66] Although this appears to be a clear example of "occupier-driven" collaboration, whereby the Nazis determined the form and limit of Czech collaboration, the matter was more complex. Based on the memory of the Czechs' alleged mass desertion from the Habsburg army to the Russians during the First World War, Nazi leaders apparently believed that their Protectorate subjects would be more of a hindrance than a help on the front lines.[67] Hitler

---

[63] Jiří Pernes, *Až na dno zrady: Emanuel Moravec* (Prague: Themis, 1997), 6, 96, 132, and *passim*.

[64] "Kuratorium," Příloha 10, k č.j. Z/II-31366/45, Státní oblastní archiv (SOA) Prague, MLS-Praha, Pres. 1; Mastny, *Czechs under Nazi Rule*, 202.

[65] Brandes, *Die Tschechen*, I:140, I:148–49, II:26.

[66] Pernes, *Až na dno*, 193.

[67] In fact, only a small minority (16 percent) of the Czech and Slovak prisoners-of-war held in Russia opted to join the battle against their native Austria-Hungary during the First World War. Nonetheless, the myth of mass desertion gained universal currency both in interwar Czechoslovakia (were it played an important role in Czech national mythology)

even refused to allow Czechs to serve in police units because he deemed them "irredeemable and traitorous."[68] The Fuehrer was not mistaken. When the Germans finally decided to throw the Government Militia into action in northern Italy in May 1944, the Czechs suffered ten dead and fifteen wounded in their first (and only) foray. Most revealing, irregular Italian partisans "captured" 800 Czech troops.[69] That ended the Czech military contribution to the New Order: In October the rest of the militiamen were disarmed and sent to work building defensive fortifications.[70]

The Government Militiamen's transformation from passive instruments to rebellious deserters illustrates the ambiguity of Czechs' responses to the occupation. Vojtech Mastny commented on life in the Protectorate: "The frontiers between collaboration and resistance were fluid and often the same persons participated in both."[71] Some of the most nationalist Czechs, like Moravec, who pushed the country to fight Germany in 1938, turned defeatist after the Munich Pact and offered their services to the country's new Nazi masters. Others served the Germans in the first years of occupation, only to discover their Czech patriotism after Stalingrad. After March 1939, Jindřich Kozák, a disgruntled former Communist, became an enthusiastic fascist who distributed pro-German leaflets and regularly used the "Hitler salute." When the tide of war shifted, Kozák did, too: He began by posting anti-German leaflets and ended as the leader of a guerilla unit that sabotaged railway cars, stole Wehrmacht weapons, and even killed German soldiers.[72] Many postwar trials were complicated by the ambiguous combination of patriotic and treacherous deeds committed by the same person, for example, a Protectorate minister or union leader who publicly called on Czechs to collaborate and denounce while privately donating money and providing information to the underground.[73] Czechs in responsible positions, in particular, faced the obligation to obey Nazi commands

---

and apparently in Germany too. Alon Rachamimov, *POWs and the Great War: Captivity on the Eastern Front* (Oxford, England: Berg, 2002), 12, 119.

[68] Brandes, *Die Tschechen*, II:25.

[69] Brandes, *Die Tschechen*, II:26.

[70] Tomášek and Kvaček, *Obžalována je vláda*, 113.

[71] Mastny, *Czechs under Nazi Rule*, 165.

[72] MS no. MLS Uh. Hradiště/46-12.9 (31 October 1946) to KPR, AKPR, s. D-11377/47 (B), k. 262.

[73] See, for example, the cases of Dominik Čipera and Arnošt Hais in Chapter 7.

while enjoying the power to intervene on behalf of compatriots. On the one hand, guards at Prague's Pankrác prison watched over other Czechs who had been imprisoned by the Nazis, and thereby saved German manpower. On the other hand, these same Czech guards also smuggled in messages and food for the prisoners from their families. At night the guards brought news of Soviet advances and even facilitated meetings between inmates. Needless to say, they did so at great risk to themselves: In autumn 1944 the Gestapo arrested a number of Pankrác guards.[74]

Most Czechs, however, resembled neither the Pankrác guards nor Jindřich Kozák in either of his incarnations. Instead, like most people throughout occupied Europe, Czechs accommodated themselves to Nazi rule and awaited the outcome of the war. Joseph Rothschild summarized, "[The Czechs] simply kept a pragmatically low profile and avoided the risks of resistance and reprisals."[75] After the war a waiter who had served German restaurant guests during the occupation explained his conduct (and that of his compatriots) to an American observer:

Yes, why did I wait on them? Why did the workers produce for them? Why did the peasants deliver their butter and Vítkovice [arms workers] their guns and the journalists their articles and the miners their coal?...Because you have to live. And to eat. I worked for them as a waiter, because that was the only thing I knew.[76]

Perhaps aware of his foreign audience, the waiter added that he had spied on his German guests and passed on information to the underground. This awkward balancing act – openly adapting to the system while secretly trying to undo it – may recall the character of Josef Schweik (Švejk), Jaroslav Hašek's protagonist of the classic antiwar novel *The Good Soldier Schweik*, who managed to destabilize the Austro-Hungarian Army while apparently attempting to serve it. Although critics have long debated whether Schweik, in fact, consciously aimed to undermine authority with his shenanigans, he was a national character of reference for contemporary Czechs. While many may not have viewed Hašek's protagonist positively, others saw in him a means

---

[74] Jaroslav Drábek, *Z časů dobrých a zlých* (Prague: Naše vojsko, 1992), 73–75, 84–85, 90.

[75] Joseph Rothschild, *Return to Diversity: A Political History of East Central Europe since World War II* (New York: Oxford University Press, 1989), 33.

[76] Joseph Wechsberg, *Homecoming* (New York: Alfred A. Knopf, 1946), 87–88.

to explain and even justify their conduct under Nazi rule. Edvard Beneš, for example, once remarked, "I don't like Schweik, but there'll apparently be nothing for us to do but to wait out these evil times through Schweikism."[77] The Germans, too, were familiar with Hašek's work: State-Secretary Frank dismissed Protectorate Agriculture Minister Adolf Hrubý as a "Schweik."[78] Though James Scott saw "Schweikian" behavior as a form of everyday resistance, such foot dragging ultimately did more for individual and national self-esteem than for the undermining of Nazi rule. The Germans were more than willing to put up with a nation of Schweiks as long as they did not have to face armed resistance.[79]

Schweikism, however, did have its uses. In defense of his compromises, Hácha argued, "If I could no longer save the state, then at least I saved the nation."[80] To a certain extent, he was right: Accommodation saved lives, at least Gentile ones. Approximately 77,000 Jews and 7,000 Roma (Gypsies) from Bohemia, Moravia, and Silesia perished in the Holocaust. An additional 36,000 to 55,000 Gentile Czechs died at the hands of the Nazis.[81] While the occupation claimed the lives of more than two-thirds of the region's prewar Jewish community and nearly all of its Roma, losses among Czech Gentiles amounted to less than 1 percent of the population.[82] The last figure, however, does not capture the

---

[77] Jaroslav Drábek, Z časů dobrých a zlých, 35.

[78] Tomášek and Kvaček, Obžalována je vláda, 162.

[79] James C. Scott, Weapons of the Weak: Everyday Forms of Peasant Resistance (New Haven, CT: Yale University Press, 1990), xvi; Mastny, Czechs under Nazi Rule, 160.

[80] Brandes, Die Tschechen, I:19.

[81] Pavel Škorpil estimated that approximately 44,000 non-Jewish, non-Roma Czechs died violently during the war, including 4,000 who perished in Allied bombing. Approximately 6,800 Czechs and Slovaks died while fighting for the Allied armies on the eastern and western fronts. It has been estimated that 200,000 Sudeten Germans also lost their lives fighting for Nazi Germany. At least 766 antifascist Sudeten Germans perished at the hands of the Nazis, but that number includes only members of the Social Democratic Party. Kučera, Populace České republiky, 48; Rhode, "The Protectorate," 319; Pavel Škorpil, "Problémy vyčíslení životních ztrát u československých obětí Nacionálně socialistického Německa v letech 1938–1945," in Ivona Řezanková and Václav Kural, eds., Cesta do katastrofy: Československo-německé vztahy 1938–1947 (Vrútky: NADAS – AFGH, c. 1992), 122–23; Jürgen Tampke, Czech–German Relations and the Politics of Central Europe: From Bohemia to the EU (Hampshire, UK: Palgrave Macmillan, 2003), 61.

[82] The Protectorate's Jewish population at the beginning of the occupation has been traditionally estimated at 118,000. According to Nazi records, approximately 27,000 Jews officially emigrated from the Protectorate by 1941, leaving around 90,000 in the region at the beginning of mass deportations. These sums include neither those individuals who managed to keep their Jewish identity a secret nor those Gentiles who Nazi racial laws redefined as Jews. Kárný, "Genocida českých Židů," 20–21; Kárný, "Konečne řešení", 18–20; Rhode, " The Protectorate," 318–19.

full impact of the war. After all, to count the Protectorate's highly assimilated Jewish community separately is to accept and perpetuate Nazi racial theory.[83] Moreover, certain segments of the Gentile population, particularly the Czech political and intellectual elite, bore Nazi terror incommensurately. The nationalist Sokol [Falcon] gymnastics organization, for example, experienced substantial losses during the occupation: 1,135 members were executed, 1,979 died in concentration camps and Nazi jails, and another 7,935 survived imprisonment. An additional 589 died fighting the Germans in the last week of the war.[84] The Communists, too, suffered Nazi repression disproportionately.[85] Not incidentally, the country's postwar leaders came predominantly from those sectors of the population that had experienced the harshest Nazi terror.

In light of the relatively low casualty rate for Czech Gentiles, the scale and brutality of postwar Czech retribution against Germans and their domestic collaborators may seem surprising. Insinuating that the Czechs experienced a benign occupation, one advocate of the Sudeten German cause wrote, "I have often wondered what it was that suddenly awakened such an abysmal hatred in the hearts of [the Czech] people. After all, it had come through the war better than any other nation in Europe."[86] Despite Nazi repression, the Protectorate population as a whole increased by 236,000 persons during the occupation.[87] For most

---

[83] The postwar Czechoslovak regime included Jewish dead among the state's wartime losses. In the 1930 census, which asked for "mother tongue," approximately 43,000 Jews in Bohemia, Moravia, and Silesia answered "Czechoslovak," 35,000 "German," and 37,000 "Jewish," but those figures disguise a high degree of multilingualism and predate the rise of Nazism, which drove many Jews to abandon their German identity. Kárný, "Genocida českých Židů," 23.

[84] Brandes, *Die Tschechen*, II:61.

[85] Without offering supporting evidence, official historians claimed that the Nazis murdered approximately 25,000 Czechoslovak Communists, one-third of the party's prewar membership. This suspiciously round number included Slovak party cadres who perished in the 1944 uprising and perhaps even those German Communists murdered by their conationals. A more reliable, though incomplete measure of repression was provided by Brandes, who noted that by 1942 the Nazis had already arrested 5,610 Communists in the Protectorate. Miroslav Bouček, Miloslav Klimeš, and Marta Vartíková, *Za národní osvobození, za novou republiku, 1938–1945: Vedoucí úloha KSČ v národně osvobozeneckém boji* (Prague: Svoboda, 1982), 471; Zdeněk Huňáček, Jiří Jožák, Vlastislav Kroupa, and Jan Stříbrný, eds., *Český antifašismus: Slovníková příručka* (Prague: Naše Vojsko, 1988), 154; Brandes, *Die Tschechen*, II:76.

[86] Wilhelm K. Turnwald, ed., *Documents on the Expulsion of the Sudeten Germans*, trans. by Gerda Johnson (Munich: Association for the Protection of Sudeten German Interests, 1953), 13.

[87] Rhode, "The Protectorate," 318–19.

of the war the average Czech's rations and living conditions compared favorably even to those in the Reich. But the absence of object deprivation and relatively few deaths (compared albeit to the inhumanly horrific standard of occupied Poland) could not compensate for the loss of sovereignty. Mastny explained, "Although the Nazis did not require from their subjects significantly greater material sacrifices than from their own people, the Czechs deeply resented any sacrifices for an alien cause."[88] A contemporary letter from the Protectorate captured the national mood:

Everything you look at has the hand of occupation upon it. You are ordered about by notices in the street, new notices and new orders, or perhaps just ridiculous and outrageous translations of your own notices continuously hit you in the face. Every time you pass these inscriptions you are forced to realize afresh that you are no longer master of your own country, no longer at home in your own home.

The changes penetrate into every detail of your daily life. You must see the names in your village written up in German, hear the names of the tram-stops shouted out in German....Everyday brings something bad, and every new thing is always worse. You are permanently living in anxiety, permanently afraid of what the next day will bring....

You suffer personally. You cannot get proper food. It is not the rationing itself, which brings discomfort in every country, but rather the way your food is rationed and why....Your restriction is not a necessary sacrifice which you are making for the sake of your own country, your army, your struggle. You are starving in order that the men you hate should be well fed....

It is the uncertainty – how long will it last, how much worse will it become and what will be the end of it all – which is so hard to bear. And always in the back of your mind, at the back of all these sufferings and uncertainties is the main trouble and biggest pain. You are absolutely helpless, there is nothing you can do....

The whole atmosphere is somehow unhealthy and all the details of normal life become abnormal. You are under permanent pathological tension....Now [our people] live in a sort of organized madness.[89]

As the author of the letter noted, this experience could not but leave a trace. Despite outward calm, the constant uncertainty, mounting fear, and daily humiliation of foreign occupation fed an impassioned

[88] Mastny, *Czechs under Nazi Rule*, 83–85.
[89] Shiela Grant Duff, *A German Protectorate: The Czechs under Nazi Rule* (London: Frank Cass, 1970), 241–43.

desire for postwar retribution against the occupiers and those who aided them.

After years of anxious tranquility, on 5 May 1945 armed resistance finally engulfed the heart of the Protectorate. When insurgents seized Prague radio and announced a general uprising against the occupying forces, Czechs built barricades around the capital city. In a few short days of fighting before the Red Army finally arrived, the Prague Uprising cost the lives of 935 Germans and 1,693 Czechs.[90] The insurrection came too late, however, to influence postwar political relations in the Czech provinces. In neighboring Slovakia, the Slovak resistance carried out a massive uprising in 1944 against the Germans and the Tiso regime and thereby emerged from the war strong enough to demand a role in postwar governance. The small Czech underground, by contrast, never recovered from the repression that followed Heydrich's assassination. In the end, Czechs who had fled abroad, not those who remained at home, determined how Czechoslovakia would be run after liberation. Thus, to understand the postwar period, we must turn our attention to wartime London, where the country's once-and-future president, Edvard Beneš, gathered together Czech and Slovak exiles committed to reestablishing and revolutionizing Czechoslovakia.

Although Beneš began his exile as an international pariah, an unwanted reminder of the Munich debacle, the former president rapidly regained his leading position in the nation. Already in August 1939 American diplomat George F. Kennan commented, "German clumsiness has given to Beneš's name a superficial boulevard popularity which his personality on its own merits was never able to command."[91] By the end of that year, the three major non-Communist resistance groups all accepted the former president's leadership.[92] Even the Protectorate ministers initially deferred to Beneš's authority, if only in private.[93] From

---

[90] The first forces to reach Prague and aid the insurgents were actually from General Andrei Vlasov's Russian Liberation Army, which threw aside its collaborationist service to the Third Reich at war's end and fled westwards across Czechoslovakia in the vain hope of escaping Stalin's wrath. Tomáš Staněk, *Perzekuce 1945* (Prague: Institut pro středoevropskou kulturu a politiku, 1996), 72–73, 201, fn. 40. For more on the liberation of Prague, see, Stanislav A. Auský, *Vojska generála Vlasova v Čechách* (Prague: Vyšehrad, 1992).

[91] George F. Kennan, *From Prague after Munich: Diplomatic Papers, 1938–1940* (Princeton, NJ: Princeton University Press, 1968), 224.

[92] Mastny, *Czechs under Nazi Rule*, 146.

[93] Verdict, SÚA, f. NS, Ns 10/46, 15.

London the former president and his entourage of Czech and Slovak exiles laid claim to the mantle of Czechoslovakia. By the summer of 1941 the major Allies had all recognized the Beneš government-in-exile as the legitimate representative of the Czechoslovak state. The realities of postwar geopolitics and the fortunes of war, however, ultimately determined that the London government had to share power with the Communists. In December 1943 Beneš had already committed the country to a military alliance with the Soviet Union as a guarantee against postwar German revanchism. In the winter of 1945, with the Red Army steadily advancing into Central Europe and the Western allies still struggling to cross the Rhine, it became clear that the Soviets would liberate Czechoslovakia. With that in mind, in March 1945 Beneš and an entourage of handpicked members from his exile government departed London for Moscow, where, together with Czechoslovak Communist leaders, they negotiated the form and program of a government to rule their country after the war.[94]

The postwar Czechoslovak regime comprised a formal coalition of six major political parties (four Czech, two Slovak), known collectively as the National Front. In Moscow the parties' leaders agreed to participate actively in the government and forbade any extragovernmental opposition. Individually, the four Czech parties were, from left to center (there was no right): the Communist Party of Czechoslovakia [Komunistická strana Československa (KSČ)], the Social Democratic Party [Československá sociální demokracie (ČSD)], the National Socialist Party [Československá strana národně socialistická (ČSNS)], and the People's Party [Československá strana lidová (ČSL)]. During the interwar period the Communist Party legally competed in elections, winning more than 10 percent of the statewide vote (thanks in part to strong support from national minorities). Although Communist leaders programmatically adopted an antagonistic stance toward the First Czechoslovak Republic, after the country signed a mutual defense treaty with the Soviet Union in June 1935 the Party became a loyal opposition and its parliamentary representatives even voted for Beneš in the presidential election of that year. Following Germany's invasion of the Soviet Union, the Communists forgot their awkward silence during the Nazi–Soviet alliance of 1939 to 1941, discarded their

94 Prokop Drtina, *Československo můj osud* (Toronto: Sixty-Eight Publishers, 1982), I:724.

multinational past, and vigorously demanded the expulsion of the Sudeten Germans from Czechoslovakia. Thanks to their superior organization and discipline, links to the victorious Soviet Union, and generous promises of national, social, and economic reform, the Communists emerged from the war as Czechoslovakia's most powerful political party. Within ten months after liberation, membership grew from approximately 28,000 wartime survivors to more than one million Czechs.[95]

The country's other Marxist party, the traditionally larger Social Democrats, had difficulty after the war in articulating a political platform distinct from the Communists. Although the Social Democratic leader, Zdeněk Fierlinger, initially served as government premier, the party only registered approximately 350,000 members. In contrast, the Czechoslovak National Socialist Party grew to more than 600,000 members and became the second-strongest Czech party. Despite their unfortunately familiar name, the National Socialists espoused neither Nazism nor fascism. Founded in 1897 as a non-Marxist alternative for Czech workers, the National Socialists were "the party of Czech nationalism."[96] After the war they enthusiastically advocated the expulsion of the Sudeten Germans, but within a purely Czech context the party supported representative democracy, defended the rule of law, and identified with President Beneš, who was a former National Socialist. The Czechoslovak People's Party (400,000 members) was a moderate Catholic movement, which, in the new political atmosphere, found itself to be a relatively conservative fighter for tradition, legal continuity, and individual civic rights. For the Slovaks there were the Communist Party of Slovakia [Komunistická strana Slovenska (KSS)] and the Democratic Party [Demokratická strana (DS)]. While remaining within the all-encompassing Czechoslovak party, the Slovak Communists tactically claimed to be an independent movement deserving of its own representation in government. The Democratic Party was a catchall group originally formed by non-Communist members of the resistance against the Tiso regime.[97]

---

[95] Karel Kaplan, *Nekrvavá revoluce* (Prague: Mladá fronta Archiv, 1993), 52–53; Bradley F. Abrams, "The Second World War and the East European Revolution," *East European Politics and Societies* 16 (2003): 3, 663.

[96] Kaplan, *Nekrvavá revoluce*, 54.

[97] Kaplan, *Nekrvavá revoluce*, 54–55.

The multiparty National Front ruled Czechoslovakia for nearly three years, until the Communist coup d'état of February 1948. This brief period, sometimes known as the Third Republic, was dominated by two main developments that framed the implementation of postwar retribution: the expulsion of the Sudeten Germans from the country and the political struggle that ended with the Communist imposition of a one-party regime. After the Second World War the Beneš regime set out to transform the "state of nationalities" that was interwar Czechoslovakia into a "national state" of Czechs and Slovaks.[98] Although the deportation of Hungarians from southern Slovakia faltered on international opposition, Czechoslovakia expelled nearly its entire German population in the brief postwar period. First, in the "Wild Transfer" of spring and summer 1945, vigilante violence and Czech authorities chased 660,000 native Germans from the country. Then, in the so-called Organized Transfer of 1946, Czechoslovakia deported another 2.26 million Sudeten Germans to the Allied occupation zones of Germany. Accompanying this process of "ethnic cleansing," more than 1.5 million Czech "new settlers" migrated from the Bohemian and Moravian interior to the formerly German-dominated borderlands.[99]

Politically, the Third Republic can be divided into three basic periods. From the spring of 1945 to the end of October the government formed in Moscow ruled by decree.[100] These first postwar months were marked by the Wild Transfer of the Sudeten Germans, but also by the reestablishment of legal institutions, economic life, and a vibrant, free press.[101]

[98] Beneš, *Světová krise*, 34.
[99] There these "new settlers" joined 868,250 "old settlers" – Czechs who remained in the Sudetenland during the war. *Statistická příručka Československé republiky 1948* (Prague: Státní úřad statistický 1948), 32.
[100] These decrees are commonly known as the "Beneš Decrees." The term (and its present-day use and abuse) imprecisely implies that Beneš was solely responsible for the decrees. Although the Czechoslovak President played a critical role in the early wartime decrees, in 1945 he usually limited himself to advising and often only signed measures that had been written, debated, and approved by the ministers of the government cabinet.
[101] There was no formal censorship in postwar Czechoslovakia, but certain areas were understood to be off limits: for example, criticism of the president, the country's nationalization program, and its alliance with the Soviet Union. The government also restricted the number of newspapers and required that each be formally linked to an authorized organization or political party. Nonetheless, within these limits the Czech press questioned official policies and engaged actively in political debate. The major Czech daily newspapers referenced in this work are the Communist *Rudé právo* [*Red Right*] (average daily sale 500,000), the National Socialist *Svobodné slovo* [*Free Word*] (300,000), the official labor union's *Práce* [*Labor*] (250,000), the Social Democratic *Právo lidu* [*Right*

The second period began on 28 October 1945 with the first meeting of the Provisional National Assembly, a parliament appointed by the leaders of the National Front. Despite the existence of this legislative body, political power remained in the hands of the government cabinet and party leaderships (as it did throughout the Third Republic). By the end of 1945, the Red Army withdrew from the country in conjunction with the American Army, which had liberated a small sliver of southwestern Bohemia. During the winter and spring, as the Organized Transfer got underway and retribution trials proceeded apace, the political parties prepared for the country's first elections on 26 May 1946. On that day, the Communists scored a stunning victory in the Czech provinces, winning forty percent of the vote. As a result of the party's statewide plurality, Klement Gottwald became government premier and the Communists retained their control over the Interior Ministry and other key institutions. The third period that followed the elections was dominated by increasing tensions between the Communists and their political partners. Internationally, Beneš's ill-fated attempts to make his country a "bridge between the East and the West" faltered with the onset of the Cold War – a development that became plainly apparent in July 1947 when the Soviets forced Czechoslovakia to disavow its expressed interest in the American Marshall Plan. At home, disputes over the communization of the police and fabricated plots to discredit non-Communist politicians reached their climax in February 1948, when ministers from the National Socialist, People's, and Democratic Parties resigned from the cabinet. A five-day crisis, during which the Communists shut down opposition papers, arrested political competitors, and mobilized militant supporters on the streets, was resolved when Beneš appointed a new cabinet chosen by Gottwald. The February coup brought an end to the Third Republic and initiated more than four decades of one-party rule in Czechoslovakia.

of the People] (190,000), the People's Party's *Lidová demokracie* [*People's Democracy*] (185,000), the Czechoslovak Youth Union's *Mladá fronta* [*Young Front*] (80,000), and the independent (but formally affiliated with the Union of Cultural Organizations) *Svobodné noviny* [*Free Press*] (68,000). Karel Kaplan, "Cenzura 1945–1953," *Sešity* 22 (1994), 8; Kaplan, *Nekrvavá revoluce*, 46; William Diamond, *Czechoslovakia between East and West* (London: Stevens and Sons, 1947), 55; Karl F. Zieris, "The New Czech Press," in *Newspapers and Newspapermen in Czechoslovakia* (Prague: Union of Czech Journalists, 1947), 32–33.

I

WILD RETRIBUTION

In May 1939, nearly a decade before he coined the term "containment," American diplomat George F. Kennan reported from Prague, "If the tide ever turns, Czech retaliation will be fearful to contemplate."[1] And that was before the Second World War even began. Hitler's imposition of a "Protectorate of Bohemia and Moravia" in March 1939 – while the rest of Europe was still at peace – meant that the Czech provinces submitted to Nazi occupation earlier than any other major non-German region on the continent. First occupied, the Protectorate was also the last to be liberated – the Red Army did not reach Prague until 9 May 1945, the day after the Armistice was signed in Berlin. In the meantime Czechs had more than six years to brood over the injustice of the Munich Pact, the humiliation of foreign occupation, the suffering of the persecuted, and the treachery of friends and neighbors. Six long years to hope for justice and plot revenge. In the spring of 1945 Kennan's prediction proved terribly true. As the nightmare of foreign occupation drew to a close, the Czech provinces exploded in an orgy of violence.

This chapter examines the causes and nature of "wild retribution" – extralegal acts of violence based at least in theory on retaliation for wartime collaboration.[2] Formal retribution courts and tribunals did not begin fully operating until the summer of 1945; some did not try their first cases until the winter of 1945–1946. In the meantime, vigilantes murdered thousands and brutalized thousands more. Wild

[1] George F. Kennan, *From Prague after Munich: Diplomatic Papers, 1938–1940* (Princeton, NJ: Princeton University Press, 1968), 178.
[2] "Wild retribution" is an adaptation of the French "*épuration sauvage*" and a counterpart to the Czech "Wild Transfer" [*Divoký odsun*] of the Sudeten Germans.

retribution was integrally linked to the expulsion of the country's German population. In the first months following the war, approximately 660,000 Germans were driven from the provinces of Bohemia, Moravia, and Silesia. During the subsequent Organized Transfer, beginning in January 1946, Czechoslovakia deported another 2.26 million to Allied occupation zones in Germany.[3] The combined toll from wild retribution and the expulsion was massive: The German-Czech Commission of Historians estimated that between 19,000 and 30,000 Germans were murdered; thousands more may have died from disease, exhaustion, and other unnatural causes.[4] The number of Czechs that perished in the spring months is unknown. Thanks to the malleability of national identity and the indiscriminate nature of the violence, many of the dead Germans may once have been live Czechs.

From the outset apologists for the postwar Czechoslovak regime blamed the violence on "chaos" and "anarchy." A contemporary polemic, *Why We Want to Transfer the Germans*, explained,

No one on the Czech side wishes to deny that in the early months following the military collapse of Germany the frontier areas of the Czech territories lacked a firm hand of authority directed by a central Government in Prague. ... In these circumstances there occurred isolated attempts at a precipitous liquidation of German groups by ruthless and planless [sic] evacuation.[5]

Despite the exculpatory nature of this claim, the collapse of Nazi authority did temporarily leave pockets of territory beyond the control of any legal forces. Under such chaotic conditions, vigilantes (and ordinary criminals) could often do as they wished. Individuals seized the opportunity to revenge themselves on those who had denounced,

[3] Karel Kaplan, *Poválečné Československo: Národy a hranice* (Munich: Nár. Politika, 1985), 153.
[4] Estimates of postwar Sudeten German deaths have ranged as high as 272,000. Norman Naimark explained, "the lower numbers may well accurately reflect the number of Sudeten Germans murdered and killed in the course of their deportation; the higher numbers would include the number who died from other causes during the uprooting, detention, transport, and resettling." Společná německo-česká komise historiků, *Konfliktní společenství, katastrofa, uvolnění: Náčrt výkladu německo-českých dějin od 19. století* (Prague: Ústav mezinárodních vztahů, 1996), 29–30; Norman Naimark, *Fires of Hatred: Ethnic Cleansing in Twentieth-Century Europe* (Cambridge, MA: Harvard University Press, 2001), 118–20.
[5] Karel Šedivý, *Why We Want to Transfer the Germans* (Prague: Orbis, 1946), 73.

imprisoned, and tortured them. Events in France, where vigilantes summarily executed nearly 10,000 alleged collaborators, demonstrate that wild retribution was not specific to the Czech provinces or even to Eastern Europe.[6] In short, apologists claim, not entirely without justification, that popular anger was irrepressible and the anarchy of spring 1945 allowed it to explode.

As this chapter argues, however, wild retribution was not simply an unfortunate and inevitable by-product of the most terrible war the world has ever known. The anarchy that gripped the Czech provinces in the spring and summer months of 1945 was more violent and lasted far longer than it need have. In retrospect, wild retribution resulted from decisions taken, and not taken, by the country's leaders during and immediately following the war. To begin with, they anticipated and encouraged vigilante violence as a means to an end, as a way to maximize the immediate flight of Germans to minimize the numbers to be deported later. Second, the Beneš government-in-exile established the objective conditions necessary for anarchy to spread unchecked. Finally, in the spring and summer of 1945 the central authorities failed to act quickly and resolutely to restore order and end the violence. As a result, the country's leaders established a precarious foundation for postwar justice.

THREATS AND PROMISES

In November 1939, when the German occupation authorities arrested more than 1,000 Czech students and shut down all Czech universities, a resistance group noted that the public mood was growing more radical with every passing day. A message to Czech exiles explained, "The nation lives today only in the hope of revenge...and any moralizing to that effect is just putting oil on the fire!"[7] Fifteen months later, after SS leader Reinhard Heydrich became Acting Protector and carried out an intense terror campaign against the Protectorate's denizens, a source in the Czech underground reported, "Besides for...a few directly paid

---

[6] Rousso, "L'épuration," in Klaus-Dietmar Henke and Hans Woller, eds., *Politische Säuberung in Europa* (Munich: Deutscher Taschenbuch Verlag, 1991), 201–202.

[7] Jitka Vondrová, ed., *Češi a sudetoněmecká otázka, 1939–1945: Dokumenty* (Prague: Ústav mezinárodních vztahů, 1994), doc. 15, 34–35.

servants of the German regime, there is not a single Czech who today does not feel the sharpest hatred toward all things German. Nobody here makes any distinctions among the Germans."[8] But the repression that followed Heydrich's arrival paled next to that unleashed after the attack on the Nazi leader by two Czechoslovak agents affiliated with the government-in-exile. Amid Nazi roundups and the summary execution of hundreds, on 2 June 1942 underground operatives claimed that every Czech in Prague had already been assigned someone to get once liberation came. The killing would allegedly begin with German children, so that there could be no more new Nazis. The days of any Czech who failed to maintain solidarity, the message also explained, "like the fate of Czech traitors bought by the Nazis, are numbered."[9] One week later, after Heydrich succumbed to his wounds, the SS razed the village of Lidice and executed its entire male population, irreversibly cementing Czech resolve to bring an end to the German presence in Bohemia, Moravia, and Silesia.

Nonetheless, as long as the occupation remained unshakable, the Czech underground did not exact retribution against Nazis and collaborators. Although the "activist" journalist Karel Lažnovský died under suspicious circumstances in 1941, it was probably natural causes, not resistance activities, that caused the death of the notorious collaborator.[10]

---

[8] Reports from Czechoslovakia (6 February 1942), Columbia University Rare Books and Manuscripts Library, New York (CU), Jaromír Smutný papers, box 12.

[9] Zprávy z domova (2 June 1942) VIII/9, Archiv Kanceláře prezidenta republiky (AKPR), f. J. Smutného, O 3201/61 no. VIII.

[10] In October 1941 one of the leading Czech advocates of collaboration, Karel Lažnovský, died after he and several of his fellow "activist" editors fell sick following a meal with the Protectorate Prime Minister, Alois Eliáš. The Nazis immediately claimed that Eliáš had poisoned the men on direct orders from Beneš in London. According to archival records, however, the German doctor who attended to Lažnovský reported first the flu, then typhus, and finally heart failure as the ultimate cause of death. Since then a number of rumors have circulated regarding Lažnovský's death. In 1948, a Czech serving a life sentence alleged that the so-called "sandwich scandal" [chlebíčková aféra] was actually a failed Gestapo plot to frame Eliáš. Decades after the end of the war a former member of the resistance claimed that the underground had in fact killed Lažnovský on orders from London. He alleged that the matter was hushed up because the Communists were not involved, but that hardly explains why this important act of resistance was not publicized by its perpetrators in the period before February 1948. Both stories – one from a convicted felon, the other four decades after the fact – are vague and without supporting evidence. Vojtěch Dolejší, Noviny a novináři: Z poznámek a vzpomínek (Prague: Nakladatelství politické literatury, 1963), 406–10; interrogation of Bohumil Seibert, Archiv Ministerstva vnitra (AMV) Prague, aj. 305–606–6, l. 49–50; Jindřich Schwippel, "Ivan Málek (1909–1994) Mikrobiologe: Betrogener Kämpfer für eine bessere Welt," in Monika

When underground leaders learned of the government-in-exile's plan to kill Heydrich, they desperately pleaded for the assassination to be called off or at least for another target to be selected. A message to London implored, "If it is necessary for reasons of foreign relations to make some sort of gesture, then let it be done to a domestic quisling, first and foremost, to E. M." – Emanuel Moravec.[11] After the June 1942 Lidice massacre and the accompanying Nazi crackdown, the underground was in no mood or position to carry out further assassinations and risk further reprisals. As a result, unlike elsewhere in Europe, in the Protectorate no prominent collaborators were executed until the very end of the war. Beneš eventually did approve an attack on Moravec, but the Czech Quisling survived until he committed suicide on 5 May 1945.[12]

Perhaps the first case of fatal retribution against Czech collaborators occurred in the autumn of 1944. In early October a village mayor informed the local Czech police that General Radomír Luža, one of the foremost leaders of the underground, was resting in a pub nearby. A patrol cornered the general and, when he resisted arrest, shot him dead. As Luža's son and namesake explained decades later, his resistance group's decision to retaliate against the Czech policemen represented a new departure for the underground: "Father ... had generally opposed this sort of exemplary mass assassination in the past. The resistance, Father thought, was not supposed to be in the business of terrorism."[13] In retaliation, an "execution party" of Czechs and Russian partisans captured and shot four Czech police officers, only one of whom survived.[14] Revealingly, the younger Luža recalled that all but one of the gendarmes believed up until the last moment that they had nothing to fear – a clear illustration that the underground did not pose a regular

Gletter and Alena Míšková, eds., *Prager Professoren 1938–1948: Zwischen Wissenschaft und Politik*, Veröffentlichungen zur Kultur und Geschichte im östlichen Europa, Band 17 (Essen: Klartext, 2001), 596–97.

[11] Earlier in the war resistance groups had made at least two unsuccessful attempts on Moravec's life. ÚVOD dispatch (11 May 1942), in Vladimír Krajina, *Vysoká hra: Vzpomínky* (Prague: Eva, 1994), 89; Jaroslav Drábek, *Z časů dobrých a zlých* (Prague: Naše vojsko, 1992), 53; Detlef Brandes, *Die Tschechen unter deutschem Protektorat*, 2 vols. (Munich: R. Oldenbourg, 1969 and 1975), I:192, 205.

[12] Libuše Otáhalová and Milada Červinková, eds., *Dokumenty z historie československé politiky 1939–1943*, 2 vols. (Prague: Academia, 1966), doc. 259, 310.

[13] Radomír Luža (with Christina Vella), *The Hitler Kiss: A Memoir of the Czech Resistance* (Baton Rouge: Louisiana State University Press, 2002), 164–65.

[14] The mayor avoided resistance retaliation during the occupation and was acquitted by a postwar court. Václav Černý, *Paměti*, 3 vols. (Brno: Atlantis, 1992–1994), II:348.

threat to the lives of collaborators. To alter this widespread perception, the attackers left behind a message: "This is what happens to those who fight against our resistance. These people killed resisters and suffered a just punishment." In his memoirs the younger Luža clearly exaggerated when he claimed that the incident stopped collaboration between Czech gendarmes and Nazis and marked the "beginning of the Czech guerilla war."[15] For the first time, however, Czech collaborators had to be seriously concerned about the possibility of resistance retaliation. In November 1944 Protectorate Agriculture Minister Adolf Hrubý finally decided to get a pistol for self-defense after partisans threatened his friend and fellow collaborator.[16]

In retrospect, the lack of wartime retribution arguably magnified postwar retribution. More Czechs likely collaborated than would have if resistance retaliation had posed an imminent danger to their lives. The failure to liquidate collaborators during the war also left them alive to be reckoned with afterward. Most fatefully, the public's thirst for justice and vengeance remained unsatiated. Whereas the Poles collectively acted out their desire for revenge during the war, the Czechs nurtured it in their breasts. They maintained outward compliance, while seething within. Echoing Kennan's prediction, one underground dispatch reported that the people "clench their teeth and fists and wait for the moment when it all will begin to give way. Then it will be terrible."[17] Three decades later, during the "Normalization" period of post-1968 Communist repression, Czech dissident Václav Havel described the fearful consequences of such behavior:

Even if they never speak of it, people have a very acute appreciation of the price they have paid for outward peace and quiet: the permanent humiliation of their human dignity. The less direct resistance they put up to it – comforting themselves by driving it from their mind and deceiving themselves with the thought that it is of no account, or else simply gritting their teeth – the deeper

---

[15] Luža, *Hitler Kiss*, 158–71; Černý, *Paměti*, II:348; Karel Veselý-Štainer, *Cestou národního odboje: Bojový vývoj domácího odbojového hnutí v letech 1938–1945* (Prague: Sfinx, 1947), 142.

[16] Six armed men apparently broke into the home of František Zmeškal, where they found only his wife. They threatened her that if her husband did not move away, they would return and kill him. In addition to procuring a gun for himself, Hrubý arranged for a new apartment for Zmeškal in a safer part of the country. Dušan Tomášek and Robert Kvaček, *Obžalována je vláda* (Prague: Themis, 1999), 117.

[17] Reports from Czechoslovakia (6 February 1942), CU, Smutný papers, box 12.

the experience etches itself in their emotional memory. The man who can resist humiliation can quickly forget it; but the man who can long tolerate it must long remember it. In actual fact, nothing remains forgotten. All the fear one has endured, the dissimulation one has been forced into, all the painful and degrading buffoonery, and worst of all, perhaps, the feeling of having displayed one's cowardice – all this settles and accumulates somewhere in the bottom of our social consciousness, quietly fermenting....

Left untreated the abscesses suppurate; the pus cannot escape from the body, and the malady spreads throughout the organism....

No wonder, then, when the crust cracks and the lava of life rolls out, there appear not only well-considered attempts to rectify old wrongs, not only searchings for truth and for reforms matching life's needs, but also symptoms of bilious hatred, vengeful wrath, and a feverish desire for immediate compensation for all the degradation endured.[18]

Havel's fears for the future – unfounded as it turned out – were likely based on his troubled memory of the past.[19] If the 1989 Czechoslovak revolution was made of "velvet," the 1945 version was written in blood.

Resigned to passivity for most of the war, the small Czech underground repeatedly called on the government-in-exile to threaten collaborators with retribution. Resistance operatives forwarded the names of informers to be read on London radio broadcasts to the Protectorate. The underground also demanded threats against Czechs who, like one chief official at the Brno tramworks, "made [themselves] out to be German." Another message from home admonished Czech students not to study in the Reich and promised that their lost semesters – due to the Nazi closure of Czech universities – could be made up after the war.[20] One dispatch to the government-in-exile revealed that preparations were also being made for postwar retribution: "It is especially effective when

---

[18] Václav Havel, "Dear Dr. Husák," in Open Letters: Selected Writings, 1965–1990, ed. and trans. by Paul Wilson (New York: Knopf, 1991), 78–79.

[19] Havel commented, "I can remember all those postwar avengers after the Second World War – usually the most energetic ones were themselves the most guilty." Despite Havel's fears, one of the most remarkable aspects of the 1989 Velvet Revolution and its aftermath was the marked absence of vigilante retribution against Communist functionaries, the secret police, or their agents. Adam Michnik and Václav Havel, "An Interview with President Václav Havel," in Neil Kritz, ed., Transitional Justice: How Emerging Democracies Reckon with Former Regimes, 3 vols. (Washington, DC: United States Institute of Peace Press, 1995), II:537.

[20] Zprávy z domova, no. 116/41/dův. (26 January 1941); no. 143/41/dův. (10 February 1941); no. 230/41/dův. (10 February 1941); no. 146/41/dův. (10 February 1941); no. 331/41/dův. (13 March 1941), CU, Smutný papers, box 11, folder 1.

you promise that all scoundrels will be punished. Entire local catalogues of them are being created. Therefore repeat the threat several more times."[21] The exiles responded positively to such appeals. Soon after the fall of France, the future Justice Minister, Prokop Drtina, warned in a radio broadcast that the exile government knew "precisely what was going on at home and how everyone was behaving." He stressed that he spoke not of out-and-out fascists, who were beyond the pale, but of those who failed their nation in its hour of need. With a flourish, he proclaimed, "Someday all these [offenders] will be strictly prosecuted – this time they will not be forgiven!"[22] In one message home Beneš declared that the fate of the country's Germans was "sealed." "Wait for the right moment," he counseled. "Retaliation, which will certainly come, will be horrible." In a bout of hyperbole, he explained what "horrible" meant: "Every crime, every act of violence, every murder committed by the Nazi henchmen in Czechoslovakia ... must be and will be revenged and atoned for a thousand times over."[23]

Beneš and his government-in-exile did more than just promise horrible revenge on the Germans and severe justice for Czech collaborators. Wild retribution was not simply an organic explosion of antipathy; it was consciously desired, planned, and executed by Czech leaders. The exiles hoped that vigilante violence would terrorize Sudeten Germans into fleeing the country of their own accord, thereby greatly reducing the number to be deported later.[24] In the president's name, Drtina urged the underground to take matters into its own hands: "It is up to you at home to make sure that the Germans are repulsed and driven out as much and as far as possible. We're counting here on [the fact] that it will be bloody and not a stroll down Wenceslas Square like it was in 1918."[25] In his last message from abroad Beneš similarly instructed underground leaders: "We must take care of many [Germans] immediately in the first days after liberation so that the greatest possible number of guilty Nazis flee in fear of a civil uprising against them ... and so that the greatest number of Nazis who will resist are killed in the revolution." The Czechoslovak

[21] Zprávy z domova, no. 562/41/dův. (3 January 1941), CU, Smutný papers, box 11, folder 1.

[22] Prokop Drtina, *A nyní promluví Pavel Svatý. ... Londýnské rozhlasové epištoly z let 1940–1945* (Prague: Vladimír Žikeš, 1945), 42–44.

[23] "President Beneš Československému národu," *Čechoslovák* III:41 (10 October 1941), 1.

[24] Kaplan, *Poválečné Československo*, 142–43.

[25] Vondrová, *Češi a sudetoněmecká otázka*, doc. 42, 80.

president did not expect the killing to stop with German Nazis: "Whoever deserves death should be totally liquidated [*vylikvidován*] either in the popular storm or by military might immediately after the revolution." He then repeated, to stress the point, "Incontrovertible traitors should disappear in the first upsurge of the revolution."[26]

LIBERATION AND RETALIATION

"If one could stop the clock in, let us say, January 1944," Tony Judt noted, "most of occupied Europe would have had little of which to complain by contrast with what was to come." Bohemia and Moravia, in particular, experienced favorable economic conditions and limited civil unrest for another year.[27] In the spring of 1945, however, as the front finally drew near and then crossed into the Protectorate, partisan attacks intensified and SS units engaged in increasingly brutal acts of repression, torching some villages and executing their occupants. Death marches from Nazi extermination camps in the East wound their way across the land, presenting locals with graphic evidence of German atrocities.[28] Guards at the Theresienstadt Small Fortress executed Czech political prisoners, while down the road in the ghetto, deportations of Jews drew to a gruesome close.[29] Amid the May 1945 Prague Uprising, German

[26] Beneš apparently believed that vigilante murders would be less divisive than trials and executions. Jiří Šolc, ed., *Vzkazy do vlasti* (Prague: HÚ AČR, 1996), doc. 83, 185–86. Part of the translation is taken from Zbyněk Zeman and Antonín Klimek, *The Life of Edvard Beneš: Czechoslovakia in Peace and War* (Oxford: Clarendon Press, 1997), 199.

[27] Tony Judt, "The Past Is Another Country: Myth and Memory in Postwar Europe," *Daedalus* 121:4 (1992), 85.

[28] "Report of the Czechoslovak Ministry of the Interior...on Crimes Committed by the Allgemeine SS and the Waffen SS in Czechoslovakia," in *Trial of the Major War Criminals before the International Military Tribunal* (Nuremberg, 1949), 86–93; Radomír Luža, *The Transfer of the Sudeten Germans: A Study of Czech–German Relations, 1933–1962* (New York: New York University Press, 1964), 261; Jaroslav Toms, *Od Mnichova po osvobození: Přehled dějin Čechů a Slováků v letech 1938–1945* (Pilsen: Západočeská univerzita, 1995), 137; Jürgen Tampke, *Czech–German Relations and the Politics of Central Europe: From Bohemia to the EU* (Hampshire, UK: Palgrave Macmillan, 2003), 71–72, 86–87.

[29] On 2 May 1945 guards executed 51 prisoners in the Small Fortress, among the last of the 8,000 who died there during the war. In all, 33,430 Jews perished in the Theresienstadt ghetto; 88,000 others were deported to death camps, only 3,500 of whom survived the war. Zdeněk Huňáček, Jiří Jožák, Vlastislav Kroupa, and Jan Stříbrný, eds., *Český antifašismus: Slovníková příručka* (Prague: Naše vojsko, 1988), 462–64; Eva Schmidtová-Hartmannová, "Ztráty československého židovského obyvatelstva 1938–1945," in Livie Rothkirchenová, Eva Schmidtová-Hartmannová, and Avigdora Dagana, eds., *Osud Židů v Protektorátu 1939–1945* (Prague: Trizonia, 1991), 93–95.

soldiers murdered civilians and set alight the capital's Old Town Hall. As Czechs awaited liberation by Allied armies, these final weeks of uncertainty and terror erased memories of the relatively calmer years of Nazi occupation. An American observer commented on the aftermath of a German massacre of ten Czechs:

Compared with the devastation I had witnessed in Russian Ukraine... the scene before me was neither horrifying nor particularly impressive, if only because on neighboring streets houses, barns, trees were untouched. Yet to this village the memory of the shootings and the burnings must for generations to come fan an undying ember of hate for the enemy and for everything he symbolized.[30]

In May 1945 Czech leaders fanned this "undying ember of hate." In his first speech in liberated Prague, Beneš called for the "liquidation" of the country's Germans and Magyars "in the interest of a united national state of Czechs and Slovaks."[31] Drtina used his first speech in the country to proclaim, "We must begin immediately, this very moment, to expel the Germans from our lands. We must use all possible means – nothing can be allowed to cause us to stop or even to hesitate."[32] For their part, Communist leaders encouraged wild retribution against both Germans and Czech collaborators. The day hostilities ended in Prague they told the country the struggle was not over: "Only the occupiers have been defeated and expelled. But their lackeys are still here among the ranks of our nation.... Away with them, uncover and seize them! You must immediately chase them before your own just court – before a people's revolutionary court."[33] A few days later, Party leader Klement Gottwald appealed on radio for local authorities to "immediately commence" the "severe" punishment of Germans.[34] The Communist daily,

---

[30] Maurice Hindus, *The Bright Passage* (New York: Doubleday, Inc., 1947), 54.

[31] Recalling the president's repeated resort to the term "to liquidate," Václav Černý commented, "The word [*vylikvidovat*] was horrifying.... It smacked of revenge, not punishment." "Projev na Staroměstském náměstí v Praze" (16 May 1945), in Karel Novotný, ed., *Edvard Beneš: Odsun Němců z Československa: Výbor z pamětí, projevů a dokumentů 1940–1947* (Prague: Dita, 1996), 139; Černý, *Paměti*, III:42.

[32] Vilém Hejl, *Zpráva o organizovaném násilí* (Prague: Univerzum, 1990), 12.

[33] Tomáš Staněk, *Perzekuce 1945* (Prague: Institut pro středoevropskou kulturu a politiku, 1996), 72.

[34] Kaplan, *Poválečné Československo*, 138.

Rudé právo, demanded an immediate reckoning with "war and political criminals, their helpers, and traitors."[35]

The people heeded their leaders' calls and immediately began to "cleanse" the country of Nazis, Germans, and their Czech collaborators. Until the Armistice, vigilante retribution could be justified as a form of resistance, a contribution, albeit belated and inconsequential, to the liberation of the country from foreign occupation. Long after hostilities had ceased, however, the death toll continued to mount until the totals were horrifying: in Nový Bydžov 77 captured German soldiers were executed; in the mountain town of Špindlerův Mlýn, now a popular Czech ski resort, 30 German civilians were murdered along with 50 soldiers; near Přerov 265 were killed, including 120 women and 74 children younger than 14 years of age. In Postoloprty a Czech investigative team later unearthed the corpses of 763 Germans who had been concentrated in the area and liquidated.[36]

Although scholars have traditionally focused on the German victims of wild retribution, an unknown number of Czechs also perished in the wave of violence that engulfed the region in the spring of 1945. Vigilantes attacked notorious Czech collaborators, while individuals used the chaos to eliminate personal enemies or rival claimants. Sadists often did not distinguish their prey by nationality, nor did lynch mobs always pause to check the documents of victims. The fate of journalist Michal Mareš's father hints at the toll that anti-German violence took on Czech bystanders. In early May a mob invaded the Prague hospital where the elder Mareš lay convalescing. Upon learning the name of his home town, a village in the overwhelmingly German Sudetenland, the vigilantes beat him to death, without pausing to determine that he was, in fact, Czech.[37] It is hardly suprising that Mareš subsequently became one of the most outspoken critics of postwar Czech "excesses."

Vigilantism was sometimes dressed up as a "revolutionary court" and covered by a fig leaf of procedure. In what must have been one of the first such trials, on the day the Red Army liberated Brno a six-man "court" in the city condemned a woman to death for having denounced

[35] Staněk, *Perzekuce*, 72.
[36] Staněk, *Perzekuce*, 77, 109–113, 119.
[37] Michal Mareš, *Ze vzpomínek anarchisty, reportéra a válečného zločince* (Prague: Prostor, 1999), 252.

Czechs to the Gestapo. She was immediately hanged in a school court-yard.[38] In Lanškroun a public tribunal, headed by a non-Communist resistance leader, brutally executed up to two dozen Germans, some of them by drowning. In Rumburk local leaders sentenced to death and shot a Reich German who had been accused of being a concentration camp guard. Near Třeboň a camp survivor chaired a "people's court," which put fourteen Germans to death. In Kadaň a wave of executions began with one on the town square, followed by seventy-two others at the local court over the next three weeks.[39] All in all, the German *Ost-Dokumentation* estimated that "people's tribunals" executed at least 1,000 Germans in the weeks after the war.[40]

Revolutionary courts executed Czechs as well. On 18 May 1945 a makeshift tribunal in Tábor convicted Zdeněk Král and Jaroslav Ryneš of "collaboration with the Germans and treachery against the Czech nation." Under interrogation Král admitted to contacts with the local SS leader and to being the regional chief of the fascist Banner movement. During the occupation he had prominently displayed a blacklist in town with the names of Gentiles who had maintained relations with Jews. To top it off, Král was listed as an informer for the Gestapo. Ryneš was also a fascist and a virulent anti-Semite. In addition to being a local leader of Banner, he had proposed expelling pupils from school for socializing with Jews and for refusing to use the "Aryan salute." The two men were publicly hanged on the town square that very day.[41]

During the months after the Red Army liberated most of Czechoslovakia, Soviet soldiers contributed to the wave of violence through rape, murder, and pandemic theft.[42] In the southwestern sliver of Bohemia

[38] SZ Brno (8 June 1945) to MS no. 13763/45-III/4. Státní ústřední archiv (SÚA), Prague, f. MS (Org), k. 1928.
[39] Staněk, *Perzekuce*, 55, 64, 78, 83–86.
[40] Staněk, *Perzekuce*, 163–64.
[41] Státní zastupitelství (SZ) Tábor (29 May 1945) to MS no.14685/45-III/4, SÚA, f. MS (Org), k. 1928; "Soud nad zrádci národa v Táboře," *Práce* (24 May 1945), SÚA, f. MZV-VA II (j81), k. 215.
[42] Amid mass rape, indiscriminate shootings, and ubiquitous plunder, expellee memoirists also recalled acts of kindness by Russians and even instances where Soviet soldiers interfered to protect them from Czechs. Naimark, *Fires of Hatred*, 116–17; Theodor Schieder, ed., *The Expulsion of the German Population from Czechoslovakia* (Bonn: Federal Ministry for Expellees, 1960), 361, 401, 415, 484; Jeremy King, *Budweisers into Czechs and Germans: A Local History of Bohemian Politics, 1848–1948* (Princeton, NJ: Princeton University Press, 2003), 188; Zeman, *Life of Edvard Beneš*, 222–23; Joseph Wechsberg, *Homecoming* (New York: Alfred A. Knopf, 1946), 111–12.

liberated by the U.S. Army, however, Czechs accused American troops of preventing justifiable retribution against Germans. One Czech editor commented, "The situation is bizarre: in the American zone the people want the Russians to come so that the Germans lose their protection; in the Soviet zone, by contrast, people yearn for the Americans so that they can rid themselves of the pillaging Red Army."[43] For his part, the U.S. Ambassador expressed relief that the American Army had responsibility for only a small region. Otherwise, he argued, the troops' reluctance to tolerate anti-German violence might have convinced Czechs that Soviet occupation was preferable.[44] In the end, the presence of two foreign armies proved fortuitous for Czechoslovakia. When, under instructions from Moscow, the Communist Party pressed for the removal of American forces, the United States successfully insisted on a mutual withdrawal. By the end of 1945 both foreign armies had pulled out, leaving Czechoslovakia unoccupied and sovereign – the only country in the region that could make that claim.[45] In the meantime, the contrast between the two occupation zones indicated that order could be established, if the authorities – American, Soviet, or Czech – wished it so.

CREATING CHAOS

In addition to planning for a wave of vigilantism, the Czech exiles created conditions that subsequently made it difficult to reestablish order and bring vigilante violence under control. Perhaps the greatest contributing factor to the chaos of spring 1945 – and to many of the injustices that plagued the Czech provinces for the next three years – was the exile government's decision to revolutionize the country's system of local administration. In December 1944 President Beneš decreed that "national committees" [národní výbory] be created on all liberated

---

[43] Ladislav Feierabend, Politické vzpomínky, 3 vols. (Brno: Atlantis, 1994–1996), III:238; Toms, Od Mnichova, 145.

[44] Karel Kaplan, ed., ČSR a SSSR: Dokumenty mezivládních jednání, 1945–1948 (Brno: Doplněk, 1997, doc. 75, 162.

[45] U.S. Ambassador to Czechoslovakia Laurence Steinhardt took credit for the Red Army's withdrawal, exclaiming, "I got them out." Kaplan, ČSR a SSSR, doc. 11 and 75, 34–35, 161–62; P. Prokš, "Politická moc a sovětizace (1945–1948)," in Miroslav Tejchman, ed., Sovětizace východní Evropy (Prague: Historický ústav, 1995), 45; Toms, Od Mnichova, 141–46; Foreign Relations of the United States Diplomatic Papers (Washington, DC: U.S. Government Printing Office, 1968), vol. IV (1945), 460–509.

territory and act as fully sovereign bodies until such time as the central government could assume its superior role.[46] The April 1945 Košice Program, which set forth the postwar regime's political aims, declared,

In contrast to the previous bureaucracy, [which was] an administrative apparatus alienated from the people, popularly elected national committees will be formed in communities, districts, and provinces as new organs of state and public administration.... In their jurisdictions the national committees will administer all public affairs, control the subordinate democratic bureaucracy, and take care of public security in concert with both central and local police forces. The government will carry out its policies via the national committees and rely fully upon them.[47]

Both the December 1944 decree and the Košice Program spoke of "popularly elected" organs, but neither spelled out just how the elections were to take place. Service on national committees was restricted to individuals of Slavic origin who were deemed "reliable" and had not been members of any banned political party. In areas where the majority of the population was not "politically reliable," that is, where German-speakers predominated, the government appointed "commissars" or "administrative commissions" [*správní komise*] to serve until local Czechs (often new migrants to the borderlands) could assume control.

The national committee system has not received the attention it merits from historians.[48] In addition to playing a critical role in postwar retribution, these new local institutions helped to undermine Czechoslovak democracy. The elimination of prewar structures, Gottwald told a gathering of Slovak Communist functionaries in Košice, was integral to the Party's plan to seize power. With the exception of President Beneš, he explained, there existed no firm continuity with the interwar

---

[46] Decree no. 18/1944, in Karel Jech and Karel Kaplan, eds., *Dekrety prezidenta republiky, 1940–1945: Dokumenty* (Brno: Ústav pro soudobé dějiny, 1995), doc. 6, I:123–24; Karel Bertelmann,*Vývoj národních výborů do ústavy 9. května (1945–1948)* (Prague: Československá akademie věd, 1964), 107–109.

[47] Jiří Grospič, Jaroslav Chovanec, and Juraj Vysokaj, eds., *Košický vládní program* (Prague: Státní pedagogické nakladatelství, 1977), 128.

[48] There are no studies of the subject in English or even in German, while in Czech the only relevant works date from the Communist period. See Karel Bertelmann, *Vývoj národních výborů do ústavy 9. května (1945–1948)* (Prague: Československá akademie věd, 1964).

republic. Gottwald gloated, "When it comes to the state administration and apparatus we have a clean slate." He called national committees "a thorn in the side" of the Communists' partners and identified them as "the main arena for the political struggle."[49] The danger inherent in national committees was immediately apparent to some. During the war, Jaroslav Stránský, the Justice Minister of the government-in-exile, warned against giving inexperienced men too much power. "This could be a new source of fascist moods [nálady], tendencies and agitation," he predicted. "It could be a source of disorder because in such a situation the government would be powerless." Stránský futilely argued that the popular will could be best and most competently carried out through "responsible, decisive men" acting in the name of the president and government.[50] Years later, Ota Hora, one of the Communists' most vigorous critics, reflected, "Above all, national committees...were at the beginning of the tragedy for the building of a democratic and free Czechoslovakia."[51]

The postwar regime ultimately established three levels of national committees in the Czech provinces. First, each community (11,533 in all) had its own Local National Committee [Místní národní výbor (MNV)], which assumed the responsibilities of a mayor or town council. Second, multiple Local National Committees were grouped in turn under the auspices of a District National Committee [Okresní národní výbor (ONV)] or, in the case of major cities, a Central National Committee [Ústřední národní výbor (ÚNV)]. The 156 ONVs and six ÚNVs assumed control over most police functions, including the investigation of non-political crimes and the maintenance of public order and "moral

---

[49] Speech of Gottwald at a conference of Communist Party of Slovakia functionaries (8 April 1945) in Košice, SÚA, f. 1, sv. 1, aj. 1, 12–13. The Communist Party of Czechoslovakia could not have been disappointed by the results: In 1945 Communists made up thirty-seven percent of District National Committee members in Bohemia and thirty-two percent in Moravia. By the beginning of 1946 Communists headed forty-six percent of all national committees. After the 1946 elections the Party's stranglehold on the national committees grew even tighter: in the Czech provinces seventy-eight percent of all District National Committee chairmen were Communist Party members; in Bohemia the number was a staggering eighty-nine percent. Bertelmann, Národní výbory, 172, 179; František Hanzlík, Únor 1948: Výsledek nerovného zápasu: Tajné služby na cestě k moci (Prague: Prewon, 1997), 47.

[50] Jech, Dekrety, doc. 6.5, I:133–34; Stránský (29 June 1944) to Nosek, SÚA, f. 100/24, sv. 75, aj. 1562.

[51] Ota Hora, Svědectví o puči (Prague: Melantrich, 1991), 124.

security." They regulated civic organizations and the press and issued gun and hunting licenses. The committees even determined citizenship and nationality, and issued passports, identification cards, and certificates of "national" and "political reliability." As a result, during the postwar expulsion local officials, not the central government, decided precisely which individuals could stay in the country and which were to be "transferred." Most importantly for this study, the committees' investigative commissions prepared cases for prosecution by retribution tribunals. Third, Provincial National Committees [Zemské národní výbory (ZNV)] in Prague, Brno, and Ostrava, oversaw the work of the District Committees in Bohemia, Moravia, and Silesia, respectively. The Provincial National Committees were appellate, not controlling bodies; the District National Committees were actually subordinate to the Interior Ministry. Matters of public security fell ambiguously between the competencies of local and central authorities.[52] This ambiguity, added to the parochial interests of local figures and the inexperience of new administrators, contributed significantly to the postwar chaos.

In the spring of 1945 the dismissal of the existing bureaucracy created a power vacuum that national committees attempted to fill. Communist scholar Karel Bertelmann explained, "The national committees functioned *de facto* well beyond 9 May 1945 as the *sole power* at the community and district level."[53] National committee members arrested, interrogated, and sometimes executed suspected collaborators. They seized and redistributed property (often to themselves and their cronies). By the time the central government belatedly began to demand that such "excesses" cease, it discovered that many national committees had become Frankenstein monsters, unresponsive to their creators and a danger to the public. A series of plaintive directives and circulars

[52] Each District National Committee was responsible for security within its jurisdiction and therefore issued orders to the local division of the National Security Corps [Sbor národní bezpečnosti (SNB)]. A District National Committee, however, could not "interfere in the direct exercise of those duties which the SNB must carry out according to the laws, directives and orders of its controlling commanders." Parallel to the national committee system there existed a hierarchical structure for the police stretching upwards to the Interior Ministry in Prague. In the Interior Ministry itself, separate departments oversaw the national committees and the police. Bertelmann, *Vývoj národních výborů*, 122–25; Stanislav Šulc, *Národní výbory: Vývoj, právní základy, poslání, práce* (Brno: ZÁR, 1946), 298–300; *Rukověť' pro národní výbory v zemi české a moravskoslezské pro rok 1947* (Prague: Státní tiskárna, 1947), 378–94.
[53] Italics in original. Bertelmann, *Vývoj národních výborů*, 94.

clearly show, first, that government orders were widely ignored and, second, that the central authorities were powerless to do anything about it.[54] Nothing so well demonstrates the arbitrary nature of local rule than the punishment of Czechs married to Germans. Despite the central government's repeated orders not to mistreat intermarried couples and their families, some national committees forced them to wear armbands marking them as German, evicted them from their homes, interned them in camps, and occasionally even expelled them from the country. Local leaders dismissed Prague's ineffectual criticism of their illegal acts with such weak excuses as, "We haven't yet had a chance to study [the government directives]," "We never received them," or even, "We lost them."[55]

In parts of the former Sudetenland the elimination of prewar structures and the lack of an indigenous Czech population combined to produce an especially lawless environment. Carpetbaggers, charlatans, and criminals flocked to the borderlands, a new Wild West where no one had a past and crimes usually went unpunished. In Liberec (Reichenberg), the former capital of the Nazi Sudetenland, the Czech district attorney later reported, "Conditions... particularly in the first days, were very chaotic." A local shoe salesman assumed the post of police chief, only to be replaced "when due to his inexperience he committed numerous, gross mistakes." Another Czech, a postal inspector, arrived in Liberec with Interior Ministry papers appointing him "government commissar" of the city. By the time the document had been exposed as a forgery and the impostor had been arrested, he had managed to enrich himself and his entourage with a considerable amount of seized property. Then there was the man who posed as a Russian official and accepted bribes from desperate Germans in exchange for worthless "residence permits." Topping off these charades was an event so absurd that it poignantly captures the uncertainty of the time. A local German Communist cell prepared a pamphlet declaring the creation of a Communist-run,

---

[54] Tomáš Staněk, *Tábory v českých zemích 1945–1948* (Ostrava: Tilia, 1996), 21, 24–25, 36–37.

[55] "Co bude se smíšenými manželstvími?" *Lidová demokracie* (13 October 1945), 1; "Pořádek do věci smíšených manželství," *Lidová demokracie* (25 November 1945), 1–2; "Ještě smíšená manželství," *Lidová demokracie* (6 November 1945), 1–2. For more on the treatment of intermarried families, see Benjamin Frommer, "Expulsion or Integration: Unmixing Interethnic Marriage in Postwar Czechoslovakia," *East European Politics and Societies* 14:2 (Spring 2000), 381–410.

self-governing, Sudeten German region. The Czech district attorney later reported, "Their self-confidence about the success of their gambit went so far that [their leader]... began to hand down written orders to arrest as a fascist any Czech who refused to recognize the creation of the autonomous region." The Soviet presence made suppression of the irredentists all the more difficult; the Red Army apparently had difficulty distinguishing between Slavic communists and Teutonic ones.[56] Into this disorder stepped Revolutionary Guards – Czech paramilitaries who quickly earned the moniker "Ransacking Guards."[57] Upon entering Liberec on 20 May they immediately executed several Germans. Nearby, five women and three children were murdered, apparently by Nazis intent on eliminating potential witnesses to their crimes.[58] Attempts to restore order were hampered by the unwillingness of paramilitary groups to submit to any authority. The local Communist secretariat reported that the chief of the Revolutionary Guards had dismissed criticism: "We don't give a damn about Interior Ministry orders." Eventually the Liberec authorities had to threaten to shoot robbers and vandals on sight.[59]

On 12 May Czechoslovak Premier Zdeněk Fierlinger called on the government to issue a radio appeal for the public to cease acts of violence against innocent Germans. Irrespective of political affiliation, his fellow cabinet ministers universally dismissed the "lynchings and tyrannization" referred to by the premier as "isolated phenomena of the revolutionary period." They argued that a public appeal by the government was neither possible nor in the country's interest. Instead, the Interior Minister pledged to call a meeting of the leaders of the security forces to convey the government's concerns privately.[60] One can only

---

[56] SZ Liberec (27 June 1945) to MS no. 16437/45-III/4, SÚA, f. MS (Org), k. 1928.

[57] In Czech, "Rabovací gardy." Václav Jiřík, *Nedaleko od Norimberku: Z dějin Mimořádného lidového soudu v Chebu v letech 1946 až 1948* (Cheb: Svět křídel, 2000), 38.

[58] SZ Liberec (27 June 1945) to MS no. 16437/45-III/4, SÚA, f. MS (Org), k. 1928.

[59] Staněk, *Perzekuce*, 93.

[60] Fierlinger, the leader of the Social Democratic Party, is typically remembered as a weak-willed Communist fellow-traveler who facilitated the February 1948 coup, but to his credit after the war he ocassionally maintained a more liberal attitude toward the Sudeten Germans than his colleagues on the left or right. Government meeting (12 May 1945), SÚA, f. 100/24, aj. 1494, sv. 137, 1. For another example of Fierlinger's tolerance, see Frommer, "Unmixing Marriage," 384, n. 10.

wonder how many lives might have been saved if the other ministers had heeded Fierlinger's advice and immediately called on the public and paramilitaries to cease and desist. Only at the end of the month did the Interior Ministry order local authorities not to execute or prosecute suspected war criminals and collaborators.[61] Not until early June were orders issued to disband the Revolutionary Guards.[62]

MASS ARRESTS

Amid the epidemic of vigilante killings, Czechs rounded up thousands of Germans, suspected war criminals, and alleged collaborators. As early as 16 April 1944, with the Red Army on the borders of prewar Czechoslovakia, the government-in-exile had called on Czechs to "immediately remove from all public functions citizens of enemy states and individuals who betrayed the Czechoslovak Republic or who collaborated with the enemy. And detain all these individuals so they do not escape."[63] The exiles did not, however, clearly instruct which traitors and collaborators were to be arrested, where they were to be interned, and how they were to be treated. These lapses were compounded by the lack of a law to govern the prosecution and punishment of collaborators and war criminals. In late February 1945 President Beneš had signed a decree establishing retribution courts, but the government shelved it in the hope that an agreement could be reached with dissenting parties. In the absence of clear instructions from the central government, the Olomouc national committee issued its own guidelines for arrests at the end of May 1945. A large, red poster called on citizens in the district to turn in war criminals, traitors, and collaborators and demanded the punishment of the following categories of individuals:

1. All of Hitler's war criminals from the German population who in some way transgressed against the Czech working people.
2. All traitors from the Czech banking, industrial, commercial, trading, and agricultural circles, who – voluntarily, directly or indirectly, clandestinely or openly, or with extraordinarily zeal – served the German

---

[61] Staněk, *Tábory*, 18.
[62] Huňáček, *Český antifašismus*, 394.
[63] Jech, *Dekrety*, doc. 6.1, I:125–26.

occupiers and helped plunder, bleed dry, and impoverish the Czech national economy.

3. All profiteers and opportunists of whatever type who enriched themselves at the expense of the Czech nation.

4. All other traitors, collaborators, and open or hidden fascists from the ranks of the Czech population who in any way transgressed against the Czech people and their national honor.

Although the poster was printed nearly a month after mass detentions had begun, the Olomouc national committee still called for more arrests and encouraged more denunciations: "It is not enough just to talk about the cleansing of public life. Every offense must be reported immediately."[64]

Without a retribution law establishing a clear definition of collaboration, officials, many of them self-appointed, indiscriminately dumped suspects into local jails and makeshift camps.[65] "In these chaotic conditions," the Liberec district attorney reported in June, "provisional police (volunteers), Revolutionary Guards, the army, and other groups arrested whomever wherever, without the agreement, often without even the permission, of the national committee." When he reviewed the cases the district attorney found that the paramilitary groups had not furnished any proof, save some forced confessions, to accompany arrested suspects. Investigations had to be carried out *ex post facto* to determine the crimes committed by those already in detention. Of the approximately 3,000 people detained, only 60 had been charged by the end of June. The district attorney complained, "There's still no clear overview of either the total number [of prisoners] or the cause of their arrests."[66] An official from Mladá Boleslav similarly reported, "The manner of arrests was not quite uniform.... The nationality of many persons has not yet been determined.... It is simply not possible to comment with certainty, particularly on the number of detained persons."[67] The Interior Ministry later commented, "It has been demonstrably shown that many individuals were arrested and persecuted without there even being a concrete accusation or evidence on hand."[68]

[64] MS no. 14019/45, SÚA, f. MS, k. 1928.
[65] Staněk, *Tábory*, 18.
[66] SZ Liberec (27 June 1945) to MS no. 16437/45-III/4, SÚA, f. MS (Org), k. 1928.
[67] SZ Mladá Boleslav to MS no. 13748/45-III/4 (8 June 1945), SÚA, f. MS (Org), k. 1928.
[68] Staněk, *Tábory*, 21.

An August 1945 inventory of the 245 prisoners held in the eastern Bohemian town of Čáslav provides a detailed look at the haphazard nature of postwar detention. In addition to informers and members of Czech fascist groups, there were many prisoners whose alleged crimes were either uncertain or simply unknown. Typical entries in the prison log include "probably denounced," "probably collaborated with Germans," and even "so far unclear" and "doubtful." Others were apparently arrested because they were the "friend of" a notorious collaborator. One woman was even detained as "the girlfriend of" a "friend of" a notorious collaborator. Fraternization with Germans was reason enough for numerous Czech women and at least two Czech men to be arrested by local authorities. Even mixed marriage was considered sufficient cause: The German husband of a Czech wife perished after one night in detention; the daughter of an intermarried couple still sat in prison in August.[69] Summing up the dire situation throughout the country, an internal government report admitted in August, "There is no comprehensive information about the countryside, the number of prisoners interned there, their interrogation or even about camp conditions."[70]

The sheer number of those detained overwhelmed the existing system of jails and prisons. The glamorous Czech film actress Adina Mandlová, who had been arrested for collaboration (see Figure 1), commented, with a bit of hyperbole, "Every police station, every school, church or public building was transformed into a detainment center for prisoners."[71] In his extensive study of the topic, Tomáš Staněk estimated that in 1945 about 500 camps and other facilities were used to hold Germans and suspected collaborators.[72] By mid-June Prague's Pankrác prison alone held 4,000 suspects; throughout the city some 20,000 had been detained in thirty-seven different locations.[73] In August an official survey of Bohemian detention camps for war criminals and collaborators counted

[69] "Seznam osob zajištěných...ve věznici okresního soudu v Čáslavi ve věci týkající se kolaborantů a zrádců," Státní okresní archiv (SOkA), Kutná Hora (KH), ONV-Čáslav, k. 75.
[70] Staněk, Tábory, 41.
[71] Adina Mandlová, Dneska už se tomu směju (Toronto: Sixty-Eight Publishers, 1976), 161.
[72] Staněk, Tábory, 27–28. According to the Interior Ministry, as of 26 November 1945 there were 221 internment camps in the Czech provinces: 5 in Prague, 114 in the rest of Bohemia, and 102 in Moravia. MS no. 43654/45-IV/1 (27 November 1945), SÚA, f. MS (Org), k. 1934.
[73] "Kdy zahájí činnost Lidové soudy?" Mladá fronta (15 June 1945), 1; "Co je vlastně KVNB," Mladá fronta (22 June 1945), 2.

Figure 1. Adina Mandlová in Pankrác Prison. Česká tisková kancelář (Czech Press Agency), date unknown. Reproduced with permission.

more than 69,000 prisoners, including 8,275 considered to be Czech.[74] At the end of November the Interior Ministry estimated that 10,000 Czechs were in custody.[75]

Arrests were often violent affairs, but detention was worse. A man from Příbram described his encounter with an angry mob: "On the way from the car to the court – a mere twenty meters – one of my front teeth was knocked out, I received a stab wound above my left eye... another to my left cheek, to my forehead." The police did not behave themselves much better – they beat him regularly during

[74] Staněk, *Tábory*, 46.
[75] MS no. 43654/45-IV/1 (27 November 1945), SÚA, f. MS (Org), k. 1934.

interrogations.[76] In her memoirs Mandlová described prisoners returning from interrogations covered in blood: "Every face spoke of the horrors they had endured."[77] In the Theresienstadt small fortress, where the Nazis had murdered more than 8,000 Czechs during the occupation, after the war a doctor fatally injected forty-five German prisoners from the SS and the Gestapo.[78] In response to reports of Czech sadism, the Interior Ministry complained that national committees had subjected "utterly innocent people to methods which were employed during the occupation by the Gestapo." Repeatedly and with increasing despair, the Ministry commanded, then implored national committees to abide by the published guidelines and to desist from illegal violations of procedure.[79]

The guards at these jails and prisons were an eclectic, and often self-selected, group. Uniformed police, Revolutionary Guards, former partisans, factory militia, and even Red Army soldiers patrolled detention facilities.[80] In a twist of fate, survivors of wartime imprisonment became the jailers of Nazis and suspected collaborators. Other former prisoners who had actually been arrested for nonpolitical crimes such as theft and murder passed themselves off as victims of Nazism and became guards or even camp commandants.[81] One brutal guard suspected of murdering Germans was later discovered to have been a Slovak fascist on the lam from retribution charges.[82] The Soviet People's Commisariat of Internal Affairs (NKVD) and Soviet secret police and military intelligence seized and deported countless Germans and even Czechs. Official records are full of murky references to Soviet authorities appearing at camps and disappearing with dozens, even

[76] The man was sentenced to eighteen years imprisonment for his role in fascist organizations. The final insult apparently came in February 1946 when the local newspaper erroneously announced his death in the military prison. He later commented in a plea for commutation of his sentence, "Perhaps they will correct it and announce that I have temporarily revived." AKPR, s. D-11377/47, k. 262, B-prominut.

[77] Mandlová, *Dneska*, 162.

[78] Staněk estimated that there were seventy violent deaths in the Theresienstadt fortress after the war. According to a recent study, between 1945 and 1948, 550 of the 3,725 German prisoners in Theresienstadt died. "Excesses," SÚA, f. MS (Drtina), k. 2111; Staněk, *Tábory*, 78; "Studie über deutsche Opfer in Theresienstadt," *Frankfurter Allgemeine Zeitung* (28 July 1997), 5.

[79] Staněk, *Tábory*, 21, 24–25, 36–37.

[80] Staněk, *Tábory*, 30.

[81] Staněk, *Tábory*, 86.

[82] MS no. 13714/46-IV/3, "Excesses," SÚA, f. MS (Drtina), k. 2111.

hundreds of prisoners. The Čáslav prison list, for example, ominously recorded a German, a Czech, and a Slovak woman as "detained for the NKVD."[83]

Behind walls and fences Czech guards committed terrifying acts of violence and cruelty. In his analysis of the camps, Staněk catalogued dozens of locations where prisoners were executed or died as a result of beatings.[84] Two facilities stand out: the Hanke internment camp near Ostrava and the Kolín camp for suspected collaborators. Police sources reported that 231 Hanke internees perished violently in the month from 15 May to 20 June 1945.[85] According to eyewitness testimony,

Apart from the drinking bouts, the guards' orgies with interned women, and the torture during interrogations, there were regular executions. Some guards even invited their friends to watch. After attempts to kill by 220-volt electric current did not succeed, death was by hanging. . . . Sometimes there were also shootings, but only in individual cases when there wasn't enough time for ceremonial executions. . . . Everyone who was to be executed was first tortured until he signed the confession he was given.[86]

In Kolín, Bedřich Kárník, a former prisoner of the Nazis turned camp commandant, subjected Czech suspects to a daily regimen of threats and vicious beatings. Under his watch and guidance guards regularly knocked out prisoners' teeth and stomped on their hands and heads. When the blood and screams disturbed the neighbors, who could easily see into the prison yard, Kárník ordered that the beatings be continued indoors. Despite public knowledge of the guards' crimes, the Kolín camp was the scene of vicious violence as late as 23–24 September 1945. Only after a "Bartholomew's night" of carnage were Kárník and several guards arrested.[87]

In jails and detention centers, guards sadistically subjected female prisoners to sexual torture. For example, investigators in Chrudim

[83] SZ Mladá Boleslav (8 June 1945) to MS no. 13748/45-III/4; SZ Olomouc (9 June 1945) to MS no. 14019/45-III/4; SZ Nový Jičín (12 June 1945) to MS no. 14228/45-III/4 (26 June 1945), SÚA, f. MS (Org), k. 1928; Staněk, *Perzekuce*, 85; Hejl, *Zpráva*, 15; "Seznam osob zajištěných," SOkA-KH, ONV-Čáslav, k. 75.

[84] Staněk, *Tábory*, 78–79.

[85] Staněk, *Tábory*, 74–75.

[86] Ota Hora, *Svědectví o puči* (Toronto: Sixty-Eight Publishers, 1978), 134–35.

[87] Interpolation no. 629, Hora, *Svědectví* (1978), 262–63.

forced two women to strip naked for their interrogation.[88] Elsewhere jailers delivered incarcerated women to be raped by Red Army soldiers. Sometimes the Russians were let in to the detention centers to personally choose their victims.[89] While most female victims of misogynistic violence were German, Czech women were targets, too, especially if they could be accused of having fraternized with German men during the war. In desperation one woman wrote an anonymous letter to the Czechoslovak president to plead for her nineteen-year-old sister, an arrested fraternizer. The woman explained,

My sister has been in prison for ten weeks already. What she's suffered for such a small offense is so inhuman as to be incomprehensible. They have treated her from the very beginning as if she were the worst criminal. National committee members came into her cell drunk, ordered her to strip naked, thrashed her so roughly that her body was like a map, they cut her exquisite hair and after the beating they doused her in water. That was repeated several nights in a row.

The sister added with emphasis, "There are more such cases with girls in my parents' village near Prague." Unfortunately, the letter likely failed to ameliorate her sister's condition. Even if it found a sympathetic audience, its author was too afraid to sign her name or even reveal the name of the village concerned.[90]

ESTABLISHING ORDER

National committees, for all their faults, had a vested interest in establishing order within their jurisdictions and concentrating power in their own hands, not those of vigilantes and paramilitaries. On 11 May 1945 the Třebíč national committee publicly proclaimed its commitment to punish war criminals, traitors, and collaborators. In four brief points the national committee also made clear that it would not tolerate disorder. First and foremost, it declared, "Vigilante punishment of

[88] MS no. 49910/45, "Excesses," SÚA, f. MS (Drtina), k. 2111. For a particularly horrifying example, see Staněk, *Tábory*, 218, n. 108.

[89] MS no. 12195/46, "Excesses," SÚA, f. MS (Drtina), k. 2111; Archiv Kanceláře Prezidenta Republiky (AKPR), f. D-11169/47 "Anonymy," vec: D; AKPR no. R-7678/45 (28 July 1945); Mandlová, *Dneska*, 171; Turnwald, *Documents on the Expulsion*, 8–9, 42–43, 87, 96–97, 113.

[90] Anonymous letter to the president, KPR no. R-7678/45 (28 July 1945), AKPR, f. D-11169/47 (Anonymy), D.

any crime is forbidden." Second, it established a concentration camp to house suspects and an "investigative commission" to interrogate them. Third, it mandated that all reports had to be signed with the full name and address of the informant: "Anonymous denunciations will not be considered." Finally, the national committee warned, "Made-up accusations, for example, those based on personal vengeance and hatred, will be punished." Unfortunately, the last threat failed to dissuade. At the end of the month, and then again one week later, the Třebíč national committee felt obliged to issue more appeals against false denunciations, which were apparently being used "solely so that personal, entirely unsubstantiated, vengefulness is satiated."[91]

Even "revolutionary justice" could be an attempt to reestablish order. At the end of May one national committee warned, "We will deal with the Germans harshly ... but we do not want and will never operate using Gestapo methods. ... No tyrannizing, torture or bullying will be tolerated. Whoever violates this order will be put on trial."[92] On 31 May 1945 the town of Havlíčkův Brod inaugurated an unofficial retribution tribunal. Six judges presided; none of them were lawyers – the chairman was a veterinarian, his deputy a school principal. A German couple accused of being paid informers for the Gestapo took the dock first. The evidence against them was overwhelming: Numerous witnesses came forward to condemn the couple. Both were convicted and shot that very day. The court then turned its attention from wartime collaboration to a more recent matter, the case of two Czech workers who had impersonated national committee officials. Without authorization the men had conducted armed searches of German villages, arrested peasants, and seized their possessions. The tribunal punished one culprit with twenty years' imprisonment, the other with ten. Each also had to submit to public pillory for a period of ten hours and do forced labor for the remainder of his sentence. Clearly, the Havlíčkův Brod national committee sought to quench the popular thirst for justice while at the same time it aimed to discourage vigilantism.[93]

---

[91] Třebíč notices (11 May, 30 May, and 6 June 1945), MS no. 13823/45, SÚA, f. MS (Org), k. 1928.
[92] Staněk, *Perzekuce*, 54.
[93] When it subsequently learned of the executions, the Justice Ministry declined to intervene because the tribunal was a "revolutionary manifestation." For the convicted Czechs, however, the Ministry noted that there would be chance to review the verdicts later. OS

Although most perpetrators went free, the police and local authorities did arrest some vigilantes, particularly if they had committed crimes against other Czechs. The Interior Ministry later reported that 3,173 suspects had been arrested for plundering property.[94] In cases of violent crime, however, many if not most of those detained were soon released and never prosecuted.[95] For example, when a Communist worker shot the alleged denouncer of his wife and two sisters, he was arrested. Although he was himself suspected of working for the Gestapo, he was shortly released. Elsewhere, the police also detained and soon let go some men who shot three alleged collaborators, two of them after a "partisan court" in a local pub. In another case, a court official and several national committee members were suspected of abusing prisoners and stealing their property. The one suspect arrested was nonetheless released and the matter was dropped altogether.[96] Despite their horrific crimes, Kolín camp commandant Kárník and his subordinates were released from jail after six weeks.[97] Attempts to bring perpetrators to justice often caused anguish to whistle-blowers. They were accused of being "Germanophiles" and of protecting collaborators. One policeman who had arrested a guard for beating prisoners was himself disciplined.[98] Elsewhere the police allegedly reprimanded a Czech landlord when he attempted to report an attack on a German woman.[99] The message was quickly assimilated that there was no penalty for violence against Germans and collaborators, but there was a price to pay for attempting to prevent it.

In time the Interior Ministry and regional and local authorities attempted to assert their authority over the arrest and detention of suspects. The scope of the challenge they faced is demonstrated by repeated orders detailing who *not* to detain. In May the police in various cities exempted certain groups from arrest, including pregnant women, invalids, infants and their mothers, as well as members of mixed-marriage

Havlíčkův Brod (4 June 1945) to SZ Kutná Hora MS no. 13492/45-III/4, SÚA, f. MS (Org), k. 1928; MS no. 13492/45-III/4 (12 June 1945), SÚA, f. MS (Org), k. 1928.

[94] Nosek address to PNS (26 April 1946), Luža, *Transfer*, 269, n. 9.

[95] Tomáš Staněk, *Odsun Němců z Československa 1945–1947* (Prague: Naše vojsko, 1991), 202.

[96] "Excesses," SÚA, f. MS (Drtina), k. 2111.

[97] Hora, *Svědectví* (1978), 263.

[98] Staněk, *Tábory*, 86–87.

[99] Turnwald, *Documents on the Expulsion*, doc. 92, 211.

NATIONAL CLEANSING

families who had committed no crime against the state or the nation.[100] From Prague the Interior Ministry ordered that Czechs not be detained unless it could be demonstrated that they were "traitors against the nation, saboteurs and subversives, or collaborators." Any Czech guilty only of a minor offense was to be conditionally released. The Interior Ministry also called on other government departments not to issue their own orders for arrests. In Moravia and Silesia, the respective police headquarters in Brno and Ostrava assumed command of operations. In early June the Prague national committee formed a commission to systematize and direct the arrest and subsequent interrogations of suspects.[101]

These attempts to restore order were severely hampered by the absence of a final version of a retribution law. The Pardubice national committee pleaded with the Justice Ministry to have such a law passed as soon as possible. In the meantime, the committee faced a deluge of denunciations – many of which it suspected to be based solely on revenge – but could not do anything with them.[102] On 21 June 1945 the České Budějovice district attorney similarly complained that the work of investigators had been "slowed down by the uncertainty...caused by the fact that the people's court decree in its exact form is not known."[103] Thanks to these delays, by the time the government finally promulgated the retribution decree specifying exactly what crimes and which criminals were to be prosecuted, thousands of suspected collaborators and war criminals were already in jail.

CONCLUSION

The spring and summer months of 1945 were a brutal time in the Czech provinces of Bohemia, Moravia, and Silesia, but the scale of the violence was not unique. Vigilantes executed as many as 10,000 individuals by extralegal means in contemporary France.[104] In the eastern territories seized by the Soviet Union and Poland, millions of Germans

---

[100] NBS Ostrava (17–18 May 1945), NBS Brno (20 May 1945), NBS Opava (28 May 1945), Staněk, *Tábory*, 15.
[101] Staněk, *Tábory*, 17, 36–37.
[102] ONV Pardubice (26 May 1945) to ÚPV, SÚA, f. ÚPV-běž., k. 808, sign. 801/4.
[103] SZ České Budějovice (21 June 1945) to MS no. 15031/45-III/4, SÚA, f. MS (Org), k. 1928.
[104] Rousso, "L'épuration," in *Politische Säuberung*, 201–202.

60

were put to flight; hundreds of thousands perished.[105] With the end of the war some degree of chaos was inevitable. No government, certainly not one returning from six years in exile, could have prevented vigilante acts of retribution, particularly those aimed at notorious servants of the occupying regime.

As this chapter has argued, however, Czechoslovak leaders did not seek to suppress vigilantism. In fact, they repeatedly encouraged violence as a means to magnify the Wild Transfer and summarily reduce the country's German population. One of the country's foremost liberals, Pavel Tigrid, commented in retrospect,

> The "revolutionary retaliation" did not become "unstoppable." It was carefully thought out, prepared, and imported from Moscow by the new postwar rulers. It was decreed from above by an unelected power elite that did not bother to ask anyone – certainly not the Czech people who at every step it invoked and praised – about anything. Until the people finally said to themselves: if the bosses are going to play that tune, why shouldn't we dance?[106]

The creation of national committees further contributed to the chaos by depriving local government of administrative continuity. For postwar justice, the government's crimes of omission were perhaps worse. Despite planning for years, the exiles returned without clear and final instructions regarding whom to imprison or even what offenses to prosecute. Mass, indiscriminate arrests created an untenable situation, whereby either accused persons had to be released or laws had to be created to match their alleged crimes. As subsequent chapters explain, the country's leaders ultimately chose the latter option.

Scholars have traditionally depicted a postwar struggle between Czechoslovak Communists, who sought to establish a Soviet-style dictatorship, and "democrats," who fought to stop them.[107] In fact, most of the so-called "democrats" were not adherents of liberal democracy, especially when it came to Germans and alleged collaborators. If, as Tigrid stated, the violence was "imported from Moscow," then it only made

---

[105] Naimark, *Fires of Hatred*, 126.

[106] Pavel Tigrid, *Kapesní průvodce inteligentní ženy po vlastním osudu* (Toronto: Sixty-Eight Publishers, 1988), 290.

[107] For a brief version of this thesis, see Radomír Luža, "Czechoslovakia between Democracy and Communism," in Victor S. Mamatey and Radomír Luža, eds., *A History of the Czechoslovak Republic, 1918–1948* (Princeton, NJ: Princeton University Press, 1973), 387–415.

a brief stopover there on the way from London to Prague. Long before the Britain-based exiles decamped for their short stay in the Soviet capital, Beneš and his followers had already anticipated and welcomed wild retribution. Back in Czechoslovakia, Communist leaders may have encouraged violence with greater zeal, but their non-Communist partners did not intervene to stop vigilantism or restore order. Like the Communists, the "democrats" saw utility in anarchy. Whereas the former planned for chaos to facilitate revolution, the latter hoped that disorder would rid the country of undesirable minorities. These policies were not without consequences. Staněk explained, "The democrats' competition with the Communists to enforce vigorous measures against Germans and suspected collaborators...quickly put them [the 'democrats'] in a position from which it was not easy to block or lessen unleashed passions."[108] Before the retribution courts began their trials, the principle that vengeance was in the nation's interest and the knowledge that vigilantes would go unpunished had been widely assimilated.

---

[108] Staněk, *Perzekuce,* 176.

2

THE GREAT DECREE

On 22 May 1945 two representatives of the Brno national committee arrived in Prague with troubling news for the Justice Ministry. Tempers in Czechoslovakia's second-largest city had reached the boiling point. Paramilitary forces and local police had interned around 1,600 suspected collaborators and war criminals in a local dormitory. Most prisoners were German, but the group included approximately 100 Czechs. The delegates anxiously reported,

In the last few days there have been riots in front of the building. A mob of people has demanded that the prisoners either be handed over to it or be tried immediately by a people's court. Only the positioning of guards with machine guns has prevented the riotous crowd from storming the building and carrying out justice on the spot.

The Brno officials expressly refused to assume the burden of firing on the people. They apparently had only managed to calm matters down by promising the mob that the committee's representatives would return from Prague with either a functioning court or their resignations in hand. To emphasize the gravity of their predicament, they revealed that in the nearby village of Husovice the "people themselves had spontaneously established a people's court that ... condemned a woman to death and carried out the verdict." Two weeks after the war had officially ended, the officials implored the government to allow Brno to begin formal trials of collaborators. The alternative, they warned, was a mass lynching.[1]

---

[1] MS no. 12809/45-Pr/4 (22 May 1945), Státní ústřední archiv (SÚA), Prague, f. MS (Org), k. 1935.

The Czechoslovak cabinet met at once. On the Justice Ministry's recommendation, the central government succumbed to the threat of popular violence and issued orders to create the first legal People's Court in the Czech provinces.[2] Unfortunately, thanks to bickering between Czech and Slovak leaders, as well as political infighting between the Communists and their political partners, the government had yet to promulgate a final version of a retribution decree to govern the new court. Law or no law, on 8 June 1945 the Brno court tried the very first cases of officially sanctioned retribution. The public's thirst for justice and revenge made the trial a spectacle. According to one reporter, "The courtroom ... was filled to the very last seat."[3] After a brief session, the People's Court convicted all three defendants. The judges sentenced to death a sixty-one-year-old Gestapo official responsible for sending many Brno residents to concentration camps. A sixty-four-year-old concierge was also given a capital sentence because, "although he was a Czech, he turned in other Czechs for listening to foreign radio broadcasts and thereby caused their deaths." The court then sentenced the third defendant, a German, to eight years for the crime of denunciation. At six in the evening the Gestapo official and the Czech informer were executed publicly in the courtyard of a former German gymnastic organization.[4]

A full month passed after the Brno trial before the Czechoslovak government promulgated the so-called Great Decree for the punishment of "Nazi criminals, traitors, and their accomplices." That decree, however, only applied to the Czech provinces of Bohemia, Moravia, and Silesia. By then Slovak leaders had created their own system of courts with their own guidelines. Unfortunately, the government did not use the extra time to improve the measure that its predecessor, the Beneš government-in-exile, had written in London. Though the Great Decree clearly established guidelines for the prosecution and punishment of collaborators and war criminals, it restricted the courts to such a degree that it severely handicapped judges' ability to ensure due process and just verdicts.

---

[2] Government meeting (23 May 1945), SÚA, f. 100/24, aj. 1494, sv. 137.

[3] "Lidové soudy zahájily činnost," *Zemědělské noviny* (10 June 1945), SÚA, f. MZV-VA II (j81), k. 215.

[4] "První zrádci před mimořádným lidovým soudem," *Svobodné slovo* (9 June 1945), SÚA, MZV-VA II (j81), k. 215; "První hlavy padly," *Mladá fronta* (10 June 1945), 2.

As the Second World War drew to a close, governments-in-exile and resistance groups throughout Europe prepared plans to punish Nazi war criminals and collaborators. The similarities of postwar retribution in such diverse countries as France, Norway, and Czechoslovakia demonstrate clearly that the desire to purge was not unique to any one state. The universal demand for justice did not lead, however, to uniform systems of prosecution and punishment. If retribution was a continent-wide phenomenon, the form it took was nonetheless dependent on the decisions of individuals in power. In each European country these decisions created different courts and yielded different results. This chapter argues that the Czechoslovak government-in-exile led by Edvard Beneš constructed a retribution system that was inherently flawed. Given a popular mandate to bring heinous war criminals to justice, entrusted with a mission that was as necessary as it was moral, the country's leaders failed. Though the final law differed only slightly from those of other countries, these differences made postwar Czech retribution one of the bloodiest of its kind.

THE ORIGINS OF CZECH RETRIBUTION: FROM LONDON TO PRAGUE

Czech retribution did not originate in the East. The severe punishment meted out to collaborators after the war was not the result of a plot hatched by Czechoslovak Communists under the direction of Joseph Stalin. As long as the Soviet Union maintained its nefarious alliance with Nazi Germany, Klement Gottwald and his comrades could not credibly demand retribution against anyone who collaborated with the occupying forces at home. Only after Germany attacked the Soviet Union did the Czechoslovak Communists emerge from the shadows, but even then their voice was hardly the decisive one. In 1943 they declined an invitation to join the exile government, though the Party did participate in the State Council, the Czechoslovak parliament-in-exile. With only occasional input from the Communists, the London "democrats" led by Beneš wrote the retribution decree that punished tens of thousands of their compatriots after the war. It was then imported from the West.

In a speech to the Czechoslovak State Council in London Beneš proclaimed retribution to be "one of the most important" issues facing postwar Europe. After 1918, the president explained, the successor states to Austria-Hungary had let bygones be bygones. This time, he continued, "it will be the direct responsibility of every member of the nation and state to carry out punishment against the quislings and internal collaborationists without mercy and without hesitation." Otherwise, Beneš warned, they risked sowing the seeds for another "catastrophe."[5] Czechoslovakia's exiled leaders, like their allies big and small, believed that the failure to prosecute the German Kaiser and his followers after World War One led directly to the rise of Hitler and the outbreak of the Second World War.[6] Accordingly, the exiles viewed retribution as an essential safeguard of the postwar order. Not long after receiving recognition from the Allies in the summer of 1941, the Czechoslovak government-in-exile and its Polish counterpart publicly declared their commitment to hold the Nazis accountable for their crimes.[7] In the January 1942 St. James Declaration, the two exile governments and seven others pronounced the punishment of war criminals to be among their countries' foremost war aims. The signatories committed themselves to seek, arrest, extradite, try, and convict the guilty regardless of nationality. Most significantly, the governments promised to punish not only the occupiers, but also any of their own citizens who had committed war crimes.[8]

A year later, the United States and Great Britain joined the St. James Declaration signatories and formed the United Nations War Crimes

---

[5] Edvard Beneš, *Šest let exilu a druhé světové války: Řeči, projevy a dokumenty z r. 1938–45* (Prague: Orbis, 1947), 326–28.

[6] Despite elaborate negotiations and noble pledges to seek just retribution for the crimes of the Kaiser and his army, the victorious powers did not force the Netherlands to hand the exiled Wilhelm II over for prosecution. The international community also yielded to the Weimar government's demand to prosecute its own citizens before the German High Court in Leipzig, where the original list of 3,000 war criminals was whittled down to 900 and then finally to twelve. In the end, the Leipzig court convicted only six defendants and even they received minimal sentences. Legal scholar Michael Marrus commented, "As precedent, in the opinion of almost every Allied leader who remembered these events, the experience of the Leipzig trials was something strenuously to be avoided." Michael R. Marrus, *The Nuremberg War Crimes Trial, 1945–46: A Documentary History* (Boston: Bedford Books, 1997), 3–4, 8–12; Anton Rašla *L'udové súdy v Československu po II. svetovej vojne ako forma mimoriadneho súdnictva* (Bratislava: SAV, 1969), 9–14, 18–19.

[7] Text of the "Joint Czechoslovak–Polish declaration on the punishment of crimes committed by Germans in occupied territories," SÚA, f. MS-L, k. 4 (IV-4).

[8] The St. James Declaration was named after the London palace in which the discussions were held. It is also known as the London Declaration. Rašla, *L'udové súdy,* 18–21.

Commission (UNWCC).[9] Over the following years the Czechoslovak representative to the commission, Bohuslav Ečer, played a leading role in the drafting of international norms on capturing and punishing war criminals. In particular, it was he who first argued that the Nazi leaders be tried for the crime of "aggressive war," a charge that later became central to the Nuremberg Trial.[10] Ultimately, however, the International Military Tribunal at Nuremberg (IMT) was neither a catalyst nor even a model for Czechoslovak retribution. After all, the Allies did not officially agree on the IMT until 8 August 1945, two months after the first legal Czech retribution trial.

What began with international declarations soon took national forms. At the end of June 1943, the Czechoslovak Justice Minister-in-exile, Jaroslav Stránský,[11] formally asked the government-in-exile's Legal Council to consider measures to augment existing laws to facilitate the punishment of "individuals who had violated the responsibilities of an ordinary citizen of the republic during the German occupation."[12] Within several weeks a first draft had been prepared, and on 11 February 1943 the Legal Council presented Stránský with its final proposal. The Justice Ministry, however, chose to write its own draft and requested that

[9] The Soviet Union declined to participate when the Allies refused its demand for separate representation for all seven of its republics devastated in the war. The Soviets formed their own commission and only joined international structures in time for the Nuremberg trial. Bohuslav Ečer, *Jak jsem je stíhal*, ed. by Edvard Cenek (Prague: Naše vojsko, 1946), 148–49.

[10] Arieh J. Kochavi, *Prelude to Nuremberg: Allied War Crimes Policy and the Question of Punishment* (Chapel Hill, NC: University of North Carolina Press, 1998), 97–100.

[11] Jaroslav Stránský, scion of one of the great Czech political families, had an illustrious carreer both prior to and after the war. A long-time parliamentary representative (1918 to 1921, 1929 to 1939), Stránský had cofounded the National Democratic Party after the First World War, only to break ranks with it when it adopted an anti-Masaryk policy. After the 1925 elections he joined the Czechoslovak National Socialist Party and for the rest of his life he remained one of the party's leading figures at home and in exile. In the 1930s he succeeded his father as editor-in-chief of the country's leading liberal newspaper, *Lidové noviny* (renamed *Svobodné noviny* after the war). He was also a law professor at Masaryk University in Brno, a position that prepared him for his service as Justice Minister in the exile government and its postwar successor. In November 1945, when Drtina took over the Justice Ministry, Stránský became Deputy Premier and Minister of Education. After the Communist coup of February 1948 Stránský fled to the West, where he once again became a leader of the Czechoslovak exile movement. Milan Churáň et al., *Kdo byl kdo v našich dějinách ve 20. století* (Prague: Libri, 1994), 494–95.

[12] The Legal Council was both a substitute high court for the exile community and an advisory body to assist its leaders in crafting new laws. Stránský letter (25 June 1943), Archiv Kanceláře prezidenta republiky (AKPR), f. LA, k. 17, inv. č. 12; Zápis 2. zasedání Právní rady (17 March 1942), AKPR, f. LA, k.4.

the Legal Council review it, which it did in 34 meetings from September 1943 until January 1944. At that point the State Council began its own lengthy, intermittent deliberations. Frustrated with the pace of progress on the retribution decree, Stránský commented that it appeared as if "the government and the State Council were trying to outdo each other to see who could not complete it first."[13]

Despite universal agreement that the guilty had to be punished, writing and passing a retribution law proved no easy feat for the Czechoslovak government-in-exile. Finance Minister Ladislav Feierabend recalled, "There was no longer nor more passionate debate in the government than over the draft of the retribution law."[14] In a speech to the State Council, Deputy Chairman Vladimír Klecanda revealed the depth of disagreement among the exiled leaders:

I ... understand well the fears of many of my colleagues that retribution might destroy the unity of our people. I myself have the same fears. I also understand the concerns of some colleagues that we not unequally punish some strata of our population and I recognize the objections of others that we cannot allow cruel justice itself to weaken the core of our people. We cannot drive the guilty into the camp of the international, anti-democratic opposition, for we cannot allow ourselves to forget that after this war it will organize itself – perhaps underground – in every corner of Europe....

I am aware of the seriousness of these objections and questions, but I cannot avoid seeing the other side to our problem – the cleansing and restoration to health of the broken spirit of our nation....

We cannot permit the people to linger with disbelief in human justice. Through many years of suffering they have seen it trampled on, humiliated, and completely helpless. If we do not give the nation back a secure belief in the justness of Czechoslovakia, which the Western democracies betrayed and for a time abandoned, it will never fully recover.[15]

There was no discord among the exiles over the guilt of the Germans, but when it came to Czechs and Slovaks, fissures quickly appeared. These disagreements in London merely foreshadowed greater conflicts that waited at home.

[13] Zápis XL. plenární shůze (26 September 1944), AKPR, f. LA-SR, k.2, 2. Karel Jech, ed., *Dodatky k edici dokumentů Dekrety prezidenta republiky 1940–1945*, unpublished manuscript.
[14] Ladislav Feierabend, *Politické vzpomínky*, 3 vols. (Brno: Atlantis, 1994–1996), III:44.
[15] "Projev prof. Dra. Klecandy, referenta retribučního dekretu, ve schůzi politického výboru Státní rady v červnu 1944 v Londýně," SÚA, f. MS (Drtina), k. 2113.

Communist leaders in London and Moscow unsuccessfully pushed for a retribution law that would explicitly punish economic and political collaborators from the Czech and Slovak elite. On 28 October 1943 – the twenty-fifth anniversary of Czechoslovak independence – the Moscow Czechs called on the London government "to pass a law to punish anyone who collaborates with the occupiers or supports the Hácha and Tiso governments." The communiqué further demanded, "The law should explicitly concern business circles that are helping the Germans maintain their war production as well as the state bureaucracy at all levels if it is assisting the Germans in public administration."[16] In London Václav Nosek, the future Interior Minister, repeated the Communist Party's demand for the retribution law to specifically criminalize membership in the Hácha and Tiso governments. Concerned that the others hoped to let bourgeois collaborators off, he argued for a law "so clear that there can be not the smallest doubt that [it] punishes first and foremost these main criminals." Nosek called for explicit mention of not only ministers and leading bureaucrats, but also those who ran the justice system and the country's economy. Without representation in the government-in-exile, however, the Communists' role in the drafting of the retribution decree was minimal. From his position on the State Council, Nosek did not have the leverage to force government ministers to name names. Instead, Stránský successfully insisted that the exiles let "the law remain a law and not resolve individual cases."[17]

In contrast to the Communists, other exiles believed that the proposed law unfairly punished Czechs and Slovaks. In particular, Feierabend objected strenuously to the blanket condemnation of the Protectorate government and other domestic political leaders. Of course, as a former Protectorate minister, Feierabend had a personal stake in the matter.[18] Another delegate argued that penalties should

[16] Libuše Otáhalová and Milada Červinková, eds., *Dokumenty z historie československé politiky 1939–1943*, 2 vols. (Prague: Academia, 1966), doc. 318, II:389.
[17] Zápis SR, XL. schůze (26 September 1944) in Jech, *Dodatky*, 7, 10.
[18] Feierabend, *Politické vzpomínky*, III:44. Ladislav Feierabend served as Finance Minister in the Second Republic government and remained in that position after March 1939, while at the same time participating in the Czech underground. In January 1940 he escaped to France and later joined the Beneš government-in-exile in London, where he served once again as Finance Minister. After the war Feierabend joined the National Socialist Party, but his past prominence in the banned Agrarian Party prevented him from playing a significant role in postwar politics. After February 1948 he fled Czechoslovakia again. Churáň et al., *Kdo byl kdo*, 107.

differ according to nationality because the Germans were collectively guilty, while Czech and Slovak collaborators only bore individual responsibility for their crimes.[19] The neutral language of the draft likely reflected Beneš's instructions, given with an eye to international relations, that "under no circumstances should it appear like retribution solely against the Germans."[20] For most of the exiles the promise of egalitarian punishment seemed to pose no threat to national unity because they believed Czech collaborators to be a small minority that could be easily identified and isolated. Summing up this view, Beneš publicly proclaimed that the guilty would be punished irrespective of nationality, but that "there will be few Czechs, more Slovaks, and the most Germans."[21]

The London Slovaks feared the consequences of Beneš's belief that there were many more collaborators to be found among their conationals than among the Czechs. The Slovak exiles, despite their opposition to Tiso, were unwilling to return to the interwar unitary state. Even those who remained loyal to the once-and-future president advocated Slovak autonomy, though they deplored its present, fascist form. They were on guard for anything in the retribution decree that promoted administrative centralization or singled out the Slovak people for special punishment. The London Slovaks also had personal reasons to be wary of the retribution decree: Ján Paulíny-Toth, who most vigorously opposed the draft's violations of traditional law, had signed the October 1938 Žilina Accord on Slovak autonomy.[22] Moreover, like Feierabend, most of the Slovaks on the Council had come from the Agrarian

---

[19] The National Socialist František Uhlíř objected to the draft on these grounds. Karel Jech and Karel Kaplan, eds., *Dekrety prezidenta republiky, 1940–1945: Dokumenty* (Brno: Ústav pro soudobé dějiny, 1995), I:178, n. 1.

[20] "Záznam názorů E. Beneše na trestání válečných zločinců," in Jech, *Dekrety*, doc. 8.1, 180.

[21] Beneš repeated this statement to Stalin. Karel Novotný, ed., *Edvard Beneš: Odsun Němců z Československa: Výbor z pamětí, projevů a dokumentů 1940–1947* (Prague: Dita, 1996), 112; Vojtěch Mastný, "Záznam o prvním politickém rozhovorou...," *Svědectví* 12:47 (1974), 483.

[22] In the interwar republic Paulíny-Toth had been a leader of the Slovak National Party, which demanded decentralization of the state. His signature on the October 1938 Žilina Accord, which devolved substantial power to Bratislava, was entirely consistent with his party's longtime advocacy of Slovak autonomy. Despite his agreement with the Slovak People's Party on this issue, Paulíny-Toth opposed Tiso's rule and in 1939 fled into exile. Josef Tomeš and Alena Léblová, eds., *Československý biografický slovník* (Prague: Academia, 1992), 525.

Party, which the Beneš group blamed for undermining the president at Munich, persecuting political opponents during the Second Republic, and ultimately surrendering the rump state in March 1939. In fact, all but one of the votes in London against the retribution decree, whether in the State Council or the government cabinet, came from men who had served in the Agrarian Party.[23]

After years of deliberation and months of delay, in the summer of 1944 the government-in-exile rushed to complete the retribution decree. Although Beneš had repeatedly stated that he wished to issue the measure once back on Czechoslovak territory, in August 1944 he declared that the decree was ready and should be signed at once.[24] External events had forced the exile government's hand. First, the Red Army had crossed the borders of prewar Czechoslovakia.[25] Second, on 31 August 1944 a massive uprising against the Tiso regime and the Nazis temporarily liberated a large portion of central Slovakia. The opportunity to punish Germans and collaborators had finally arrived, but there was still no retribution law.[26] On 28 September the State Council voted in favor of the Justice Ministry's draft and forwarded it to the government cabinet. The cabinet approved the Justice Ministry's retribution proposal during the first week of October 1944, but Beneš did not sign it until 1 February 1945.[27] A leading Slovak Communist later claimed that the delays demonstrated Beneš's reluctance to carry out retribution.[28] This is questionable – it is inconceivable that the government-in-exile, which Beneš had selected and directed, would

---

[23] The exception was Pauliny-Toth. Despite opposition from Slovaks and the Czech Agrarians, the State Council approved the Justice Ministry draft with only five votes against. Among government ministers, only Feierabend and Jan Lichner dissented. Bohumil Laštovička, V Londýně za války: Zápasy o novou ČSR 1939–1945 (Prague: Svoboda, 1978), 625, n. 1; Feierabend, Politické vzpomínky, III:168.

[24] Jech, Dekrety, doc. 6.6, I:135; Miloš Klimeš, ed., Cesta ke Květnu: Vznik lidové demokracie v Československu (Prague: Československá akademie věd, 1965), doc. 33, 162 n. 1; Laštovička, V Londýně za války, 625, n. 1.

[25] Mečislav Borák, Spravedlnost podle dekretu: Retribuční soudnictví v ČSR a Mimořádný lidový soud v Ostravě (1945–1948) (Ostrava: Tilia, 1998), 27.

[26] In fact, as Drtina soon learned, the leaders of the Slovak National Uprising were not yet interested in carrying out retribution. Besieged from all sides by the Germans, Slovak resistance leaders chose to leave the punishment of collaborators and war criminals to a later date. Klimeš et al., Cesta ke Květnu, 420.

[27] Jech, Dekrety, I:178–79, n. 1; Borák, Spravedlnost podle dekretu, 26–27.

[28] Laštovička, V Londýně za války, 625, n. 1.

have acted against his wishes.[29] According to Feierabend, the president "was precisely informed about [retribution] and fully approved of it."[30] The Czechoslovak government-in-exile finally promulgated the London retribution decree (Decree no. 6/1945) on the eve of Beneš's departure for Moscow at the end of February 1945.[31]

In all likelihood, the exile government issued the decree while still in London to create a fait accompli for upcoming discussions in Moscow. Just the previous month the Czechoslovak Communists had developed their own retribution draft. Thirty-six paragraphs long, the "Law for the Punishment of Nazi Criminals, Traitors and Collaborators" was clearly meant as a communist alternative to the London retribution decree. The preamble was dramatic: "The tears and blood of the Czechoslovak people call for unlimited redress, for national cleansing and for the extinction of even the last traces of the Nazi and fascist evil from the soil and life of the liberated republic." Unsurprisingly, the Communist version permitted the courts far greater latitude in determining guilt. It criminalized service in the enemy's military, including the failure to desert even if one had been forcibly impressed. The draft specifically punished anyone who had supported the enemy "financially," but then explicitly excluded from retribution "members of the working classes who involuntarily serve the occupation and military machine in order to save their lives or livelihoods." Finally, the draft empowered national committees to erect emergency "people's courts" during the liberation of the country.[32]

When Beneš and handpicked members of his London government arrived in Moscow, the Communist leaders presented them with a political

[29] Edward Taborsky, "Politics in Exile, 1939–1945," in Victor S. Mamatey and Radomír Luža, eds., *A History of the Czechoslovak Republic, 1918–1948* (Princeton, NJ: Princeton University Press, 1973), 323.

[30] Feierabend, *Politické vzpomínky*, III:106.

[31] By then, other countries had beaten Czechoslovakia to the punch. On 30 March 1943 the London Poles became the first of the signatories of the St. James Declaration to promulgate a retribution law. The Yugoslav Partisans proclaimed their rules to punish collaborators in early May 1944; the Free French government formally announced a retribution law soon after the Allied landings in Normandy; the Communist Polish government issued its decree at the end of August, and the Netherlands completed its law in September 1944. Even the Hungarians, erstwhile allies of the Germans, proclaimed their own retribution code earlier than the Czechoslovak government-in-exile. Borák, *Spravedlnost podle dekretu*, 24; Rašla, *L'udové súdy*, 64–71.

[32] This may be the first mention of the term "national cleansing." Jech, *Dekrety*, doc. 8.3, I:186–94.

program for postwar Czechoslovakia. Historian Karel Kaplan commented, "The Communist proposal . . . contained such deep and expansive changes in the political, social, and economic spheres that it was nothing less than a project to construct a new regime."[33] After minor amendments, the new government promulgated the proposal when it first met on liberated territory in the eastern Slovak town of Košice on 5 April 1945. The Košice Program, as it came to be known, began by declaring the new regime's commitment to overthrow Nazi rule. The army was to be rebuilt along Soviet lines, complete with political commissars. In the tenor of the day, the government promised to introduce firm price controls on essential goods, to expand the social welfare system, and to nationalize banks, lending houses, insurance companies, power plants, and other major industrial concerns. The Czechs also acknowledged the reality created by the 1944 insurrection and recognized the Slovak National Council [Slovenská národná rada (SNR)], the umbrella organization of the resistance movement, as the supreme legislative and administrative body in Slovakia.

Despite its call for greater democracy and revolutionary socioeconomic reforms, the Košice Program, "threatened more than it promised."[34] It announced the denaturalization of all Germans and Magyars who could not prove their antifascist credentials, and declared that guilty Germans and Magyars were to be expelled from the Republic. The Program further demanded the "fastest possible cleansing of all traitorous, collaborationist, anti-democratic and anti-popular elements from the army." It barred "traitors to the nation, fascists and open or masked enemies of the people" from participation in politics and disenfranchised "all traitors to the nation and helpers of the enemy." The Košice Program also formally banned allegedly collaborationist parties, including the country's largest prewar political party, the Czechoslovak Agrarians. Finally, in Point IX, the government promised to "take as its highest responsibility and its moral duty before the Czech and Slovak nations to capture, prosecute, and punish all war criminals, all traitors, all conscious and active helpers of the German and Magyar repressors."[35]

---

33 Karel Kaplan, *Nekrvavá revoluce* (Prague: Mladá fronta Archiv, 1993), 19.
34 Radomír Luža, "Czechoslovakia between Democracy and Communism," in Victor S. Mamatey and Radomír Luža, eds., *A History of the Czechoslovak Republic, 1918–1948* (Princeton, NJ: Princeton University Press, 1973), 392.
35 Due perhaps to the unsettled international situation, the Program did not openly declare the government's intent to expel the Sudeten German population as a whole. Point VIII

Although Point IX began with the government's plans for German and Magyar war criminals, the emphasis was clearly on the internal enemy, on "traitors, collaborators and fascist elements from the ranks of the Czech and Slovak nations." For the first time the Program mentioned the creation of a "National Court" to try the most prominent Czech and Slovak collaborators. Though Nosek's demand that individuals be named did not find its way into the London decree, it received prominence in the Košice Program. The government explicitly committed itself to prosecute Hácha, Tiso, and all the members of their governments from March 1939 until the end of the war. Some leeway was granted for ordinary bureaucrats, who were not to be considered guilty simply because of their service, but the Program declared that a thorough purge of the state apparatus was necessary. Consistent with the London decree, Point IX also promised to punish functionaries from a wide range of Czech and Slovak fascist organizations. The Košice Program also specifically targeted "treacherous journalists" and, more significantly, "traitors from the ranks of banking, industrial, and agrarian magnates."[36]

In contrast to the lengthy deliberations in London, in Moscow the assembled party leaders approved Point IX after a short debate. Although the London Czechs argued with the Communists over the politicization of the army and over Czech–Slovak relations, retribution provoked virtually no controversy.[37] In fact, the discussion of retribution was of so

deprived most Germans of their citizenship, but did not say that they were to deported. In fact, the Program seemed to leave the door open for regaining citizenship on a case-by-case basis. Only those Germans and Magyars convicted of specific crimes were to be "banished from the republic forever, as long as they are not given a capital sentence." Point IX promised internment only for members of Nazi and fascist organizations and military formations. Even Point X spoke not of the confiscation of all German property, but only of the expropriation of those Germans who had "actively helped in the destruction and occupation of Czechoslovakia." Jiří Grospič, Jaroslav Chovanec, and Juraj Vysokaj, eds., *Košický vládní program* (Prague: Státní pedagogické nakladatelství, 1977), 128–34.

[36] Grospič et al., *Košický vládní program*, 131–33.

[37] There were disagreements over the imposition of political commissars on the army, the foreign orientation of the postwar republic, and the national committee system. Czech–Slovak relations, however, proved to be the most contentious issue, as Drtina and his National Socialist colleagues fought to maintain the principle that a "Czechoslovak" nation, as opposed to separate Czech and Slovak nations, existed. This quixotic argument served only to divide the non-Communist camp into mutually distrusting Czech and Slovak sides, a fatal error that the Czech "democrats" repeated time and time again until they had ultimately helped to undermine their potential allies in Slovakia. Klimeš, *Cesta ke Květnu*, doc. 131–38, 391–453.

little importance that Prokop Drtina, the future Justice Minister, failed even to mention it in his memoirs. Stránský did object to the novel introduction of a "National Court," but quickly gave in to the Communists' demand. The only substantive discussion of the retribution clause was a disagreement among the National Socialists themselves. In an interjection that must have delighted Gottwald and his comrades, Drtina criticized his elder colleague Stránský for arguing that Hácha's greatest guilt consisted not in his actions of March 1939, but in his conduct thereafter.[38] Nonetheless, although the wording of Point IX clearly expressed the Communists' view of collaboration, the Program did not mention the retribution proposal that the party had completed in January. Instead, Point IX explicitly endorsed the London decree as the basis for postwar retribution in Czechoslovakia.[39]

Although the Košice Program concerned the entire country, Slovak representatives did not take part in the discussion of retribution in Moscow. For months the London exiles and the Slovak National Council had struggled over their relationship, with the Slovaks claiming the right to determine domestic policy and the Beneš government insisting that the SNR was merely its representative on the ground. The exiles had expressed their willingness "to study" proposals that the Slovak leaders forwarded, but unambiguously declared, "There cannot, however, be some policies applied in Slovakia and others in the Czech lands, for example, for retribution, administrative and economic measures."[40] The SNR ignored this admonition and on 28 April 1945 presented Stránský with the draft of a retribution law just for Slovakia. Noticeably disturbed by this unexpected development, the Justice Minister objected strenuously to the creation of a separate Slovak system to punish collaborators. He warned, "If the SNR issues an independent retribution statute, then the government will take no responsibility for it."[41]

In a cantankerous government meeting, Stránský and his non-Communist allies argued that the London decree had been hammered out over many years of discussions, approved by the country's

[38] This and other proretribution statements may have encouraged the Communists to accept Drtina as Justice Minister in the mistaken belief that he would be amenable to their approach to the punishment of collaborators. Klimeš et al., *Cesta ke Květnu*, doc. 132, 419.

[39] Grospič et al., *Košický vládní program*, 131–32.

[40] Rašla, *L'udové súdy*, 50–51.

[41] Jech, *Dekrety*, I:250.

parliament-in-exile, signed by the president, and confirmed in the Košice Program. Despite their agreement in Moscow, the Czech Communists now claimed that the Slovak draft was superior to the London decree, possibly because its terse vagueness and uncompromising severity more closely fit their conception of retribution.[42] After all, in London Nosek had argued for simplicity: "We need a law that is brief and comprehensible by every layman."[43] The Party's leaders also likely saw the law as a means to promote Slovak autonomy in the misguided belief that the Communists had more support in Slovakia than subsequent events soon demonstrated.[44] In direct contradiction to the wishes of the country's Justice Minister, Gottwald encouraged the Slovaks to go ahead and publicize their decree for "psychological and political" reasons.[45]

On 15 May 1945 the Slovak National Council issued its own retribution law. It was a rushed job: Slovak Communist leader Gustáv Husák apparently wrote the whole text in a single evening.[46] On 19 May

---

[42] Unlike the Great Decree, the Slovak retribution statue (No. 33/1945) made no attempt to anchor itself in legal precedent; nowhere did it refer to the existing criminal code, even in reference to murder. The opening five paragraphs of the statute haphazardly and redundantly established the material basis of the law. The paragraphs themselves were not even parallel: four cover broad classes of criminals; one is focused on a specific type of crime. Criminals were roughly divided into four categories: "fascist occupiers"; "domestic traitors," who were defined as "domestic criminals who helped the German and Magyar fascists"; "collaborators," defined as "significant co-workers of the occupiers"; and, lastly, "petty criminals of the fascist regime." Added to this was a self-standing crime: "Treachery against the [1944] Uprising." The guidelines for punishing these vaguely defined crimes were extraordinarily severe. Paragraph Three not unreasonably created a maximum penalty of thirty years' imprisonment for "collaborators." Paragraph Five commensurately threatened "fascist delinquents" with two years' imprisonment plus the loss of civic rights for up to fifteen years. But for the crimes outlined in the other three paragraphs, the Slovak Statute mandated the death penalty as *the only possible sentence*. This was true not only for military treachery and racial persecution, but also for a whole range of lesser offenses. Anyone convicted, for example, of having "publicly defended or praised" the suppression of the Slovak National Uprising was to be executed. The Slovak statute even mandated the death penalty for any Czechoslovak citizen found guilty of having "publicly denigrate[d] the Union of Soviet Socialist Republics, the allies, or their state systems and armies." Rašla, *L'udové súdy*, 59, 63–64; "Dôvodová zpráva," k SNR Nariadenie L'udové súdy, Archiv Akademie věd České republiky, Prague, f. Zd. Nejedlý, veřejná činnost, k. 10, str. 3; Jech, *Dekrety*, I:255–62.

[43] Laštovička, *V Londýně za války*, 624 n. 1.

[44] Michal Barnovský, *Na ceste k monopolu moci: Mocenskopolitické zápasy na Slovensku v rokoch 1945–1948* (Bratislava: Archa, 1993), 50–51.

[45] Jech, *Dekrety*, doc. 13.1, I:250–51.

[46] Borák, *Spravedlnost podle dekretu*, 82–83.

the central government met in a last, vain attempt to reconcile Czech and Slovak differences. Stránský claimed that the Slovaks' intransigence had created a crisis and accused them of violating the Košice Program. But they could not be convinced to abandon their plans. Once again the Communists pushed for statewide adoption of the more radical Slovak retribution law. The Health Minister (from the People's Party), Adolf Procházka, voiced another concern when he commented, "The SNR at least has the advantage that its statute is not the work of a group of emigrants." He argued that the London decree needed to be amended through input from the home front for "moral, psychological, and political reasons." Stránský's proposal that the government address this problem by allowing the Provincial National Committees to comment on the London decree met with approval from his colleagues. Plans for consultation with "the people" were delayed, however, pending the outcome of a commission formed to reconcile differences between the Czech and Slovak leaders.[47]

Ultimately, the government neither resolved Czech-Slovak differences nor consulted meaningfully with representatives of the home front.[48] On 4 June the government finally approved the retribution decree for use only in the Czech provinces. Commonly known as the "Great Decree," Decree no. 16/1945 for the punishment of "Nazi criminals, traitors, and their accomplices" differed only slightly from the statute drafted by the London government-in-exile. On 19 June President Beneš signed it into law together with Decree no. 17/1945 establishing a National Court in Prague. The Czech retribution decrees were then publicly promulgated on 9 July 1945. Finally, two months after the end of the war, the inhabitants of the Czech provinces learned what crimes the government planned to punish and how it planned to punish them.[49]

---

[47] Twentieth meeting of the first government (19 May 1945), SÚA, f. 100/24, aj. 1494, sv. 137; see also Jech, Dekrety, doc. 13.3, I:262–65.

[48] Jaroslav Drábek, concentration camp survivor and veteran resistance member, who became National Prosecutor after the war, commented, "The retribution law was very flimsy [chabý], we at home had not the slightest influence on its wording." Jaroslav Drábek, Z časů dobrých a zlých (Prague: Naše vojsko, 1992), 106.

[49] The daily newspapers printed the full text of the Great Decree on 12 July 1945. See "Lid bude jediným a nejvyšším soudcem," Mladá fronta (12 July 1945), 1; "Mimořádné lidové soudy," Lidová demokracie (12 July 1945), SÚA, f. MZV-VA II, j81, k. 215.

Figure 2. The People's Judges are Sworn In, Prague Pankrác Courthouse. Česka tisková kancelář (Czech Press Agency), 1 September 1945. Reproduced with permission.

THE GREAT DECREE

The Great Decree (Appendix 1) established a system of twenty-four Extraordinary People's Courts located at the sites of regular Regional Courts throughout the Czech provinces. The courts were "extraordinary" because they were originally authorized only for a one-year period to punish a specific set of crimes through expedited procedure. The term "people's" reflected the courts' composition: Each judicial panel comprised a professional chief justice plus four "people's judges," laypersons appointed by national committees and approved by the central government (Figure 2). The London decree on retribution had authorized only two people's judges, but the postwar government added another two. The change not only strengthened the say of untrained laypeople at the expense of the professional jurist. The additions also represented a further step in the politicization of postwar Czech life. The number four was no accident: It was assumed that each of the four legal Czech parties would have a people's judge on every panel. Such a configuration might ensure that the courts not be used for political intrigue within the ruling coalition, but it did little to protect members of banned parties like the Agrarians. Despite their extraordinary nature, People's Court trials were open to the public and the accused had the right to choose his or her own counsel. If the defendant could not afford a lawyer or refused to select one, the Great Decree stipulated that the court appoint defense counsel on his or her behalf.

The Great Decree outlined eleven types of crimes, divided into four categories: Crimes against the State, Crimes against Persons, Crimes against Property, and the self-standing crime of "Denunciation." The first four paragraphs of the decree punished "Crimes against the State." Paragraph One relied directly on the interwar Law for the Protection of the Republic to punish conspiracy, espionage, and treachery with sentences ranging from twenty years' imprisonment to death. In 1923, after a young anarchist assassinated the Czechoslovak finance minister, parliament passed a stringent law designed to prevent extremism on both the left and the right and to secure the state against national minorities' attempts to undermine it.[50] More than two decades later, the Great Decree's use of the Law for the Protection of the Republic relied on the "theory of legal continuity" that Beneš had formulated during the war. According to the once-and-future president, the German invasion of March 1939 and the Franco-British failure to uphold their guarantees of rump Czechoslovakia had violated, and thereby invalidated, the Munich Pact of September 1938. As a result, all that had come to pass after Munich, including Beneš's own resignation, was null and void. In short, he argued, "Our state never stopped legally existing.... Everything that occurred after 19 September 1938 happened illegally, unconstitutionally, and was forced upon us by threats, terror,

---

[50] The parliament modeled the 1923 law on a similar Weimar Republic law enacted the previous year after the assassination of German Foreign Minister Walther Rathenau. The Czechoslovak law toughened penalties for acts against the constitution, the democratic system, the state's integrity, and public officials – for example, insulting the president was declared a criminal offense. Certain crimes were removed from the purview of the ordinary courts and put under the jurisdiction of a newly established "state court" (an institution that the Communists recreated in the fall of 1948 to punish alleged enemies of socialism). In the interwar parliament the Law for the Protection of the Republic was opposed primarily by national minorities, the Communists, and representatives from the Slovak People's Party, who accurately predicted that the law might one day be used against them. Members of the National Socialist Party who voted against the law were expelled from the party, but at nearly the same moment the National Socialists gained a new, prominent member – Edvard Beneš. Ferdinand Peroutka, *Budování státu*, 4 vols. (Prague: Lidové noviny, 1991), IV:1742–53.

and violence."[51] According to this theory, Beneš remained president, the First Republic still existed, and, most importantly for postwar retribution, Czechoslovakia's criminal code and especially its laws against sedition applied throughout the occupation to all of the dismembered country's citizens.[52]

Paragraphs Two and Three punished support for the occupation including participation in Nazi and fascist groups. In London Beneš had proposed the criminalization of membership as a clever way of getting around his prohibition on separate measures for Czechs and Germans. He suggested, "It is worth considering, however, whether it would not be useful to specifically criminalize membership ... in Henlein's party, the SA, SS, Gestapo or even service in the German army."[53] Because many organizations were overwhelmingly or entirely German in nature, punishment of specific groups would be nationally selective in practice if not in law. The Great Decree divided Nazi and fascist organizations into two categories. Paragraph Two outlawed membership in paramilitary formations, such as the SS, SA, and Sudeten German Freikorps. According to Paragraph Three, only leaders and functionaries of political organizations, such as the Nazi Party, the Sudetendeutsche Partei (SdP), and Czech fascist groups, were to be punished. For both paragraphs the penalty was five to twenty years' imprisonment, but for paramilitary members life incarceration was also a possibility.

Paragraph Four was the most blatantly political aspect of the decree. Five to ten years in prison was mandated for any "Czechoslovak citizen who ... *while abroad* subverted the movement to liberate the Czechoslovak Republic in its pre-Munich constitutional form and unity, or who otherwise consciously harmed the interests of the Czechoslovak Republic."[54] This measure retroactively threatened anyone who had

---

[51] Edvard Beneš, *Paměti: Od Mnichova k nové válce a k novému vítězství* (Prague: Orbis, 1947), 156 (see also pp. 98, 113–14, 168–70).

[52] In exile Charles de Gaulle adopted a policy strikingly similar to that of Beneš. The Free French declared that the formation of the Pétain cabinet on 17 June 1940 was illegal. As a result, the Vichy regime was a "usurper," the Armistice it signed was invalid, and Franco-German hostilities had never ceased. Like that of the Czechoslovak First Republic, the legal code of the French Third Republic theoretically remained in force throughout the war. Peter Novick, *The Resistance versus Vichy: The Purge of Collaborators in Liberated France* (New York: Columbia University Press, 1968), 142.

[53] "Záznam názorů E. Beneše na trestání válečných zločinců," in Jech, *Dekrety*, doc. 8.1, 180.

[54] Italics added. Jech, *Dekrety*, I:169, doc. 8 §4.

challenged the authority of Beneš or his government-in-exile. In addition to those Czechs who opposed the president and his coterie, Paragraph Four could have been applied to any antifascist German or Slovak exile who did not wish to reestablish the interwar state along centralist lines. In London Paulíny-Toth pointedly asked "whether these provisions were maybe intended to punish anyone... who has reservations about the... 1920 [centralist] constitution." Stránský's response confirmed that those in power reserved the right to subjectively determine what constituted treachery abroad. The Justice Minister promised that the government would "distinguish between well-intentioned criticism and those who increasingly disassociated themselves from us."[55] Although the paragraph was rarely used, the threat likely served to keep the Beneš regime's political opponents from returning to Czechoslovakia after the war.[56]

The next section (Paragraphs Five through Seven) punished Crimes against Persons. Paragraph Five relied heavily on the Austrian criminal codes of 1852 and 1878 to punish violent crimes like robbery, assault, and murder. As strange as it might seem that the Great Decree reached nearly a century back for precedent, there was actually no alternative. The interwar republic had never managed to fully replace the Habsburg criminal code with one of its own. In fact, not until after February 1948 was a new, unitary code for Czechoslovakia enacted. Recycling the 1852 law against slavery for use against the Nazis, Paragraph Five covered the crime of "public violence via the enslavement of a human being." Paragraph Six took this concept a step further and explicitly criminalized participation in the organization of "forced or mandatory labor" to the benefit of Nazi Germany. To punish police, judges, and other participants in the Nazis' repressive apparatus, Paragraph Seven criminalized actions that contributed to the imprisonment of, harm to, or legal judgment against inhabitants of the Czechoslovak Republic.

[55] Zápis XL. schůze (26 September 1944), AKPR, f. LA-SR, k. 2. Jech, *Dodatky*.
[56] Anton Rašla claimed that no one was convicted under Paragraph Four, but in May 1947 the National Court convicted Jan Antonín Bat'a *in absentia* for declining to join, and keeping his employees from joining, the Czechoslovak resistance movement abroad. Rudolf Beran was also indicted under Paragraph Four (for having assisted in creating a rival resistance group in Poland) and acquitted of the charge. Rašla, *L'udové súdy*, 80; "Usnesení Nejvyššího soudu České republiky ze dne 20.7.1994 sp. zn. Tzn. 51/93," *Sbírka soudních rozhodnutí a stanovisek České republiky* (1994), no. 62, 291; Verdict against Rudolf Beran (21 April 1947), SÚA, f. NS, TNs 1/47. 4.

Paragraphs Eight through Ten concerned Crimes against Property. Paragraph Eight covered vandalism, arson, burglary, and breaking and entering. Paragraph Nine addressed those who participated in the confiscation and expropriation of the property of the Czechoslovak state or any of its citizens. Paragraph Ten punished anyone who "exploited the distress caused by national, political, or racial persecution to enrich himself at the expense of the state," a business, or an individual. The mention of "racial" enrichment was an oblique reference to "Aryanization," the process by which the Nazis expropriated and redistributed Jews' property. Nonetheless, in tune with contemporary practice throughout formerly occupied Europe, nowhere did the Great Decree specifically refer to the Jews as victims or to the Holocaust as an event.

Of all the offenses, only Paragraph Eleven, "Denunciation," had not been part of the decree developed in London. In retrospect, this is surprising. During the war the underground had repeatedly called on the government-in-exile to "threaten before all else severe punishment to those who denounce to the Gestapo or simply threaten others with the Gestapo." A typical message provided the name and address of a denouncer and asked London radio to warn the public about him. In one instance the underground identified a woman who had been sent to Vienna for Gestapo training. Back in the Protectorate her method was simple: "She seeks acquaintance with men of any age and ruthlessly denounces them." Apparently she had eighty lives on her conscience.[57] The Premier of the government-in-exile, Jan Šrámek, did point out the need for a means to punish denunciation, but his colleagues did not pursue the matter further until they returned home after the war.[58] There they quickly came to appreciate the Czech public's passionate hatred for those who had betrayed their compatriots to the occupation authorities. The last-minute addition of Paragraph Eleven in spring 1945 can thus be seen as the home front's only substantive, if indirect, contribution to the Great Decree.

The addition of Paragraph Eleven criminalized wartime denunciation, but the Great Decree offered the People's Courts no means to penalize Czechs who after the war falsely accused others of collaboration

---

[57] "Zprávy z domova" no. 625/41/dův. (29 April 1941), no. 116/41/dův. (26 January 1941), no. 143/41/dův. (10 February 1941), CU, Smutný papers, box 11, folder 1.

[58] Government meeting (4 June 1945), SÚA, f. 100/24, aj. 1494, sv. 137.

for personal or political reasons.[59] The Decree failed to mention other offenses that later became the subject of much debate and consternation. Considering the infamous horrors of Gestapo interrogation, it is especially surprising that there was no specific measure concerning torture.[60] The men who wrote the Decree also neglected to include a clause specifically punishing rape.[61] Proponents of harsh retribution soon found a litany of lesser offenses not covered by the Great Decree and pressed for a new law to punish alleged collaborators who could not be tried by the People's Courts.

In contrast to contemporaries who wished to expand the Great Decree, Vilém Hejl retrospectively argued that the regular legal code, augmented by the Law for the Protection of the Republic, would have sufficed "to judge all the crimes from the occupation period."[62] In other words, there was no need for a special, retroactive measure at all. In reference to French retribution, Peter Novick explained, "It would be hard to find a principle more fundamental not only to traditional concepts of law, but to the layman's instincts of equity" than the legal principles of *nullum crimen sine lege* and *nulla poene sine lege*.[63] The former, "no crime without a law," denies a regime the power to declare an act illegal after it has been committed. The latter, "no penalty without a law," prevents a regime from increasing the penalties for a particular crime after the fact. The Czechoslovak Legal Council in London was acutely aware of the dangers inherent in retroactive law, but argued that the step was necessary and justified: "Without denying that the principles *nullum crimen sine lege* and *nulla poene sine lege* are among the most valued achievements of human civilization, this is a situation so extraordinary, with crimes so unconscionable and horrendous, that a temporary departure from the mentioned principles is justified not only by valid constitutional law but also by moral, criminal, and political considerations."[64] The Legal Council also claimed that the framers of the country's 1920 constitution would have undoubtedly approved of the retroactive nature of the retribution decree. Moreover, if legal

---

[59] Bedřich Bobek, "Konec retribuce," *Obzory* III:18 (3 May 1947), 233.

[60] "Skončení retribučního soudnictví," MLS Brno přednosta, f. MS (Org.), k. 1942.

[61] Amos Pokorný, "Lidové soudy," *Dnešek* II:1 (3 April 1947), 11.

[62] Vilém Hejl, *Zpráva o organizovaném násilí* (Prague: Univerzum, 1990), 21.

[63] Novick, *Resistance versus Vichy*, 141.

[64] Notes to Paragraph One. "Notes to the law for the punishment of Nazi crimes by special people's courts." AKPR, f. LA, inv. č. 12, k. 17, H.

principles were religiously adhered to, then vicious war criminals would escape justice and remain a dire threat to the security of the state and the safety of its citizens. Finally, it was argued, retroactive retribution was in agreement with popular and learned opinion in Czechoslovakia and throughout the world.[65] Perhaps Herbert Pell, the U.S. representative to the UNWCC, put it best when he explained, "We are either statesmen preparing new laws for new conditions or solicitors' clerks torturing precedents and twisting rules to make them fit cases which unquestionably were not in the minds of the judges who originally enunciated them."[66]

The retribution decree clearly violated the principle of *nulla poene sine lege*. Almost every paragraph mandated longer prison sentences than were in the regular criminal code. Even for existing crimes, such as murder or arson, the penalties were toughened. Moreover, the court could mandate that sentences be served in labor battalions, a new institution that aimed to force convicted collaborators and war criminals to undo some of the damage they had caused. Judges could also order the confiscation of part or all of a convict's property. This penalty provided both the state and individual beneficiaries of its largesse a financial incentive to convict defendants, especially wealthy ones. Most fatefully, the Great Decree expanded the range of crimes subject to the death penalty. Unlike in some other European countries, capital punishment did not have to be formally reintroduced to Czechoslovakia – the interwar state had permitted execution in particularly egregious cases of military treachery. The retribution decree's framers argued that during war political crimes against the state are a form of military treachery and therefore punishable by death according to the 1923 Law for the Protection of the Republic.[67] The Great Decree, however, added a new

---

[65] In terms of constitutional law, the Czechoslovak government-in-exile was fortunate that the country's 1920 constitution did not forbid the implementation of retroactive legislation. The Dutch government-in-exile, by contrast, had to pass a specific measure to override its constitution's ban on *ex post facto* law. To justify its stance, the Czechoslovak Legal Council also cited a leading British jurist, who defended retroactive law in the House of Lords (7 October 1942). Henry L. Mason, *The Purge of Dutch Quislings: Emergency Justice in the Netherlands* (The Hague: Martinus Nijhoff, 1952), 62; "Uvozovací dekret," AKPR, f. LA, inv. c. 3, k. 4.

[66] Kochavi, *Prelude to Nuremberg*, 241.

[67] The Legal Council further justified the death penalty on grounds of internal and international security. "Notes to the law for the punishment of Nazi crimes by special people's courts," §1, AKPR, f. LA, inv. č. 12, k. 17, H.

wrinkle to executions: A court could order that a prisoner be hanged in public. It was argued that in particularly horrendous cases public executions would serve a psychological end: "Before the eyes of the people, who had been condemned for years to look helplessly upon Nazi crimes, just retribution will be enacted. Public execution will underline the end of the Nazi reign of terror."[68]

Retribution judges could also sentence a convict to a novel penalty, the "loss of civic honor," for a mandated period of time up to life. The "loss of civic honor" precluded the right to hold elected office and the right to vote. Any state honors or awards received by the convict prior to the verdict were invalidated, as was any payment therewith associated. In the military, guilty noncommissioned officers were to be degraded; higher-ranking officers were to be cashiered. These measures were perhaps appropriate to the crime of treachery and could be justified as means to ensure the future security of the state, but the "loss of civic honor" went further. Without "civic honor" one could not assume any position of responsibility for others, whether in a public institution, private business, or volunteer organization. A degraded individual could not own, operate, or edit any newspaper or journal, be a teacher, or give public lectures on any topic. Even the so-called "free professions" – medicine and law – were verboten. Essentially all that remained to the convicted collaborator was to be a simple worker.[69]

As foreign as the term "loss of civic honor" may sound today, Czechoslovakia was not the only country to enforce this novel sanction after the war. France had a similar punishment called "national degradation" [dégradation nationale], which barred the guilty from all public employment and could even include a ban on residency in a given area. Danish courts, for their part, sentenced collaborators to the loss of "common confidence" for a period from a minimum of five years to life. In the Netherlands tribunals could deprive convicts of their civic rights and ban them from certain occupations and "functions" for life.[70] In fact, Czechoslovak exiles actually borrowed the concept of "civic

---

[68] "Notes to the law for the punishment of Nazi crimes by special People's Courts," §30, AKPR, f. LA, inv. č. 12, k. 17, H.

[69] Sbírka zákonů a nařízení Republiky československé (Prague, 1946), no. 16/1945, §15.

[70] Novick, Resistance versus Vichy, 148–49; Carl Christian Givskov, "The Danish Purge Laws," in Neil J. Kritz, ed., Transitional Justice (Washington, DC: United States Institute of Peace Press, 1995), II:133; Mason, Dutch Quislings, 64–65.

honor" from the King of Norway's January 1942 order for members of Quisling's Nasjonal Samling organization to be punished with the "loss of public trust."[71]

"People's judges" also existed in one form or another across post-war Europe. Throughout the continent the belief prevailed that, when it came to retribution, trained jurists were not qualified to rule alone, especially since the judiciary had been compromised in many countries by its service during the occupation.[72] Like the Czech courts, judicial panels in France comprised one professionally trained judge accompanied by four laypersons chosen from the resistance. In Denmark there were two jurors for every judge and in the Netherlands a secondary system of tribunals empowered to rule on minor offenses included one judge and two members of the resistance.[73] As for the criminalization of membership in Nazi and fascist organizations – another novel aspect of the Great Decree – the International Military Tribunal at Nuremberg endorsed this approach when it collectively convicted the Gestapo, SS, and Nazi Party leadership.[74]

The Great Decree broke ranks with Western Europe, however, when it came to judicial procedure. In London Beneš argued that the sooner retribution was concluded, the sooner everyday life and the justice system could return to normal. Therefore, he recommended that the government set a deadline for the completion of the punishment of war criminals and collaborators. In order to speed up retribution, Beneš proposed that the length of individual trials be limited so that each case could be disposed of as quickly as possible. This line of reasoning led the Czechoslovak president to an extraordinary conclusion: A retribution court's verdict should be final. He argued, "Trials should be as short as possible and [I] would be hard-pressed to recommend that the verdicts of these courts be subject to appeal."[75] When Paulíny-Toth objected to the proposal that the convicted have no right to appeal, Stránský responded

---

[71] The Committee for Criminal Law Reform (21 July 1942), AKPR, f. L-PR, k. 4, inv. č. 3, no. 17.

[72] In France, for example, all judges save one lone stalwart had sworn an oath of allegiance to Pétain. Novick, *Resistance versus Vichy*, 84.

[73] Novick, *Resistance versus Vichy*, 152; Givskov, "The Danish Purge Laws," in *Transitional Justice*, II:135; Mason, *Purge of Dutch Quislings*, 69.

[74] As Chapter 6 explains, the Great Decree's criminalization of the SA caused the courts problems after the IMT ruled that SA membership in and of itself was not criminal.

[75] Jech, *Dekrety*, doc. 8.1, 179–80.

that the defendants did not deserve any special consideration. The Justice Minister explained, "We consider the category of these accused to be particularly contemptible and despicable."[76] With that prevailing opinion, the government-in-exile dutifully wrote Beneš's recommendation into law. Paragraph thirty-one of the Great Decree reads, "Against the verdict of the Extraordinary People's Courts there are no means of legal redress."[77]

In London the Legal Council justified the denial of appeal on the grounds that the Second World War represented a state of emergency writ large. Austrian (Habsburg) law had allowed for summary judgments and denied judicial review in cases where criminality in a specific area escaped beyond control. The exiles mistakenly believed that the courts would begin operating before the conflict ended and that postwar Czechoslovakia might resemble Weimar Germany in its first years, beset with armed and hostile paramilitary groups.[78] The courts, thus, were to operate in a summary fashion, as if on the battlefield or in a state of civil unrest.[79] As it turned out, the exiles planned for a situation that did not arise – the courts were not officially authorized until two months after armed hostilities ended. Moreover, the marauding bands in the Czech provinces were not seditious; they were progovernment. Even when it became obvious that the punishment of collaborators would take years, the regime stuck to its commitment to summary justice while abandoning its hope for swift retribution. Although Beneš originally proposed that retribution last only three months, the Great Decree authorized the People's Courts for a year and parliament later extended them for yet another. The ban on appeals, however, remained unaltered.

The total denial of the defendant's right to appeal was largely responsible for the inconsistent and unfair nature of postwar Czech retribution.

[76] Zápis XL. plenární shůze (26 Sept. 1944). Jech, *Dodatky*, 7.
[77] *Sbírka zákonů*, no. 16/1945, §31.
[78] "Notes to the law for the punishment of Nazi crimes by special People's Courts," §1, AKPR, f. LA, inv. c. 12, k. 17, H.
[79] In November 1943, a Czechoslovak legal expert vainly presented a detailed case against this application of summary law for retribution. He argued that the purpose of retribution – to punish egregious crimes committed in the past – was wholly different than that of emergency law, which aimed to make a "frightening example" to deter crime thenceforth. According to Czechoslovak law, the expert maintained, summary courts should have only tried crimes that had just been committed, where the guilt was beyond doubt, and where the only possible penalty was death. "Druhé vyjádření dra. Schwelba," AKPR, f. LA-PR, k. 4, inv. č. 3, 4.

Other countries restricted appeals, but nowhere in Western Europe was a lower court's verdict absolutely beyond review.[80] Even Hungary had an appellate body that could review a sentence if the lower court's judges consented.[81] Without the right of appeal, a person convicted by a Czech People's Court had no means to redress prejudiced, incommensurate, or aberrant verdicts. There was also no procedure to iron out inconsistencies in sentencing. In one important sense, however, the Great Decree enshrined the concept of fair play: If the defense could not appeal, then neither could the prosecution.[82] This total denial of any judicial review, unless new evidence came to light, proved a critical check on the politicization of the retribution courts. Judges could rule, confident that the government could not overturn verdicts it found objectionable.

Judges' hands were further tied by mandatory minimum sentences of five to twenty years. In London the ever-skeptical Pauliny-Toth accurately predicted, "If a court views the minimum sentence as too high and too harsh, it could easily result in the defendant being freed."[83] The courts could also not consider traditionally recognized mitigating circumstances like a defendant's character, background, or the welfare of his or her minor children. Eduard Táborský, Beneš's personal secretary, criticized this restriction and advocated leaving the matter to the discretion of the judges.[84] His concerns, however, were also ignored – the first clause of Paragraph Sixteen of the Great Decree categorically states, "A sentence of imprisonment cannot be reduced below the minimum penalty, nor replaced with a more lenient type of punishment." The second clause, however, opened a window for judges:

---

[80] In Denmark, for example, a defendant could request a retrial if his or her sentence was greater than ten years. In the Netherlands a defendant could appeal if the judges who had issued the verdict in question approved. Later this measure was changed to permit appeals of sentences greater than six years. Givskov, "Danish Purge Laws," 135; Mason, *Dutch Quislings*, 60.

[81] László Karsai, "The People's Courts and Revolutionary Justice in Hungary, 1945–46," in István Deák, Jan T. Gross, and Tony Judt, eds., *The Politics of Retribution in Europe: World War II and Its Aftermath* (Princeton, NJ: Princeton University Press, 2000), 236.

[82] To the benefit of defendants, the final draft did not incorporate the Legal Council's proposal that the prosecution should be able to appeal an acquittal. "Notes to the law for the punishment of Nazi crimes by special people's courts," §24, AKPR, f. LA, inv. c. 12, k. 17, H.

[83] Zápis XL. plenární shůze (26 Sept. 1944). Jech, *Dodatky*, 5.

[84] Táborský, "Záznam ke konečné osnově retribučního dekretu," AKPR, f. LA, k. 17, H.

According to Paragraph Sixteen a sentence could be reduced or even commuted if subsequent to the crime the perpetrator acted to undo the damage he or she had caused by helping to liberate the country. The courts could also lessen a penalty if the defendant had openly collaborated to conceal resistance activity, but only "if it [was] generally known or [could] be proven without delay that the accused acted with the intent to benefit the Czech or Slovak nations or the Czechoslovak Republic or its allies." The Decree left it up to the judges to decide just what constituted such patriotic action and to what extent it was to be recognized in sentencing.

The ban on appeals and the limits on mitigating circumstances were exacerbated by the most egregious aspect of the Czech retribution decree. According to Paragraph Thirty-One, "The death penalty, as a rule, is to be carried out *within two hours* after the pronouncement of the verdict. At the express request of the condemned, the time limit may be extended for an additional hour."[85] The condemned had the right to request clemency from the country's president, but such a plea did not delay the summary enactment of the verdict. If the president did not respond positively within the mandated three hours, the execution proceeded as planned. In reality, only the most prominent cases could hope for clemency; even if the court telegrammed a defendant's plea to Prague, the president did not devote his days to reviewing and commuting sentences. The absurdity of the three-hour limit was demonstrated by the case of Olga Trpišková, a notorious informer. Because Trpišková's conviction was all but certain and she was accused of capital crimes, her parents did not await the verdict, but petitioned in advance of the trial for presidential clemency in case their daughter received the death penalty.[86] In light of the rushed and prejudicial nature of many trials, there is little doubt that the three-hour limit led to the death of at least some innocents.

Without the right to appeal and without reasonable hope of presidential clemency, a staggeringly high percentage of death sentences resulted in speedy executions. Herein lies perhaps the greatest difference between

---

[85] Italics added. *Sbírka zákonů*, no. 16/1945, §31.

[86] Trpišková was convicted of informing for the Sicherheitsdienst and was given a life sentence. See Chapter 4 for more on the Trpišková case. Letter from Trpišková's parents (25 September 1945), AKPR, s. D-11377/47, k. 262, B-prominut; "Doživotní žalář dr. Trpiškové," *Lidová demokracie* (28 September 1945), SÚA, f MZV-VA II (j81), k. 215.

Czech retribution and that practiced elsewhere in Europe. The number of defendants sentenced to death by Czech courts was high, but not entirely disproportionate, especially considering the great variations in conditions under Nazi occupation. As Table 1 illustrates, however, the rate of execution was a different story. Leaving aside Norway, where only a handful of defendants received the death penalty, none of the other countries for which statistics are available came remotely close to the Czech rate of execution. Denmark carried out nearly sixty percent of its death sentences, but, as in Norway, the absolute number was relatively small. Similar to their Czech comrades, the Hungarian Communists wielded disproportionate power within their country's multiparty government, but Hungary's rate of execution was still less than 40 percent.[87] France, the country that sentenced the highest number of defendants to death, executed a mere one-ninth of them. Even when we discount for the 4,397 defendants sentenced to death *in absentia* (without doing so for Czechoslovakia or any other country), the French rate of execution was still only thirty percent.[88] As a result the Czech provinces, with one-fourth of the French population, executed almost as many defendants as France. Aside from Bulgaria, where a Stalinizing regime liquidated thousands before the war even ended,[89] Czech retribution courts apparently sent more defendants to death per capita than anywhere else in Europe.

The effect of the ban on appeals and the three-hour rule can clearly be seen in comparison with developments in Slovakia. The Slovak retribution law also did not permit appeals.[90] As in the Czech provinces, in Slovakia a defendant's only hope was to make a plea for mercy, but the Slovak statute gave forty-eight hours, not a mere three, for higher authorities to review the case. In practice, clemency cases dragged on for much longer and defendants sometimes sat in prison for months

[87] Death sentences in Hungary had to be approved by the Allied Control Commission. Karsai, "The People's Courts," in *Politics of Retribution*, 236–37.
[88] Rousso, "L'Épuration," in Klaus-Dietmar Henke and Hans Wollar, eds., *Politische Säuberung in Europa* (Munich: Deutscher Taschenbuch Verlag, 1991), 217.
[89] Robert Lee Wolff, *The Balkans in Our Time* (Cambridge, MA: Harvard University Press, 1967), 293.
[90] The original Slovak retribution draft allowed for appeals, but in subsequent negotiations this provision was dropped, possibly in the fruitless attempt to reconcile it with the Czech decree. Woller, *Dekrety*, I:253–54.

Table 1. *Postwar Retribution Death Sentences and Executions by Country*

Country or Region	Death Sentences	Executions Carried Out	Percentage Executed
Czech provinces[a]	723	686	94.9
Slovakia[a]	65	27	41.5
Belgium[b]	2,940	242	8.2
Bulgaria[c]	2,618	1,576	60.2
Denmark[d]	78	46	59.0
France[e]	7,037	791	11.2
Hungary[f]	476	189	39.7
Netherlands[g]	138	36	26.1
Norway[h]	25	22	88.0

[a] Prior to the Communist takeover of February 1948. One parliamentarian claimed that 693 of 713 death sentences in the Czech provinces were carried out, for an execution rate in excess of 97 percent. "Výsledky retribuce," Vojenský historický archiv (VHA), f. Čepička, sv. 23, aj. 168; Otakar Liška et al., *Vykonané tresty smrti Československo 1918–1989* (Prague: Úřad dokumentace a vyšetřování zločinů komunismu, 2000); Hobza, ÚNS 56 (10 June 1947), 46.

[b] Martin Conway, "Justice in Postwar Belgium: Popular Passions and Political Realities," *Cahiers d'Histoire du Temps Présent* 2 (1997), 8. Mason counted 4,170 death sentences and 230 executions by December 1949. Henry Lloyd Mason, *The Purge of the Dutch Quislings* (The Hague: Nijhoff, 1952), 177, n. 20.

[c] Jan Rychlík, "Proces s Jozefom Tisem v roce 1947," *Český časopis historický* 96:3 (1998), 579, n. 16.

[d] Carl Christian Givskov, "The Danish Purge Laws," in *Transitional Justice*, Neil J. Kritz, ed. (Washington, DC: United States Institute of Peace Press, 1995), 128.

[e] Henri Rousso, "L'Épuration: Die politische Säuberung in Frankreich," in Klaus-Dietmar Henke and Hans Woller, eds., *Politische Säuberung in Europa* (Munich: Deutscher Taschenbuch Verlag, 1991), 217. Kupferman counted a total of 6,763 death sentences, of which 3,910 were *in absentia*, and only 767 were carried out. Fred Kupferman, *Le Procès de Vichy: Pucheu, Pétain, Laval* (Brussels: Editions Complexe, 1980), 22.

[f] István Deák, "Resistance, Collaboration, and Retribution during World War II and its Aftermath," *Hungarian Quarterly* 35:134 (1994), 73. Rašla credits postwar Hungarian retribution with 332 death sentences and 146 executions (44.0 percent). Anton Rašla, *L'udové súdy v Československu po II. svetovej vojne ako forma mimoriadneho súdnictva* (Bratislava: SAV, 1969), 71.

[g] Prior to December 1950. Mason, *Dutch Quislings*, 64.

[h] These figures are only for "Norwegians." Twelve Germans were also executed in Norway. Stein U. Larsen, "Die Ausschaltung der Quislinge in Norwegen," in Klaus-Dietmar Henke and Hans Woller, eds., *Politische Säuberung in Europa* (Munich: Deutscher Taschenbuch Verlag, 1991), 243, 260.

awaiting a response.[91] In contrast to the summary execution that faced defendants in the western half of the country, in Slovakia the wheels of justice were given time to slowly turn. Tempers were allowed to cool and mitigating circumstances could be taken into account. As a result the authorities decided to grant mercy with great regularity and the Slovak execution rate of 41.5 percent was less than half the Czech rate.

The case of Peter Starinský demonstrates the differences between appeals for mercy in the Czech provinces and Slovakia. Starinský had started the war as a district commander of the Hlinka Guards, the local version of Mussolini's Blackshirts. In that role, the Bratislava National Court concluded, he "carried out all orders entrusted to him . . . particularly those that concerned anti-Jewish and anticommunist measures." Starinský's diligent work earned him a promotion in 1941 to Chief of Central State Security, where, among other duties, he oversaw the notorious Slovak prison at Ilava. He was responsible for the interrogation of political prisoners and, at the very least, did nothing to prevent his underlings from employing torture to obtain confessions. He worked with the SS and the Gestapo and personally profited from the "Aryanization" of Jewish property. In the final stages of the war, Starinský organized search and destroy parties to hunt down partisans and participated fully in the German suppression of the 1944 Slovak National Uprising. He defended himself by claiming that he had acted the same as "any other state employee." On 9 December 1946 the Slovak National Court sentenced Starinský to death.

Unlike in the Czech provinces, the hangman did not immediately step forward to carry out his lethal duties. Instead, the Bratislava National Court listened to Starinský's plea for clemency and forwarded it to Prague with the recommendation that his death sentence be commuted to thirty years' imprisonment. The Slovak Commissioner of Justice argued that the penalty be reduced even further, to twenty years. Starinský, it seems, had played a clever double game. He had hidden a Jewish woman in his apartment and had refused to hand over French prisoners-of-war to the Nazis. More importantly, he had intervened

---

[91] In one Slovak case Justice Minister Drtina even argued that the lengthy delay between the defendant's conviction and his prospective execution constituted an unintended, onerous increase in his original sentence, essentially adding a fourteen-month prison term to the death penalty. The government agreed and commuted the defendant's sentence. Government meeting (13 June 1947), SÚA, f. 100/24, a.j. 1494, sv. 142.

to release from prison two resistance leaders who later became vice chairmen of the Slovak National Council, the body responsible for administering postwar Slovakia. It was certainly not to his disadvantage that Starinský had allowed Igor Daxner, the Chief Justice of the Slovak National Court, to be interned during the war in a hospital instead of a prison. The Justice Ministry in Prague concurred with the National Court's recommendation and, over the objections of the Slovak National Prosecutor, recommended commutation. On 17 June 1947 the Czechoslovak government unanimously approved the reduction of Starinský's sentence to thirty years. By then more than six months had elapsed since the verdict was announced – time enough for concerns about the police chief's two minor children to be raised; time enough for passions to cool and clemency to be considered.[92] The same pattern – death sentences commuted to lesser terms with the passage of time – can be observed throughout postwar Europe, from Slovakia to France to the Allied military tribunals in occupied Germany. Only in the Czech provinces did the laws preclude a reasonable chance at clemency. The result was an execution rate well in excess of 90 percent.

CONCLUSION

As this chapter has endeavored to illustrate, Czech retribution was not at its roots a Communist program. "That unintelligible determination of war criminals," Czech National Prosecutor Jaroslav Drábek dismissively recalled, "was thought up in London."[93] Even those elements of the law that most offended traditional Western jurisprudence – retroactivity, the ban on appeals, and summary executions – originated not in the shadow of the Kremlin, but in the offices of Beneš and his coterie, a group that included many men trained in the law. Though the Košice Program did represent a victory for the broad Communist definition of collaboration, it was the decree written and passed in London that provided the legal structure and guidelines for postwar retribution in the Czech provinces. Ironically, the major innovation adopted from the Košice Program, the National Court, turned out to be the institution

---

[92] "Návrh Ministerstva spravedlnosti...na prominutí trestu smrti Dru. Petersu Starinskému," MS no. 44.645/1947-IV/8, SÚA, f. MS (VI/y), k. 1111, folder 19; Government meeting (17 June 1947), SÚA, f. 100/24, a.j. 1494, sv. 144.
[93] Drábek, Z časů dobrých a zlých, 106.

that caused the Communist Party the greatest headaches after the war. Far from being a kangaroo court, it proved highly resistant to political pressure even under the most trying of circumstances.

At the close of this consideration of Czech retribution's origins, it is necessary to note again that Czechoslovakia was not alone in its attempt to punish war criminals and collaborators. The Beneš government's desire for retribution was not in and of itself wrong headed; it was in many ways a highly moral endeavor. The atrocities of the Second World War demanded a response, and the universality of postwar trials across state boundaries clearly demonstrates that far more than political revenge was at stake. Nevertheless, the Beneš government did err in the type of law it created. The framers of this fundamentally flawed document – this "fateful and shameful decree"[94] – included measures that permitted, even encouraged, gross abuses to be perpetrated later. In the end, courts can only be as fair as the laws they are given to interpret.

[94] Pavel Tigrid, *Kapesní průvodce inteligentní ženy po vlastním osudu* (Toronto: Sixty-Eight Publishers, 1988), 327.

3

PEOPLE'S COURTS AND POPULAR JUSTICE

The term that the Czechoslovak government-in-exile chose to describe its retribution tribunals was hardly an auspicious one. Over the previous decade Europe had become familiar with the Nazi People's Court (Volksgericht), an institution that dealt mercilessly with alleged enemies of the Third Reich. After the war the negative connotations of the term "People's Court" led one Czech columnist to argue that the exiles should have adopted a different name: "In a populist fervor we have taken...too much from Nazism...'Volksgerichte' are linked frightfully with the image of horror, suffering, cruelty, lawlessness. Let our courts...be linked with the image of law and truth."[1] If the term did not please Czech ears in 1945, then it sounded even worse after the February 1948 coup d'état, when the victorious Communist Party made People's Courts a fixture of Stalinist justice. Despite the similarity in nomenclature, however, the postwar Extraordinary People's Courts bore little resemblance to either the Nazi tribunals that preceded them or the Communists ones that followed. Thanks to the efforts of prosecutors, professional judges, and even "people's judges," with time the Czech courts overcame the pernicious legacy of wild retribution and the excessively harsh limitations of the Great Decree. In the words of a contemporary commentator, the People's Courts, "despite all difficulties, particularly despite the thoroughly inappropriate legal regulations, completed an immense task; a task that was vitally necessary."[2]

---

[1] F. Klátil, "Suďte přísně, ale spravedlivě," *Svobodné slovo* (14 June 1945), Státní ústřední archiv (SÚA), Prague, f. MZV-VA II (j81), k. 215.

[2] Jaroslav Morávek, "Lidové soudy skončily," *Mladá fronta* (6 May 1947), SÚA, f. MZV-VA II (j81), k. 217.

In May 1947 the Justice Minister told the country's parliament that Czech national committees had forwarded 132,549 cases to public prosecutors, but only 38,316 cases had thereafter gone to trial. The largest part of the difference between the two figures consisted of cases that prosecutors had dismissed because of insufficient evidence. In fact, over the course of retribution prosecutors dismissed more cases (40,534) than they ultimately tried.[3] Vilém Hejl commented,

One interpretation of this fact says that the same or nearly the same number were imprisoned or persecuted innocently. Correctly speaking, however, it is possible to object that this number also represents the enduring civic, legal, and human honor of those who dealt with these cases and did not submit to pressure or to the hateful psychosis of revenge.[4]

This encomium could be extended to the judges as well, for they acquitted nearly 30 percent of defendants who came before the courts. Even when a case resulted in conviction, the judges often gave a defendant fewer years in prison than the very harsh law mandated. Both the rate of conviction and the average length of sentences decreased over the course of retribution. With time, the revolutionary courts became institutionalized, as people's judges became, de facto if not de jure, professionals.

Neither the preponderance of dismissals nor the significant share of acquittals can mask the fact that retribution was an onerous and debilitating process for many more people than simply those defendants who were tried and convicted. As this chapter will describe, however, many of the injustices ascribed by critics to retribution courts actually occurred long before cases reached trial, if they ever did. When analyzing postwar retribution it is necessary to distinguish between arrests and detention on the one hand and trials and convictions on the other.

[3] According to Drtina, another 31,793 cases were discontinued because the accused either had died or could not be located. As Chapter 6 explains, another 14,879 persons, mainly Germans, were released from indictment in order to facilitate their deportation from the country. Prosecutors referred 4,592 cases directly to regular courts, either because they were ordinary criminal matters or collaboration offenses too complex or uncertain to be tried in the minimum three days originally allotted to People's Court trials. Finally, due to time constraints, prosecutors never managed to try 2,435 cases. Prokop Drtina, *Na soudu národa: Tři projevy ministra spravedlnosti dr. Prokopa Drtiny o činnosti Mimořádných lidových soudů a Národního soudu* (Prague: Min. Spravedlnosti, 1947), 11–12.
[4] Vilém Hejl, *Zpráva o organizovaném násilí* (Prague: Univerzum, 1990), 26.

The former were almost entirely the responsibility of the security forces controlled ultimately by the Interior Ministry, headed by a Communist, Václav Nosek. The latter were the domain of prosecutors and judges under the watch of the Justice Ministry, directed by a National Socialist, Prokop Drtina.[5] Along this fault line between the police and the courts, between the Interior and the Justice Ministries, some of the greatest conflicts in postwar Czechoslovakia occurred. Once materials passed from the hands of the police to those of prosecutors and judges, a defendant's prospects improved dramatically.

A BLOODY BEGINNING

In the beginning the Czech People's Courts ruled mercilessly. During the months leading up to 1 October 1945, judges convicted ninety-seven percent of the defendants whose trials ended in a verdict. Nearly one in every eight defendants was given a death sentence.[6] Thus, when Josef Pfitzner took the stand on 5 September 1945 as the first defendant before the Prague People's Court, his prospects were not good. Formerly a professor at the city's German university, in 1939 Pfitzner became the Nazi mayor of the occupied capital. Among other charges, he stood accused of complicity in the execution of his predecessor, the former Czech mayor, Otakar Klapka, and in the desecration of Czechoslovakia's Grave of the Unknown Soldier. An active member of Henlein's SdP movement before the war, during the occupation Pfitzner became Standartenführer of the SA in Prague. The German professor's alleged crimes included his scholarly activity, which, according to the Czech prosecutor, "falsified

---

[5] Born into a prominent Czech family, Prokop Drtina (1900–1980) earned a degree in law and served in President Masaryk's office before becoming the personal secretary of Edvard Beneš in 1936. After the Nazi occupation Drtina helped to organize the Czech underground before he fled abroad in late 1939 under threat of Gestapo arrest. In London he rejoined Beneš and served as the president-in-exile's political aide, in which role he delivered a number of public addresses to the home front on British radio (BBC). Milan Churáň et al., *Kdo byl kdo v našich dějinách ve 20. století* (Prague: Libri, 1994), 87–88.

[6] In the period before 1 October 1945, the People's Courts collectively convicted 202 defendants (twenty-five were sentenced to death, eleven to life, 165 to prison terms, and one was given no penalty), and acquitted only six. Another twenty cases were transferred to the regular criminal courts for adjudication. Summary Justice Ministry figures have been revised according to my calculations based on the original submissions from individual courts. MS no. 34474/45-III/4, SÚA, f. MS (Org.) k. 1930, sv. 1; MS 64989/46-III/2, SÚA, f. MS (Z.tr.), k. 2076.

Figure 3. The Execution of Josef Pfitzner. Česká tisková kancelář (Czech Press Agency), 6 September 1945. Reproduced with permission.

our history."[7] After a two-day trial, the Prague People's Court sentenced Pfitzner to death and ordered that he be hanged in public.

As the Great Decree mandated, within hours Pfitzner stood on the scaffold. The scene, one newspaper explained, was intended to evoke the 1621 execution of twenty-seven Bohemian rebels by Habsburg imperial forces after the province's defeat at the Battle of the White Mountain. In any case, there was clearly some poetic justice in the execution site's backdrop: Pankrác prison, where Czech resisters had been jailed and tortured during the occupation. The newspaper dramatically recaptured the event for its readers (Figure 3):

Streams of people flowed to Heroes' Square....the police...estimated participation at more than 30,000 people.... By the execution site the Extraordinary People's Court chief justice read [Pfitzner] the verdict one more time...in the blaze of the setting sun and the shadows of the...gallows....The words sounded rather historic, as if the entire six years of suffering marched before us. On one side the setting sun, on the other the darkening wall and empty window of a burned-out home, to this day indicting the German brutality.

---

[7] Mečislav Borák, *Spravedlnost podle dekretu: Retribuční soudnictví v ČSR a Mimořádný lidový soud v Ostravě (1945–1948)* (Ostrava: Tilia, 1998), 50; Prokop Drtina, *Československo můj osud* (Toronto: Sixty-Eight Publishers, 1982), II:124.

Then the chief justice of the People's Court delivered Pfitzner into the hands of the executioners. The executioner's two assistants took him by the underarms and led him to the execution-place under the gallows. Hardly anyone could notice that Pfitzner's mouth had opened. "I die for Germany!" he said, but he lied. For no hero died here, only a Czechoslovak citizen, a state employee, who gave his word to the republic....

The body of the hanged, as the old police regulations demand, remained hanging on the execution-place for another whole hour. Thus ended the life of a traitor and recently still the lord of the capital of the republic.[8]

Drtina later considered Pfitzner's public execution to be excessive. In his memoirs, the Justice Minister commented that the German history professor "was not the type of Gestapo cut-throat for whom that type of degradation would probably have been justifiable."[9]

At the time, however, Drtina and his fellow government ministers were mainly distressed that women and children had watched Pfitzner's execution. From the vantage point of a Pankrác jail cell, a German prisoner described a ghoulishly festive atmosphere: "Mothers pushed their perambulators and children of school age climbed on the tops of the cars."[10] In his memoirs, Jaroslav Drábek, the Czech National Prosecutor, commented disapprovingly on the scene: "It reminded me too much of pictures from the French Revolution."[11] In the end, the public hanging, intended to satiate popular anger, instead provoked an outcry. Before the next defendant could be executed, Czech workers destroyed the scaffolds in front of Pankrác prison.[12] To prevent similar scenes from recurring, the government immediately passed a resolution mandating that future executions take place in closed areas that could not be seen from neighboring houses. Only individuals holding approved passes would be allowed to observe and, above all, no minors could attend.[13]

The demands of frequent executions unnerved some towns and caused problems for some courts. When civic leaders of Marienbad

---

[8] "Pfitzner odsouzen na smrt," *Svobodné slovo* (7 September 1945), SÚA, f. MZV-VA II (j. 81), k. 215.

[9] Drtina, *Československo*, II:125.

[10] Wilhelm K. Turnwald, ed., *Documents on the Expulsion of the Sudeten Germans*, trans. by Gerda Johnson (Munich: Association for the Protection of Sudeten German Interests, 1953), 29.

[11] Jaroslav Drábek, *Z časů dobrých a zlých* (Prague: Naše vojsko, 1992), 107.

[12] Borák, *Spravedlnost podle dekretu*, 50–51.

[13] First government, meeting fifty-four (14 September 1945), 16–17, SÚA, f. 100/24 (KG), sv. 138.

(Mariánské Lázně) learned that retribution trials might take place in their town, they feared that defendants might be sentenced to death and executed on the spot. The Marienbaders appealed directly to Drtina:

Insomuch as Marienbad is exclusively a spa town and this year will already be attending to foreign guests, such circumstances would have catastrophic effects on our spa business. It is understandable from the psychological perspective that domestic and foreign guests, who above all are seeking spiritual relaxation, would avoid a spa resort where executions are taking place.[14]

Others towns asked for trials not to be held in their area at all.[15] For some courts, finding hangmen to do the job proved a difficult task. After all, skilled individuals who had practiced that profession during the war could hardly be employed: The Pilsen People's Court, for example, gave capital sentences to three Czechs who had worked as executioners for the Nazis.[16] The Tábor People's Court had to delay capital trials because it could not find anyone qualified to carry out the verdicts summarily as the law required. Not until the middle of October 1945 did the District National Committee hire an executioner, but he turned out to be under contract with the České Budějovice court, which claimed his services on the same days that he was expected in Tábor. Finally, on 21 November the Tábor court found its own hangman.[17]

In October 1945 the Prague People's Court printed up detailed instructions for steps to be taken in the case of a trial for a capital crime. First of all, the Justice Ministry needed to be informed. Then the court's executioner had to be put on call for the entire day. After the verdict the court was to contact a priest, the prison doctor, the coroner, the warden, the municipal authorities, the chief justice of the relevant Regional Court, and Zdeněk Marjanko, the Justice Ministry official responsible for retribution (whose home and office phone numbers were both

---

[14] The spa town of Františkovy Lázně (Franzensbad) had a similar request refused by the Justice Ministry. Místní správní komise, Mariánské Lázně (16 May 1946) to Drtina, SÚA, f. MS (Org), k. 1943, sv. 1. See also Václav Jiřík, "Retribuční realita a Chebsko," in Frank Boldt, ed., *Velké dějiny, malý národ* (Havlíčkův Brod: Český spisovatel, 1995), 217.

[15] Both Mělník and Rakovník petitioned the Prague People's Court not to hold sessions in their towns. Slaný and Kladno, by contrast, requested local trials of war criminals. Pres. 376-3/45 (30 October 1945), Pres. 378-3/45 (20 October 1945), Pres. 234-3/45 (2 January 1946), Pres. 253-3/45 (7 December 1945), Státní oblastní archiv (SOA) Prague, f. MLS-PR, Pres. 3.

[16] Ls 495/46, MLS Plzeň (MS no. 76271/46-IV/5), SÚA, f. MS (Org), k. 1932, sv. 9.

[17] MLS Tábor (9 January 1946) to MS no. 3727/46-IV/5, SÚA, f. MS (Org), k. 1929.

listed, just in case). Finally, the chief justice asked that court "employees, especially women, not go as spectators to the executions."[18] After an execution, came the question of how to dispose a defendant's corpse: The Prague People's Court donated fifty-five bodies for scientific research.[19] Over time, hangings changed from public spectacles, worthy of national attention, to the daily routine of the Czech People's Courts, until by May 1947 nearly 700 defendants had been executed.

DELAYS, DISAGREEMENTS, DISMISSALS

The severity of the early months failed to satisfy the leaders of the Communist Party. When the government cabinet met on 24 October 1945, they accused Jaroslav Stránský, Justice Minister at that time, of intentionally sabotaging the prosecution of Czech collaborators. The Communist Minister of Information, Václav Kopecký, charged Stránský with "running away" from the task of retribution, even though the London government had "denounced and stigmatized thousands of people." Kopecký blamed this development on the alleged fact that the Justice Ministry was "under the influence of the wealthiest stratum of the population." Coming to the support of his comrade, party leader Gottwald criticized the Great Decree as insufficient.[20]

Throughout this discussion the Communist ministers adopted a tone that suggested that they did not consider themselves responsible for Czech retribution. In fact, from the very beginning Gottwald and his comrades seem to have intentionally abandoned the administration of justice to their political competitors. Stránský and the other London Czechs had been forewarned in Moscow when Kopecký told them, "We are keeping to *your* system... of extraordinary summary people's courts."[21] During the May 1945 Prague Uprising, Communist

---

[18] "Opatření po rozsudku smrti," oběžník č. 2 (18 October 1945), SOA-Prague, f. MLS-PR, Pres. 16. In two Cheb cases at least the court dutifully telephoned the Ministry of Justice – both requests for clemency were denied. Václav Jiřík, *Nedaleko od Norimberku: Z dějin Mimořádného lidového soudu v Chebu v letech 1946 až 1948* (Cheb: Svět křídel, 2000), 168, 244.

[19] "Záznam o vydaných mrtvolách k účelům vědeckým," SOA-Prague, f. MLS-PR, Pres. 16.

[20] First government, meeting ninety-four (24 October 1945), 4-12, SÚA, f. 100/24 (KG), sign. 1494, sv. 138.

[21] Italics added. Miloš Klimeš, eds., *Cesta ke Květnu: Vznik lidové demokracie v Československu* (Prague: Československá akademie věd, 1965), doc. 132, 419.

resistance leader Josef Smrkovský made sure that the only two non-Communists on the Czech National Council were designated to the National Bank and the Justice Ministry.[22] In the postwar government the non-Communist ministers of Foreign Affairs (the former president's son, Jan Masaryk) and Foreign Trade (Hubert Ripka) were each saddled with a Communist deputy, but Justice Ministers Stránský and Drtina suffered no such assistance. In fact, Justice was the only powerful ministry that did not include a Communist or party sympathizer in its leadership.[23] Despite the Party's outspoken desire for harsh retribution, leading Communists may have ultimately preferred to avoid responsibility for a process that promised to divide the nation. Drtina described the burden he felt when he became Justice Minister: "Simply put, I did not envy Stránský that he had to carry out retribution. And now I myself was to have that unenviable task? That was my main inhibition; [that was] why I did not want the Justice Ministry."[24]

The Communists' willingness to let go of retribution may have also stemmed from a simple calculation: There was a limit to how many powerful ministries the other parties would allow them to control. After the 1946 elections, Drtina later explained, "We [National Socialists] did not insist that we had to receive [the Justice] Ministry and we would have been satisfied with another ministry, perhaps the Ministry of Interior or National Defense, or the Ministry of Agriculture."[25] In response, Gottwald angrily rejected any suggestion that his party surrender the Interior portfolio: "The Communists will never give up that ministry." When the National Socialists then asked to appoint one of

---

[22] Ota Hora, *Svědectví o puči* (Toronto: Sixty-Eight Publishers, 1978), 67.

[23] The Czechoslovak Communist Party, together with its Slovak affiliate, claimed only seven of the twenty-five cabinet positions in the postwar government cabinet, but it controlled the most powerful ministries and managed to neutralize many others. With Július Ďuriš as Minister of Agriculture the Party gained the power of patronage thanks to the distribution of land expropriated from Sudeten Germans and alleged collaborators. With Václav Kopecký as Minister of Information, the Communists had command of the airwaves and the means to punish unsympathetic newspapers. Most significantly, the Communist Party claimed the post of Interior Minister for Václav Nosek. At first glance, it appears that non-Communists also secured some important positions, but Ludvík Svoboda, the supposedly nonpartisan Minister of National Defense, was Stalin's willing lieutenant, and Zdeněk Nejedlý, the allegedly unaffiliated Education Minister, did not conceal his Communist affinities.

[24] In his memoirs, Drtina admitted that in the end he took the position because he was ambitious and did not want to let the opportunity pass him by. Drtina, *Československo*, II:107–108.

[25] Drtina, *Na soudu národa*, 36.

Figure 4. Prokop Drtina, Czechoslovak Minister of Justice (1945–1948). Česká tisková kancelář (Czech Press Agency), 5 April 1946. Reproduced with permission.

their men regional director for security of Bohemia, Kopecký threatened, "If the National Socialists get that position, there will be conflict on the streets."[26] Unlike the Interior Ministry, which had direct control over the police and security forces, the Justice Ministry did not legally have the power to force judges to obey its orders in specific trials. The Communist leaders probably believed that the judiciary, an independent-minded and largely conservative elite, would be difficult to tame and thus was better left for a later time.

When Drtina replaced Stránský as Justice Minister at the beginning of November 1945, the Communists (and the country) may have expected him to push for the harsh punishment of collaborators. After all, on London radio Drtina had been the voice of uncompromising retribution, repeatedly promising that traitors would receive no mercy after the war (Figure 4).[27] Six months after the end of the war, however, Drtina had moderated his tone. Only a few days after assuming his position, he

[26] Hejl, *Zprávy*, 50.
[27] See, for example, Drtina's radio addresses, "Warning to Traitors," "Warning to Collaborators," and "The Execution of Pierre Pucheu." Prokop Drtina, *A nyní promluví Pavel*

told his new subordinates in the Justice Ministry that retribution must be carried out "as rapidly as possible." He further stressed that their task was not only to punish the guilty, but also to release from detention the many innocent people who had never betrayed the nation.[28] When Drtina met a month later with the chief justices and prosecutors of the People's Courts, he emphasized that the Czech nation had maintained its honor during the war. According to the new minister, "Treacherous politics were mainly the work of individuals, who had no experience or political will, or of insignificant trash."[29] With his new gospel of tolerance toward Czechs, Drtina soon faced the barrage of criticism that Stránský had weathered: By the middle of January the Justice Minister felt it necessary to demand, unsuccessfully, that Communist ministers stop their party's public criticism of retribution.[30]

At the 24 October 1945 government meeting Kopecký provocatively accused Stránský of intentionally delaying retribution trials for more than four months.[31] The People's Courts did get off to a slow start: The Brno court tried its first case in June, but the next court, in Uherské Hradiště, was not established until the first of August. By the end of that month only five courts were operating. Another ten People's Courts, including the one in Prague, began in September; seven started in October, one in November, and one, the Cheb court, not until the following year.[32] Despite Kopecký's accusations of Justice Ministry subterfuge, there was a simpler explanation for the courts' delays. After six years of foreign occupation the Czech judicial system was in a disastrous state, hardly prepared to assume its regular responsibilities, not to mention the massive process of trying thousands of alleged collaborators and war criminals. In Ostrava, the courthouse had been bombed, so trials temporarily had to take place in city hall. In Pilsen, an outbreak of infectious disease meant that the jail had to be quarantined and work

---

Svatý... Londýnské rozhlasové epištoly z let 1940–1945 (Prague: Vladimír Žikeš, 1945), 42–45, 128–31, 396–400.

[28] "Úkoly justiční správy," *Svobodné slovo* (9 November 1945), 1.

[29] "Zápis o poradě" (12 December 1945), MS no. 50296/45-IV/5, SÚA, f. MS (Org), k. 1927.

[30] Second government, meeting twenty-four (18 January 1946), 1-4, SÚA, f. 100/24 (KG), aj. 1494, sv. 139.

[31] First government, meeting ninety-four (24 October 1945), 4-12, SÚA, f. 100/24 (KG), sign. 1494, sv. 138.

[32] "Přehled činnosti veřejných žalobců u mimořádných lidových soudů," SÚA, f. MS, k. 1929.

consequently delayed. District attorneys noted a dearth of typewriters, a shortage of paper, and a debilitating absence of light and, especially, heat. Reports from prosecutors complained of abysmal pay, advanced age, and unreasonably lengthy commutes – one had to catch a daily train at four in the morning to reach the court on time. Another problem was the court staff, which was insufficient and too often untrained.[33] Drtina called the judicial system "the Cinderella of state administration."[34] In December 1946 he had to petition the parliament's budgetary committee for more funds because the Justice Ministry faced a *decrease* of 13.5 million crowns in its yearly allocation.[35]

A Justice Ministry report from the end of 1945 commented that the judiciary "had never been in such a precarious state as now."[36] Drtina estimated that there was a shortfall of 800 judges in the Czech provinces.[37] Apparently, only half of all prewar judges and state attorneys remained fit to carry out their official functions. Only about three-fourths of all court personnel were available for the daunting tasks of postwar justice. The reactivation of retired judges did not suffice, especially with the new needs to replace German judges in the borderlands and carry out retribution.[38] A purge of compromised judges deprived Czech courts of more. Seventy-five judges in all were referred to a disciplinary commission. By July 1947, twenty-one of the judges had been acquitted or had their cases dismissed, thirty-three had been disciplined, and eight had been released from service.[39] The purge would certainly have been greater had the Nazi imposition of a superior system of German courts in the Protectorate not spared Czech judges the responsibility of adjudicating wartime political crimes.[40]

---

[33] MS no. 1493/46-IV/5, no. 2777/45-IV/5 (8 January 1946), no. 3224/46-IV/5 (9 January 1946), no. 4182/46-IV/5 (10 January 1946), no. 5302/46-IV/5, SÚA, f. MS (Org), k. 1929.

[34] Prokop Drtina, *O soudcovské nezávislosti, lidovém soudnictví a jiných časových otázkách československé justice* (Prague: Mladá fronta, 1946), 22–23.

[35] "Beran a Syrový v nejbližší době před soud," *Svobodné slovo* (4 December 1946), SÚA, f. MZV-VA II (j81), k. 216.

[36] Brožovský (30 December 1945), SÚA, f. MS (Drtina), k. 2111.

[37] Drtina, *Československo*, Appendix IV, II:252.

[38] Drtina, *O soudcovské nezávislosti*, 22–23.

[39] "Výsledky očistného řízení...proti soudcovským úředníkům" (23 June 1947), SÚA, f. MS (Drtina), k. 2113; Drtina, *Na soudu národa*, 69.

[40] In the Protectorate, German courts assumed jurisdiction for political crimes. Trials of resistance members were conducted by local German courts, by military courts-martial, or by courts in the Reich itself. Gerhard Jacoby, *Racial State: The German Nationalities*

In response to Communist criticism, Stránský and Drtina blamed national committees for the delays. Despite repeated appeals, the national committees were slow to nominate Czechs to serve as people's judges.[41] This tardiness, however, was the least of the problems caused by the new "people's administration." In the spring and summer of 1945 national committees created "investigative commissions" and delegated to them the task of preparing cases against suspected collaborators. According to an official pamphlet, the new commissions were necessary because the old police had been compromised by their service during the Protectorate.[42] Investigative commissions were staffed by political appointees, who often had little or no legal training. An anonymous letter to the Czechoslovak President commented despondently on the commissions: "To look for the law there would be a joke."[43] Only after an investigative commission transferred a suspect and his or her dossier to the courts could prosecutors and judges begin their work. Until a person's case file was forwarded, he or she remained under the watch of the national committee, in the custody of the police, not the court. In the meantime, prosecutors and judges could not release a suspect or dismiss a case.[44]

The investigative commissions caused more problems than they solved. In January 1946 the Mladá Boleslav public prosecutor complained,

Above all, it is necessary to note that cases charged by the investigative commissions were more often than not insufficient, or even investigated deficiently – in numerous cases without regard for the provisions of the retribution decree. The investigation was incomplete, fragmentary; there were even cases where the material consisted only of a report about the arrest of the suspect, without declaring the causes or facts on which the suspicion was based, [and] at the most attached a brief record of the accused's partial testimony. The materials are almost never catalogued; more often than not a

Policy in the Protectorate of Bohemia and Moravia (New York: Institute of Jewish Affairs of the AJC and WJC, 1944), 99–105.

[41] First government, meeting ninety-four (24 October 1945), 8, SÚA, f. 100/24 (KG), aj. 1494, sv. 138.

[42] Stanislav Šulc, Národní výbory: Vývoj, právní základy, poslání, práce (Brno: ZÁR, 1946), 301.

[43] Anonymous letter (14 September 1945), KPR no. 13196/45, Archiv Kanceláře prezidenta republiky (AKPR), f. D-11169/47 (Anonymy-f).

[44] Drtina, O soudcovské nezávislosti, 17–18.

summary of the materials, personal account, and the like were absent. From several records it was not even clear how long the suspect had languished in custody.[45]

In an effort to rectify the situation, the Justice Ministry designated judges to work on investigative commissions.[46] Although there was some improvement, problems persisted until the very end of the courts' operations. In their final reports to the Justice Ministry, prosecutors and judges complained that their tasks had been greatly complicated by the work of investigative commissions. The Uherské Hradiště head prosecutor called the commissions unprofessional: They swamped the courts with cases that were confusing and often baseless. The Nový Jičín chief justice complained that a case had to be completely reconstructed once a trial began.[47] Confronted with insufficiently and incompetently prepared dossiers, prosecutors had to retread the ground covered by investigation commissions, a process that led to considerable delays.

At the 24 October 1945 government meeting the Communist ministers not only accused the Justice Ministry of stalling. Gottwald complained that prosecutors had released "out-and-out collaborators and traitors" and claimed that this development had "worsened public morale."[48] Over the next several years this accusation became a primary theme of the Communist critique of retribution. A January 1946 article in *Pochodeň* [*Torch*], a weekly journal for party cadres, lambasted prosecutors for dismissing numerous cases. The author, a Communist parliamentary deputy, complained, for example, about the releases of Anna Freitová, who had allegedly denounced her neighbor during the war for having a radio; Jiří Hubený, who had voluntarily served in the German army; Michal Kyselka, who had apparently administered confiscated Jewish property; and Josef Malina, a former functionary of the National Fascist Community organization. Prosecutors had also dismissed charges against Josef Neuman, who had

---

[45] MLS Mladá Boleslav prosecutor (8 January 1946) to MS no. 3128/46-IV/5, SÚA, f. MS (Org), k. 1929.
[46] Drtina, *O soudcovské nezávislosti*, 17.
[47] "Skončení retribučního soudnictví," Vedoucí veřejný žálobce (v.v.ž.), MLS-UH, přednosta MLS-NJ, v.v.ž. MLS-OL, v.v.ž. MLS-KL, přednosta MLS-LT, v.v.ž. MLS-PR, v.v.ž. MLS-KH, SÚA, f. MS (Org), k. 1942.
[48] First government, meeting ninety-four (24 October 1945), 4-12, SÚA, f. 100/24 (KG), sign. 1494, sv. 138, 5-6.

allegedly supported the suppression of the Communist movement, and Alois Rossman, who had run a factory that made tanks. The article argued that prosecutors who freed collaborators should be punished for aiding and abetting them. In conclusion, the author claimed, there could be no "people's justice" without a "rectification" of the prosecutors' role.[49]

In response to such charges Drtina argued that when a prosecutor returned a case to a national committee, he was not demonstrating his disagreement with the "people," but his dissatisfaction with the work of the investigative commission.[50] Dismissals, like delays, were partly a product of incompetence and partisanship on the part of those who originally prepared the cases. Investigative commissions forwarded large numbers of cases that had no business being tried by retribution courts. A common complaint of prosecutors was that they simply had no idea why a defendant had been arrested in the first place. Many cases rested on little more than on innuendo, "neighbor's gossip," or second-hand knowledge. Others were simply the result of personal scores being settled. In many instances, the purported offense was not even a crime according to the Great Decree: for example, membership in the German Red Cross or denunciation of a neighbor to the police for theft. Some such charges, like fraternization with Germans or the adoption of German nationality, later became the subject of punishment by national committees for "offenses against national honor." Other cases were dismissed because the accused had been "forced" to join the SA or some other fascist group. Prosecutors also terminated proceedings because the suspect had been a mere member, not a leader or functionary, of the Nazi party, Banner movement, or other banned organization.[51]

By May 1947, when the People's Courts were disbanded, prosecutors had dismissed 40,534 cases for insufficient evidence. An additional 31,793 cases had been discontinued because the accused either had died

---

[49] Josef Tesla, "Kam kráčíš, spravedlnosti?" *Pochodeň* II:1 (4 January 1946), 1, 3.
[50] Drtina, *O soudcovské nezávislosti*, 30–33.
[51] "Výkazy o věcech napadlých pro lidový soud," MLS-Ostrava to MS, SÚA, f. MS (Org), k. 289; "Seznam zastavených spisů u veřejného žalobce u mimoř. lid. soudu v Kutné Hoře," Archiv Ministerstva vnitra (AMV) Prague, no. 12793, 2–4; Květa Jechová, "Deník žalobce jako přístupová cesta k porozumění fondu mimořádného lidového soudu a nebo jen oklika?" in Mečislav Borák, ed., *Retribuce v ČSR a národní podoby antisemitismu: Židovská problematika a antisemitismus ve spisech mimořádných lidových soudů a trestních komisí ONV v letech 1945–1948* (Prague: Ústav, pro soudobé dějiny AVČR, 2002), 110.

or could not be located. As Chapter 6 explains, another 14,879 persons, mainly Germans, were released from indictment to facilitate their deportation from the country. Prosecutors referred 4,592 cases directly to regular courts, either because they were ordinary criminal matters, or because they concerned collaboration offenses too complex or uncertain to be tried in the maximum three days originally allotted to People's Court trials.[52] Finally, due to time constraints, prosecutors never managed to try 2,435 cases. In all, of the 132,549 cases forwarded by investigative commissions and the police, the People's Courts ultimately judged only 38,316, approximately 31 percent of the original total.[53] At first glance, it may appear that Czech prosecutors failed to execute their duties, but prior to the war they had only tried about 27 percent of all cases they received from the police.[54]

The investigative commissions were responsible not only for delays and dismissals, but also for acquittals. The commissions lost valuable evidence and forwarded numerous cases without supporting documentation. Without knowledge of incriminatory materials, the prosecutor often had to submit a rough indictment and then make the best of it when the court found the case weak. Frequently, the investigative organs only prepared the case against a defendant and suppressed any evidence that might speak in his or her favor. As a result, the defense sometimes had an advantage over the prosecution, which was surprised to learn during the trial of exculpatory information that undermined the state's case. Columnist Edvard Valenta commented that in the courtroom the judge "sometimes ... resembled a poorly prepared schoolchild" as he rifled through a case file in the attempt to discover what critical evidence had been ignored.[55] The Mladá Boleslav chief justice attributed these problems to inexperience and the "revolutionary mood," a mood that was responsible for brutality and deception. He commented, "This came to light during the trials when the indictment rested on the accused's confession, while the accused objected that the confession had been forced out of him by abuse." Some judges suspected that there was a more insidious

---

[52] The first revision to the Great Decree permitted prosecutors to extend trials beyond the originally mandated maximum three days. Law no. 22/1946 (24 January 1946), *Sbírka zákonů a nařízení Republiky československé* (Prague, 1946), 161.

[53] Drtina, *Na soudu národa*, 11–12.

[54] Drtina, *Na soudu národa*, 43.

[55] Edvard Valenta, "Soudce, agitátor a anonym," *Dnešek* I:48 (20 February 1947), 753.

cause for the apparent incompetence of the investigative commissions. In numerous cases incriminatory materials were forwarded either at the last minute or even after the verdict. One judge did not disguise his belief that the delays were meant to produce a situation where the courts could be criticized for their leniency.[56]

The machinations of some national committees did not end when investigative commissions forwarded suspects' dossiers to the courts. The Pilsen prosecutor complained vehemently about numerous interventions by national committees, factory councils, and resistance organizations, especially in cases that had already been dismissed. Some individuals were rearrested after the court had released them.[57] Václav Stieber, an investigative judge in Kladno, got into hot water when he refused to allow four members of a local factory committee to be present at an interrogation. When he then freed the accused, the local Communist newspaper published a series of *ad hominem* attacks, including articles entitled: "Dr. Stieber – the Type of Judge That Should Not Be" and "The Peak of Dr. Stieber's Impudence." The judge responded by suing two national committee members for defamation of character.[58] In an even more controversial case, judge Josef Malý ordered the conditional release of six persons because of prison overcrowding (and, apparently, a lack of cookware). The men were part of a larger group of twelve suspects that a district national committee had arrested without any substantiating information. As minor criminals with permanent residences in the area, Malý argued, the suspects were no threat to flee. The local Communist secretary saw matters otherwise and publicly called for the people to take matters into their own hands. The police immediately rearrested the six men, four of whom Malý then released for the second time. Like Stieber, Malý did not stop there. The judge ordered the arrest of several local Communist functionaries.[59]

Although Stieber initially won his defamation suit, a regional court later overturned the verdict and the Justice Ministry dismissed him. As for Malý, the warrants he issued were rescinded and he was quickly

---

[56] "Skončení," v.v.ž. MLS-LT, v.v.ž. MLS-MB, přednosta MLS-HK, přednosta MLS-MB, přednosta MLS-UH, v.v.ž. MLS-PR, přednosta MLS-UH, SÚA, f. MS (Org), k. 1942.

[57] "Skončení," v.v.ž. MLS-PL, SÚA, f. MS (Org), k. 1942.

[58] Reports on judges, "Václav Stieber," SÚA, f. MS (Drtina), k. 2111.

[59] Reports on judges, "Josef Malý," SÚA, f. MS (Drtina), k. 2111.

reassigned to another district.[60] Others were not as strong willed. According to the Nový Jičín chief justice, the press forced prosecutors to try cases that had no place under retribution law.[61] The Most chief justice concurred, "The public prosecutor did not conceal the fact that he wanted to avoid attacks from the public and he therefore consciously tried cases that should have been stopped or at most transferred [to a regular court]."[62] Press attacks also led courts to take up some cases that prosecutors had already dismissed. The Communist weekly *Torch* boasted that its complaints about two dismissals had led to the defendants being tried, convicted, and sentenced to five and eight years, respectively.[63] Pressure, however, occasionally came from opposite directions. A judge in Chomutov explained, "Releasing some of the less serious cases... is too odious considering the repeated newspaper attacks on the courts and yet almost daily employers' requests are received for the release of employees whose arrests threaten the operations of the entire firm."[64]

The Union of Liberated Political Prisoners [Svaz osvobozených politických vězňů (SOPV)][65] pressed the government and the courts to punish collaborators and war criminals to the fullest extent.[66] Representing victims of Nazi persecution, the SOPV claimed 62,000 members in 6,000 local chapters. The group had a "purge commission" in Prague to collect incriminatory material for trials of major war criminals and even ran its own investigative team in Germany, which worked to get the Allies to extradite suspects back to Czechoslovakia.[67] The courts, for their part, sometimes relied on the organization to identify suspects. The Cheb People's Court, for example, regularly sent photographs of former

[60] Reports on judges, "Václav Stieber" and "Josef Malý," SÚA, f. MS (Drtina), k. 2111.
[61] "Skončení," přednosta MLS-NJ, SÚA, f. MS (Org), k. 1942.
[62] "Skončení," přednosta MLS-MO, SÚA, f. MS (Org), k. 1942.
[63] Jindra Uher, "Trestní, či osvobozující komise dle malého dekretu?" *Pochodeň* II:25 (21 June 1946), 1.
[64] OS Chomutov (12 February 1946) to Presidium KS Most, SÚA, f. MS (Org), k. 1934, sv. 3.
[65] The organization's full name was the Union of Liberated Political Prisoners and Surviving Kin of the Victims of Nazism [Svaz osvobozených politických vězňů a pozůstalých po obětech nacismu].
[66] See, for example, Resolution of SOPVP ve Vejprnicích (24 August 1946) to MV. SUA f. MVII-N, inv.c. 80, sign. 561, k. 143.
[67] "SOPVP od VIII. sjezdu KSČ do února 1948," SÚA, f. 100/1, sv. 30, č.j. 240.

concentration camp guards to the SOPV central office in Prague. The organization then contacted its members to determine whether any had witnessed the guards' crimes.[68] To reach the general public the SOPV also placed calls in national and local newspapers for information about indicted war criminals. These notices encouraged Czechs to report to the commission and testify before the courts. In one such insert, the group sought information about the conduct of a specific SS guard, members of the Prague Gestapo, and whether one suspect had been an executioner at Theresienstadt.[69] The SOPV also protested, often vigorously, against what it viewed as unjustified acquittals and lenient sentences.[70]

While demanding severe justice, the SOPV could also stress fairness. One chapter, which sent a harshly worded resolution to the Communist Party demanding a "thorough cleansing of public life ... of traitors, reactionaries, and collaborators," also insisted that the courts "must try individual cases only on the basis of thoroughly and conscientiously developed indictments, based on the deposition of all witnesses for and against, and with the cooperation of political prisoners."[71] In general, the SOPV's early pronouncements expressed support for the government, the demand to participate in the punishment of collaborators, and growing disappointment with the results of retribution. Some statements reveal an aggrieved sense that the nation was ignoring those who had suffered on its behalf.[72] After February 1948, in a bid to avoid a purge, the Union's leaders retrospectively boasted that Communists within the group had eventually prevailed over members of the National Socialist and People's parties. That assessment squares with the recollections of the non-Communist National Prosecutor, Jaroslav Drábek, that the SOPV began the postwar period as a nonpartisan organization, but was progressively subverted from within.[73] Even after Communists wrested control, however, the group was arguably not their pliant instrument.

[68] Jiřík, *Nedaleko od Norimberku*, 75, 161, 215, 308, 311–13, 326, 329.

[69] *Lidová demokracie* (11 September 1947), 4.

[70] See, for example, "Pro posouzení veřejnosti!" *Kutnohorský kraj* II:29 (19 July 1946), 3.

[71] SOPV + PON pobočka v Sušici (15 March 1946) to the KSČ, SÚA, f. 100/24, sv. 38, ar.j. 822, l. 3–4.

[72] Resoluce delegátů první pracovní konference vojenského odboru SOPVON (15/16 June 1946), SÚA, f. 100/24, sv. 38, ar.j. 822, l. 7-11; SOPV (12 April 1946) to Gen. Sekretariát KSČ (p. gen. taj. R. Slánský), SÚA, f. 100/24, sv. 38, ar.j. 822, l. 26.

[73] "SOPVP od VIII. sjezdu KSČ do února 1948," SÚA, f. 100/1, sv. 30, č.j. 240; Drábek, *Z časů dobrých a zlých*, 102. Early on, in September 1945, an informer even accused one section of the SOPV of anti-Communist sentiments. Supposedly members opposed the

To the contrary, the Communists cadres who ran the Union likely pressured the Party leadership to maintain an unflinching demand for harsh punishment.

NATIONAL INSECURITY AND CZECH "GESTAPOISM"

The difficulties faced by the courts were part of a larger problem involving not only national committees, but also the police and national security forces, none of which regularly respected the prerogative of judges to determine guilt and innocence. In January 1946 the Justice Ministry complained, "The approach of organs subordinate to the Interior Ministry not only undermines the authority of the courts . . . in the eyes of the public, it is also a serious violation of the principle that justice is at all levels separate from administration."[74] If the public behavior of officials subordinate to the Interior Ministry seemed disturbing, what went on in private was far worse. The police and the national committees were not only unprofessional; they were all too often sadistic. On trial, many defendants credibly claimed that they had been forced to confess by illegal methods.[75] In a rousing speech to parliament in December 1945, Ota Hora, a young National Socialist deputy, called for an end to "excesses" – the contemporary euphemism used to describe everything from vandalism and theft to rape and murder. Evoking President Tomáš G. Masaryk's 1918 appeal for the Czechs to de-Austrianize themselves, Hora exhorted the country to "de-Nazify" itself: "De-Nazify, everywhere and in all things, in the state administration and the security forces. Yes, de-Nazify in those police jails where . . . utterly innocent people have suffered."[76]

Attempts to "de-Nazify" the country were dealt a severe setback in May 1946, when the parliament passed Law no. 115/46 to exonerate Czechs of any crimes committed in the struggle for their nation's liberation. Certainly, a need existed to legalize genuine acts of wartime resistance, but the law also aimed to shield postwar instigators of

nationalization of banks and called the Communist program an "unfortunate legacy of the revolution." SÚA, f. 100/24, sv. 38, ar.j. 822, 8–9.

[74] MS no. 7563/46-IV/1 (31 Jan. 1946), SÚA, f. MS (Org), k. 1934, sv. 3.

[75] "Skončení," v.v.ž. MLS-MB, SÚA, f. MS (Org), k. 1942; Jiřík, *Nedaleko od Norimberku*, 50, 221; Trial transcript, SOA-Praha, MLS-PR, Ls 1026/45, 232–33.

[76] Hora, *Svědectví* (1978), 163–69; "Bezpečnost základem pořádku v státu," *Svobodné slovo* (22 Nov. 1945), 1.

revolutionary courts and the perpetrators of "excesses" against all suits and prosecution. Originally, the Justice Ministry had prepared a bill to amnesty acts committed against Germans, Magyars, and collaborators, as defined by the retribution decrees. That draft covered a perpetrator of vigilante justice if he or she had believed his or her target to be a collaborator. Crimes committed "out of greed, lust, or to conceal or enable another criminal act" were explicitly excluded from the amnesty. Importantly, the proposed amnesty was limited to acts committed before 9 July 1945, the date when the Great Decree officially took effect.

On 20 December 1945 the government proposed passing a law of impunity rather than simply declaring an amnesty. Whereas an amnesty would have merely protected the perpetrators from punishment, the proposed law essentially declared that no crimes had ever been committed. The government also extended the period of impunity by another three and one-half months to 28 October 1945, the date when the parliament first met. No crimes were explicitly excluded from the proposed law; even acts of greed or "lust" could be covered if they had been committed as expressions of opposition to the enemies of the Czech and Slovak nations or their state. In other words, any crime, even rape or murder, committed against a German, Magyar, or a person thought to be a collaborator was potentially no crime at all. Parliament finally passed a measure that neither declared an amnesty nor handed out broad impunity – Law no. 115/46 simply declared acts of wild retribution committed before 28 October 1945 to have been legal. In a dry understatement, Drtina later told parliament, "The final version of this question went somewhat farther than the Justice Ministry had intended."[77]

In February 1947 a military court in Pilsen (Plzeň) heard a case against four policemen indicted for their inhumane treatment of prisoners in May 1945.[78] The defendants had brutally beaten their former captain and several of their former colleagues, who had been arrested for alleged collaboration with the Germans. After being punched, kicked, and beaten with a truncheon, the former captain, František Bureš, was then shackled for forty-eight hours. He died shortly after he was

---

[77] Drtina, *Na soudu národa*, 53–55.
[78] Military tribunals handled disciplinary procedures against the police.

finally taken to a hospital. Although the military court determined that three of the defendants were responsible for brutally beating prisoners, thanks to Law no. 115/46 the policemen could not be held accountable. The four officers were immediately released. The Communist flagship *Rudé právo* greeted the verdict with approbation: "By this just decision an attack of compromised denouncers on the [police] has been repulsed."[79]

Others were less ecstatic. What offended the Social Democratic weekly *Cíl* [*Goal*] most was the defendants' failure to admit to their crimes, irrespective of their inevitable acquittal. For in the absence of demonstrated guilt, the police officers continued to serve, however they might choose to exercise the public trust. Summing up the fears of many Czechs, the weekly asked incredulously whether the verdict meant that "People, who in police service transgressed against the basic principles of their profession, against the proper meaning for the existence of the whole police corps in a normal state, will protect your... and everyone else's security?" In decrying the "First Verdict of Its Kind in the Republic," *Cíl* called on parliament to amend Law no. 115/46.[80] Other journals echoed the demand, but to little effect.[81] In the midst of the preparations for Law no. 115/46, the Justice Ministry ordered prosecutors to release individuals being held for crimes committed against Germans and suspected collaborators. Judicial proceedings against them were suspended. In May 1947 Drtina announced that public prosecutors had received 104 cases of postwar "Gestapoism," of which 79 were considered to be serious matters. By then 41 cases had still not been fully investigated, 4 had been dismissed (likely for procedural reasons), and only 4 had resulted in convictions. The remaining 30 cases had been dismissed thanks to Law no. 115/46.[82] One Czech journalist distressingly concluded, "The fact, that after a hideous war, criminal cases against honor, health, and life... have remained unpunished, has so shaken trust in the law, rights, and government, that it will take a long time before trust again returns and establishes itself."[83]

---

[79] "Po časopisech," *Právní prakse* XI (1947/48), 30–31.
[80] "Rozsudek první svého druhu v republice," *Cíl* III:6 (21 February 1947), 1.
[81] Tomáš Staněk, *Odsun Němců z Československa 1945–1947* (Prague: Naše vojsko, 1991), 204.
[82] Two of the four convictions were for the crime of rape. Drtina, *Na soudu národa*, 61.
[83] Staněk, *Odsun*, 202–204.

Even after parliament granted immunity to acts of "revolutionary" brutality, the courts still offered victims of abuse their best opportunity to have their stories heard and their pleas addressed. Shortly before the Pilsen military court tried the four officers, the Prague People's Court exposed a harrowing tale of police brutality and the bungled attempt to cover it up. The trial initially centered on a depressingly familiar crime: Zdenka Holubová and Anna Velíšková stood accused of having betrayed several Czech men, including both of their husbands, to the Gestapo for listening to foreign radio. The prosecution focused on the denunciation of Adolf Pytrus, Holubová's former husband, who, unlike the other two victims, did not survive his internment in a Nazi concentration camp. More than thirty-eight witnesses took the stand, many of them with contradictory testimony. After the war Adolf's son Jiří had first turned in Velíšková for the crime; then Pytrus's brother denounced Holubová. Pytrus's father blamed his son's former wife, but the spouse of one of the other men arrested by the Gestapo accused Velíšková of the crime. Each defendant unsurprisingly tried to pin guilt on the other.

What appeared to be an ordinary trial of denunciation changed its tenor when Velíšková revealed that the Czech police had physically coerced her to confess to the crime. Another woman, Marie Kaňková, testified that the police had brought her in for questioning in October 1945 and pressured her to recant her testimony against Holubová and implicate Velíšková instead. When she refused, two police officers, Ladislav Čadek and Josef Volf, viciously beat her and then confronted her with Velíšková, whereupon the two women were forced to strike each other. Several former inmates and guards of Pankrác prison credibly testified that when Kaňková returned from police interrogation, she was bleeding profusely and covered with horrible bruises from her shoulders down to her backside. Only after three days was she finally taken to the prison hospital.

After her release from detention Kaňková attempted to press charges against the two officers. At a time when police were basically a law unto themselves, her decision to pursue the case was extraordinarily courageous, if seemingly hopeless. A military tribunal did investigate her accusations, but rejected them because she was unable to identify officers Čadek and Volf in court. At that point, the matter was laid to rest. Later, however, People's Court Judge Karel Černík, who had been assigned the trial of Velíšková and Holubová, reexamined the case records and discovered that the "Čadek" brought before the military tribunal had the first name Tomáš, whereas the man who had allegedly beaten Kaňková was named Ladislav. As for Josef Volf, the man presented to Kaňková by the military court spelled his surname with a "W" not a "V." The military prosecutors had gotten the wrong men, in all likelihood intentionally. One week before the trial was to begin, Černík summoned Kaňková's actual tormentors, officers Ladislav Čadek and Josef Volf, to the courthouse. They arrived under the impression that they were to give depositions regarding the upcoming trial of Velíšková and Holubová. To their surprise, court bailiffs seized their weapons and Černík declared that they were under arrest for aiding and abetting a collaborator, a crime according to Paragraph Twenty of the Great Decree.[84]

The arrrests of the two officers turned an all too ordinary case of denunciation into a national scandal. Much of the Czech press expressed horror at the abuses revealed by Kaňková's testimony. Newspapers described the beatings as evidence of Czech "Gestapoism" – the distressing tendency of many Czech policemen to behave like their German predecessors (Figure 5). Others used the opportunity to condemn the erosion of civic rights and defend the principle of judicial independence. The Communist press, by contrast, unleashed a campaign against the court. *Rudé právo* decried the equation of law officers and collaborators and accused the presiding judge of intentionally sullying the name of the 1945 "revolution." In an unconvential response, Černík interrupted the trial and addressed the gallery and, by extension, the Czech public: "The revolution is [not] being judged by me... unless that term also embraces the beating of witnesses. There has been no attempt to discredit the National Security Corps, only... an endeavor to cleanse the nation of denouncers and their accomplices, as the retribution law demands."[85] This appeal failed to dissuade *Rudé právo*, which vehemently attacked the court for allegedly privileging the word of denouncers over that of patriotic policemen. Above all, the newspaper demanded that the charges against Čadek and Volf be dismissed immediately. As in less sensational cases, such pressure soon paid dividends. On Justice Ministry

[84] Protokol s Karlem Černíkem (23 February 1948), AMV, 305-49-4, L. 89–99.
[85] Trial transcript, SOA-Praha, MLS-PR, Ls 1026/45, SOA-Praha, MLS-PR, Ls 1026/45, 220.

ZNÁRODNĚNÝ ŠATNÍK ANEB PŮJČOVNA MASEK III

„Že jsme se ničemu nenaučili, Kaňková a Vlíškovál"   Kreslil H. Jonda

Figure 5. The Nationalization of a Wardrobe or the Borrowing of Masks. "So, we didn't learn anything? Kaňková? Vlíšková?" Cartoon from the Social Democratic Journal *Cíl*, vol. III, no. 6, 1947.

orders, the two cases were separated and the Prague People's Court proceeded only with the indictment against Holubová and Velíšková.[86]

As if the trial had not been dramatic enough, several days into the proceedings a surprise witness suddenly materialized. Jaroslava Ledererová, a pregnant twenty-four-year-old, dramatically took the stand cradling a small baby wrapped in a blanket. She described the day in May 1945 when she, like so many other Czechs, found herself arrested and imprisoned "by mistake." Ledererová testified that in a group holding cell she had overheard Velíšková claim responsibility for turning in her "old man." The prosecutor, who already had reason to doubt the charges, demanded to know how the two women could ever have met. The encounter that Ledererová described as taking place in the infamous Bartholomew Street police headquarters was an impossibility – by the time Ledererová arrived there, Velíšková had already been transferred to Pankrác prison. The prosecutor turned on Ledererová and threatened her with severe penalties for perjury. After brief discussion with her lawyer, who noted that she could not be punished if she changed her testimony while still on the stand, the surprise witness told an entirely different story.

Ledererová broke down in tears, admitted that she had made a mistake, and begged Velíšková for forgiveness. When the prosecutor pursued the matter further, Ledererová revealed that earlier the same day she had told her cousin, who was a police official, that she recognized the defendant. Together with two of his colleagues, the cousin whisked Ledererová off to a free lunch and from there immediately to a police station, where she hurriedly gave her sworn testimony. The entire deposition apparently took only two to three minutes. The officers told her that someone from the police was mixed up in the matter and they did not want to leave him in the lurch. Her cousin also warned her not to reveal their familial relation. When later in court a lay judge read Ledererová's protocol aloud, she claimed that several statements were not even her own. The prosecutor condemned the young woman for her perjury, but did not press charges because of her pregnancy and her infant. In a twist on Agatha Christie's *Witness for the Prosecution*, Ledererová's intervention only served to further weaken the case against

---

[86] "Protokol sepsaný dne 23.2.1948 u Ostb. v Praze s JUDrem. Karlem Černíkem," AMV a.č. 305-49-4, L. 91.

Velíšková. Ultimately, after three and one-half hours of deliberation, the judges acquitted Velíšková and sentenced Holubová to fifteen years in prison for the death of Adolf Pytrus.[87]

Why Čadek and Volf originally intervened on behalf of Holubová remains a mystery, but it seems clear that she was not the reason for the cover-up. In its coverage of the trial *Rudé právo* vigorously defended the actions of the police, but left the fate of the accused women to the court. When Holubová was convicted and Velíšková acquitted, the Communist flagship reported the verdict in a factual manner, and no "spontaneous" protests erupted. The cover-up undoubtedly stemmed from a concern to protect the police from an investigation that could have exposed far worse abuses of power, but that alone does not explain why the Interior Ministry pursued the matter with such urgency. Josef Volf, it seems, was no ordinary policeman. According to a secret Interior Ministry report, "because of his special service, personal bearing, trustworthiness and capability, [in July 1946] he was assigned to the personal bodyguard of Mr. Chairman of the Government, Klement Gottwald."[88] Left unmentioned was Gottwald's other role – Chairman of the Communist Party. In striking a blow against police brutality, Černík had hit uncomfortably close to one of the most powerful men in the country. Once the matter was taken out of the judge's hands, however, the policemen found

[87] "Dva příslušníci SNB před lidovým soudem," *Lidová demokracie* (29 January 1947), 2; "Dva členové státní policie vyslechnuti," *Lidová demokracie* (30 January 1947), 2; "Doznané falešné svědectví v případě Pitrus," *Rudé právo* (3 February 1947), 3. "Udavačky před lidovým soudem," *Mladá fronta* (29 January 1947); "U lidového soudu se věří udavačům?" *Rudé právo* (30 January 1947); "Svědectví o gestapismu?" *Národní osvobození* (30 January 1947); "Veřejný žalobce hájí nezávislost...," *Národní osvobození* (31 January 1947); "Wolf a Čadek vyloučeni z řízení...," *Národní osvobození* (31 January 1947); "Výslech – či mučení?" *Národní osvobození* (1 February 1947); "Mimořádný lidový soud hájí svoji nezávislost," *Národní osvobození* (2 February 1947); "Bude konečně jasno v udavačském procesu?" *Právo lidu* (4 February 1947); "Boj o nezávislost mimořádného lidového soudu pokračuje," *Národní osvobození* (4 February 1947); "Právnicky neudržitelné stanovisko předsedy lidového soudu," *Rudé právo* (5 February 1946); "Vyšetřování falešného svědectví u lidového soudu," *Rudé právo* (5 February 1946); "Závažné obvinění vyšetřovacího aparátu SNB," *Národní osvobození* (5 February 1947); "Rozsudek nad Velíškovou a Holubovou v pátek," *Rudé právo* (6 February 1946); "V pátek bude vynesen rozsudek v udavačském případu," *Právo lidu* (6 February 1947); "Policisté o výslechu svědkyně Ledererová," *Národní osvobození* (6 February 1947); "Naše slovo k případu A. Pytrus," *Právo lidu* (7 February 1947); "Epilog vrušujícího procesu na Pankráci," *Právo lidu* (8 February 1947); "Holubová 15 let těžkého žaláře," *Rudé právo* (8 February 1947), SÚA, f. MZV-VA II (j81), k. 217.
[88] "Zpráva" (1 February 1947), AMV, 305-85-4, L. 23.

a more sympathetic hearing. On 8 May 1947 *Rudé právo* announced that Čadek and Volf had been released and the charges against them dismissed.[89]

The Holubová–Velíšková trial makes for depressing reading. From the men imprisoned by the Nazis for listening to foreign radio to the women "mistakenly" arrested by postwar Czech authorities, the curse of denunciation and the horror of police brutality respected no change in regime. Many Czech policemen were apparently as willing as their Nazi predecessors to torture suspects and witnesses to produce desired testimony, and, with very few exceptions, the perpetrators were free to do as they pleased. Even if the exculpatory laws did not cover their bestialities, their bosses in the Interior Ministry shielded them from prosecution. The only extraordinary thing about Čadek and Volf was that they were caught and exposed. Even if they only served three months in jail – considerably less than they deserved – this was far more than most other brutal policemen who had terrorized suspected collaborators after the war. The court, most significantly, revealed to the public how the two policemen, like so many of their colleagues, had conducted themselves. The judge's resilience offered positive encouragement to others distressed by the political manipulation of retribution. In a report to the Justice Ministry, a court interpreter commented, "Dr. Černík, who vigorously resisted the intervention of high officials of the Interior Ministry, as well as the irresponsible invective and bullying approach of *Rudé právo*,... earned a reputation as an intrepid defender of judicial independence."[90] Despite its outcome, the Holubová–Velíšková case illustrates how trials of collaborators paradoxically provided both the initial justification for the mistreatment of suspects and ultimately the sole means to seek redress for such brutality. In the end, only the retribution courts had the power to expose and make amends for the crimes committed in retribution's name.

COLLABORATORS WITH AND WITHOUT STARS

Although retribution trials offered individuals an opportunity to clear their names, it was still preferable to avoid charges of collaboration

[89] "Povede státní zastupitelstvo proti Volfovi a Čadkovi řízení na svobodě?" *Rudé právo* (2 February 1947), 3; "Čadek a Volf zproštěni žaloby lidového soudu," *Rudé právo* (8 May 1947), SÚA, f. MZV-VA II (j81), k. 217.
[90] Ladislav Drůbek, "Poznatky od mimořádných soudů," SÚA, f. MS (Drtina), k. 2111.

altogether. After all, some of the accused did not live long enough to get their day in court. The mayor of Cheb, for example, died under mysterious conditions in police custody.[91] Others emerged from detention irrecoverably scarred. According to a Kutná Hora weekly, a local leader of the pro-Nazi Kuratorium youth movement "was shot and crippled for the rest of his life . . . in an unfortunate accident during an interrogation."[92] Thousands languished in jail for months before they earned an acquittal. Kazimierz Moroz, for example, was detained from June 1945 until a regular criminal court finally acquitted him on 10 October 1947 – five months after the People's Courts had been disbanded. In fact, counting his wartime internment in the Buchenwald concentration camp, he spent more than four years behind bars and barbed wire.[93] For some defendants, an acquittal did not signal the end of their travails, but, rather, the beginning of an odyssey through a maze of legal maneuvers. The Kutná Hora People's Court acquitted Antonín Matlach on 2 October 1945, but the prosecutor immediately proposed retrying him before a regular criminal court. Over the course of the next year, various juridical agencies disagreed over whether to pursue the case, until a new trial date was finally set for 28 January 1947. The trial was rescheduled for 25 February and then for 14 March, when for the second time Matlach was acquitted of the charges. Even after this second acquittal the prosecutor forwarded the case to a national committee for punishment as an "offense against national honor," for which Matlach could still face up to a year in prison.[94]

Aware of the dangers and, in the best case, the inconveniences that lay in wait for anyone accused of collaboration, many Czechs did not

---

[91] Jiřík, *Nedaleko od Norimberku*, 153.

[92] Probably in recognition of this "unfortunate accident," the court rejected the prosecutor's request of ten years' imprisonment and sentenced the defendant to eighteen months instead. "Lidový soud v Kutné Hoře," *Kutnohorský kraj* II:50 (13 December 1946), 3.

[93] Kaz. Moroz, KPR no. R-10536/47, R-15049/47, AKPR, f. D-11377/47 (prominut.-B), k. 262.

[94] Matlach, a forty-four-year-old cobbler of Czech nationality, was indicted for having denounced a barman who had refused in March 1939 to accept a German two-mark silver coin in payment of the tab. The barman had allegedly pronounced his desire to defecate on both the coin and on Hitler himself. In the end, the fact that no one had suffered any serious consequences – the German police immediately released the barman after a short interrogation – was decisive: On 2 October 1945 the Kutná Hora People's Court acquitted Matlach of the charges. Verdict against A. Matlach (2 October 1945) and related correspondence, SOA Prague, f. MLS-KH, Ls 5/45.

put their faith in the rule of law. A safer policy was "might makes right." In the words of one farmer who was threatened with indictment,

I am not afraid, but it is all this unpleasantness which I mind. They cannot even start a case against me. But they will ask me questions, me and the wife and the children; I will have to travel to the district town several times, and that costs money; neighbors will start talking – they'll say that there is no smoke without fire – why should I go through all that? That is why I entered the [Communist] Party, and since then everything is all right. We want peace, you know; didn't we have trouble enough during the occupation?[95]

Although one cannot determine the exact extent of the phenomenon, there is substantial anecdotal evidence that numerous collaborators sought shelter in the Communist Party after the war. They hoped, not unreasonably, that membership would save them from prosecution – in the contemporary French expression, they tried "to become Red to whitewash their past" (*"devenir rouge pour se faire blanchir"*).[96] For example, a police sergeant, who had allegedly worked for the Gestapo during the war, joined the Communist Party afterward and became director of security for the Rokycany national committee. The Communist head of the Marienbad national committee had allegedly taught workers German during the occupation and had even become a German himself. An anonymous letter to the president summed up the widespread belief that the most vigorous proponents of retribution were themselves guilty: "Collaborators with [red] stars are trying collaborators without stars."[97]

In September 1946 the Communist Party Central Committee discussed the need to "cleanse" the party of undesirable elements. One member commented, "We audited several different locations and discovered that, although pre-registration had already been carried out, there

---

[95] Jan Stransky, *East Wind over Prague* (New York: Random House, 1951), 83.

[96] Peter Novick, *The Resistance versus Vichy: The Purge of Collaborators in Liberated France* (New York: Columbia University Press, 1968), 75, n. 38.

[97] Hora, *Svědectví* (1978), 176–77; Vlastislav Chalupa, Ivan Gad'ourek, and Mojmír Povolný, eds., *Tři roky: Přehledy a dokumenty k Československé politice v letech 1945–1948*, 3 vols (Brno: Právnická fakulta Masarykovy univerzity, 1991), II:360–61; anonymous letter to the president KPR no. R-14799/46 (6 November 1946), AKPR, f. D-11169/47 (Anonymy-f). See also "Národní správci," *Obzory* III:10 (8 March 1947), 145–46; Vladimír Krajina, *Vysoká hra: Vzpomínky* (Prague: Eva, 1994), 154; Hora, *Svědectví* (1978), 99, 132–3, 173.

were twenty-two individuals who at any moment could be seized by the [police]. That would be humiliating for the entire party." Another delegate insisted that local cadres must purge party members whose pasts raised the danger that they might be thrown into prison "with their party card in their pocket." Unsurprisingly, the situation was the worst in the borderlands. There, in particular, one delegate insisted, "Our comrades...must expel from our ranks anyone whose membership is only a means to plunder or who wants to hide behind his membership." Faced with overwhelming evidence that collaborators and ordinary criminals had joined the party in large numbers, the Central Committee instructed local secretariats to carry out a more thorough purge. In a revealing circular the leadership proclaimed, "We want the entire public to know that we do not tolerate among us people who transgressed against their own nation during the occupation."[98]

The Communists also accused their political competitors of welcoming collaborators into their ranks. Although the numbers were likely smaller, this charge was not all bluster. In part, it depends on how one defines the term "collaborator," for if former members of the banned Agrarian Party are included, then the National Socialists also had their fair share of collaborators. In his memoirs, prominent Czech critic Václav Černý noted that every party sheltered "compromised" individuals and "cowards," but he reserved his harshest criticism for the Communists and National Socialists.[99] The ubiquitous presence of compromised individuals spurred efforts to discover damaging information about one's political competitors. The Communist Party was at a considerable advantage thanks to its control of military intelligence, the Interior Ministry, and 95 percent of national committee security departments. The Party used information collected in the course of retribution investigations and through interrogation of incarcerated Nazis to blackmail an unknown number of Czechs, including members of other political parties.[100]

Retribution also justified the creation of specialized secret police forces that were then exploited for nefarious purposes. The Provincial

[98] Comments by Novák, David, and Hromádko, and "Dopis zaslaný OV KSČ," Zasedání ÚV KSČ (25–26 September 1946), SÚA, f. 1, sv. 2, aj. 13.

[99] Václav Černý, Paměti, 3 vols. (Brno: Atlantis, 1992–1994), III:56.

[100] František Hanzlík, Únor 1948: Výsledek nerovného zápasu: Tajné služby na cestě k moci (Prague: Prewon, 1997), 146–48.

Bureau of Security [Zemský odbor bezpečnosti], originally formed to search for war criminals, was used by its Communist masters to spy on political opponents. When parliament finally passed a law in July 1947 to regulate the police, the Provincial Bureau of Security was to have been abolished, but was merged into other Interior Ministry sections instead. Another security unit, "Department F," originally concentrated on the purge of collaborators in the military and on gathering information against former entrepreneurs. Formed in summer 1946, this illegal police unit, staffed by twenty trusted Communists, interrogated Gestapo officers about the conduct of Czechs who had been in the wartime resistance or imprisoned in concentration camps. The non-Communists also managed to get Department F legally abolished, but it continued to work in secret and intimidate the Party's opponents.[101] Historian František Hanzlík concluded, "The main problem of the retribution decrees consisted of the fact that, although they enabled the just punishment of criminals, they also... enabled their abuse for the benefit of attaining specific political goals."[102]

Communist abuse of security for political goals came to light in the trial of Leopold Pospíšil, a former intelligence officer in the Czechoslovak air force. After the Germans destroyed Czechoslovakia, Pospíšil organized the escape of 182 soldiers, including many pilots, to Poland. He also smuggled out information regarding Germany's V1 rocket program. Immediately after the war Pospíšil was arrested and, in gross violation of the law, he languished in police custody for more than fifteen months. After he nearly perished from maltreatment, he finally went on trial in September 1946 before a regular criminal court. The case against him rested on the testimony of several Gestapo officers, who claimed that Pospíšil had been one of their agents. It soon emerged, however, that security officials had promised the Gestapo officers their freedom if they testified against the Czech resistance leader. On 23 September 1946, the court finally acquitted Pospíšil, but the two Communist national committee members who contrived the whole plot went unpunished.[103] Their attempt to discredit the non-Communist resistance had nonetheless backfired: On 18 October 1946 Drtina ordered that

---

[101] Karel Kaplan, *Nekrvavá revoluce* (Prague: Mladá fronta Archiv, 1993), 128–29.
[102] Hanzlík, *Únor 1948*, 149.
[103] After the Communist takeover, the courts retried Pospíšil and convicted him. On 18 June 1969 the Prague City Court overturned the conviction. Chalupa, *Tři roky*, II:237–38,

unsubstantiated Gestapo testimony against Czechs be inadmissible before People's Courts.[104]

Revelations about police abuses that emerged from trials like those of Pospíšil and Velíšková undermined popular confidence in the justness of postwar retribution. According to the chief prosecutor in Jičín,

The publicizing of the Dr. Pospíšil case...caused a considerable shock to the People's Courts' outlook because readers of such articles carried over a suspicion of tendentious witness testimony and...investigation to other cases. The public was willing to believe that everyone who stood before a [People's Court] was being done an injustice.[105]

Doubts only grew as more and more witnesses disavowed the depositions they had made in the spring of 1945. As early as February 1946, *Svobodné slovo* reported a disturbing trend. The National Socialist daily remarked, "And you see something interesting: how many people have a short memory. How many of those, who in the May days vociferously pounced upon collaborators, [now] distance themselves from their declarations and testimony breaks down!" According to the newspaper, some people had found the ground under their feet and now confidently spoke the truth, whereas others who had denounced for personal reasons changed their stories and now said, "No, I never claimed or tried to prove anything like that."[106] Proponents of harsh retribution, by contrast, chalked up the many cases of disavowed testimony to what they considered to be a wholly different disturbing trend. Starting as early as the winter of 1946, the Communist press complained that

262, 294–99; Hubert Ripka, *Czechoslovakia Enslaved: The Story of the Communist Coup d'Etat* (London: Victor Gollancz, 1950), 159; Hejl, *Zpráva*, 127–28.

[104] A similar, but more infamous case resulted from an attempt to defame the General Secretary of the National Socialist Party, Vladimír Krajina, whose wartime resistance and imprisonment undermined the Communists' claim that only they had resisted the occupation. Without the approval of the Justice Ministry, an Interior Ministry official interrogated Karl Hermann Frank and produced a deposition detailing extensive collaboration between Krajina and the Nazis. When a prosecutor later confronted Frank with this statement, the Nazi leader expressed surprise at his supposed testimony and told a very different story: He had been forced to sign the document which he could not even read because it was written in Czech. Drtina, *Československo*, II:116–17, 134–47; Krajina, *Vysoká hra*, 161–63, 209; Drtina, *Na soudu národa*, 62–64.

[105] "Skončení," v.v.ž. MLS-Jičín, SÚA, f. MS (Org), k. 1942.

[106] "Cesta spravedlnosti," *Svobodné slovo* (28 February 1946), SÚA, f. MZV-VA II (j81), k. 216.

collaborators were suing their accusers for defamation of character.[107] Although the government had failed to outlaw false denunciation, victims of that odious practice had apparently found a means to strike back at their persecutors. Faced with the threat of a lawsuit for slander, many denouncers were dissuaded from following through on their accusations. Regardless of whether the witnesses had lied under interrogation or later on the stand, the courts could no longer rely on their testimony.

PEOPLE'S JUDGES

The conduct of professional judges – above all, the unwillingness of many to submit to political pressure – confirmed their roles as conservative guarantors of the legal order. That much may have been expected of them. They did not, however, sit alone in judgment. On each People's Court panel four lay judges outnumbered the professional chairman. The framers of the Great Decree likely expected "people's judges" to force the courts to adopt a strict interpretation of the law and, above all, to mete out severe popular justice. Final reports submitted by the twenty-four chief justices of the People's Courts paint a very different picture. According to the professional justices, their lay colleagues did not remain radical for long. As the people's judges became acculturated to the court environment and familiar with the laws, they developed a working relationship with their fellow justices and eventually became something akin to professionals themselves.

Tigrid denigrated the people's judges as "self-selected."[108] Although this may have been true for the "revolutionary courts" that sprang up in spring 1945, it does not accurately reflect the twenty-four Extraordinary People's Courts. The Great Decree required national committees to prepare lists of potential people's judges, who then had to be approved by the government before they could assume their roles. The official procedure for selecting people's judges may not have been respected in every case, but records indicate that the central government

---

[107] "Žaloby kolaborantů a zrádců," *Rudé právo* (3 March 1946), 3.
[108] Pavel Tigrid, *Kapesní průvodce inteligentní ženy po vlastním osudu* (Toronto: Sixty-Eight Publishers, 1988), 382.

regularly reviewed and approved official lists of nominees.[109] Although a national committee could blacklist individuals with whom it disagreed, it could not select the final form of a court. Ultimately, the decision to impanel people's judges for a specific case was the prerogative of the presiding professional judge, a responsibility different justices likely exercised with greater or lesser care. Some established regular panels and intentionally balanced political factions to prevent one party from gaining two lay judgeships at the same trial. Establishing political parity was apparently difficult in the beginning, when the political affiliations of many people's judges were not yet clear. As time elapsed, however, the professionals became more adept at designing fair panels, or so some claimed. The Pilsen chief justice, for example, explained that problematic people's judges were merely replaced. Compared to the investigative commissions and the police, there were few complaints about the people's judges. The chief justices of the Most and Pilsen courts even credited the national committees with selecting responsible individuals.[110] An anonymous letter to the president, which otherwise condemned retribution as "victor's justice," nonetheless praised the quality of the lay judges: "We are ... impressed by the people named to the People's Court."[111]

People's Court judges were not presumed to be impartial. On the contrary, the employment of concentration camp survivors and former resistance fighters as lay judges was sanctioned and even encouraged – for service on the National Court it was explicitly urged by presidential decree. The government of former exiles may have hoped that this practice would mollify interest groups of former prisoners and partisans. Moreover, the lay judges' unimpeachable "national honor" might insulate the People's Courts from criticism. Finally, proponents of harsh retribution probably expected that survivors and resisters would display much less sympathy toward collaborators than might ordinary citizens who had accommodated themselves to the Nazi occupation. In practice,

[109] See SÚA, f. 100/24 (KG), sign. 1494.
[110] "Skončení," přednosta MLS-BR, přednosta MLS-LT, v.v.ž. MLS-BR, v.v.ž. MLS-UH, v.v.ž. MLS-HK, přednosta MLS-UH, přednosta MLS-PL, přednosta MLS-MO, přednosta MLS-PL, SÚA, f. MS (Org), k. 1942.
[111] Anonymous letter (14 September 1945), KPR no. 13196/45, AKPR, f. D-11169/47 (Anonymy-f).

the recommendation that Nazi victims be appointed as lay judges surprisingly proved to be a popular one with some professional judges. The Mladá Boleslav chief justice, for example, questioned the fairness of letting former prisoners be judges, but nonetheless noted that they often were the most careful in apportioning penalties. The Olomouc prosecutor wrote that judges who "had themselves tasted the cruelty of the Nazi order" fairly assessed cases. The Nový Jičín chief justice believed that former political prisoners, especially members of the intelligentsia, proved to be the best judges. Far from being a handicap, their personal experience with injustice and imprisonment led them to be careful in determining guilt and punishment.[112]

The 4:1 ratio of people's judges to professional jurist aimed to ensure that the latter could not abuse his greater knowledge and experience to deceive or intimidate his lay colleagues into acceding to his will. When it came to deciding the verdict and sentence, the Great Decree stipulated that the people's judges vote first, from eldest to youngest, followed finally by the professional chairman of the court. In practice, when the people's judges outvoted their professional chairman, he was put in a difficult situation because he alone had the legal training to justify the verdict in writing. Thus, in some cases, even though he disagreed with the verdict, the Brno chief justice reported that he had "to conjure up" the reasons for his lay colleagues' decision. It seems, however, that such instances were rare. The Brno chief justice concluded with some condescension that the courts had been successful because professional judges had been able to restrain their lay colleagues and guide their decision making. For their part, the Hradec Králové and Česká Lípa chief justices reported that in general the lay judges followed their professional colleague's guidance.[113] Given the enormous gap in legal knowledge between a court's chairman and its people's judges, and the traditional deference shown by laymen to wearers of judicial robes (and by contemporary Czechs to university-educated authorities), it is hardly surprising that professional jurists were able to make their opinions prevail. Even among the people's judges themselves, disharmony was not the rule.

[112] "Skončení," přednosta MLS-KH, přednosta MLS-PR, přednosta MLS-MB, v.v.ž. MLS-OL, přednosta MLS-NJ, SÚA, f. MS (Org), k. 1942.
[113] "Skončení," přednosta MLS-MO, přednosta MLS-BR, přednosta MLS-BR, přednosta MLS-HK, přednosta MLS-CL, SÚA, f. MS (Org), k. 1942.

Several chief justices reported that most verdicts were made unanimously and that strong disagreements were few and far between.[114]

The chief justices were critical of specific people's judges. The Česká Lípa chief justice explained, "One cannot give a single opinion about the quality of the lay judges." Some took their role seriously, whereas others, the judge revealingly complained, were "stubborn" and refused to be taught by the professional. The Ostrava chief justice cited two examples of questionable behavior. In one trial, the presiding professional judge gained the clear impression that his lay colleagues were well informed about the case before the proceedings began. In the other, the presiding judge caught two of his lay colleagues conferring with the prosecutor – they were apparently trying to convince him to expand the indictment so that the defendant could be charged with a capital crime. The Nový Jičín chief justice believed that the lay judges had been frequently influenced by events beyond the courtroom: "During the trial proceedings and in voting, the professional judges showed a firm hand. Only their efforts ensured that the Extraordinary People's Court in Nový Jičín represented a court tribunal, and not a street tribunal, and that its verdicts were basically acts of law and not acts of vengeance." The Most chief justice concluded that the people's judges did a good job under extraordinary circumstances, but that working with them was difficult and time consuming.[115]

Problems with people's judges apparently stemmed from several sources. The chief justices from Prague and Tábor complained that some lay judges simply were not smart enough to understand the intricacies of the law. The chief justice from Nový Jičín categorically declared female people's judges to be inferior to male ones, while his counterpart in Písek chauvinistically claimed that women occasionally allowed themselves to be overcome by emotion. The Ostrava head prosecutor remarked that relatives had tried to influence some lay judges. In one Kutná Hora trial two lay judges excused themselves from voting at the last moment, thereby invalidating the verdict. It later emerged that a defense witness had sent one of them a threatening letter: "Dear friend, I ask you, and at the same time advise you, to get sick on the 13th and not to go to the

[114] "Skončení," přednosta MLS-LB, přednosta MLS-MO, přednosta MLS-UH, SÚA, f. MS (Org), k. 1942.
[115] "Skončení," přednosta MLS-CL, přednosta MLS-OS, přednosta MLS-NJ, přednosta MLS-MO, SÚA, f. MS (Org), k. 1942.

People's Court. It will be best for you that way."[116] When a court held its session at the scene of the crime or the judges came from that locality, an overly harsh verdict sometimes ensued, often as a result of petty personal and financial scores being settled.[117] The press also apparently managed to sway lay judges against some defendants.[118]

Other complaints concerned political maneuvering, which was hardly surprising considering that people's judges were usually selected according to party affiliation. Some lay judges were apparently "instructed" or given orders before the trial; others allegedly ruled according to public opinion or the socioeconomic standing of a defendant.[119] The Česká Lípa chief justice noted two cases where political or class affiliation affected the voting. In the first, one lay judge claimed, "He's a comrade; I won't vote." Although the professional judge argued for a ten-year sentence, his lay colleagues demurred. In the second case, the defendant's guilt could not be proven, but a people's judge nonetheless commented, "I know that he didn't commit it, but he was a big man at the labor office so I vote to convict."[120]

Overall, however, the chief justices had a positive view of their lay colleagues.[121] Some even lauded the people's judges' conduct in effusive terms. The Litoměřice chief justice wrote that his lay colleagues suffered pressure and political manipulation throughout their tenure but did not submit. The České Budějovice and the Klatovy chief justices both claimed that even when lay judges arrived with preconceived notions and political instructions, they usually set them aside, examined the case critically, and decided on an objective basis. In some cases, the people's judges declared and demonstrated their willingness to suffer

---

[116] "Skončení," přednosta MLS-TA, přednosta MLS-PR, přednosta MLS-PI, přednosta MLS-NJ, v.v.ž. MLS-OS, v.v.ž. MLS-KH, SÚA, f. MS (Org), k. 1942.

[117] "Skončení," přednosta MLS-UH, v.v.ž. MLS-JH, v.v.ž. MLS-TA, přednosta MLS-NJ, SÚA, f. MS (Org), k. 1942.

[118] "Skončení," přednosta MLS-CR, přednosta MLS-OL, v.v.ž. MLS-CR, v.v.ž. MLS-TA, přednosta MLS-OS, přednosta MLS-JH, přednosta MLS-TA, SÚA, f. MS (Org), k. 1942.

[119] "Skončení," přednosta MLS-TA, SÚA, f. MS (Org), k. 1942.

[120] "Skončení," přednosta MLS-CL, SÚA, f. MS (Org), k. 1942.

[121] "Skončení," v.v.ž. MLS-OP, přednosta MLS-PI, v.v.ž. MLS-JH, přednosta MLS-CH, v.v.ž. MLS-CR, přednosta MLS-HK, přednosta MLS-MB, přednosta MLS-NJ, v.v.ž. MLS-OL, v.v.ž. MLS-TA, přednosta MLS-KH, přednosta MLS-KL, v.v.ž. MLS-UH, přednosta MLS-JH, v.v.ž. MLS-MB, přednosta MLS-LT, přednosta MLS-MO, v.v.ž. MLS-PR, přednosta MLS-PR, přednosta MLS-LB, přednosta MLS-PL, v.v.ž. MLS-OS, přednosta MLS-BR, SÚA, f. MS (Org), k. 1942.

the problems that ensued from a vote contrary to the opinion of their acquaintances or members of their political group. In the opinion of the Jihlava and Jičín chief prosecutors, the press did have an effect on the lay judges, but tendentious articles frequently achieved the opposite result of what their authors had intended. In an effort to demonstrate that they were independent, the people's judges voted against the press' recommendation. The Cheb chief justice concluded that the lay judges were "the best."[122]

TAKING THE EDGE OFF THE GREAT DECREE

When the professional judges and prosecutors complained about people's judges, they usually focused on the early months of retribution. There was a general impression that, with experience, the lay judges had become progressively more judicious and reliable.[123] The Uherské Hradiště chief justice commented, "On the whole, the people's judges proved themselves and with time they became positive actors in decision-making. [Their] original severity and frequent partiality... lost its sharpness and towards the end changed into perhaps unjustifiable leniency."[124] In their final reports to the Justice Ministry, almost every judge and prosecutor mentioned that the courts, and particularly the people's judges, became more lenient as time elapsed. As early as September 1945, *Národní osvobození* [*National Liberation*] accurately predicted the coming trend. The newspaper warned, "Big collaborators and traitors live for the meantime in the pleasant hope that with the passage of time there will come leniency in judging their acts."[125] Whereas in 1945 the People's Courts convicted more than eighty-eight percent of defendants, by 1947 only fifty-five percent of completed trials ended with a conviction. Month by month the rate of acquittal climbed, from a mere 2.6 percent through the end of September 1945, to 8.3 percent in October 1945, 16.9 percent in April 1946, 28.8 percent in October

---

[122] "Skončení," přednosta MLS-LT; přednosta MLS-CB; přednosta MLS-KL; v.v.ž. MLS-JH; v.v.ž. MLS-JC; přednosta MLS-CH, SÚA, f. MS (Org), k. 1942.

[123] "Skončení," přednosta MLS-UH, v.v.ž. MLS-ZN, přednosta MLS-TA, přednosta MLS-ZN, přednosta MLS-OL, v.v.ž. MLS-PR, SÚA, f. MS (Org), k. 1942.

[124] "Skončení," přednosta MLS-UH, SÚA, f. MS (Org), k. 1942.

[125] The newspaper blamed the Interior Ministry for inexplicable slowness in forwarding cases to the prosecutors and courts. "Kdo zdržuje očistu?" *Národní osvobození* (15 September 1945), SÚA, f. MZV-VA II (j. 81), k. 215.

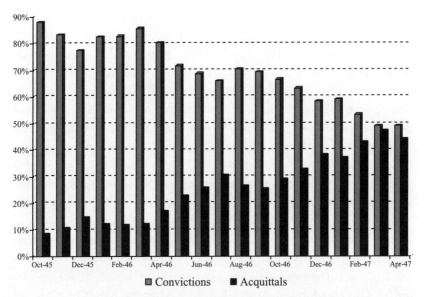

Chart 1. Rate of Convictions and Acquittals by Month.

1946, upward until it reached a high of 47.4 percent in March 1947 (see Chart 1).[126]

There were a number of causes for the trend toward leniency, including the steady increase in the proportion of defendants who were Czech (a development examined in Chapter 6) and the fallout from the relatively light sentences given by the National Court to prominent Czech collaborators (whose cases are discussed in Chapter 7). The prime contributor to the rising acquittal rate, however, was the waning of popular passion as the war's horrors began to fade from memory and the public's attention increasingly focused on issues other than retribution. In the first months after the occupation ended lay judges, and professional ones as well, ruled in the shadow of Nazi atrocities and German oppression. In later months the courts faced a greater awareness of postwar police abuses, like those exposed by the trials of Pospíšil and Velíšková. The growing number of witnesses who denied the veracity of their own depositions also contributed to the trend toward leniency, not only by

---

[126] These totals reflect all trials that ended in a conviction or an acquittal. In 1945 the People's Courts transferred 155 cases to be tried by regular criminal courts. In 1946 and 1947 the corresponding figures were 912 and 437, respectively. The conviction total includes cases where the court ruled the defendant guilty but did not assess any penalty. Monthly summary reports, SÚA, f. MS (org), k. 1930–33, f. MS (Z.tr.), k. 2076–77.

undermining the prosecution, but also by feeding judges' general skepticism about the value of testimony extracted by the police.

As the People's Courts dragged on into their second year, much of the public became weary of the trials and began to yearn for a return to normalcy. The judges themselves were not immune to "retribution fatigue." The Hradec Králové chief justice reported that over time even concentration camp survivors become more lenient.[127] Tardiness and absenteeism on the part of lay judges also became more common, until operations of some courts were threatened. The Prague chief justice reported in June 1946 that people's judges were increasingly failing to attend court sessions, causing delays and even mistrials. Some delinquent lay judges apparently no longer even bothered to think up excuses. An internal Justice Ministry report noted that similar complaints had arrived from other People's Courts.[128] In the 18 December 1946 revision of the Great Decree, the Parliament felt obliged to introduce sanctions for people's judges who failed to fulfill their duties.[129] After thousands of trials, retribution proved to be an unwelcome burden not only to prosecutors and professional jurists, but to lay judges as well. By May 1947 the Most chief justice commented, "All the people's judges . . . without distinction expressed great satisfaction that the [People's Court] was finally ending its operation and that they would never again have to decide about the fate of their fellow citizens."[130]

The trend toward leniency, many chief justices and head prosecutors indicated, occurred not so much in the determination of guilt and innocence as in the apportionment of punishment. The Olomouc prosecutor cited three trials of former mayors to demonstrate the inconsistency of "people's justice." The first to be tried was sentenced to twenty years

---

[127] "Skončení," v.v.ž. MLS-HK, přednosta MLS-ZN, v.v.ž. MLS-LB, přednosta MLS-HK, SÚA, f. MS (Org), k. 1942.

[128] The problem was further complicated by the fact that the original lists of potential people's judges had been all but used up and it was necessary for the national committees to find more candidates. "Mimořádný lidový soud v Praze – soudce z lidu," MS no. 42158/46-I/3 (21 June 1946) to MV, SÚA, f. MV-NR (B-2523/11), k. 2312.

[129] A people's judge who failed to exercise his or her "civic duty" by missing a court session or by leaving one early could be fined up to 10,000 crowns or sentenced to a maximum of eight days in prison. If the lay judge's delinquency prevented a scheduled trial from taking place, he or she could also be made to compensate for the costs incurred. Sbírka zákonů, Law no. 245/46 (18 December 1946).

[130] "Skončení," přednosta MLS-MO, SÚA, f. MS (Org), k. 1942.

in prison. The second received a five-year sentence for his membership in the SA, but was acquitted on charges of propagating and supporting Nazism. The third, tried in February 1947, was convicted, but absolved of punishment even though, the prosecutor noted, his guilt was greater than that of the first defendant.[131] The average prison sentence for convicted defendants decreased from a high of 10.1 years in the period leading up to 1 October 1945 to a low of 6.3 years in February 1947. Overall, the average prison sentence was 7.3 years.[132]

The Great Decree aimed to prevent leniency in sentencing. Each paragraph established minimum sentences, the lowest of which amounted to five years in prison. A mechanism did exist to lessen the harsh minimum sentences, but the rules for mitigating circumstances laid out in Paragraph Sixteen of the Great Decree were very stringent. The paragraph somewhat convolutedly declared,

> The court may reduce the sentence below the minimum penalty . . . [or] in cases deserving particular consideration, may . . . abstain from imposing a sentence, if it is generally known or can be proven without delay that the accused acted with the intent to benefit the Czech or Slovak nations or the Czechoslovak Republic or its allies . . . or if he later rendered outstanding service toward the liberation of the republic from the enemy power, or if he attempted to rectify or minimize the evil caused by the enemy, and remained steadfast after his return to the path of duty. This provision cannot, however, be applied in cases in which the damage caused by the perpetrator disproportionately outweighs the general good that he pursued.

People's Courts could not consider factors such as a defendant's character, personal history, or familial relationships – for example, whether he or she had any dependent children. As a result, one judge complained, the court effectively orphaned numerous minors, who then became wards of the state.[133] The wording of Paragraph Sixteen also meant that in practice it could be used more effectively by men who were in positions of authority and could claim that they had remained in their jobs to avoid a greater evil. Most women, by contrast, were at a

---

[131] "Skončení," v.v.ž. MLS-OL, SÚA, f. MS (Org), k. 1942.
[132] These averages do not include convictions that resulted in death and life sentences or no sentence at all. Monthly summary reports, SÚA, f. MS (org), k. 1930–33, f. MS (Z.tr.), k. 2076–77.
[133] "Skončení," přednosta MLS-OP, SÚA, f. MS (Org), k. 1942.

considerable disadvantage.[134] Moreover, the emphasis on patriotic activity and resistance work meant that Czech defendants were far more likely to successfully invoke mitigating circumstances than were their German equivalents. The sympathies of the judges could only have exacerbated this difference.

As early as January 1946, the Opava public prosecutor reported that his region's People's Court frequently employed Paragraph Sixteen as means to reconcile the harsh punishment mandated by the law with the minor crimes committed by the accused.[135] Nearly every Czech who stood before the Uherské Hradiště court in the first few months made some claim for mitigating circumstances. For the most part, the court listened to them and handed down lighter sentences than the decree mandated. František Zapletal was found guilty of denunciation, but toward the end of the occupation he had hidden a Russian prisoner of war and delivered him to the partisans. Thanks to this act Zapletal received a two-year sentence and lost only one-fifth of his property. L. Charvat, the former leader of a local chapter of the fascist organization Green Swastika, earned a reduced sentence of two years because he compensated for years of pro-Nazi activity by hiding and arming partisans at the end of the war. M. Kopetsche, a former Czech who became a German during the war, had threatened Czechs that they would be sent to Siberia, argued that Beneš should not be permitted to return, and called the Russians "Bolshevik pigs." Although Kopetsche was also judged guilty of denunciation, he had helped Gestapo prisoners and protected the family of an emigré soldier, so the court gave him a two-year sentence. In other cases, Paragraph Sixteen may have saved the defendant from execution. The Uherské Hradiště court sentenced O. Tlust'ák to twenty years in prison, but had he not procured food for Czech prisoners, his denunciation of six people likely would have cost him more. Even J. Hanzlíková, a German woman, successfully invoked Paragraph Sixteen. She had denounced a man who had escaped from forced labor, but thanks to her later efforts to free the prisoner's father from jail, the People's Court gave her only a two-year sentence. In total, of the nineteen cases adjudicated by the Uherské Hradiště court in

---

[134] "Skončení," přednosta MLS-NJ, SÚA, f. MS (Org), k. 1942.
[135] Public prosecutor MLS Opava (15 January 1945) to MS no. 5620/46-IV/5, SÚA, f. MS (Org), k. 1929. See also, "Skončení," přednosta MLS-CL, SÚA, f. MS (Org), k. 1942.

the latter half of October 1945, seven involved the use of Paragraph Sixteen to lessen the penalty, in one case to a verdict of guilty with no punishment.[136]

As time elapsed, judges apparently employed Paragraph Sixteen with ever greater frequency even when there were no legitimate grounds for doing so.[137] The Kutná Hora chief prosecutor cited several cases where the defendants' actions hardly constituted resistance. Josef Mrázek received a lesser sentence because he had a "weak mental state." Emil Brejcha was convicted but absolved of punishment because he had "listened to London radio at home and in a pub, spoken Czech even with members of the Hitler Youth, avoided the flying of flags, never greeted with the Nazi salute, and did not wear the Swastika symbol." Marie Štíchová had her sentence reduced because she had not committed "any further denunciation."[138] The Česká Lípa chief prosecutor also reported that the use of Paragraph Sixteen increased "especially...towards the end...when the people's judges' exhaustion and distaste for carrying out their offices was apparent."[139]

The Legal Commission of the Communist Party Central Committee singled out Paragraph Sixteen as the most abused element of postwar retribution. Despite the "clear" language of the paragraph, individuals who had allegedly betrayed their nation used it to great effect. The commission commented, "These malefactors frequently sat on two chairs. Among us they acted like patriots and simultaneously collaborated with the Germans." When they were brought before the court, however, they stressed their resistance activity: They "pulled from the fire that iron which suited them." They solicited testimonials to their loyalty in an attempt to fool the people. As resistance activity they claimed that they listened to foreign radio and spread the news, or even that they knew others who listened to foreign radio and did not denounce them. Such activity, the Legal Commission stressed, was not resistance: "It is not enough after Stalingrad or later, when it was already clear to everyone how the war would turn out, for someone to turn around and make himself out to be a

---

[136] MLS Uherské Hradiště summary (16–30 October 1945), SÚA, f. MS (Org), k. 1930, sv. 1.

[137] "Skončení," v.v.ž. MLS-CR, v.v.ž. MLS-BR, v.v.ž. MLS-CL, v.v.ž. MLS-OS, SÚA, f. MS (Org), k. 1942.

[138] "Skončení," v.v.ž. MLS-KH, SÚA, f. MS (Org), k. 1942.

[139] "Skončení," v.v.ž. MLS-CL, SÚA, f. MS (Org), k. 1942.

patriot." The Commission demanded a stricter standard of judgment for employment of Paragraph Sixteen.[140] In December 1946, when the parliament extended the retribution courts for a second time, the deputies approved an amendment to the Great Decree to make it more difficult for defendants to claim mitigating circumstances. Thenceforth, the votes of four judges (out of five) were necessary for Paragraph Sixteen to be invoked.[141]

The professional judges also complained that the inflexibility of the retribution laws, especially the high minimum sentences, tied their hands and deprived them of the ability to tailor penalties to individual defendants.[142] The head prosecutor and the chief justice of the Prague People's Court noted, however, that the people's judges found a way around the limitations of the Great Decree: When they saw fit, they simply voted for a penalty of fewer than five years, even though this was contrary to the law. The Mladá Boleslav chief justice reported that in four cases the people's judges gave out suspended sentences even after the professional chairman explained that the retribution law did not permit such a decision. When the Brno public prosecutor complained that the People's Court had given an informant a mere six years even though the law mandated at least ten, the Justice Ministry responded that there was nothing it could do. "After all," a ministry official commented, "it cannot be excluded that lay judges consciously vote for a lesser punishment wanting in specific ... cases to moderate the otherwise just severity of the retribution decree." In some cases, the court preferred to free a defendant rather than give the minimum sentence. In one Kutná Hora trial, the people's judges voted to acquit even though the defendant's guilt had been proven. One of the lay judges responded to the prosecutor's attempt to continue the case by stating, "Don't be so harsh on him. He's young and we didn't want to ruin him. Let him work for the republic."[143] In another case, two lay judges from the Havlíčkův

[140] "§16 retribučního zákona," Právnická komise ÚV KSČ, SÚA, f. 29, aj. 96, str. 35–37.
[141] Sbírka zákonů, Law no. 245/46 (18 Dec. 1946).
[142] "Skončení," v.v.ž. MLS-KL, v.v.ž. MLS-TA, přednosta MLS-KL, přednosta MLS-UH, přednosta MLS-CL, přednosta MLS-KH, přednosta MLS-MB, přednosta MLS-NJ, v.v.ž. MLS-PL, v.v.ž. MLS-UH, přednosta MLS-JH, v.v.ž. MLS-PR, přednosta MLS-PR, přednosta MLS-BR, SÚA, f. MS (Org), k. 1942.
[143] "Skončení," v.v.ž. MLS-PR, přednosta MLS-PR, přednosta MLS-MB, v.v.ž. MLS-PR, přednosta MLS-PR, v.v.ž. MLS-KH, v.v.ž. MLS-KH, SÚA, f. MS (Org), k. 1942, MS no. 15,547/46-IV/1 (22 Feb. 1946), SÚA, f. MS (Org), k. 1934, sv. 3.

Brod court walked out of deliberations in a successful ploy to prevent a guilty verdict against the defendant.[144] In his tribute to the lay judges, the Cheb chief justice wrote, "They carefully followed the case, deliberated, and sometimes, when the law was too harsh or the case had not been sufficiently demonstrated, they adopted the correct position, which was also in accord with the legal perspective."[145]

Despite mandatory minimum sentences and restrictions on mitigating circumstances, in the end 222 of the 357 sentences handed down by the Mladá Boleslav People's Court were for fewer than five years' imprisonment. Another 26 defendants were found guilty but given no punishment. Overall, nearly two-thirds (64.8 percent) of all guilty verdicts were for less than the mandated minimum sentence. In other words, through the use of Paragraph Sixteen Mladá Boleslav judges ruled that a substantial majority of convicted collaborators deserved recognition for their patriotic service to the Czech nation or state during the war.[146] In Nový Jičín the court was less forgiving, but still in 278 of the 639 guilty verdicts the judges handed down sentences of fewer than five years.[147] According to the aggregate Justice Ministry figures, the twenty-four People's Courts absolved 781 convicted persons entirely of punishment. Aside from those defendants, the tabulations do not provide enough information to determine just how often judges ignored the minimum sentences or to what extent they utilized Paragraph Sixteen. Nonetheless, the overall average sentence of 7.3 years suggests that many convicted defendants successfully convinced judges to give them only a few years in prison.[148]

[144] Drtina explained that this was why the government felt the need to include fines for negligent people's judges in the revised retribution decree. Third government, meeting forty-seven (13 December 1946), 31–33, SÚA, f. 100/24 (KG), aj. 1494, sv. 142.
[145] "Skončení," přednosta MLS-CH, SÚA, f. MS (Org), k. 1942.
[146] In fact, the judges may have resorted to Paragraph Sixteen even more frequently since many of the longer sentences could still have been reduced below the mandated minimum for the specific crime. "Skončení," přednosta MLS-MB, SÚA, f. MS (Org), k. 1942.
[147] "Skončení," v.v.ž. MLS-NJ, SÚA, f. MS (Org), k. 1942.
[148] When Drtina delivered his final report on retribution to the Czechoslovak parliament, he claimed that the average People's Court sentence amounted to more than 10 years in prison (10.4 to be exact). However, the Justice Ministry's own tabulations paint a very different picture. The cumulative reports from 1945 to 1947 show an average sentence of 7.3 years; an internal Justice Ministry report from 1949 (which includes 1948 retribution cases) indicates that sentences averaged only 7.1 years. The close correlation between the two internal Justice Ministry tabulations makes Drtina's public claim questionable. Although it cannot be proven decades later, it seems that the Justice Minister may very well have lied in his June 1947 address to parliament. Rather than face the

CONCLUSION

After the courts wrapped up their operations in May 1947, one columnist reflected, "A journalist, who month after month followed countless trials...comes to the conclusion that, though retributive justice essentially fulfilled its mission, in individual cases it did not manage to avoid quite severe blemishes."[149] Designed to be summary tribunals, constrained by time limits, and hampered by poorly prepared cases and political pressure, the Czech People's Courts undeniably issued many unfair and inconsistent sentences. In a normal system of justice such discrepancies could have been ironed out in the appeals and review processes. In the Czech provinces, however, the Great Decree offered defendants no such hope and courts no such safeguard. Instead, People's Courts judges, professional and lay alike, bore the burden of determining the ultimate fate of defendants. It is no wonder that many greeted the end of retribution with relief.

With almost 700 defendants executed and more than 20,000 imprisoned, Czech retribution appears in retrospect to have been very harsh indeed. At the time, however, the People's Courts faced considerable criticism for their leniency. The Communist press reserved its harshest condemnation for prosecutors and professional justices, but proponents of harsh retribution ultimately expressed disappointment in the people's judges as well. In an unwitting testament to the lay judges, the Communist regime later attributed their conduct to a flawed selection process. In December 1948 Justice Minister Alexej Čepička claimed that prior to the coup professional judges had either excluded "honorable members of the working class" from service on the People's Courts or had limited their numbers so that their voices were drowned out.[150] Gottwald's son-in-law Čepička was hardly the most honest of characters, but his complaint illustrates the collective failure of people's judges to hew the Party's line. Assessing retribution as a whole, a May 1947 article in *Mladá fronta* praised the laypeople's unwillingness to be bound by the Great Decree: "We can only thank the people's judges for the fact that...the edge of the simply inappropriate law was dulled

outrage of deputies, Drtina apparently chose to inflate the average sentence. Drtina, *Na soudu národa*, 12; "Poznámky KPR k statistice ministerstva spravedlnosti o výsledcích retribuce," Vojenský historický archiv (VHA), f. Čepička, sv. 23, aj. 168, str. 1–2.

[149] "Nad retribuční bilancí," *Národní osvobození* (10 May 1947), 1.

[150] Alexej Čepička, *Zlidovění soudnictví* (Prague: Min. informací a osvěty, 1949), 15–16.

and that solutions to problems, for which the law did not provide, were frequently found."[151] In the span of less than two years Czech retribution underwent a remarkable evolution. Despite their many flaws, the People's Courts developed into professional tribunals that offered many indicted collaborators and war criminals an opportunity to defend themselves, voice their stories, and even clear their names.

[151] Jaroslav Morávek, "Lidové soudy skončily," *Mladá fronta* (6 May 1947), SÚA, f. MZV-VA II (j81), k. 217.

4

DENUNCIATION

"The Disease of Our Times"

When Czechoslovakia's exile leaders returned home after the Second World War, they brought with them an extensive retribution decree designed to punish "Nazi criminals, traitors, and their accomplices." Thirty-three paragraphs long, the London decree spelled out the penalties for a wide range of offenses, from membership in Nazi organizations to arson, enslavement, and murder. Despite the document's considerable length, the former exiles soon learned that there was an offense they had neglected to include. As accusations mounted and thousands of suspects were detained, it became abundantly clear that one of Czech society's prime concerns was bringing to justice individuals who had betrayed their coworkers, neighbors, and family members to the German authorities. So, when the country's leaders finally promulgated the Great Decree, they added one paragraph (Paragraph Eleven) that created a new type of crime: "Denunciation."

Justice Minister Drtina captured the general sentiment when he called denunciation the "worst phenomenon and most revolting crime of the occupation period."[1] When the time finally came for retribution trials, Czechs turned first on the denouncers among them. At the Brno People's Court in June 1945, the first three persons legally tried by a postwar Czech tribunal were all charged with denunciation. In the months leading up to October 1945 prosecutors indicted at least two-fifths of

[1] P. Drtina, *Těsnopisecké zprávy Prozatímního národního shromáždění Republiky československé* (PNS) 32 (20 February 1946), 5; Prokop Drtina, *O soudcovské nezávislosti, lidovém soudnictví a jiných časových otázkách československé justice* (Prague: Mladá fronta, 1946), 13–14.

all defendants for violations of Paragraph Eleven.[2] Over the next two years Czech People's Courts convicted thousands of denouncers and sentenced hundreds of them to death. The public watched a seemingly endless parade of individuals who betrayed their compatriots for listening to foreign radio, fraternizing with Jews, or speaking ill of the Nazis. Despite this concerted and protracted effort to purge society of denouncers, in February 1947 a Czech journalist noted with great regret, "the vice called denunciation, which was born on 15 March 1939, lives on." While the People's Courts prosecuted the guilty from the occupation period, he remarked, "A new army of denouncers is already being born among us." Far from being eradicated, denunciation, the "disease of our times," had spread.[3]

This chapter examines the phenomenon of denunciation in Nazi-occupied Bohemia and Moravia during the war and its punishment by Czech People's Courts after liberation. In the form of witness depositions, trial transcripts, and other documentary evidence, postwar retribution has bequeathed historians unparalleled sources for reconstructing the darker side of everyday life during the occupation, a period about which we still know remarkably little. Historians Edward Muir and Guido Ruggiero warned that trials present a hegemonic view of the past: Legal paragraphs determine the parameters of debate, testimony is tailored toward proving innocence or guilt, and all activity is "polluted by [the] authority" of the state and its representatives in court, the prosecutors and the judges.[4] This is especially true when it comes to the prosecution of denunciation, an ostensibly legal act at the time of its commission that is only retroactively criminalized by successor regimes. Keeping in mind the nature and limitations of the evidence, this chapter employs court records to evaluate the causes of wartime denunciation and the motives of its perpetrators. In particular, the role of denunciation in facilitating the deportation of Czech Jewry will be explored through an examination of the Protectorate tabloid

[2] "Přehled činnosti MLS do 1. října 1945," MS no. 64989/46–III/2, Státní ústřední archiv (SÚA), Prague, f. MS, k. 2076.

[3] Jiří Bílý, "O udavačství jako nemoci doby," Masarykův lid XVI:4 (February 1947), 3–4.

[4] Edward Muir and Guido Ruggiero, "Introduction: The Crime of History," in Edward Muir and Guido Ruggiero, eds., History from Crime (Baltimore: Johns Hopkins University Press, 1994), viii–ix.

Aryan Struggle and the postwar prosecution of its editors and contributors. Finally, the chapter ends by considering retribution's contribution to postwar denunciation and its consequences for Czech society.

PARAGRAPH ELEVEN

Denunciation stood alone in the Great Decree, separate from Crimes against the State, Persons, and Property. Paragraph Eleven mandated, "Any person who . . . in the service or interest of the enemy, or by exploiting the situation created by the enemy occupation, denounced another for some real or invented activity, shall be sentenced to imprisonment for five to ten years." In a variation on the biblical "eye for an eye," Paragraph Eleven tied a perpetrator's sentence to the ultimate fate of his or her victim. If the crime had no consequences, the maximum sentence was ten years. If the denunciation led to arrest of a "Czechoslovak citizen," then the penalty was increased to a mandatory ten to twenty years. If the denunciation resulted "directly or indirectly" in the victim's injury or in the incarceration of multiple individuals, then the perpetrator was to be punished with life imprisonment. For a denunciation that ultimately led to the victim's death, through either his or her execution or expiration while under detention, the punishment was death. The new paragraph never specified, however, just what constituted "denunciation." The definition of criminal denunciation was only limited by the proviso that the act had to have been committed "in the service or interest of the enemy, or by exploiting the situation created by the enemy occupation."[5]

Sheila Fitzpatrick and Robert Gellately defined "denunciations" as "spontaneous communications from individual citizens to the state (or to another authority such as the church) containing accusations of wrongdoing by other citizens or officials and implicitly or explicitly calling for punishment."[6] Under normal circumstances, such communication is not only legal; it is regarded as the duty of a good citizen

[5] Paragraph Eleven, Decree no. 16/1945, in Karel Jech and Karel Kaplan, eds., *Dekrety prezidenta republiky, 1940–1945: Dokumenty* (Brno: Ústav pro soudobé dějiny, 1995), I:241.

[6] Sheila Fitzpatrick and Robert Gellately, "Introduction to the Practices of Denunciation in Modern European History," in Sheila Fitzpatrick and Robert Gellately, eds., *Accusatory Practices: Denunciation in Modern European History, 1789–1989* (Chicago: University of Chicago Press, 1997), 1.

and recognized as legitimate by the general public. For that reason, the crafters of Paragraph Eleven had no choice but to violate the principle of *nullum crimen sine lege* – after all, the prewar Czechoslovak criminal code had no law against reporting offenses to the authorities. Technically, denunciation remained legal during the war, too, according to Nazi law. Fitzpatrick and Gellately noted that the concept "denunciation" has a dual meaning: It can signify both the honorable exposure of a criminal and the despicable betrayal of a compatriot. Even under governments recognized as legitimate, the citizen can feel torn between loyalty to the state and solidarity with family, friends, or ideological comrades.[7] During the Second World War, however, under a foreign occupation that Czechs universally considered illegitimate, reporting offenders to the authorities was widely regarded as a vile act of personal and national treason. For most subjects of the Nazi-occupied Protectorate, thus, there was little ambiguity: Denunciation represented a clear betrayal of the "community of prisoners."[8]

The gray area between the legitimate duties of a subject and the popular revulsion for denunciation meant that the verdicts of the Czech People's Courts for this crime were perhaps less consistent than for any other. In his final report to the Justice Ministry, the Kutná Hora chief prosecutor cited two similar cases of denunciation to illustrate vagaries in sentencing. The first defendant, Božena Šišková, had denounced her husband and his mother to the police for hiding weapons. Both were imprisoned and her husband subsequently died. The second defendant, Josef Horák, had denounced his son to the police for illegally butchering two pigs. His son was arrested and also perished. The same panel of judges tried both Šišková and Horák, but sentenced the former to death and the latter to twenty years' imprisonment. According to the exasperated prosecutor, the judges did not take into account the fact that Šišková was the mother of three children, ages six to twelve. By contrast, they reduced Horák's sentence because of his advanced age, his lack of a prior record, and because he was allegedly motivated by "anger ensuing from cheerless family relations" – even though long before he finally acted, he had publicly declared his intent "to rid" himself of his son.[9]

---

[7] Fitzpatrick and Gellately, "Introduction to the Practices of Denunciation," 17.

[8] Fitzpatrick and Gellately, "Introduction to the Practices of Denunciation," 19–20.

[9] "Skončení retribučního soudnictví," Vedoucí veřejný žalobce (v.v.ž.), MLS-KH, SÚA, f. MS (Org), k. 1942.

Paragraph Eleven left it to the courts to determine what constituted acts committed "in the service or interest of the enemy, or by exploiting the situation created by the enemy occupation." The Ostrava court acquitted Božena Chýlková, even though she had denounced her daughter for wartime fraternization with a French prisoner of war. The judges creatively determined that the denunciation was not "in the interest" of Nazi Germany, but the verdict likely reflected the reputation of the daughter, who had two illegitimate children and a venereal disease.[10] In many cases it was unclear whether the "denunciation" was even a form of collaboration. After all, under foreign rule, ordinary thefts, assaults, and murders still occurred and were investigated by the police. Black market dealings by farmers and other producers – an activity that became illegal only during the occupation (but remained so after liberation) – was often selfish profiteering, not patriotic resistance. A high Czech government official later argued that wartime denunciation of black market activity should not be punished because profiteering was wrong, regardless of when it occurred.[11]

The ascribed responsibility of the denouncer for the ultimate fate of his or her victim especially led to unfair verdicts, for when it came to sentencing, the perpetrator's intent was secondary to the consequences of his or her actions. For example, a People's Court sentenced a retiree who had denounced some acquaintances for singing the "International" in a pub to fifteen years' imprisonment because the Germans had arrested his victims. In another case, however, the court only gave a worker a three-month sentence because his victim, who had allegedly failed to black out some playing field lights, suffered no consequences.[12] Unforeseen and even undesired circumstances beyond the denouncer's control determined his or her punishment after the war. Individuals who maliciously intended to harm their victims sometimes failed to do so because alert Czech postal workers intercepted letters addressed to the Gestapo and other German authorities.[13] In other cases, local officials dissuaded individuals from denouncing their spouses or drinking

---

[10] Mečislav Borák, *Spravedlnost podle dekretu: Retribuční soudnictví v ČSR a Mimořádný lidový soud v Ostravě (1945–1948)* (Ostrava: Tilia, 1998), 227–28.
[11] Letter from Fr. Dvořák (1 March 1946) to MS, SÚA, f. MS (org), k. 1934, sv. 3.
[12] Borák, *Spravedlnost podle dekretu*, 230.
[13] "Neoslavovaní hrdinové," *Kutnohorský kraj* II:41 (11 October 1946), 2; Borák, *Spravedlnost podle dekretu*, 233.

partners by encouraging them to return home and think it over.[14] Such courageous acts clearly saved potential victims from arrest, imprisonment, and death, but they also inadvertently lessened the punishment handed down to the denouncers after the war. Thanks to the intervention of a Czech policeman, the Germans never learned that Žofie Lukšová had denounced a couple who were her tenants for distributing Communist leaflets. In the absence of serious consequences, the Ostrava People's Court only sentenced the landlady to one year in prison.[15] Had the policeman not intervened, the denunciation could have led to the couple's execution, a consequence that might have prompted the People's Court to sentence Lukšová to death. Josef Semerád did not have her good fortune. The Tábor People's Court sentenced him to life imprisonment because his victim later died in a concentration camp. The chief justice noted that the defendant's intent had not been murder: "The perpetrator did not predict [the victim's death], certainly did not aim for that, and certainly did not want it."[16] Despite the fact that he personally played no immediate role in his victim's murder, Semerád was held accountable for the ultimate consequences of his denunciation.

The wording of Paragraph Eleven caused other inequalities in judgment. For one, the paragraph alternately employed the terms "Czechoslovak citizen," "people," and "another" to describe the victim(s) of a denunciation. After Czechoslovakia revoked the citizenship of the country's Germans in August 1945, the People's Courts never reached a satisfactory consensus as to whether the denunciation of a denaturalized German was even a crime. Second, the mandatory minimum sentence was particularly limiting in the case of denunciation. The chief justice for the Písek People's Court objected that five years was often an excessive penalty, especially for "lesser denunciation of an economic sort." The head prosecutor in Jičín also called for different penalties for economic and political denunciation, especially when the case concerned financial officials whose job was to report economic infractions. The Opava head prosecutor argued for shorter sentences in cases when denunciation only resulted in a brief interrogation. The Kutná

---

[14] Václav Jiřík, "Retribuční realita a Chebsko," in Frank Boldt, ed., *Velké dějiny, malý národ* (Havlíčkův Brod: Český spisovatel, 1995), 217; Borák, *Spravedlnost podle dekretu*, 226.

[15] Borák, *Spravedlnost podle dekretu*, 231.

[16] "Skončení," přednosta MLS-TA, SÚA, f. MS (Org), k. 1942.

Hora chief justice, for his part, complained that Paragraph Eleven punished all denunciation, even if there were no consequences. The judge also regretted that the concept "denunciation" had not been clearly defined in the law. This was especially problematic when a "chain" of denunciations occurred: when one person spoke to another who then spoke to a third person, eventually leading to an arrest. Sometimes one member of the "chain" was convicted, while others were acquitted or not even tried.[17] In a speech before parliament, Drtina remarked on the problem of judging "forced" denunciation – when an individual betrayed a companion under interrogation or torture.[18] Summing up their frustration with the law, the Znojmo head prosecutor and chief justice both complained that certain paragraphs of the Great Decree, including Paragraph Eleven, "allowed such a broad interpretation that [they] probably did not reflect the original intent of the law [and] led often to chicanery."[19]

THE USES OF DENUNCIATION

At the end of October 1945 one of the country's leading dailies, *Mladá fronta* [*Young Front*], declared denunciation to be "an immense disgrace for many Czech people."[20] Though depressingly frequent in the Protectorate, the crime was not a particularly Czech phenomenon. For one, focus on Czech denouncers ignores the prevalence of the practice among the region's Germans, who had greater opportunity to communicate directly to the occupation authorities through formal relationships in Nazi organizations and informal contacts with individual Nazis.[21] Second, denunciation was a feature of Nazi rule everywhere,

[17] "Skončení," v.v.ž. MLS-CL, přednosta MLS-PI, v.v.ž. MLS-JC, v.v.ž. MLS-OP, přednosta MLS-KH, přednosta MLS-CL, SÚA, f. MS (Org), k. 1942.

[18] Prokop Drtina, *Na soudu národa: Tři projevy ministra spravedlnosti dr. Prokopa Drtiny o činnosti Mimořádných lidových soudů a Národního soudu* (Prague: Min. spravedlnosti, 1947), 19.

[19] "Skončení," v.v.ž. MLS-ZN, přednosta MLS-ZN, SÚA, f. MS (Org), k. 1942. There were numerous other complaints about Paragraph Eleven. See "Skončení," v.v.ž. MLS-CL, přednosta MLS-NJ, přednosta MLS-PI, v.v.ž. MLS-BR, v.v.ž. MLS-NJ, v.v.ž. MLS-TA, přednosta MLS-KH, v.v.ž. MLS-PL, přednosta MLS-KL, přednosta MLS-TA, přednosta MLS-OP, SÚA, f. MS (Org), k. 1942.

[20] "Udavačka zavinila smrt dvou žen," *Mladá fronta* (26 October 1945), SÚA, f. MZV-VA II (j81), k. 215.

[21] Borák, *Spravedlnost podle dekretu*, 224.

from its beginnings in Germany through its expansion across nearly all of Europe. André Halimi estimated that during the war the French sent between three and five million denunciatory letters to the occupation authorities of their country.[22] Even in occupied Poland, an area famed for its resistance to Nazism, the diary of Zygmunt Klukowski indicates that Poles denounced with disturbing regularity. Commenting on his hometown, the doctor sorrowfully noted, "The commandant of the gendarmes said that if he listened to all denunciations, half of Szczebrzeszyn would either be in jail or have been executed."[23]

Denunciation was common throughout occupied Europe because it served a critical function in maintaining repressive rule. In his groundbreaking study of the Soviet occupation of eastern Poland from 1939 to 1941, Jan Gross wrote, "The principal mechanism for the penetration of the state into the private realm is the practice of denunciation." Thanks to informers the authorities can learn what goes on in workplaces, social forums, and even homes. Armed with a denunciation the police can intervene to prevent acts of resistance or preemptively disarm potential opposition. In a state that promotes denunciation, inhabitants live in constant terror of each other and are incapable of group action against the regime. Gross explained, however, that denunciation does not only allow the private realm to be publicized; it also enables the "privatization of the public realm." He wrote, "The real power of a totalitarian state results from its being at the disposal of every inhabitant, available for hire at a moment's notice." Under totalitarian rule any individual can potentially harm anyone else, through a legitimate exercise of the right to denounce. Everyone thus has "direct access to the coercive apparatus of the state."[24] Thanks to the authorities' propensity to act on denunciations, individuals can employ the police to settle their own personal grudges or eliminate undesirable persons. For those without direct access to power, denunciation could function, Phillipe Burrin

---

[22] André Halimi, *La délation sous l'occupation* (Paris: Alain Moreau, 1983), 7; Phillipe Burrin, *France under the Germans: Collaboration and Compromise*, transl. by Janet Lloyd (New York: New Press, 1996), 208.

[23] Zygmunt Klukowski, *Diary from the Years of Occupation, 1939–1944*, transl. by George Klukowski (Urbana: University of Illinois Press, 1993), 189 (see also pp. 57, 77–78, 85–87, 89, 110, 136–37, 196, 253).

[24] Jan T. Gross, *Revolution from Abroad: The Soviet Conquest of Poland's Western Ukraine and Western Belorussia* (Princeton, NJ: Princeton University Press, 1988), 117–21.

commented, as a "weapon of the weak" that enabled them to indirectly utilize the police for their own ends.[25] Unlike in James Scott's classic study of Malaysian peasantry, however, this "weapon of the weak" was far from a form of everyday resistance. It was, to quote Fitzpatrick and Gellately, the "*Alltag* of popular collaboration."[26]

The People's Courts offer plenty of evidence for the "privatization of the public realm." Disputes over money and property normally sour relations and often result in legal suits, but during the occupation the authorities offered another way to resolve financial disagreements. A frequent dispute was between lessor and lessee, for example, the baker who denounced his tenant for listening to foreign radio and stealing wood.[27] Another common conflict was between relatives over land or an inheritance. During the occupation František Bureš denounced his son Miroslav for illegally holding on to firearms. According to the son, the trouble began when the father remarried, placing the family's inheritance in doubt. František made his denunciation immediately after a civil court had decided the dispute in favor of his son, but it was Miroslav who ultimately managed to rid himself of his father. In November 1945 the Kutná Hora People's Court sentenced the disabled retiree to six years in prison, with two years to be spent in a labor battalion. In the end, the family squabble backfired on everyone concerned: As part of the verdict the state confiscated one-half of the father's property.[28]

Marital strife, unpleasant enough in peacetime, led to arrest and death during the occupation. When Pavla Maříková denounced her husband in 1942 for listening to foreign radio broadcasts, she brought an end to four trying years during which events had repeatedly conspired against the couple. In 1938 Pavla Armstark, the daughter of a mixed Czech-German marriage, wed Rudolf Mařík, a Czech, and the two settled in the Bohemian borderland. "From the beginning," Rudolf later testified, "the marriage was not alright." It probably did not help that he was thirty-one years older than Pavla, but history was not kind to the couple either. Soon after their marriage, Germany's annexation of the

---

[25] Burrin, *France under the Germans*, 209.
[26] Fitzpatrick and Gellately, "Introduction to the Practices of Denunciation," in *Accusatory Practices*, 10; James C. Scott, *Weapons of the Weak: Everyday Forms of Peasant Resistance* (New Haven, CT: Yale University Press, 1990).
[27] Borák, *Spravedlnost podle dekretu*, 231.
[28] F. Bureš verdict (15 November 1945), Státní oblastní archiv (SOA) Prague, f. MLS-KH, Ls 50/45.

Sudetenland forced them to flee to the Bohemian interior, where they un-wisely settled near an eighteenth-century military town named Terezín in Czech, Theresienstadt in German. Two years later the town became the Protectorate's main ghetto for Jews and its nearby fortress a concen-tration camp for political prisoners. In the meantime, Rudolf had struck up a friendship with a fellow Czech refugee from the Sudetenland who himself had to move a second time when the ghetto was established. The two regularly listened to foreign radio at the latter's home. When Pavla denounced her husband to the Gestapo, he broke under interro-gation and betrayed his accomplice. The Nazi court gave both men two years' imprisonment. Pavla celebrated their arrest by declaring herself "German." After the war the Litoměřice People's Court sentenced Pavla Maříková to five years in prison.[29]

Spousal denunciation often stemmed from extramarital affairs. Af-ter a twenty-three-year marriage Anežka Kupčíková's husband divorced her, threw her out of their apartment, refused to pay alimony, and in-vited another woman to live with him. Kupčíková got her revenge by denouncing him for listening to foreign radio, an act for which he paid with his life. After the war the Ostrava People's Court sentenced her to twenty-five years in prison. Other denouncers aimed to rid themselves of spouses so that they could start up with lovers. Štěpánka Bortoliová and Augustina Musiálková, for example, both denounced their hus-bands to pave the way for extramarital relationships.[30] The Holubová–Velíšková trial described in the previous chapter may have been a sim-ilar case. After her husband was deported to a concentration camp, Zdenka (Pytrusová) Holubová invited his friend to move into her apart-ment. Once the newly ensconced couple learned of the husband's death, they were immediately married. In its February 1947 verdict the Prague People's Court noted,

Because divorce or separation costs money, sometimes takes quite a long time until the spouses are free, and there are other difficulties and scandals associated with it, during the occupation wives helped themselves to other, easier and quicker means: simply, they denounced their husbands themselves, through their acquaintances or anonymously to the Gestapo and the husband disappeared without a divorce trial.[31]

[29] P. Maříková verdict, SOA-Litoměřice, f. MLS-Litoměřice, Lsp 19/46.
[30] Borák, *Spravedlnost podle dekretu*, 228–29.
[31] Verdict, SOA-Praha, MLS-PR, Ls 1026/45, 89.

It is not clear to what extent the judges' assessment in this case reflects a gender bias or the fact that men did not have to resort to "divorce through denunciation" because they found it far easier to end their marriages through ordinary legal channels or simple abandonment. In his study of the Ostrava court, Mečislav Borák concluded that spouse-denouncing "interestingly was almost exclusively the domain of women, insulted or calculating wives."[32] That statement is only true, however, if one distinguishes between wives and ex-wives. Karel Svoboda, for example, turned in his former wife, while Vladimír Němeček found denunciation to be an effective means to smite his ex-wife's new husband.[33]

For some denunciation may have offered an escape from an intolerable situation. In September 1943 Anna Böhmová denounced her husband for listening to foreign radio, whereupon he was immediately arrested and eventually sent to the Sachsenhausen concentration camp, at which point all trace of him was lost. Nonetheless, Böhmová was no Nazi; in fact, before the war both she and her husband had been members of the Communist Party. The Nazis had arrested her brother and her two nephews for being Communists. Böhmová's motivation was personal, not political: As she admitted to a postwar court, she had acted to rid herself of her physically abusive husband. Perhaps outraged at the denunciation of a Communist, the judges gave little weight to Böhmová's marital suffering and sentenced her to twenty years in prison.[34] Some men also employed denunciation as a "weapon of the weak" to rid themselves of their tormentors. František Zeman, for example, turned in the brother who beat him, but the judges proved more sympathetic to him. The Ostrava People's Court acquitted Zeman because of his "weak mental state."[35]

Even the most fundamental family ties were challenged by the lure of denunciation. People's Court records reveal depressing cases of children who ratted on their parents and parents who turned on their

---

[32] Borák, *Spravedlnost podle dekretu*, 228.

[33] K. Svoboda verdict (11 September 1945), SOA Praha, f. Mimořádný lidový soud (MLS) Kutná Hora (KH), Ls 1/45; Borák, *Spravedlnost podle dekretu*, 229.

[34] Böhmová served seven years of the sentence before being deported to Germany in 1953. Jiřík, "Retribuční realita," in *Velké dějiny*, 217.

[35] Borák, *Spravedlnost podle dekretu*, 227.

children. Ludmila Schremplová, for example, denounced her daughter for listening to foreign radio. The daughter was imprisoned; after the war the mother received a ten-year sentence.[36] In a twist on the infamous Soviet hero, Pavlik Morozov, who denounced his father for antistate activity, a twenty-two-year-old Czech student was convicted in February 1946 for having betrayed his parents during the occupation. In a letter to the "Czech Quisling" Emanuel Moravec, the boy had asked what he should do with his parents, who due to their "intellectual backwardness and reactionariness [weren't] capable of understanding Hitler's New Europe." This betrayal was just one of his crimes: He also denounced his history teacher for speaking against Nazism and a classmate for tearing a picture of Hitler out of a magazine. Both victims perished as a result. In the end, the perpetrator was saved from the gallows by the fact that he had denounced his victims while he was still a minor. The court sentenced him to the maximum fifteen years instead.[37]

Committed fascists and so-called national renegades were particularly prone to betray their compatriots to the authorities. The Nazi Sicherheitsdienst (SD) and the Gestapo found the Czech fascist Banner movement to be a repository of willing denouncers.[38] "Renegades" – individuals who before the war were considered to be Czech but who declared themselves German during the occupation – provided another group that was not inhibited from denouncing by the illegitimacy of the Nazi regime. After all, by renouncing their Czech identity they had revoked their membership in the "community of prisoners." Like Pavla Maříková, Hermína Rippová and her husband declared in 1940 that they were actually Germans. The husband's reward for joining the German nation was to be drafted into the Wehrmacht and ultimately to die in April 1945 defending the Reich. With her husband away, Rippová turned on his family, who shared her house. She caught her brother-in-law, a former lieutenant colonel in the Czechoslovak military, entrusting an illegal weapon to a friend, a carpenter, who was, in turn, to bring it to a third conspirator, a pharmacist. After Rippová denounced the group,

[36] Borák, *Spravedlnost podle dekretu*, 227.
[37] "Moravcův odchovanec," *Svobodné Československo* (10 February 1946), SÚA, f. MZV-VA II (j81), k. 216.
[38] Tomáš Pasák, *Český fašismus (1922–1945) a kolaborace (1939–1945)* (Prague: Práh, 1999), 304–305, 341, 344–45.

the Gestapo went to work and arrested the brother-in-law, his wife (who was apparently of Jewish descent), the carpenter, and the pharmacist, all of whom were executed. Subsequently, neighbors' hostile behavior led Rippová to ask the Gestapo to find her a more suitable place to live – the villa of a Dr. Křemen, whom she also denounced for concealing a weapon. In the end, the case was cut-and-dried. Despite Rippová's denials, a Gestapo interpreter testified that she had betrayed her relatives and their friends. The People's Court judges deliberated for a mere quarter-hour before returning the expected verdict: the death sentence. Rippová requested the permitted extra hour of life and was executed in Prague at 3 P.M. on 9 October 1945.[39]

The trial of Antonín Prokop, a Czech farmer, illustrates how denunciation could be but one weapon in an ideologue's arsenal. In addition to denouncing eight persons, Prokop also provided the SD and the Gestapo with information about the popular mood and individual Czechs' opinions. According to the postwar verdict against him, he praised Nazism and Hitler at every possible opportunity, railed against Communists and Jews, and encouraged other Czechs, including his son, to collaborate. At the trial the prosecutor produced a receipt in Prokop's name for a 20,000-crown donation to the German Red Cross. Faced with such a lengthy list of offenses, the Kutná Hora People's Court sentenced Antonín Prokop to twenty years in prison, including ten years in a labor battalion, and the loss of one-fourth of his property and his civic rights in perpetuity.[40]

Thanks to his formal relationship with the SD and Gestapo, Prokop might be judged an "informer," not a denouncer. Fitzpatrick and Gellately defined an informer as a regular agent of the police who usually receives some form of remuneration for his services.[41] Their studies, thus, distinguished between "spontaneous communications" and regular reporting, but an individual like Prokop engaged in both activities: He regularly informed the Germans about public opinion and he also spontaneously denounced fellow Czechs on his own intiative. The Great Decree, for its part, made no distinction between denouncers and

---

[39] "Udavačka H. Rippová popravena," *Právo lidu* (10 October 1945), SÚA, f. MZV-VA II (j81), k. 215.
[40] A. Prokop verdict (12 June 1946), SOA-Prague, f. MLS-KH, Ls 15/45.
[41] Fitzpatrick and Gellately, "Introduction to the Practices of Denunciation," 1.

informers: People's Courts tried both according to Paragraph Eleven. Moreover, while contemporary Czechs spoke of Gestapo "informants" and "agents," they labeled repeat offenders "professional denouncers" [řemeslní udavači].

Judging by the records of the People's Courts, "professional denouncers" served the Nazis throughout the Protectorate in all sorts of communities. Ladislav Kamberec, a Czech teacher, terrorized a small village near Kutná Hora. Thanks to the support of the Germans and the Banner movement, Kamberec became "government commissar," a role he executed with particular zeal. As commissar he ordered Nazi flags and then forced the villagers to pay for them. As a teacher he inculcated the pupils with pro-Nazi propaganda. He betrayed one colleague for not participating in mandatory snow shoveling. After the war twenty-three former pupils, including six children under the age of fourteen, testified against him at his trial. The Kutná Hora People's Court sentenced Kamberec to fifteen years in prison and the loss of all of his property.[42] Another "professional denouncer," thirty-eight-year-old František Ježek denounced twenty-four officials of the Slavie Bank, three of whom were executed. Thanks to his initiative, another twenty-five individuals were betrayed; seven of them were executed. Ježek, who apparently was of "Czech nationality" but had "German citizenship," petitioned after the war for the return of his Czechoslovak citizenship on the grounds that he had been a political prisoner of the Germans. Instead, he received the death penalty.[43] František Eliášek and his mother Růžena were found guilty of denouncing fifty-five persons, leading to the death of thirty of them. The pair's victims came from the Czech elite, including one prewar parliamentary deputy, a senator, a mayor, and several newspaper editors. In August 1946 the son was sentenced to death, his mother to life imprisonment.[44]

The case of Karel Svoboda, the first man tried and executed by the Kutná Hora People's Court, demonstrates that "professional" informers and occasional denouncers were often one and the same. According to the indictment, the thirty-eight-year-old Czech factory guard had

---

[42] L. Kamberec verdict (22 February 1946), SOA-Prague, f. MLS-KH, Ls 19/46.
[43] "Trest smrti udavači...," Právo lidu (9 February 1946), SÚA, f. MZV-VA II (j81), k. 216.
[44] "Dva rozsudky smrti – jeden na doživotí," Právo lidu (25 August 1946), SÚA, f. MZV-VA II (j81), k. 216.

denounced twenty-eight persons who had allegedly spoken against the German Reich, lauded the assassination of Heydrich, or carried out acts of sabotage. The prosecutor also charged him with "praising and supporting" fascism for his contributions to the anti-Semitic weekly *Aryan Struggle*. Svoboda had clearly expressed an ideological commitment to National Socialism and had helped the Germans maintain their authority over the Protectorate. He did not, however, limit his collaboration to the denunciation of Jews and betrayal of coworkers; he also turned in his ex-wife for calling him a "whoremonger like Hitler." Although the language he employed in this case clearly aimed to appeal to the German authorities, Svoboda's underlying motive for the denunciation was apparently economic. Under oath he explained, "It's true that I informed on my former wife, but I only did it because she didn't want to till the field."[45] A clearer example of privatizing the public realm would be hard to find.

THE FEMININE CRIME

In October 1945 Czech journalist Jiří Hrbas penned a pseudoscientific analysis of denunciation for the Communist daily, *Rudé právo*. To incarnate the typical denouncer, Hrbas chose Olga Trpišková, a schoolteacher who had betrayed thirty colleagues to the Gestapo. Trpišková had repeatedly instigated anti-German conversations as a ruse to entrap her victims. One unfortunate student, who unwittingly showed her the Red Army's advance on a classroom map, paid for his naiveté with his life in a German concentration camp. Hrbas voyeuristically evoked Trpišková for the reader: "She wasn't particularly beautiful . . . her erotic life was not balanced. She was strongly romantic, I'd say falsely romantic. She longed for distinguished acquaintances." If the typical denouncer was an unsatisfied woman, then all denouncers were apparently effeminate deviants. They were "like peas in a pod," Hrbas explained; they were "cowards, criminals with inferiority complexes, sexual degenerates. . . . Take off their uniforms, take away their badge and you have before yourself wretched, mangy sorts of inhuman creatures, trembling

---

[45] K. Svoboda verdict (11 September 1945), A-Prague, f. MLS-KH, Ls 1/45.

from fear and terrible guilt."[46] Other journalists mocked the school-teacher's allegedly unrequited infatuation with her German secret police controller. When the Prague People's Court sentenced Trpišková to life imprisonment, the Czech press welcomed what it considered just punishment for a woman who was the "nastiest [sort of] provocateur."[47]

After her conviction Trpišková soon faded from public concern, but the conflation of denouncer and woman lives on in scholarly accounts today. In his analysis of the Ostrava People's Court, Borák concluded that women there were three times as likely as men to be tried for denunciation. He explained this gender gap by reference to "an apparent psychological connection" between the defendants' gender and their crimes.[48] Another Czech historian, Václav Jiřík, similarly claimed, "It is evident that denunciation was to a certain degree the domain of the fairer sex."[49] Burrin cited reports from two regions in France that indicate that the majority of defendants tried there for denunciation were female.[50] Several studies on Nazi Germany have demonstrated, to the contrary, that a majority of German denouncers were male.[51] In the Czech case a sample analysis of retribution court records from the month of June 1946 challenges the common opinion expressed by Hrbas, Borák, and Jiřík. Contrary to the belief that denunciation was a particularly female act, the postwar Czech People's Courts were actually far more likely to punish men for denunciation. If denunciation was a "weapon of the weak," then it was apparently one wielded more often by men than by women.

When we examine the June 1946 results of all twenty-four People's Courts, we find that Czech men were far more likely to have faced

<hr/>

[46] Jiří Hrbas, "Denunciant," *Rudé právo* (3 October 1945), SÚA, f. MZV-VA II (j81), k. 215.
[47] "Doživotní žalář dr. Trpiškové," *Lidová demokracie*; "Žena číslo V 274 odsouzena na doživotí," *Práce*; "Lidový soud nad českou profesorkou-udavačkou," *Rudé právo* (28 September 1945), SÚA, f. MZV-VA II (j81), k. 215.
[48] Borák, *Spravedlnost podle dekretu*, 224, 274.
[49] Václav Jiřík, *Nedaleko od Norimberku. Z dějin Mimořádného lidového soudu v Chebu v letech 1946 až 1948* (Cheb: Svět křídel, 2000), 376.
[50] Burrin, *France under the Germans*, 209.
[51] Robert Gellately, "Denunciations in Twentieth-Century Germany: Aspects of Self-Policing in the Third Reich and the German Democratic Republic," in Sheila Fitzpatrick and Robert Gellately, eds., *Accusatory Practices: Denunciation in Modern European History, 1789–1989* (Chicago: University of Chicago Press, 1997), 215.

Table 2. *Defendants Tried for Denunciation (Paragraph Eleven) in June 1946*

Nationality/Sex	Only §11[a]	Incl. §11[b]	Not §11[c]
Czech women	67%	75%	25%
Czech men	35%	50%	50%
German women	30%	45%	55%
German men	6%	16%	84%

[a] Defendants tried only for Paragraph Eleven.
[b] Defendants tried for Paragraph Eleven in conjunction with other offenses.
[c] Defendants not tried for Paragraph Eleven.

charges of denunciation than Czech women.[52] In total, 97 Czech women and 234 Czech men were tried that month for violations of Paragraph Eleven (sometimes in combination with other offenses). For Germans the gender gap was somewhat smaller, but men charged with denunciation still outnumbered women by the considerable margin of 101 to 55. In other words, in June 1946 the People's Courts tried more than twice as many men as women for crimes listed under Paragraph Eleven. How, then, did denunciation come to be associated primarily with women? The answer may lie in the frequency with which female defendants were prosecuted for this specific offense (see Table 2). Although in June 1946 the courts tried more men *in total* for denunciation, those women who faced judgment were *proportionately* more likely to be charged with Paragraph Eleven. Of the 129 Czech women were brought before the courts in June 1946, three-fourths faced charges involving denunciation. There were, by contrast, 464 Czech male defendants, but barely half were tried for denunciation. For Germans the difference between the sexes was greater, though at considerably lower levels: while 45 percent of German women faced charges of denunciation, only 16 percent of German men did.

[52] June 1946 roughly represented the temporal midpoint of postwar retribution, one year after the first official trial and eleven months before the last. The blood lust of the early postwar months had subsided, but the courts still convicted more than two-thirds of defendants. According to Justice Ministry records, in June 1946 the People's Courts tried 1,360 defendants including 249 women. In all, approximately 36 percent of defendants that month faced charges based on Paragraph Eleven. The calculations in the subsequent text are based on these records. "Přehled činnosti MLS v době od 1. do 30.6.1946," MS no. 49.500/46-IV/5, Archiv Ministerstva vnitra (AMV) Prague, no. 12365.

Table 3. *Conviction Rates for Denunciation (Paragraph Eleven) for June 1946*

Nationality/Sex	Only §11[a]	Incl. §11[b]
Czech women	47%	48%
Czech men	59%	63%
German women	57%	62%
German men	74%	84%

[a] Defendants tried only for Paragraph Eleven.
[b] Defendants tried for Paragraph Eleven in conjunction with other offenses.

On closer examination, the figures cited by Borák for the entire operations of the Ostrava court actually confirm this interpretation and challenge his insinuation that denunciation was a particularly female crime. He wrote, "women were three times as likely as men to stand before courts for the crime of denunciation." This statement, however, applies to female *defendants* only. A female defendant in Ostrava was three times more likely than her male counterpart to have been tried for denunciation, but the Ostrava court tried more than nine times as many men as women. Of those men, 423 faced charges of denunciation, while only 182 women did.[53] If we assume that men and women were equally represented in the population as a whole, then the average man from the Ostrava region was actually 2.3 times more likely than the average female Ostravan to be tried for denunciation. In fact, this ratio was likely greater because of the contemporary gender imbalance that resulted from wartime German male casualties, soldiers missing in action, and prisoners of war.

As Table 3 indicates, the gender gap in denunciation cases only grew in the course of adjudication. On average, slightly more than two-thirds of all defendants were convicted in June 1946. Among Czech women tried for denunciation (alone or together with other offenses), however, fewer than half were convicted. For Czech men the corresponding rate was 63 percent. In other words, not only were more Czech men tried for Paragraph Eleven offenses, but they were also substantially more likely to be convicted of the charge once brought before a court. That Germans were more likely to be convicted is hardly surprising considering the greater participation of Germans in Nazism and the

[53] Borák, *Spravedlnost podle dekretu*, 224.

virulent hatred of contemporary Czechs (including Czech judges) for all things German. Even so, the gender gap among Germans was even greater than that among Czechs: The courts convicted 84 percent of German men tried for denunciation, but only 62 percent of German women.

The strikingly different conviction rates could have stemmed from several causes. Prosecutors and judges might have treated women more leniently in the belief that collaboration, like war, was a male business.[54] Courts may have been particularly reluctant to imprison mothers for extended periods of time. Chauvinism, however, could cut both ways: While some courts might have assumed that members of the "weaker sex" were less responsible for their actions, other courts could have held women to a harsher, idealized standard of noble feminine behavior. Had the judges treated women more leniently, this approach should have also been reflected in sentencing. In June 1946, however, Czech female defendants only received slightly shorter sentences on average than Czech male defendants. In cases where denunciation was the only crime, Czech women's sentences averaged 5.4 years and Czech men's sentences 5.9 years. In cases where denunciation was charged along with other crimes, Czech females received an 8.7-year sentence on average and Czech males an average 9.6-year sentence.

Ultimately, from the available evidence one cannot conclusively determine the effect of gender bias on the conviction rates. Even if we could, we also would have to consider the cumulative effect of the gender bias of the people who turned in alleged denouncers, the police who interrogated them, and the prosecutors who chose to indict them. If we accept that the courts' verdicts were not based on erratic whim, however, then the different conviction rates for men and women vividly illustrate a striking discrepancy in the merits of the cases tried. In other words, the public, police, and prosecution combined to put forward a considerable number of poorly grounded cases against women in general and Czech women in particular. The extraordinarily low conviction rate for Czech women thus may reveal a commensurately high incidence of false

---

[54] Jennifer Turpin, "Many Faces: Women Confronting War," in Lois Ann Lorentzen and Jennifer Turpin, eds., *The Women and War Reader* (New York: New York University Press, 1998), 3.

accusation against female Czechs after the war. In the frequent acquittals of female defendants we may see the consequences of a conflict between popular perception, which led to postwar arrests and indictments, and the actual prevalence of wartime denunciation. The popular conflation of female and denouncer encouraged Czechs to turn in women and courts to try them. Before the bench, however, prosecutors frequently could not prove the charges against Czech women to the satisfaction of the judges. As a result, the courts acquitted women at a significantly higher rate than men.

Granted that men likely denounced more in the aggregate than women, it still remains to be explained why male and female defendants of both nationalities were prosecuted for denunciation at such markedly different rates. If the conflation of woman and denouncer stemmed from the extraordinary frequency with which female defendants faced charges of denunciation, then what explains this frequency? The answer likely lies in the structurally gendered nature of collaboration in Nazi Europe. If we consider collaboration by nationality and gender, German men had the greatest opportunities to serve the Nazis openly during the war. As a result, male German defendants had by far the lowest rate of prosecution for denunciation afterward. Although a number of crimes make up the rest of charges against German men, among the most common were leadership and membership in all-male Nazi organizations like the SA and SS. German women had fewer such opportunities than their male compatriots, but they, too, held leadership positions in some Nazi organizations, particularly in the Nationalsozialistische Frauenschaft and the Bund Deutscher Mädel and they also functioned as party "Block" chiefs (Blockleiterin). Czech men served throughout the Protectorate bureaucracy, worked as policemen, and were active in domestic fascist groups, like the Banner movement. Czech women, by contrast, faced structural obstacles to participation in collaborationist organizations; denunciation was one of the very few ways in which they could actually interact with the occupiers. As a result, People's Courts prosecuted Czech women overwhelmingly for Paragraph Eleven offenses. In sum, though denunciation was the collaborationist crime most likely to be committed by a woman, it was no means a particularly female offense. In fact, this allegedly feminine crime likely had considerably more male perpetrators.

CHANNELING DENUNCIATION

Beyond sowing widespread suspicion, denouncers served specific goals of the Nazis in the Protectorate. To this end, the occupation authorities crafted their policies to channel denunciation toward certain targets while broadly intimidating the population as a whole. The reaction to the assassination of SS leader Reinhard Heydrich demonstrates the Nazis' resort to both broad and targeted uses of denunciation. Immediately after the 27 May 1942 attack on the acting Protector, the Germans announced a one-million mark reward for information leading to the capture of the perpetrators. Terrified of massive Nazi retaliation, the Protectorate government offered another million and urged the Czech people to reveal the names of anyone involved in the assassination. In response, approximately 1,000 tips, half of them apparently from Czechs, deluged the Gestapo's offices.[55] For example, one woman reported that a bloody man had left a bicycle in front of her shop on the day of the assassination and that a girl had later picked it up. After the war a People's Court sentenced her to nine years. In a similar case, Anežka Rožková told her husband, Cyril, a member of Banner, that she had seen a bleeding man hit a woman with his bicycle. Cyril encouraged her to report it to the police and Anežka later identified the body of one of the parachutists, Jan Kubiš. At the time, the Nazis gave them a 150,000-crown reward; in 1946 a People's Court gave them each ten years in prison.[56]

Together with the targeted attempt to find the assassination's perpetrators, the Nazi authorities encouraged a broader wave of denunciation intended to terrorize the Czech population into submission. "Praise of the assassination" became a capital crime. Františka Kocinová, a "renegade" and a member of the Nazi party, denounced a couple that had lauded the assassination of Heydrich. They were arrested and executed. In response, on 7 October 1946 the Brno People's Court sentenced the

---

[55] Vojtech Mastny, *The Czechs under Nazi Rule: The Failure of National Resistance* (New York: Columbia University Press, 1971), 210–14.

[56] The joint denunciation by Anežka Rožková and her husband Cyril illustrates the structurally gendered nature of collaboration under Nazi occupation. Thanks to his membership in the fascist Banner organization, Cyril had access to power and thus acted as a conduit for information from his wife. "Udavačka z heydrichiády před soudem," *Národní osvobození* (22 November 1946), SÚA, f. MZV-VA II (j81), k. 216; *Lidová demokracie* (26 February 1946), 2; *Právo lidu* (26 February 1946), SÚA, f. MZV-VA II (j81), k. 216.

forty-four-year-old denouncer to death.[57] In all, the Nazis executed 477 Czechs for "approving the assassination."[58] Although the aftermath of Heydrich's assassination represented the worst of Nazi repression, speech crimes were a prime cause for denunciation throughout the war. After all, just about any Czech could be accused of slandering Hitler, grumbling about the occupation, or expressing hope for Allied victory. For example, Banner member Eliáš Baziv denounced Jan Žák to the Gestapo for predicting in August 1943 that the war would be over in two to three months and that once the Russians arrived, they would "thoroughly settle accounts with the Germans." For this unwise statement, the seventy-year old Žák spent six months in detention. After the war a People's Court convicted Baziv and sentenced him to twelve years' imprisonment.[59]

The ability of the Nazi regime to turn anyone into a potential informer made public spaces particularly dangerous. In normal times a barroom fight might result a bloody lip or a black eye, not to mention a painful hangover the next day, but under foreign occupation the pub was sometimes the antechamber to the jailhouse. For example, one farmer reported on his drinking buddies because they had beaten him up and torn off his swastika insignia. In another case, a metalworker denounced four men for cheating him at cards. With their lips loosened by liquor, Czechs said unwise things that landed them in jail. Sometimes another guest turned them in to the police, but proprietors also acted as informants. One at the Beskyd Hotel in Frýdlant turned in a man who had insulted Hitler; another barkeeper denounced a customer who had sung Polish and Czech songs.[60]

Listening could be as dangerous as speaking. Denouncers frequently turned in their victims for the crime of "listening to foreign radio." In the Protectorate, as in core Nazi Germany, individuals caught following the BBC, Radio Moscow, or other foreign sources could be punished with the death penalty and executed.[61] Unlike active resistance, which was

---

[57] "Trest smrti udavače," *Národní osvobození* (8 October 1946), SÚA, f. MZV-VA II (j81), k. 216.

[58] Detlef Brandes, *Die Tschechen unter deutschem Protektorat*, 2 vols. (Munich: R. Oldenbourg, 1969, 1975), I:266.

[59] Baziv, verdict (12 December 1946), 153–55, SOA-Prague, f. MLS-KH, Ls 597/46.

[60] Borák, *Spravedlnost podle dekretu*, 230–31.

[61] The confiscation of all radios in Czech hands was initially rejected because it would have undermined the Nazis' ability to propagate their own message. In 1943, however,

practiced by a few stalwarts, ordinary Czechs (and Germans) regularly followed the BBC and therefore were liable to arrest and execution. As we have seen, Anna Böhmová, Anežka Kupčíková, and Pavla Maříková all denounced their husbands for listening to foreign radio. From the evidence, however, the radio decrees failed to prevent people from listening to foreign broadcasts, although they were probably dissuaded from spreading the news they heard to friends and neighbors.[62]

Nazi attempts to suppress black market activity met with similarly limited success, although denouncers contributed their share of victims for this offense, too. Baziv, who turned in the seventy-year-old Žák for anti-Reich speech, also allegedly reported on another Czech for illegally butchering a pig.[63] After being summarily dismissed from work, Josef Dlapal denounced his former employers, the Cejnar couple, on the grounds that they dealt in the black market and kept double accounting ledgers. Fortunately for the Cejnars, Dlapal only sent his letters to the Supreme Price Control Office and the Economics Ministry, which carried out two audits and determined that the charges were groundless. This self-proclaimed "friend of the German nation" then threatened to take his case to the German military authorities and even signed his denunciation letter with the name of another employee, Václav Bažant. Thanks to Dlapal's machinations, the Cejnars were fined 30,000 crowns and the unfortunate Bažant suffered through five handwriting analyses by the Germans and another investigation by the Czech police after the war. The Kutná Hora People's Court concluded that this was a simple case of revenge, where black market activity was a mere pretext.[64]

THE *ARYAN STRUGGLE* FOR DENUNCIATION

Exposure of black market commerce may have suppressed attempts to evade fixed prices and rationing, and denunciations of radio listening

the Nazis disabled the short-wave capacity of more than one million radios in the Protectorate. Gellately, "Denunciations in Twentieth-Century Germany," 192–93; Zdeněk Huňáček, Jiří Jožák, Vlastislav Kroupa, and Jan Stříbrný, *Český antifašismus a odboj: Slovníková příručka* (Prague: Naše vojsko, 1987), 397.

[62] Brandes, *Die Tschechen*, II:18; Jan Stransky, *East Wind over Prague* (New York: Random House, 1951), 75.

[63] Baziv verdict (12 December 1946), 153, SOA-Prague, f. MLS-KH, Ls 597/46.

[64] The Kutná Hora People's Court accepted Dlapal's excuse that he feared deportation to Germany after his dismissal and therefore reduced his sentence to three years. J. Dlapal verdict (30 April 1947), SOA-Prague, f. MLS-KH, Ls 96/47.

and anti-Reich speech likely prevented many Czechs from communicating freely with each other, but these illegal activities still flourished throughout the occupation regardless of how many practitioners were betrayed and punished. By contrast, the Nazis' encouragement of denunciation yielded deadly success in the genocide of the Protectorate's Jews. Nazi racial laws, which prohibited and punished contacts between Jews and Gentiles, directed denunciations against individuals who disobeyed these strictures. Anti-Semitic denunciation arguably played a critical role in deterring opposition to the deportation of Jews and thereby contributed to their extermination.

The April 1947 trial of Václav Píša depressingly revealed the contribution of Czech denouncers to the Nazi Holocaust of Protectorate Jewry. Like the archetypal fascist, Píša had a checkered past, with periods in jail and on the unemployment line, prior to his wartime elevation to prominence as a notorious anti-Semite. In 1931, the forty-three-year-old Píša, then working for a medical insurance company, was convicted of embezzlement and given a ten-month sentence, which an appeals court later tripled because of his poor character. A year later, paroled on the stipulation that he not step foot inside a whisky bar, Píša was arrested again on charges of fraud. After three years without employment, in 1936 he finally found work at various magazines from whence he graduated the next year to an editorship at the Kutná Hora newspaper of the ambiguously named Business Party of the Radical Center. Like Emanuel Moravec, at this time Píša was still a Czech nationalist who patriotically condemned the Germans. After the Munich Pact, however, Píša moved farther to the right and joined up with the fascists. When the Germans took over, the Gestapo's approach to the future editor was a classic case of blackmail. Píša later testified that he had been arrested and given the choice of becoming an agent or going to prison.[65]

In 1940 Václav Píša got his most important (and last) job as a regional editor of the weekly anti-Semitic tabloid *Aryan Struggle* [*Árijský boj*]. A Czech version of Julius Streicher's *Der Stürmer* (*The Stormer*), the paper's masthead proudly trumpeted itself as the "Central Organ of the Anti-Jewish Movement" in the Protectorate. It had a maximum print run of approximately 20,000 to 23,000 copies, but, as we shall see, its

[65] V. Píša verdict (26 April 1947), SOA-Prague, MLS-KH, Ls 646/46, 399, 419–20.

circulation had a far greater impact.[66] In a letter to Moravec, editor-in-chief Rudolf Novák described the weekly's mission: "Our paper spreads throughout the Czech countryside an antidote against Benešite whispered propaganda.... In a reporting fashion... we expose local Jew-lovers, Benešites, and the like."[67] Throughout its turbulent existence *Aryan Struggle* had three main themes: support for Nazism, the German Reich, and collaboration with it; denigration of the interwar Czechoslovak Republic, its past leaders, and its successor, the Beneš government-in-exile in London; and, primarily, the propagation of anti-Semitism and the pillorying of so-called "Jew-lovers."

As part of its enthusiastic support for the occupation, *Aryan Struggle* promoted the activities of fascist and anti-Semitic organizations. At the same time, the tabloid attacked public figures who failed to express the proper enthusiasm for Nazism. One article, for example, accused local newspapers of maintaining "two irons in the fire" and threatened to expose anyone who maintained a "Janus head."[68] Even after the tide turned on the Nazis, *Aryan Struggle* continued to promote Czech collaboration. In February 1945 the tabloid ridiculed French writer Robert Brasillach for his alleged attempts to ingratiate himself with Jews after years of anti-Semitic writings.[69] His supposed turnabout, the article accurately predicted, would not save the Frenchman. The editors proudly declared their determination to go down with the Nazi ship: "*Aryan Struggle* will still continue to implacably refute buck-passers [*alibisti*]. A warrior cannot fear for his life."[70] *Aryan Struggle* defiantly published its last issue on 4 May 1945, the day before the Prague Uprising.

For *Aryan Struggle* denouncing the interwar republic and the Czechoslovak government-in-exile was the same as denouncing the Jews. After all, the tabloid claimed, the First Republic was nothing more than a "little Palestine." Its predecessor, "the former Jew-Habsburg

[66] Vojtěch Dolejší, *Noviny a novináři: Z poznámek a vzpomínek* (Prague: Nakladatelství politické literatury, 1963), 386–87; R. Novák verdict (26 March 1947), SÚA, f. NS, TNs 6/47, 11.

[67] R. Novák verdict (26 March 1947), SÚA, f. NS, TNs 6/47, 12.

[68] "Krajinný tisk," *Árijský boj* II:4 (24 January 1942), 6, SOA-Prague, f. MLS-KH, Ls 646/46.

[69] For more on Brasillach, see Alice Kaplan, *The Collaborator: The Trial and Execution of Robert Brasillach* (Chicago: University of Chicago Press, 2000).

[70] "Případ Roberta Brasillache čili alibismus se nevyplácí," *Árijský boj* (17 February 1945), 5, SOA-Prague, f. MLS-KH, Ls 646/46.

Austria," was apparently not much better.[71] Imitating the pornography of *Der Stürmer*, the article "Alice Masaryk's Harem" accused the former president's daughter of being a lesbian who engaged in orgies. *Aryan Struggle* claimed that Alice had used a chateau in the impoverished, eastern (i.e., "oriental") Czechoslovak province of Subcarpathian Rus as a hideaway for her illicit trysts with other women. True to form, the tabloid also accused her of an abnormal, erotic longing for Jewish men.[72] As for the government-in-exile, its domination by Jews was allegedly demonstrated by the power of the Justice Minister, "the Jew Stránský" (whose grandfather had apparently converted to Christianity).[73]

A range of articles demonized Jews and justified Nazi measures against them. A few titles from one issue suffice to convey the tabloid's content: "Stalin: 'Slavic' Jew," "Jews – parasites," and "The Jew wanted this war." Other articles featured the theories of notorious anti-Semites like Houston Stewart Chamberlain. Digging up old lies, *Aryan Struggle* also lectured its readers about "Kolín Jews and ritual murder." Despite the imminent and inescapable defeat of Nazi Germany, in March 1945 editor-in-chief Novák declared victory in the anti-Semitic struggle. On the sixth anniversary of Czechoslovakia's destruction, he exulted, "The great significance of 15 March 1939 lies... in the fact that we got rid of the Jews *forever!*"[74]

For all their venom, the regular articles in *Aryan Struggle* were only window dressing for the tabloid's most insidious section: "The Floodlight." Under this heading, week after week the editors printed notices exposing Czechs, Jewish and Gentile, who violated anti-Semitic sanctions or who otherwise failed to demonstrate sufficient loyalty to the Third Reich.[75] The tabloid solicited reports from its readership: "Write us, call (our telephone number is 313–75), visit us. Take part actively in the purifying anti-Jewish struggle."[76] In response, *Aryan Struggle*

---

[71] R. Novák verdict (26 March 1947), SÚA, f. NS, TNs 6/47, 18, 20.
[72] "Harém Alice Masarykové u Jasiny," *Árijský boj* II:4 (24 January 1942), 1, SOA-Prague, f. MLS-KH, Ls 646/46.
[73] R. Novák verdict (26 March 1947), SÚA, f. NS, TNs 6/47, 6, 18, 20.
[74] *Árijský boj* IV:20 (15 May 1943), 1, 5; V:29 (15 July 1944), 5; II:7 (22 February 1941), 6; VI:10 (10 March 1945), 1, SOA-Prague, f. MLS-KH, Ls 646/46.
[75] In 1933 Streicher's *Der Stürmer* instituted a "pillory column," the likely prototype for *Aryan Struggle*'s Floodlight. Randall L. Bytwerk, *Julius Streicher* (New York: Dorset Press, 1988), 163.
[76] *Árijský boj* II:29 (26 July 1941), 3, SOA-Prague, f. MLS-KH, Ls 646/46.

received sixty denunciatory letters a day, most of them directed against Jews and so-called "Jew-lovers."[77] Some of the contributions had no particular target. For example, one anonymous letter claimed, "For its Jewish politics the former state paid the highest price: collapse and destruction.... [N]ever forget the period of Jewish rule."[78] Most contributors, however, had specific gripes about their own communities. One letter complained that the closed synagogue in Moravské Budějovice still displayed Hebrew writing that allegedly "frightened passers-by." The writer called on the town to propose a new use for the building.[79]

From his perch in the eastern Bohemian town of Čáslav, Píša used his position as regional editor to solicit, collect, and print letters in *Aryan Struggle* that singled out specific individuals. The 26 July 1941 issue, published prior to the mass deportation of Jews from the area, illustrates the wide net that local anti-Semites cast.[80] From Kutná Hora a letter exhorted, "Ban Jews from going to the market in the morning." The author expressed outrage that he had spied "the notorious Jewish card-player Weinberger" selling mushrooms there. An informer in nearby Suchdol ratted on a priest and his cook, the village mayor, a carpenter, a farmer, and several others, because they had aided a Jew. They were all members of the official National Solidarity movement[81] – even the local chairman was apparently involved. The author concluded,

---

[77] R. Novák verdict (26 March 1947), SÚA, f. NS, TNs 6/47, 11.

[78] *Árijský boj* IV:27 (3 July 1943), 6, SOA-Prague, f. MLS-KH, Ls 646/46.

[79] *Árijský boj* IV:5 (30 January 1943), SOA-Prague, f. MLS-KH, Ls 646/46.

[80] Centered around the towns of Čáslav, Kolín, and Kutná Hora, Píša's home region did not include an especially high number of Jews: In the 1930 census only 0.5 percent (2,322 persons) of the general population in the Kutná Hora court district defined itself as Jewish by religion. (By comparison, in Bohemia as a whole slightly more than 1 percent of the population was recorded as Jewish and in Prague the number topped 4 percent.) In June 1942 the Nazis deported 2,202 Jews from Kolín to the Theresienstadt ghetto in three separate transports. Only 137 of the deportees survived the war. Ministerstvo vnitra a Státní úřad statistický, *Statistický lexikon obcí v zemí české* (Prague: Orbis, 1934), xiii–xxiv, 426–31; Miroslav Kárný, *"Konečné řešení": Genocida českých Židů v německé protektorátní politice* (Prague: Academia, 1991), 152.

[81] In spring 1939 Hácha and his aides created National Solidarity [Národní souručenství], a nonpartisan, umbrella Czech movement meant to be a bulwark against domestic fascists and a counterweight to Nazi encroachments on national life. The first aim was effectively realized: The group quickly registered more than 98 percent of eligible men. But the movement failed as a Czech nationalist counterweight to German pressure because from the beginning the Nazis ignored National Solidarity's attempts to advance Czech interests by reaching out to the occupation authorities. Brandes, *Die Tschechen*, I:43–44.

"We hope that National Solidarity summons these gentlemen and dis-abuses [them] of their acts which damage the nation." In Čáslav an-other informer complained about the "white Jew" Svoboda and his wife "Sarah" and warned, "This time we'll soon be finished with the Jewess."[82] In Brandýs nad Labem the wealthy mayor had allegedly taken a Jew under his protection. From Hradec Králové came news that Růžena Nehybová, a fruit seller, had been spotted repeatedly conversing with "that moldy, old Jewish geezer Silberstern." Another contributor exposed a Jewish professional couple in Litomyšl who had hired an "Aryan" girl to shop for them during curfew hours. Finally, three youths from the same town found their names printed in the tabloid because they continued to associate with a Jewish friend. All that in a single installment of Píša's section, itself just one part of *Aryan Struggle*.[83]

The letters in *Aryan Struggle* not only demonstrate anti-Semites ea-ger to betray their neighbors to the Gestapo. The denunciations on the tabloid's pages also inadvertently reveal numerous cases of Gentiles act-ing to lessen Jews' isolation and even aid them materially. Early in the war one letter writer complained about Čáslav:

That some of our people provocatively overlook the regulations for Jews is evident from the fact that they *over-respectfully* greet Jews on the street and often stop and have friendly conversation with them. If they continue to repeat such improper conduct then those apprehended will also be marked... as apparent Jew-lovers and humiliated friends of Jews!

In the same issue the tabloid's editors reminded the people of Dolní Královice that contacts with Jews were illegal and revealed that one Jew continued to visit an "Aryan family."[84] Another informant reported in August 1941 that a local Jew with American citizenship had been seen buying bread without ration coupons. The anti-Semite denounced the baker by name and added, "It's high time for the Czech person to understand that the Jew is his greatest enemy."[85]

[82] Following Nazi terminology, "Sarah" was the name that *Aryan Struggle* employed to describe any female Jew. "White Jews" were Gentiles who fraternized with Jews.
[83] "Středočeská oblast," *Árijský boj* II:29 (26 July 1941), 6, SOA-Prague, f. MLS-KH, Ls 646/46.
[84] "Čáslav" and "Dolní Královice," *Árijský boj* (date unknown), 6, SOA-Prague, f. MLS-KH, Ls 646/46.
[85] Letter no. 22, SOA-Prague, f. MLS-KH, Ls 646/46, 50.

As the outing of the mayors of Brandýs and Suchdol demonstrated, *Aryan Struggle*'s editors paid special attention to stigmatizing prominent Czech Gentiles who failed to respect Nazi race laws, lest these "white Jews" become an example to their compatriots. In one issue, a letter accused a factory owner in Čáslav of renting space to an intermarried "Aryan." Another anonymous informer damned the entire local police force in Lipnice nad Sázavou as "protectors of Jews."[86] While such actions could not prevent the Nazis from fulfilling their fanatic commitment to the annihilation of European Jewry, the letters nonetheless showed the unwillingness of many to participate in the ostracization of the Protectorate's Jews. Exposure in *Aryan Struggle* undoubtedly intimidated those who had transgressed anti-Semitic sanctions and dissuaded many more from even attempting to do so. "Although many Czechs sympathized with the plight of their Jewish compatriots," Vojtech Mastny concluded, "for all practical purposes, the Nazis...succeeded in isolating the Jews from other people."[87] Gellately's commentary on Germany rings equally true for the Protectorate: "Without denunciation...there is no telling how many people might have helped Jews or members of other stigmatized groups or expressed solidarity with them."[88]

In the heady days of summer 1941, with the German army closing in on Moscow, the editors of *Aryan Struggle* boasted, "The Floodlights are a success." They announced, "In nearly every case about which we have written, a rectification has already been made."[89] The tabloid did not achieve "rectification" merely by intimidating Czechs, because Czechs were not *Aryan Struggle*'s only readers. In its 26 March 1947 verdict against Editor-in-Chief Novák, the Prague National Court concluded, "It has been determined that as a rule the Gestapo immediately moved against those marked [in the tabloid]."[90] The former head of the Kolín SD, Bedřich Erdman, testified that he read Píša's work with great interest.[91] In the Novák trial, Dr. Olga Koganová-Henychová, a converted

---

[86] *Árijský boj* (2 August 1941), 6, SOA-Prague, f. MLS-KH, Ls 646/46.

[87] Mastny, *Czechs under Nazi Rule*, 192.

[88] Gellately, "Denunciations in Twentieth-Century Germany," 221.

[89] "Reflektory má úspěch," *Árijský boj* 26 July 1941), 3, SOA-Prague, f. MLS-KH, Ls 646/46.

[90] R. Novák verdict (26 March 1947), SÚA, f. NS, TNs 6/47, 114.

[91] V. Píša verdict (26 April 1947), SOA-Prague, f. MLS-KH, Ls 646/46, 421.

half-Jew of Russian origin, attested that the Gestapo confronted her with an article from *Aryan Struggle* attacking her and her husband.[92] At Píša's trial witnesses testified that the Gestapo had interrogated them about specific articles and notices that had mentioned them.[93] In Würzburg, Gellately determined, "for the everyday activity of the Gestapo denunciations represented the single most important factor in initiating cases."[94] Thanks to *Aryan Struggle*, much the same seems to have been true in the Protectorate.

When German officials read the reports in *Aryan Struggle*, the consequences could be dire, especially for anyone considered to have "Jewish blood." After repeated attacks in Píša's rubric, Viktor Kačer, whose grandmother was Jewish, lost his job at the post office and was deported to work in Germany.[95] The Floodlight accused Karel Eben, a convert to Christianity, of walking around without a yellow star and of visiting his "Aryan" ex-wife. The police investigated the charge, arrested Eben, and deported him to the East, from which he never returned. The Floodlight also exposed the "Jew Amschelberg," accusing him of hiding in a sanitarium. Soon thereafter the Gestapo arrested him and sent him off to Theresienstadt, where he perished within six weeks.[96] After *Aryan Struggle* repeatedly made the "coarsest personal attacks" on the Andreses, former owners of an "Aryanized" department store in Prague, the head of the family was arrested and shipped to Theresienstadt. He survived life in the camp for only fourteen days.[97]

The postwar trial of Alfred Rziha vividly demonstrated what awaited victims in Píša's home region when the Gestapo came knocking at their doors. Until the deportation of the area's Jews, Rziha worked in the local Gestapo's "Church and Jewish Department." Later he transferred

---

[92] Deposition of Dr. Olga Koganová-Henychová (7 May 1947), SOA-Prague, f. MLS-KH, Ls 646/46, 268.

[93] V. Píša verdict, (26 April 1947), SOA-Prague, f. MLS-KH, Ls 646/46, 396, 421, 430.

[94] In particular, Gestapo actions meant to enforce Nazi anti-Semitic policies stemmed from denunciations in nearly 70 percent of all cases. Gellately, "Denunciations in Twentieth-Century Germany," 187–89.

[95] Píša testified at his trial that two of Kačer's fellow postmen had denounced him. SOA-Praha, f. MLS-KH, Ls 646/46, 388.

[96] R. Novák verdict (26 March 1947), SÚA, f. NS, TNs 6/47, 26, 114.

[97] After the war Novák testified that the denunciation came from the store's employees. AMV, aj. S-101–3, l. 9–15.

to the "anti-Marxist" department.[98] Thanks to his bilingualism – his stepmother was Czech, as was his wife – he acted as an interpreter at numerous interrogations during which he also involved himself directly in the extraction of information from prisoners. Even among the local Gestapo, Rziha's brutality was notorious. One witness revealed that other officers turned to the interpreter "when they themselves could not force some prisoners to confess." According to trial testimony, Rziha's "specialty" was kicking Jews in the chest, but he and his fellow Gestapo officers also resorted to other forms of torture. One witness related how after fourteen days he was summoned for his third interrogation, beaten with a truncheon, then made to do half-squats on a hot stove. When the Gestapo officers finally removed the stove, they placed a pointed pole underneath him and forced him to continue doing squats. At the end of the three-hour interrogation, the prisoner had two fewer teeth and an open gash on his backside. After the war the Kutná Hora People's Court determined that Rziha was personally responsible for knocking out at least sixty-four teeth and breaking at least another twenty. In addition to his predilection for punching teeth out and kicking chests in, the verdict called him "a virtuoso at slapping" and detailed his resort to other horrifying forms of torture. One hundred and seven living witnesses testified against Rziha; another twenty victims could not make it to the trial because they had died as a result of the confessions he had obtained from them. On 14 April 1947 at 8:20 in the evening, soon after the Kutná Hora People's Court sentenced him to death, Rziha was hanged. Four minutes later the court doctor declared the brutal Gestapo officer dead.[99]

After the war, in a vain attempt to lessen his shared responsibility for the Gestapo's crimes, Píša described himself under interrogation as "some sort of go-between," a role he claimed, "a person of public stature could not ... avoid."[100] Although the latter half of the statement is not

---

[98] Rziha served the Gestapo first in Kladno (June to November 1941), then in Kolín, near Kutná Hora (November 1941 to October 1944), and finally in Benešov (October 1944 to 8 May 1945). A. Rziha verdict (14 April 1947), SOA-Prague, f. MLS-KH, Ls 48/47, 496.

[99] Rziha escaped to Bavaria at the end of the war, but he was arrested in July 1946 by the U.S. military, interned in Dachau, and extradited to Czechoslovakia five months later. A. Rziha verdict (14 April 1947), SOA-Prague, f. MLS-KH, Ls 48/47, 476, 496, 499–500, 508–10, 529; "Trest smrti gestapákovi Rzihovi," *Kutnohorský kraj* (18 April 1947), 3.

[100] V. Píša verdict (26 April 1947), SOA-Prague, f. MLS-KH, Ls 646/46, 431.

credible – Píša's superiors in Prague suggestively inquired several times if the editor did not perhaps wish to resign[101] – his self-designation rings true. As the local editor of *Aryan Struggle*, Píša was a public figure to whom anti-Semites and other disgruntled would-be informants could turn with their complaints. For example, a police sergeant named Smolík once stopped Píša on the street and, "with an ironic smile," told the editor that one of his men had a Jewish wife. The officer added, "You should point that out!" Upon Píša's query, Smolík willingly divulged the policeman's name, which was printed in *Aryan Struggle* along with the recommendation that the intermarried family be given forced labor.[102] Thanks to his job Sergeant Smolík had ample opportunity to report this information directly to the Gestapo, but he chose instead to go to the editor, a fellow Czech. In another instance, Píša received a denunciatory letter that began with the disclaimer, "You don't have to publicize this; it is probably enough only for your orientation." The informant then proceeded to denounce the numerous "Aryans" who attended the funeral of the Jewess Eisnerová. In addition to calling for a ban on such activities, the anonymous anti-Semite reported that Jews were still riding bicycles in his town.[103]

Like Sergeant Smolík and the anonymous letter writer, most Czechs probably hesitated to speak to a German official, not to mention the Gestapo. After all, Czechs universally viewed the occupation authorities as illegitimate. Not only would such contact make the instigator a pariah among fellow Czechs, the act itself was risky. Contact with the Gestapo might open oneself to interrogation. Conversation or correspondence with Píša, by contrast, could be rationalized as information passed on to another Czech, who then bore responsibility for what ensued. One letter writer unwittingly revealed his discomfort with the idea of denunciation. He wrote Píša, "To begin with let me note that I

---

[101] Several letters in Píša's dossier clearly demonstrate that he was given the opportunity, and even encouraged, to resign. In November 1940, the editor-in-chief of *Aryan Struggle* accused Píša of being "choleric" and "spoiled like a little child" and asked him to "be a man, not an ever whimpering old maid." One month later the same editor asked Píša whether he wished to continue to work for the tabloid or whether a replacement should be sought. Letters from Protižidovská liga to V. Píša (11 September 1940, 23 September 1940, 28 November 1940, 9 December 1940, 20 January 1941), SOA-Prague, f. MLS-KH, Ls 646/46.

[102] Vyšetřující hlídka četnické stanice Čáslav (19 May 1945), interrogation of Píša, SOA-Prague, f. MLS-KH, Ls 646/46, 7–8.

[103] Letter no. 35, SOA-Prague, f. MLS-KH, Ls 646/46, 50.

am not and do not want to be an informant." Despite this disclaimer, the author quickly descended into a demented rant against one particular "Jew-lover."[104] The critical link that Píša provided between Czech anti-Semites and the German authorities is strikingly demonstrated by the fact that all but two of the seventy denunciatory letters in Píša's case file were written in Czech.[105] After the war an official of the Čáslav investigative commission summed up *Aryan Struggle*'s nefarious contribution to the Holocaust and Nazi repression:

The fact is that without those denunciations, Píša would have had no material for his newspaper and the Gestapo would have learned nothing about the private life of the Czech population. . . .

Under certain circumstances it is possible consequently to characterize this sort of denunciation . . . as anonymous denunciation carried out by Reich authorities via the public press.[106]

In short, Píša "domesticated" the act of denunciation and thereby enabled Czech anti-Semites to communicate indirectly with the German police. Thanks to *Aryan Struggle*, the occupation authorities overcame the inherent reluctance of potential denouncers to interact with a foreign and illegitimate regime.

THE *ARYAN STRUGGLE* COMES TO AN END

As early as February 1941, when Nazi victory in Europe seemed assured and the Germans' grip on the Protectorate was unchallenged, *Aryan Struggle*'s editors still betrayed a touch of embattled insecurity: "We warn anyone who threatens those who read our paper, just as we warn those who announce a boycott of stores which sell our paper."[107] By March 1945 anger against the anti-Semitic tabloid and confidence in the Nazis' imminent defeat had reached the point where *Aryan Struggle*'s editors were subjected to some of their own medicine. In response to an anonymous letter that threatened the tabloid with unspecified retaliation, the paper sophomorically accused the letter writer of wearing

[104] Letter no. 58, SOA-Prague, f. MLS-KH, Ls 646/46, 50.
[105] Letters nos. 1–70, SOA-Prague, f. MLS-KH, Ls 646/46, 50.
[106] Dr. Blahota, Investigative Commission ONV Čáslav (7 August 1945), SOA-Prague, f. MLS-KH, Ls 646/46, 118.
[107] *Árijský boj* II:7 (22 February 1941), 6, SOA-Prague, f. MLS-KH, Ls 646/46.

the skirt in his family.[108] Despite the bravado of the attack on Brasillach in the very same issue, the men behind *Aryan Struggle* could not have doubted what fate awaited them at the end of the war.

On 1 May 1945 Václav Píša sat down to write a personal testament. He noted, "I burned many documents so as not to hurt certain individuals. Today I regret this because many of the same have now become hostile to me." The editor named fifteen persons, including a priest, who had supplied him with information and had requested that he denounce specific individuals in *Aryan Struggle*. Píša revealed, "In Čáslav there were many who gave me material against Jews and Aryan persons and quite often they were angered that I was not radical enough." In an amendment to the testament, written on 4 May, he damned those "'secret' friends of the new order [who now] would happily... break a cane over me." The next day Píša wrote a second amendment and named three more authors of defamatory articles.[109] Then he fled Čáslav. When he returned on 9 May 1945 he was arrested.

Over the next weeks Píša continued to be a "go-between," only this time in reverse. Anyone who could be linked to him, it seems, fell under suspicion. On 8 May 1945 local authorities arrested five individuals with ties to the former editor, including his wife, Pavla.[110] The others were Antonín Kubricht, described in a prison report as a "friend of Píša and several informers"; Rudolf Bok, another "friend of Píša"; František Červený, suspected of "probable collaboration with Píša"; and Jindřich Levý, who had "former connections to Píša and Germans." The next day Pavla Gottfriedová was arrested on the grounds that she was the girlfriend of Kubricht, a "friend of Píša." At least two others, Jan Pauliš and Karel Rochovanský, who had contributed to *Aryan Struggle*, found themselves in the Čáslav jail by the end of August.[111] Under interrogation Píša added more names: Otto Havlíček from Dolní Královice; a German shoemaker and his wife; A. Štehlík, who sent reports about Jews and

[108] "Středočeská oblast," *Árijský boj* VI:10 (10 March 1945), SOA-Prague, f. MLS-KH, Ls 646/46.
[109] Píša's testament and amendments, SOA-Prague, f. MLS-KH, Ls 646/46, 71–74.
[110] Pavla Píšová committed suicide soon after she was released from jail. Letters from Pavla Píšová (18 May 1945), SOA-Prague, f. MLS-KH, Ls 646/46, 3.
[111] "Seznam osob zajištěných... ve věznici okresního soudu v Čáslavi ve věci týkající se kolaborantů a zrádců," Státní okresní archiv Kutná Hora (SOkA-KH), f. ONV-Čáslav, k. 75.

"Jew-lovers;" a newsdealer, an electrician; and several others.[112] Working through the denunciatory letters one by one, interrogators pressed the editor to remember the authors' names, but despite his apparent willingness to comply, he was often stumped.[113] Investigators sent some of the anonymous letters to various national committees in the hope that local authorities could divine their provenance.[114]

Čáslav radio soon opened another front in the hunt for *Aryan Struggle* denouncers. A public broadcast appealed for anyone wronged by Píša to personally report to the District Court on the morning of 11 June 1945. Victims were instructed to bring a brief description of their case and copies of any relevant articles from *Aryan Struggle*. One can only imagine the scene that morning as the former editor's victims congregated in the hope of justice being done. A seventy-one-year-old man, who had been exposed in the tabloid for having social relations with Jews, revealed that his wife had suffered a heart attack after reading the issue and died soon afterward.[115] Another man, whose wife *Aryan Struggle* had accused of "massaging lazy Jewish bodies," reported that the Gestapo had searched their home and that they had been economically ruined when people subsequently avoided them. Others who came forward described the consequences of being cited in the tabloid: harassment by neighbors, questioning by bosses, searches, beatings, and detention by the Gestapo. The prosecutors received numerous inquiries about the origin of denunciations that had been printed in *Aryan Struggle*. Requests for information came from as far as Prague, Český Brod, and Ústí nad Labem.[116]

It did not take long for the Kutná Hora People's Court to punish *Aryan Struggle* correspondents. Along with his many other crimes, the court's first defendant, Karel Svoboda, also wrote denunciatory letters to the tabloid. After his execution, the second in line was Rudolf Štěnička, a local newsdealer and regular contributor to *Aryan Struggle*. In addition to his letters, in which he "attacked primarily Jews and Jewish *Mischlinge*," he was the local leader of the fascist Banner movement, an

---

[112] Výš. čet. a pol. hlídka Čáslav (24 May 1945), interrogation of Píša, SOA-Prague, f. MLS-KH, Ls 646/46, 12.
[113] Výslech obviněného, Okresní soud v Čáslavi (15 June 1945), SOA-Prague, f. MLS-KH, Ls 646/46, 47–49.
[114] SOA-Prague, f. MLS-KH, Ls 646/46, 19–28.
[115] SOA-Prague, f. MLS-KH, Ls 646/46, 29–34.
[116] SOA-Prague, f. MLS-KH, Ls 646/46, nos. 2, 60, 103, 104, 116, 163–65, 413.

enthusiastic fundraiser for the German Army's Winterhilfe program, and an informant for the Gestapo and SD. Convicted on four counts of treason, propagation of Nazism, terrorization, and denunciation, Štěnička was sentenced to imprisonment, the loss of all his property, and the termination of his civic rights in perpetuity.[117] One month later the court sentenced Jan Pauliš to six years in prison, the loss of half his property, and abrogation of his civic rights for the period of his imprisonment. Against the stipulations of the retribution laws, the judges recognized as mitigating circumstances that the defendant admitted to his crimes, had an "innocent family," and – despite his virulent anti-Semitism and fervent praise for the deportation of Jews – had "integrity."[118]

The parade of *Aryan Struggle* defendants before the Kutná Hora People's Court continued. Antonín Kubricht was an agent of the SD who helped Píša prepare a list of reliable and suspect Czechs. One of his denunciations resulted in the victim's death, a consequence that in turn led to Kubricht's execution on 22 March 1946. Denunciation was apparently a family vocation: In the same trial his wife was sentenced to a six-year prison term, the loss of all her property, and the abrogation of her civic rights for a decade.[119] Another husband-and-wife team, Otto and Ludmilla Havlíček, earned twelve and five years, respectively, for providing Píša with defamatory information. The verdict declared that Otto "attacked in a coarse and racist manner Jews . . . and individuals who helped Jews."[120] In January 1946 J. Ginzel and M. Trojanová received thirteen and ten years' imprisonment, respectively, for their contributions to *Aryan Struggle*.[121] The Kutná Hora People's Court also sentenced Julie Mušková, who had submitted many articles praising anti-Jewish sanctions and denounced "interracial" fraternization, to ten years' imprisonment for her "literary" activities. A local newspaper concluded, "Kutná Hora thus rid itself of another propagandizer of German 'culture.'"[122] In all, the Kutná Hora People's Court and regular Regional Court together punished more than twenty

---

[117] R. Štěnička verdict (25 September 1945), SOA-Prague, f. MLS-KH, Ls 2/45.

[118] J. Pauliš verdict (30 October 1945), SOA-Prague, f. MLS-KH, Ls 16/45.

[119] A. Kubricht and O. Kubrichtová verdict (22 March 1946), SOA-Prague, f. MLS-KH, Ls 87/46.

[120] O. Havlíček and L. Havlíčková verdict (31 May 1946), SOA-Prague, f. MLS-KH, Ls 224/46; V. Píša verdict (26 April 1947), SOA-Prague, f. MLS-KH, Ls 646/46, 430.

[121] *Kutnohorský kraj* II:2 (11 January 1946), 1.

[122] *Kutnohorský kraj* II:7 (15 February 1946), 2.

defendants associated with *Aryan Struggle*.[123] Meanwhile, on 26 March 1947 the Prague National Court convicted and executed Píša's boss, Editor-in-Chief Rudolf Novák.[124]

Much to Píša's distress, one of his former associates escaped punishment altogether. In his first testament Píša named Václav Hluchý as a chief co-conspirator who had repeatedly encouraged and praised the editor's activities. When the police did not immediately act on the tip, Píša implored his interrogators, "once again I plead that I be also allowed to thoroughly demask...Hluchý. [He] was the *spiritus rector* of everything."[125] On 13 September 1945 the authorities finally arrested Hluchý and indicted him for having been an associate of Píša, an informant for the Gestapo, and an active member of the Czech Association for Collaboration with Germans.[126] Hluchý also faced charges of having publicly declared his belief in Germany's ultimate victory and of having denounced a victim who subsequently perished in Nazi detention. In his defense, however, twenty-six witnesses, including resistance leader General Alois Liška, testified that during the war Hluchý had been the district head of the military underground. Apparently he had been a double agent assigned by the resistance to keep tabs on "denouncers and unreliable persons." Thanks to his ties to Píša, Hluchý had allegedly been able to warn many potential victims and thereby prevent greater harm. Thanks to witness testimony, the Kutná Hora People's Court acquitted him on all charges.[127] Despite this exoneration, Hluchý's

---

[123] See also V. Píša verdict, 427; E. Baziv verdict (12 December 1946), SOA-Prague, f. MLS-KH, Ls 597/46; Monthly summary reports, SÚA, f. MS (org), k. 1930–33, f. MS (Z.tr.), k. 2076–77.

[124] R. Novák verdict (26 March 1947), SÚA, f. NS, TNs 6/47, 1.

[125] Výslech obviněného, Okresní soud v Čáslavi (4 June 1945), SOA-Prague, f. MLS-KH, Ls 646/46, 15; commentary on indictment (9 March 1947), SOA-Prague, f. MLS-KH, Ls 646/46, 272; interrogation of Pisa (13 August 1945), SOA-Prague, f. MLS-KH, Ls 646/46, 119.

[126] Appointed by Hácha in the summer of 1939, the Czech Association for Collaboration with Germans [Český svaz pro spolupráci s Němci (ČSSN)] ostensibly aimed to improve relations between Czechs and Germans and to ensure that the two nation's interests and goals coincided. Although the group's various chapters organized some events, including free German conversational circles, a visit of the Berlin chamber orchestra, and a wide range of lectures, it failed to garner the interest of the Nazis or Czechs. In September 1942 the Association's leaders disbanded the ČSSN, leaving behind a considerable debt. Interrogation of Walter Jacobi, SD Chief Prague, AMV 325–166–3, 36; "ČSSN," Příloha 9, k č.j. Z/II-31366/45, SOA-Praha, MLS-Praha, Pres. 1.

[127] Verdict, Ls 646/46, 434–37.

postwar conduct raises serious questions about his innocence. Immediately after Píša's arrest, Hluchý personally searched the editor's house and likely vetted his files before turning them over to the police.[128] Over the next two years Hluchý actively inserted himself into the investigation of Píša and made numerous inquiries about the progress of the case.[129] Hluchý may well have acted out of fear that his underground activity could be unfairly used against him. Nonetheless, his ambiguous role in the otherwise cut-and-dried Píša case illustrates the difficulties the courts faced in sorting out collaboration and resistance in the Protectorate.

Finally, in April 1947, Píša went on trial. His case had been held up, in all likelihood, so that he could testify against all those who helped him to terrorize the region for the duration of the war. The evidence against Píša was overwhelming. In addition to his partial confession and dozens of inflammatory articles from *Aryan Struggle* and other newspapers, fifty witnesses testified against him. There was no shortage of accusations to level against Píša. He was charged with twelve counts of denunciation resulting in fines, imprisonment, and the death of his victims. In one of the more inhuman episodes, Píša admitted that he had complained to the police that Gentiles were bidding farewell to Jews as they were being deported from the Čáslav train station.[130] He was also indicted for the denunciation of a philatelist club member whose arrest resulted in the detainment of fourteen others, five of whom subsequently perished. Finally, Píša was accused of "propagating and supporting Nazism and fascism" for his service as Gestapo agent "Vincent," for his public expression of joy at Franklin Delano Roosevelt's death, and for his membership in the Czech Association for Collaboration with Germans, the Anti-Jewish League, and the League against Bolshevism. Píša could hardly have expected more lenient treatment than his fellow anti-Semites received, but the editor maintained a vigorous defense and insisted on his innocence till the very end.

---

[128] Deposition of Rudolf Bok (2 April 1947), SOA-Prague, f. MLS-KH, Ls 646/46, 309; deposition of SNB guard František Rosenthal (4 April 1947), SOA-Prague, f. MLS-KH, Ls 646/46, 311; SOA-Prague, f. MLS-KH, Ls 646/46, 442.

[129] Demonstrating the bad blood between the two men, Hluchý taunted Píša by maliciously revealing to the jailed editor that his wife Pavla had committed suicide more than six months before. Verdict, SOA-Prague, f. MLS-KH, Ls 646/46, 399; Letters from Pavla Píšová (18 May 1945), SOA-Prague, f. MLS-KH, Ls 646/46, 3.

[130] V. Píša verdict (26 April 1947), SOA-Prague, f. MLS-KH, Ls 646/46, 429.

Ultimately, he was acquitted on two counts of denunciation but sentenced to death for the others. On 26 April 1947 the Kutná Hora People's Court executed Václav Píša by hanging.[131]

Critics of retribution, in postwar Czechoslovakia and elsewhere, have focused on the political nature of prosecution and dismissed trials as mere victors' justice, a means of legitimating the present, not coming to terms with the past. Hejl wrote, "Retribution did not strive for justice; its goal was retaliation, in other words, revenge."[132] Tigrid summarized the entire process as "conspicuously political justice, . . . the punishment of those who lost by the hand of the war's victors."[133] The People's Courts, and especially the National Court, do offer numerous examples of political machinations and partisan revenge. The trials of Václav Píša and his *Aryan Struggle* contributors, however, illustrate another, equally significant, side to retribution. The anti-Semites punished in Kutná Hora were part of a wider, albeit incomplete, reckoning with the perpetrators of the Holocaust in Bohemia and Moravia. Postwar Czech courts tried hundreds, perhaps thousands, of Gestapo officers, SS men, and other war criminals, including a considerable number of guards who had served at concentration camps in the Protectorate, Sudetenland, and abroad.[134] Most significantly, the Litoměřice People's Court executed both the commandant of the Theresienstadt Ghetto, Karl Rahm, and his counterpart from the town's Small Fortress prison, Heinrich Jöckel.[135] Amid condemnations of political intrigue and naked vengeance, it should not be forgotten that Czech People's Courts exacted a measure of justice for the Nazis' crimes, including their genocide of the Jews.

THE CURE BECOMES A DISEASE

Considering the terror that *Aryan Struggle* correspondents and other denouncers had wrought in the Protectorate during the six long years

[131] V. Píša verdict (26 April 1947), SOA-Prague, f. MLS-KH, Ls 646/46, 1.
[132] Vilém Hejl, *Zpráva o organizovaném násilí* (Prague: Univerzum, 1990), 21–23.
[133] Pavel Tigrid, *Kapesní průvodce inteligentní ženy po vlastním osudu* (Toronto: Sixty-Eight Publishers, 1988), 388.
[134] See, for example, Jiřík's detailed analysis of the Cheb court's prosecution of concentration camp guards. Jiřík, *Nedaleko od Norimberku*, 309–42.
[135] "Soud velitele terezínského ghetta," *Svobodné slovo* (24 April 1947); "Rozsudek nad býv. velitelem terezínského ghetta," *Lidová demokracie* (1 May 1947), SÚA, f. MZV-VA II, k. 217.

of Nazi rule, it is hardly surprising that victims jumped at the opportunity to turn in their former tormentors. In contrast to the occupation period, after liberation Czechs faced no inhibition in communicating directly with authorities they universally viewed as legitimate. In other words, there was no longer any need to domesticate denunciation. Every action, it seemed, had its equivalent reaction: Wartime denunciations led directly to postwar denunciations. For example on 25 May 1945 Rudolf Mařík got his revenge against his wife, Pavla, who had turned him in to the Gestapo. He informed the local investigative commission, "I request that my wife be taken into custody, rigorously interrogated, and punished."[136] Although actual victims likely needed no encouragement, the authorities vigorously spurred the public to denounce collaborators. One national committee even promised to punish anyone who protected an enemy of the nation, even if he or she was a family member. The pronouncement warned, "every late denunciation will be severely punished."[137]

As one denunciation led to another, the cycle of accusations began to spiral out of control. In his memoirs Václav Černý recalled the "avalanche of denunciations and slander, incriminations, and dirty tricks, [which] in ninety percent [of cases] had to do with the settling of personal, antipathetic accounts; whosoever undercut whomever else ... with the accusation of collaboration with the Germans, which the other returned to him in a similar statement."[138] Locksmith Karel Košík, for example, denounced his neighbor to the police immediately after the war, but the neighbor turned the tables by denouncing Košík as well. Called on to investigate, an Interior Ministry official disparagingly summed up the case as merely "a matter of mutual incrimination."[139] In a similar case, a landlord and his lessee turned in one other during the occupation, one for listening to foreign radio, the other for sabotage.

---

[136] For his part, Josef Kuchta submitted a request for Mařík's arrest as well. See the earlier discussion in this chapter for more details on the case. P. Maříková verdict, SOA-Litoměřice, f. MLS-Litoměřice, Lsp 19/46.

[137] Miroslav Kružík, "Spisy tzv. Malého dekretu v bývalých okresech Nové Město na Moravě a Velké Meziříčí," in Mečislav Borák, ed., *Retribuce v ČSR a národní podoby antisemitismu: Židovská problematika a antisemitismus ve spisech mimořádných lidových soudů a trestních komisí ONV v letech 1945–1948* (Prague: Ústav pro soudobé dějiny, 2002), 135–36.

[138] Václav Černý, *Paměti*, 3 vols. (Brno: Atlantis, 1992–1994), III:35.

[139] Letter from K. Košík to the KPR (18 February 1947), KPR no. R-10802/47, Archiv Kanceláře prezidenta republiky (AKPR), s. D-11377 (prominut), k. 262, B.

The renter greeted the Red Army by denouncing his nemesis, but before revolutionary justice could be enacted, the landlord denounced the lessee, who eventually received a five-year sentence from a Czech People's Court.[140]

Although the country had been liberated and the nightmare of foreign occupation finally brought to a welcome close, the new atmosphere eerily resembled the old. In the National Socialist weekly, *Masaryk's People* [*Masarykův lid*], a Czech journalist lamented,

Before, someone hurled words at you: praised the assassination, listens to foreign radio, insults the Fuehrer – and off you went. To a concentration camp or to death. Today, someone else hurls words at you: asocial, Germanophile; in some places a simple determination suffices: not a member of our party. You'll lose your job; they'll hand you over to the appropriate authorities; you'll sit 18 months in jail, and in the end it will be discovered that it's not true.[141]

As People's Courts revealed more and more cases based merely on malicious accusations, the public grew disillusioned with retribution. One letter to the country's president remarked, "It is interesting that the less property that was expropriated, the fewer the... denunciations, and nothing is made up [about] those who already have nothing and live in rented lodgings."[142] A parliamentary representative commented, "The statistics from all the investigative commissions and People's Courts speak clearly about what a high percentage of denunciations consist only of personal vengefulness and malice without objective basis. And in such cases we must have the courage to shout down these human hyenas, who feed on the suffering of their innocent neighbors."[143] Judging by the numbers of cases dismissed and acquitted, Vojta Beneš estimated that 240,000 Czechs had been falsely accused by their fellow citizens after the war.[144] One journalist justifiably argued that the greatest flaw in Paragraph Eleven turned out to be its failure to punish false denunciation.[145] In fact, the country's leaders rarely paid even lip service to

---

[140] Borák, *Spravedlnost podle dekretu*, 231.
[141] Jiří Bílý, "O udavačství jako nemoci doby," *Masarykův lid* XVI:4 (February 1947), 3–4.
[142] Letter of "České ženy ze smíšených manželství" to KPR (received 16 August 1946), SÚA, f. ÚPV-běž., k. 1032, sign. 1364/2.
[143] Hobza, PNS, thirty-fourth meeting, 38.
[144] Tigrid, *Kapesní průvodce*, 374.
[145] Bedřich Bobek, "Konec retribuce," *Obzory* III:18 (3 May 1947), 233.

the need to dissuade individuals from turning in others for fabricated crimes.

To the contrary, the Communist Party took the lead in encouraging new waves of denunciation. In a column titled "The Readers' Voices," *Rudé právo* printed letters to the editor, many of which bore a disturbing similarity to those previously featured in *Aryan Struggle*. Whereas the latter devoted an entire page to accusatory contributions, the former only featured a few letters daily, but the intent was very much the same: to stigmatize specific individuals and bring them to the attention of the police, while at the same time dissuading countless others from committing similar offenses. One contributor to The Readers' Voices expressed his anger that the Písek court had not yet punished four notorious collaborators. Another reported that his town's bank still employed a man who had "provocatively" donated a Czechoslovak military uniform to the German war effort and had even sent his two sons to a German high school. A third declared his outrage that a Russian émigré had been released from prison and subsequently disappeared. The letter demanded, "Who released this Nazi from custody? Who intervened on his behalf? Who wrote a character reference for him? Name these accomplices and pillory them!"[146]

The most common theme of the letters – themselves merely representative examples of numerous denunciations received every day by *Rudé právo*[147] – was the familiar outrage at interethnic fraternization. Where contributors to *Aryan Struggle* exposed Gentiles who associated with Jews, letters in *Rudé právo* decried Czechs who fraternized with Germans. V.R. from Vilštejn complained that in the Cheb area German women had attended many dances. Apparently, this was common behavior. V.C. from Těšice wrote that there had been three dances during Lent and that Germans had attended them all. At two firemen's balls, the Germans had even received refreshments and stayed till four in the morning. F.Z. from Seletice complained that Mr. Procházka had brought a German woman – who had been assigned to him for work – to a dance. As during the war, even children were not immune from the "disease" of denunciation. A girl from Prague informed the Communist daily's

[146] *Rudé právo* (23 February 1946), 3; (15 March 1946), 5; (19 February 1946), 5.
[147] The newspaper noted that it received many letters daily, some of which were anonymous. These, it claimed, were thrown immediately into the trash. *Rudé právo* (6 March 1946), 3.

readers that in the city's Letná Park she had run into a young Czech mother teaching her child to count in German. The letters commonly complained that, so soon after the occupation ended, the Czechs had allegedly forgotten the horrors perpetrated by the German people.[148]

During the winter of 1946–1947 the Communist Party turned its attention to the black market. In addition to calling for new sanctions, *Rudé právo* told its readers to report all profiteers. In an attempt to overcome an apparent distaste among some for turning in fellow citizens, the daily explained, "It's not denunciation. It's a patriotic and social act!" The same issue revealed that the campaign had already yielded results: 81 persons had been arrested in Moravia and another 257 warrants were outstanding. Tons of goods – from pork, lard, and wine to cigarettes, cash, and even cars – had been seized.[149] The antiprofiteer campaign offered the public a very broad channel into which it could fit its personal disputes and thereby "privatize the public realm" once more. Another round of denunciations ensued – a disturbing preview of what Communist victory would bring.

CONCLUSION

The Nazis fomented a culture of denunciation that postwar retribution inadvertently perpetuated. In particular, the Czechoslovak government's failure to punish false denunciation enabled retribution to be appropriated by ordinary citizens as a means to carry out vendettas. The wave of baseless accusations after the war arguably retarded society's recovery from the occupation and thus facilitated the consolidation of a totalitarian regime after 1948. All was not darkness, however; the "disease" of denunciation did not spread entirely unchecked, in part thanks to the retribution courts themselves. The increasing frequency of dismissals and acquittals progressively weakened the link between denunciation and detention, such that the former did not necessarily lead to the latter. As postwar denouncers increasingly disavowed their testimony on the stand, they undermined the efficacy of denunciation as a means to "privatize the public realm." Faced with government inaction, victims of postwar denunciations, moreover, sought succor in laws against

---

[148] *Rudé právo* (16 February, 27 February, 9 March 1946), 3.
[149] "SNB stupňuje boj proti šmelině" and "Na Moravě zatčeno...," *Rudé právo* (9 January 1947), 1.

defamation and slander.[150] Finally, the postwar regime greatly curtailed the opportunity to denounce when, in May 1947, it brought Czech retribution to a close. Thereafter, at least until the Communist coup d'état, the charge of collaboration could no longer be brandished so effectively to rid oneself of enemies and rivals.

[150] "Žaloby kolaborantů a zrádců," *Rudé právo* (3 March 1946), 3.

5

OFFENSES AGAINST
NATIONAL HONOR

On the eve of the Czechoslovak National Assembly's 28 October 1945 inaugural meeting, the regime worked furiously to put the final touches on the country's postwar revolutionary transformation. In the span of one week President Beneš signed more than forty decrees. Some were procedural, governing the new parliament and its wages; others dealt with cultural issues, for example, regulating the Czechoslovak Philharmonic Orchestra. Many, however, were significant pieces of legislation that merited serious debate. Preempting parliamentary oversight, the government approved decrees nationalizing mines, investment banks, private insurance firms, substantial industrial concerns, sugar and liquor factories, and large producers of chocolate, lard, and beer. Other last-minute decrees confiscated "enemy property," created a citizens' militia, and instituted forced-labor battalions for convicted collaborators.[1] Amid this wave of decrees, at the eleventh hour the government expanded the scope and radically altered the character of postwar retribution. When the new parliamentary deputies first assembled, they trumpeted the return of democratic rule. "Not until the next day," renowned journalist Ferdinand Peroutka commented, "did the deputies learn – from the newspapers – that on 27 October the president had signed the important decree on national honor."[2]

The decree on national honor (no. 138/1945) – dubbed the Small Decree [Malý dekret], in contrast to the earlier Great Decree – was extraordinarily brief and exceptionally vague. The measure granted Czech

---

[1] *Sbírka dekretů presidenta republiky: Souhrn všech dekretů, jež byly vydány* (Brno, Czechoslovakia: Zemského výkonného výboru čs. strany národně socialistické [Melantrich], c. 1945), 131–237.

[2] Ferdinand Peroutka, "A přece ...," *Svobodné noviny* (11 November 1945), 1.

national committees – administrative bodies whose members were appointed according to political affiliation – powers ordinarily reserved for courts led by trained judges. The creation of a new type of retribution tribunal, six months after the war ended, prolonged and intensified the atmosphere of legal uncertainty that had plagued the country for the previous seven years. Further sanctions, in particular disenfranchisement and the denial of "certificates of national reliability," only added to the widespread sense of insecurity. In the end, the Small Decree resulted in thoroughly predictable abuses and injustices. Nonetheless, like the People's Courts, the honor commissions ultimately stopped short of what the Communists and other proponents of harsh retribution had expected from this radical expansion of retribution.

THE SMALL DECREE

As the summer of 1945 drew to a close, the People's Courts began to approach the massive caseload that awaited them. By the end of August five courts had tried their first cases; another ten commenced operations in September.[3] With only a few months left until the Great Decree was originally set to expire, it soon became clear that there was not enough time to prosecute all of the anticipated cases. The mass arrests of spring 1945 had packed the country's jails and prisons. Police, vigilantes, paramilitary groups, and national committees had detained suspects en masse, barely pausing to determine their guilt or even record the charges against them. At the end of summer 1945 the judicial authorities still did not know the cause of arrest for a significant portion of prisoners. When prosecutors finally reviewed the cases, they authorized the dismissal of proceedings against thousands of individuals who had been arrested under false pretenses. Frequently, prosecutors discovered that a suspect's alleged offense was even not a crime according to the Great Decree.

Releases were not greeted with equanimity. In July workers at the Škoda factory in Hradec Králové went on strike to protest the discharge of alleged collaborators from jail.[4] When the authorities in Kralupy

---

[3] Seven held their first trials in October, one in November, and one (Cheb) the next year. "Přehled činnosti veřejných žalobců u mimořádných lidových soudů," Státní ústřední archiv (SÚA), Prague, f. MS, k. 1929.

[4] Katalog "Zápisů předsednictva ONV Hradec Králové," Státní okresní archiv (SOkA) Pardubice, 63.

nad Vltavou decided to release the owner of a local factory because they had serious doubts about his guilt, the local Communist Party secretary threatened that he could not be responsible for the public's reaction. He warned that the people might capture the factory owner and beat him to death. The specter of popular vengeance did the trick – "for security reasons" the investigative commission canceled its discharge order.[5] Depending on how one looked at the problem, either innocent people had been unlawfully arrested or the Great Decree had failed to criminalize all treacherous acts. The Kladno Communist secretariat took the latter view and demanded a new statute to permit national committees to punish "collaborationist, asocial, and speculative elements" that could not otherwise be brought before the People's Courts.[6]

In September 1945 Klement Gottwald called on his colleagues in the government to broaden the scope of the Great Decree and toughen its penalties. The Justice Minister, Jaroslav Stránský, countered that no additional laws were necessary.[7] After more than a month of deadlock, on 24 October the government held a heated debate about retribution and authorized an interministerial commission to draft a new decree.[8] The very next morning the Interior Minister, Václav Nosek, announced that the commission had drafted guidelines for the punishment of "offenses against national honor." Just in case anyone objected, he commented, "It's a matter of the general peace." Surprisingly, despite his earlier reservations, Stránský agreed with the proposal; he only stressed that the People's Courts must have prior jurisdiction.[9] The Great Decree, from inception to promulgation, had taken more than three years to draft; the Small Decree was apparently completed in a single evening and approved the very next day. In the end, a contemporary article explained, the law was created to match the criminal: "The Decree for the protection of national honor punishes . . . the considerable number

---

5 MS no. 26122/45-III/4 (15 September 1945), SÚA, f. MS (Org), k. 1927.
6 "Trestat i provinilce nepatřící lidovým soudům," *Lidová správa* I:2 (21 October 1945), 6.
7 First government, fifty-fourth meeting (14 September 1945), 21–3, SÚA, f. 100/24 (KG), sign. 1494, sv. 138.
8 First goverment, ninety-fourth meeting (24 October 1945), 4–12, SÚA, f. 100/24 (KG), sign. 1494, sv. 138.
9 First government, ninety-sixth meeting (25 October 1945), 1, SÚA, f. 100/24 (KG), sign. 1494, sv. 138.

of those who were detained and cannot be tried before a People's Court according to the [Great] Decree."[10]

The Small Decree lived up to its moniker. Whereas the Great Decree had thirty-four paragraphs and the National Court Decree an additional nineteen, the Small Decree had a mere four (Appendix 3). Of these, the first section of Paragraph One established both the crime and the punishment:

Whoever, during the period of heightened danger to the republic..., undermined public morale by unbecoming behavior insulting to the national sentiments of the Czech or Slovak people, will be punished – if the act is not a criminal offense punishable by the courts – by District National Committees with up to one year in prison, a fine of up to 1,000,000 Czechoslovak crowns, or public censure, or with two or three of these punishments.[11]

If a defendant was indigent, the national committees could substitute internment in lieu of a fine. The time a defendant spent in jail prior to his or her conviction was to be deducted from the sentence. The measure also established a statute of limitations of six months from the commission of an "offense against national honor" or from the promulgation of the decree.[12] In other words, by 27 April 1946 every Czech would know if he or she faced punishment for "unbecoming behavior." The decree did not define the terms "public morale" or "insulting"; the phrase "offense against national honor" appeared only in its title. People's Party deputy Helena Koželuhová pointedly remarked, "If someone can figure out from this decree what national sentiment is, then he's a magician."[13] This vagueness was qualified by the statement that subsequent "directives issued on this matter by the Interior Ministry are binding on the national committees."

In light of Stránský's initially strong opposition to revisions to the Great Decree, his later acceptance of the Small Decree seems surprising. Communist pressure may have cowed the Justice Minister and his allies into submission. After all, they faced daily reports of supposed public

---

[10] "Ochrana národní cti," *Svobodné noviny* (4 November 1945), 1.

[11] Although it speaks of the "Czech and Slovak people," the Small Decree was only applied in the provinces of Bohemia, Moravia, and Silesia. *Sbírka dekretů*, Decree no. 138/45, 236.

[12] This was a considerable reduction of the three-year period originally proposed by the Interior Ministry. Karel Jech and Karel Kaplan, eds., *Dekrety prezidenta republiky, 1940–1945: Dokumenty* (Brno: Ústav pro soudobé dějiny, 1995), doc. 43.2, I:939–43.

[13] Helena Koželuhová, "Naše národní čest," *Obzory* I:15 (15 December 1945), 229.

rage like that expressed by the workers in Hradec Králové and Kralupy. More likely, however, Stránský and his allies accepted the Small Decree (no. 138/1945) as a quid pro quo: the government simultaneously approved Decree no. 137, which mandated that within thirty days of its promulgation all prisoners in the country either had to be arraigned or released. The cabinet thus finally moved to "reestablish the guarantee of personal freedom and [end] the chaos." According to Decree no. 137, anyone arrested had to be charged within eight days – a quadrupling of the interwar standard of forty-eight hours, but still a great improvement on the contemporary norm of several months. While promising a return to normalcy, Decree no. 137 also ensured that no one would be held accountable for the "excesses" of the previous spring and summer: All arrests and detentions prior to the decree's promulgation were declared legal. No individual, no matter how clearly he or she had been wronged, could sue for unlawful deprivation of personal liberty. Ultimately, Stránský and his fellow non-Communists probably did not oppose Decrees no. 137 and 138 because, like their more radical colleagues in the cabinet, they also bore responsibility for the springtime violence and desired the legal means to protect themselves and the state from indemnity claims. The politically moderate Health Minister even argued that it was the government's duty not to leave the problem to the incoming parliament.[14] Together Decrees no. 137 and 138 retroactively established legal grounds for the arbitrary arrests and indefinite detentions of 1945.

The press, which had thus far patriotically applauded the government's every move, unexpectedly and vociferously criticized the Small Decree. Newspaper columnists suggested that the country's retribution mania had become a threat to democracy. In the People's Party daily H. Pánková sarcastically commented that some day the victims of the postwar regime might have to follow the example of the victims of Nazism and form their own organization, the "Union of Prisoners of a Free and Democratic Republic." The Small Decree, she argued, essentially approved the illegitimate activities of "revolutionary" courts and purge commissions.[15] Peroutka ventured that Czechoslovakia's

---

[14] First government, fifty-fouth meeting (14 September 1945), 21–3; ninety-fourth meeting (24 October 1945), 4–12, SÚA, f. 100/24 (KG), sign. 1494, sv. 138; Stanislav Šulc, *Národní výbory: Vývoj, právní základy, poslání, práce* (Brno: ZÁŘ, 1946), 301–302.

[15] H. Pánková, "O cti a bezecti," *Lidová demokracie* (24 November 1945), 1–2.

obsessive hunt for traitors unnecessarily damaged the country's international reputation. Pushing the limits of the permissible, he challenged the authority of the country's leaders to judge wartime collaboration. After all, they were a group of exiles who had spent the war in London and Moscow, free of the day-to-day dilemmas of life under occupation. Most parliamentarians, on the other hand, had experienced Nazi rule and could better judge their fellow citizens.[16] Raising the contentious charge of "victors' justice," Peroutka asked, "Does [the government] assume that it can judge the question of national honor better than the parliament?"[17]

The columnists were especially outraged by the circumvention of parliamentary rule. Peroutka accused the government of treating the deputies like "children" and did not even exempt the president from his criticism. He called on parliament to seize the initiative and pass guidelines for the punishment of "offenses against national honor." In November 1945, when the Interior Ministry issued its own directive and the legislature was again preempted by executive fiat, Peroutka sarcastically suggested that the deputies should create a "special committee for newspaper reading" to keep abreast of important political developments.[18] One opportunity remained to exert the legislature's authority: According to wartime Presidential Decree no. 11/1944, an elected parliament had to ratify the decrees within six months of its inauguration or they would lapse.[19] Although not a single decree had yet to face opposition, columnist Ladislav Gut called on the parliament to stand up and be counted.[20] Gottwald also recognized the matter's great importance: Before the Central Committee the Communist leader declared ratification to be the party's primary task.[21] In the end, the parliament dutifully ratified each and every decree.[22] The interwar tradition of party leaders orchestrating docile

[16] Ferdinand Peroutka, "Parlamentí úvahy," *Svobodné noviny* (8 December 1945), 1.

[17] Ferdinand Peroutka, "A přece...," 1.

[18] Ferdinand Peroutka, "Parlamentí úvahy," 1.

[19] Jech, *Dekrety*, doc. 5, I:121–22.

[20] Ladislav Gut, "Ať promluví sněmovna," *Svobodné slovo* (21 November 1945), 1.

[21] Referát s. Gottwalda, ZÚV-KSČ (18 Dec. 1945), SÚA, f. 1, sv. 1, ar.j. 8, str. 12.

[22] On the floor of the parliament, the People's Party rapporteur noted the controversy over the Small Decree, but only called for the Interior Ministry's instructions to be formally approved by the parliament or, at the very least, officially issued by the government. Despite one deputy's lone call for a thorough review by an elected parliament, on 28 March 1946 the representatives approved the decrees unanimously. Constitutional

backbenchers was not only reestablished, it was strengthened. Over the next two years the parliament did not reject a single piece of government legislation; only once did it force a vote of confidence in a minister.[23]

While the Small Decree undercut parliament's authority, it greatly enhanced the national committees' powers. They already played a critical role in the prosecution of collaborators. The People's Courts were dependent on the national committees' investigative and security commissions, which encouraged and collected denunciations, oversaw the detainment and interrogation of suspects, and decided which cases to forward to prosecutors and which to quash. District national committees were also responsible for choosing the lists of people's judges, which were then approved by the government. After the promulgation of the Small Decree, both Peroutka and Pánková accused the government of handing over a matter as critical as retribution to "political bosses."[24] After all, many national committees had already demonstrated their unwillingness to follow the laws or even obey direct orders. Communist leaders, for their part, encouraged disobedience or, as they saw it, independent initiative. In the introductory article to first issue of *Lidová správa* [*People's Administration*], a magazine published for Communist national committee members, Party General Secretary Rudolf Slánský exhorted cadres to claim the power that was rightfully theirs. He told them to do whatever was necessary, "even if they can't find a paragraph of the old law which would permit it. If they do something good and beneficial, nobody will reproach them for exceeding their authority."[25]

THE NATIONAL HONOR DIRECTIVE

On 26 November 1945 the Interior Ministry issued a directive to govern the punishment of "offenses against national honor." Whereas the Small Decree was brief and vague, the national honor directive was extensive and particular. Even so, confusion and inconsistencies prompted the

---

Law no. 57/1946 reads: "All decrees of the president of the republic are to be deemed from their inception as law." Jech, *Dekrety*, II:974–75, n. 4, 987–88, 992, 1008–1009; Řehulka, PNS 28 (12 February 1946), 12.

[23] Karel Kaplan, *Nekrvavá revoluce* (Prague: Mladá fronta Archiv, 1993), 47–49.

[24] H. Pánková, "O cti a bezecti," 1–2; Ferdinand Peroutka, "A přece...," 1.

[25] R. Slánský, "Lidová správa," *Lidová správa*, I:1 (15 October 1945), 1–2.

publishing of two official guidebooks – one by Jindřich Stach, as the first installment in a series of pamphlets for national committees, the other by Jaroslav Fusek, on behalf of the Interior Ministry – to provide more detail and answer commonly posed questions.[26] According to the directive, each District National Committee was to establish an independent Penal Adjudication Commission [Trestní nalézací komise (TNK)] composed of four members – one for each of the four Czech political parties.[27] Because tie votes (2:2) were ruled as acquittals, the assent of three members was necessary to approve a conviction. A clear continuation of the government's "to the victors belong the spoils" policy, parity was a means to prevent the commissions from becoming a weapon in the political struggle between the legal parties, but it could not protect adherents of political movements that had been suppressed.[28]

Although the directive clearly states that at least one of the four commission members had "to have acquired a doctorate in law or completed all the mandated state exams," Fusek dismissed this requirement in his pamphlet: "It is not a procedural error if one of the commission members is not legally trained."[29] In any case, the commissions did not have to defer to a professional judge nor did they have to suffer any defense lawyers. If honor commission members agreed, the accused could bring counsel to the proceedings, but once there, the lawyer had to remain silent. The defendant could not call character witnesses and could not even view the evidence – it was the commission's responsibility to assemble the case both for and against the accused. The Interior Ministry admonished commission members to be fair and judicious: "Out of official responsibility the penal commission itself ascertains everything that testifies against and in favor of the accused."[30] In short, commission members acted as investigators, prosecutors,

---

[26] Jaroslav Fusek, *Provinění proti národní cti* (Prague: V. Linhart, 1946); Dr. Jindřich Stach, *Provinění proti národní cti* (Brno: ZÁŘ, 1946).

[27] Although the directive did not explicitly spell out that each party should have one member, later Interior Ministry clarification left no doubt about the matter. "Vyjádření odd. I/2 MV (17 Sept. 1946) k dotazu p. ministra ve věci složení trestní nalézací komise u ONV," SÚA, f. MV-NR, k. 2016.

[28] Though not necessarily representative, the penal commission in the town of Rokycany consisted of four men: a Social Democratic lawyer, a Communist vocational teacher, a National Socialist lawyer, and a Populist wood seller. ONV Rokycany (29 Jan. 1946) to MV, SÚA, f. MV-NR, k. 2016.

[29] Fusek, *Provinění*, 23.

[30] Stach, *Provinění*, 19–20.

defense lawyers, and, ultimately, judges. And they did so in closed chambers from which the public was excluded.

The powers of penal commissions immediately raised concerns. Columnists argued that without professional judges there could be no justice.[31] A People's Party representative objected, "Even German pseudo-justice did not deny the accused the possibility to choose his own counsel; we cannot be worse in this regard."[32] In the Czech law journal *Legal Praxis* [*Právní praxe*], the entire directive was critiqued:

The procedure for prosecuting offenses against national honor suffers from significant deficiencies: the restriction on a defense lawyer's rights is one of the most serious. One cannot overlook that the accused has no right to look at court documents; he learns the facts of the case only during oral proceedings; witnesses cannot be prosecuted for false testimony; lay commissions are handed matters that would be a difficult mouthful even for a professional judge. If, however, a professionally trained defense lawyer is to be precluded from intervening on behalf of the accused – most of whom have no legal experience – that innovation is in conflict with the fundamental postulates of criminal procedure.[33]

When the Brno bar association, supported by the Justice Ministry, asked for the right to defend clients before penal commissions, the Interior Ministry denied the request. The ministerial department in charge of honor tribunals noted, "In our opinion, the admittance of defense lawyers would result in undesirable complications and confusion" and could lead to "unrest among the people." A second Interior Ministry department concurred: "From experience it is well-known that defense lawyers can have significant and detrimental influence, particularly on lay judges."[34] Before parliament one Communist deputy went even further: "A lawyer has nothing to look for at investigative and penal commissions.... Every intervention... will be immediately refused. If a lawyer intervenes for an illegal objective, let him be punished."[35]

[31] Ladislav Gut, "At'promluví sněmovna," *Svobodné slovo* (21 November 1945), 1; Stanislav Klíma, "Národní očista," *Lidová demokracie* (8 December 1945), 1–2.
[32] B. Bunža, PNS 34 (27 February 1946), 6.
[33] Zdeněk Sušil, "Obhájce v řízení podle dekretu o národní cti," *Právní praxe* X:2–3, 95–96.
[34] MV no. B-2220-13/6-46-I/2, SÚA, f. MV-NR (B2220), k. 2016.
[35] Škrlantová, PNS 25 (24 January 1946), 14.

The directive did offer something to defendants. First, national honor cases were to be pursued while the defendant was at liberty. Second, unlike the verdicts of People's Courts, honor rulings could be appealed to a higher authority: the Penal Appeal Commissions [Trestní odvolací komise (TOK)] of the Provincial National Committees in Prague and Brno. Moreover, in contrast to the district commissions, trained lawyers staffed the provincial appeals commissions.[36] The provincial assemblies also tended to be more moderate than individual national committees, many of which were firmly in the hands of the Communist Party.[37] Finally, a convicted defendant could seek redress from the country's Supreme Administrative Court, although this secondary appeal could not delay the implementation of a penalty. The Communists' attempt to exempt national honor cases from the Supreme Court's purview was ultimately defeated.[38]

Although the national honor directive permitted appeals, it also authorized penal commissions to try defendants who had been previously exonerated by People's Courts. When a prosecutor dismissed a case because it was unwinnable or when judges acquitted the accused because he or she did not deserve the minimum five-year sentence, the local penal commission could immediately initiate proceedings against him or her and sentence the defendant for the lesser charge of "offending national honor." In other words, the division of Czech retribution into different levels enabled a form of double jeopardy. Communist scholar Karel Bertelmann estimated that penal commissions punished 8,000 individuals previously freed by the People's Courts.[39]

Like the Small Decree, the Interior Ministry's directive did not define "national honor." Instead it outlined nine offenses for the penal commissions to punish. Acts considered to be "unbecoming behavior

---

[36] L. Kopřiva, ZNV Prague (2 May 1946) to MV, SÚA, f. MV-NR (B2220), k. 2016.

[37] Ervín Polák, *Čísla mluví o voličích a o národních výborech* (Prague: Státní tiskárna, 1947), 39.

[38] In practice, during the appeals process penal commissions delayed prison sentences, not fines, which could eventually be repaid. Josef Plzák, "Malý retribuční dekret (Dekret pres. rep. č. 138/1945 Sb.) ve světle judikatury Nejvyššího správního soudu," *Právní prakse* XI (1947/48), 113.

[39] Karel Bertelmann, *Vývoj národních výborů do ústavy 9. května (1945–1948)* (Prague: Československá akademie věd, 1964), 140.

insulting to the national sentiments of the Czech or Slovak people" were specified as follows:

a. The declaration of German or Magyar nationality without losing Czechoslovak citizenship, or conscious support of the "denationalization" efforts of Germans and Magyars.
b. Political collaboration, including participation in a fascist organization, if accompanied by excessive zeal that exceeded the normal responsibilities of a member.
c. Propagation, defense, praise, or support of Nazism, fascism, or anti-Semitism.
d. Approval, support, or defense of enemy speeches or the actions of Nazis, fascists, and Czech or Slovak traitors.
e. Professional collaboration with Germans, Magyars, and Czech or Slovak traitors in excess of normal work requirements.
f. Seeking advancement, awards, rewards, services or any other advantages from German or Magyar offices or officials. Also, offering bribes or other advantages to the occupiers.
g. Abuse of high office, acquired thanks to the occupiers, to gain or ensure personal advantage at the expense of subordinates.
h. Social relations with Germans and Magyars more than necessary. Also, economic relations more than necessary, which tended toward support of the occupiers.
i. Tyrannizing, defaming, or terrorizing Czechs or Slovaks in the service or interest of the occupiers or in an attempt to earn their favor.[40]

Unlike conventional allegiance to a state, "national honor" was not an obligation shared equally by all of Czechoslovakia's people. Aside from two offenses [clauses (g) and (i)], the Interior Ministry directive explained that the Small Decree should be applied "only against Czechoslovak citizens of Czech, Slovak or another Slavic nationality."[41] It would have been absurd, for example, to punish Germans under clause

---

[40] Paraphrased from Stach, *Provinění*, 25–26.
[41] According to the Small Decree, any Slav, not just a Czech, could be punished for an "offense against national honor." Since the Small Decree was applied only in the Czech provinces, the inclusion of the Slovaks did not play a major role. As for other Slavs, in most regions this point was largely immaterial, but in the northeast corner of the Czech provinces, around the area of Těšín, Poles formed a significant minority (for example, see the later discussion of the Zikmund Hess case). Several villages of Croats in southern Moravia were also potentially affected.

(h) for fraternization with other Germans. Germans, moreover, were expected to have maintained their own national honor, not that of the Czechs, and those who remained true to Germany earned their own special retribution: expulsion.

Most of the nine offenses were similar to Great Decree crimes, but of a less serious nature and therefore not likely to be punished by the People's Courts. Essentially, these were political offenses – lesser acts of collaboration with the occupying power, its representatives, and its supporters. In some instances, such as clause (i), "tyrannizing, defaming, or terrorizing Czechs," the directive merely restated crimes first codified in the Great Decree. Here the national honor directive followed through on the Small Decree's promise to establish a lower threshold for punishment. The Interior Ministry directive went far beyond the Great Decree, however, when it outlined two offenses, clauses (a) and (h), that defined collaboration *nationally*, not politically.

Turning briefly to some of the political crimes, under clause (b) the directive (and a later supplement) added more than three dozen groups to the Great Decree's list of fascist organizations. Some, like the National Fascist Community [Národní obec fašistická (NOF)], were homegrown movements predating the occupation. The Nazis and the Protectorate government created others during the war to organize and reward potential supporters. These ranged from anti-Semitic organizations like the Aryan Guard and the Anti-Jewish League, to pro-German interest groups like the "Union of Czech Veterans from the [First] World War, Who Fought by the Side of the German Army." Of special note was the Kuratorium pro výchovu mládeže [Board for Youth Education], a movement designed to educate Czech youth in the benefits of Nazi rule. Membership in these organizations was declared punishable only when accompanied by "especial zeal" exceeding the normal responsibilities of a member. The list also contained five mass organizations from which only functionaries who had "political influence" could be punished. These included the Czech League against Bolshevism, the Czech Association for Collaboration with Germans, and the National Union of Employees.[42] To cite a case tried under clause (b), in July 1946 the Kutná Hora honor commission sentenced Antonín Brož, a "fanatical"

[42] "Příloha ke směrnicím ministra vnitra ze dne 26. listopadu 1945, odst. 10, písm. b)," Fusek, *Provinění*, 28–29.

member of the fascist Banner movement, to ten days in jail and a hefty fine of 10,000 crowns[43] – roughly a year's salary for the average worker.[44] Another Banner member, Václav Novotný, got five months from a penal commission in Prague.[45]

In clause (c) the national honor directive explicitly made the "propagation, defense, praise or support...of anti-Semitism" a punishable offense. The Great Decree had criminalized the propagation or support of "the fascist or Nazi movement," but had only outlawed "racial persecution" when it was employed for personal enrichment (Paragraph Ten). Along with Nazism and fascism, anti-Semitism was now declared an affront to Czech "national honor," punishable by up to one year in prison and a million-crown fine. In the fallout from the Václav Píša trial (described in Chapter 4), the Kutná Hora penal commission investigated at least eight *Aryan Struggle* correspondents and punished five of them. On 29 March 1946 three men received fines ranging from 5,000 to 8,000 crowns for submitting "inflammatory" articles to the anti-Semitic weekly. One had alleged that there were many Jews and "Jew-lovers" in Kutná Hora and denounced a local shop owner for "favoring Jews to the detriment of rations for Aryans."[46] Like the prosecution of Píša and his associates by the Kutná Hora People's Court, the punishment of anti-Semitic "offenses against national honor" challenges the commonly held opinion that little to no justice was done after the war to everyday accomplices in the Holocaust.

According to clause (d), offensive speech was enough to merit proceedings. For example, the Kutná Hora commission tried a woman for having defamed the Masaryk family as "degenerates" and called Tomáš G. Masaryk, the country's founder and first president, a

[43] No. R14/94/46 (19 July 1946), SOkA Kutná Hora, f. ONV-KH, k. 88, sign. II/21b.
[44] In 1948 the average worker earned 834 crowns per month. According to Jan Michal, Czech wages increased only slightly between 1947 and 1948 while inflation remained relatively low. Milan Kučera, *Populace České republiky 1918–1991* (Prague: Česká demografická společnost, 1994), 57; Jan M. Michal, "Postwar Economic Development," in Victor S. Mamatey and Radomír Luža, eds., *A History of the Czechoslovak Republic, 1918–1948* (Princeton, NJ: Princeton University Press, 1973), 436, 446–47.
[45] ÚNV Prague TNK no. 13, case no. 1302-N-3, SOkA Kutná Hora, f. ONV-KH, k. 89, sign. III/21b/c (TNK 1947).
[46] "Protokoly o schůzích TNK" (1945–46), SOkA Kutná Hora, f. ONV-KH, kniha no. 31, 24; Trestní nález no. R14/100–46 (29 March 1946), SOkA Kutná Hora, f. ONV-KH, k. 88, sign. III/21b.

"Jew-lover," his daughter Alice a "whore," and his son Jan, the post-war Foreign Minister, an "alcoholic."[47] In another case, a worker who sent a letter to Emanuel Moravec praising his work (i.e., supporting a Czech traitor), denigrating Beneš, and recommending the persecution of intellectuals, received a fine of 10,000 crowns.[48] A librarian who was only sixteen when the war began was punished with public censure instead of a more serious penalty because the commission recognized that he had merely acted out the teenage predilection to be different and shock others. His "provocative" reading of pro-Nazi newspapers and his approval of Nazi teachings were chalked up to his immaturity.[49]

In contrast to most other offenses, neither clause (a) nor the first part of clause (h) punished an explicitly political crime. Neither mentions Nazism, fascism or "the occupiers." Instead, clause (a) refers to "German nationality" and the first part of clause (h) to "Germans."[50] In punishing the declaration of German nationality, clause (a) transformed what had thitherto been a personal choice into a criminal act with collective connotations. Clause (h), in turn, penalized Czechs who had fraternized with Germans during the war. Together, these two offenses singled out Czechs who had flirted with the imaginary boundary between the two nations. Although the Small Decree introduced the concept of "national honor," it was actually the Interior Ministry that thus created an entirely new form of treason – against the nation, not the state.

Nationality in Czechoslovakia was a complex, contentious issue. In many areas the Czech and German communities had been highly integrated (even inseparable) and bilingual individuals successfully oriented within and between both. One nationalist organization from the mountainous northeastern corner of Bohemia explained, "In our borderlands there are many inhabitants who could just as easily

[47] No. 24 (29 March 1946), SOkA Kutná Hora, f. ONV-KH, kniha č. 31, "Protokoly o schůzích TNK (1945–46)."
[48] No. R14/459/46 (4 October 1946), SOkA Kutná Hora, f. ONV-KH, k. 88, sign. III/21b.
[49] Trestní nález – ÚNV Prague no. 2907 RVNB-VIII/47-D16, TNK no. 11 (23 September 1946), SOkA Kutná Hora, f. ONV-KH, k. 89, sign. III 21b/c (TNK 1947).
[50] Clause (e), "professional collaboration," refers to "Germans" by nationality, but the clause also includes "Czech and Slovak traitors" and therefore does not define the offense in exclusively national terms. Clause (e) seems not to have been frequently used and therefore will not be examined in greater depth here.

demonstrate their Czech origin as their German."[51] It was not un-
common for people of mixed ancestry to have accented their German
identity under the Habsburg Monarchy, then stressed their Czechness
in the interwar republic, only to rediscover under the Nazis that they
were German after all. In the words of the Mladá Boleslav national
committee, "In [our] district...there are many individuals who purely
for self-serving reasons changed the representation of their nationality
according to whatever was best for themselves and their property."[52]
For many such changes were a normal part of life, not a clear political
calculation, but a *modus vivendi* for surviving and even thriving in a
world based on nations. After 1938, however, Nazi policies imbued nationality with new meaning: To become German during the occupation
was viewed as an ideological choice, an expression of support for racial
policies that ultimately aimed to eliminate the Czech nation through
radical assimilation, deportation, or even annihilation.

After the war Czechoslovakia essentially declared that the days of nation straddling, of taking sides based on the exigencies of the moment,
had passed. No longer could an individual choose his or her national
identity – in fact, everyone had already chosen it for the last time. The
day after the Potsdam Conference approved the "orderly transfer of
the German population" from Eastern Europe, President Beneš signed
Decree no. 33, which aimed, in the words of a high-ranking Interior
Ministry official, "to strip Germans...of Czechoslovak citizenship in
order to prepare their transfer from Czechoslovak territory."[53] Only
Germans who had fought actively against the occupation or had suffered
Nazi persecution could earn reinstatement as Czechoslovak citizens.
Even these "antifascists" were required to demonstrate that they had
remained loyal to the Czechoslovak Republic and had never wronged
the Czech or Slovak people. Prewar "Czechs," who during the occupation had officially declared themselves to be "German," could regain

[51] Národní jednota severočeská (18 December 1945). SÚA, f. ÚPV-běž., k. 1032, sign.
1364/2.
[52] MV internal report regarding meeting with ONV Mladá Boleslav security officer (3 April
1947), SÚA, f. MV-NR (B2220), k. 2017.
[53] The logic was deceptively simple: During the war the Germans had acquired Reich
citizenship and therefore should be repatriated after the war to their own country,
Germany. The government claimed, after all, that it was only fulfilling the Germans' wish
to go *"Heim ins Reich."* Vladimír Verner, "Státní občanství podle ústavního dekretu
presidenta republiky ze dne 2. srpna 1945, č. 33 Sb.," *Právní prakse* IX:1 (1946),
161

their Czechoslovak citizenship only if they proved that they had converted under threat or extreme duress.

In the new Republic animosity toward Germans "of Czech origin" was fierce. One article in the country's most liberal daily newspaper explicitly called for their expulsion: "The removal of 300,000 morally and nationally unreliable persons will contribute greatly to the recovery of our national life."[54] An official pamphlet claimed: "These renegades and 'Mischlinge' were the worst enemies of all things Czech."[55] Prior to the promulgation of the Small Decree, the Justice Ministry had told prosecutors to pay special attention to Czechs who had become German, especially when the conversion could be linked to another crime. The Ministry argued that under the right circumstances such a declaration could be construed as support for Nazism.[56] In practice, however, People's Courts were unlikely to punish someone solely for such a declaration. When government advisors suggested a revision to the Great Decree to permit the punishment of national "renegades," Stránský argued against the proposal on the grounds that the law could not be written for individual cases. He presciently warned that such an amendment could cause a new wave of problems and unrest.[57]

Clause (a) of the national honor directive confusingly criminalized the "Declaration of German...nationality, if it did not result in the loss of Czechoslovak citizenship." But Decree no. 33 had already denaturalized individuals who voluntarily declared themselves German, so as noncitizens such former Czechs could not be tried by a national honor commission for clause (a). Individuals who had regained their citizenship on the grounds that they had been forced to adopt German nationality could not be punished either – the national honor directive specified that anyone who had committed an offense under duress was exempt from the Small Decree. If Czechs who had become German were largely immune from prosecution, then whom did the directive

---

54 It is unclear where the author got this number, but two months later Interior Minister Nosek offered the same figure for the number of Czechs in the Sudetenland who became German under compulsion. "Tři sta tisíc odrodilců," *Svobodné noviny* (10 November 1945), 2; V. Nosek, PNS 27 (31 January 1946).

55 Josef Mucha and Karel Petrželka, *O některých současných problémech národnostně smíšených manželství* (Prague: Svoboda, 1946), 3.

56 MS (24 August 1945) to all public prosecutors (MLS no. 23505/45-III/4 pol.), SUA, f. MS (Org), k. 1927.

57 Jech, *Dekrety*, 943, n. 1; first government, ninety-fourth meeting (24 October 1945), 4–12, SÚA, f. 100/24 (KG), sign. 1494, sv. 138.

aim to punish? By process of elimination, only those Czechs who had expressed German nationality but did not legally become German were liable. An official guidebook gave the example of a Czech man who had tried to intimidate his neighbors by claiming he was a German. Because he had never formally applied for German nationality, he had not been denaturalized after the war.[58] More common were probably cases of Czechs who had applied for German citizenship, but were rejected by the Nazis as unfit. Emil Holub, a middle-aged painter, was one of those two-time losers who were first turned down by the Germans only to be later punished by the Czechs. On 11 November 1946 a Prague penal commission sentenced him to six months, twenty-two days in prison, plus a sentence of "public censure" – the verdict was to be posted in public for two weeks.[59]

Prewar Czechs who had officially become German were not supposed to escape punishment altogether. According to Stach's Interior Ministry pamphlet, "Such a person is already punished by the fact that he is now treated as a German."[60] When the national honor directive was issued, it was assumed that such "former" Czechs would be deported along with their new German compatriots and thus suffer a severe penalty for their betrayal – banishment.[61] Soon, however, Czechoslovakia's plans to expel Germans "of Czech origin" foundered on opposition from the Allied occupation authorities in Germany, which proved reluctant to accept yet more refugees, especially those who hardly seemed German.[62] While these "former Czechs" awaited resolution of their claims to re-naturalization, they existed in a legal limbo fraught with dangers, but they were beyond the reach of national honor commissions.

National committees repeatedly complained to the Interior Ministry that Czechs who had become German during the occupation were evading punishment. Local authorities feared that the Small Decree's six-month statute of limitations would expire before these "renegades" regained their citizenship and thus became eligible for prosecution for

[58] Stach, *Provinění*, 9.
[59] Archiv Ministerstva vnitra (AMV) Prague, no. 305-583-4, KS-Stb-Praha.
[60] Stach, *Provinění*, 8–9.
[61] MV no. B2220-28/11-1946-I/2 (23 December 1946), SÚA, f. MV-NR (B2220), k. 2016.
[62] In late November 1946 a high-ranking government official noted, "Soviet and American authorities are already now requesting that our offices permit the return of those Germans who were transferred and are of Czech origin." ÚPV no. 44535-II-8701/46 (25 November 1946), SÚA, f. ÚPV-běž., k. 1032, sign. 1364/2.

offenses against national honor. The disclosure of a wartime archive containing more than 100,000 requests for German citizenship only added to these concerns.[63] An Interior Ministry official admitted, "It was not known, and only now is it becoming clear, that the number of such individuals is so considerable." Afraid of the public's reaction, the official suggested a change in the national honor directive. From the beginning of 1947, commissions gained the power to prosecute successful declarations of German nationality; in fact, from then on they could punish any Slav regardless of his or her citizenship.[64]

Seeking German nationality was of the more frequently prosecuted offenses, but it does not appear to have been punished harshly. The Litoměřice penal commission, for example, convicted Josef Swatuschka for applying for German citizenship and sentenced him on 3 May 1947 to pay a 2,000-crown fine and face public censure. Jan Svatuška, Josef's next-door neighbor (and likely his relative), received a one-week jail sentence and a 500-crown fine for the same offense.[65] In Kutná Hora, Antonín Jahoda was fined 3,000 crowns for having written in a letter, "I'm unhappy that I'm a Czech, and if I knew German, I'd never call myself a Czech."[66] Another Czech who applied for German citizenship and joined the Deutsche Arbeitsfront had to pay only a 1,000-crown fine because of his ill health and two minor children.[67] Božena Dürschmiedová was fined 1,000 crowns for having declared herself German. The penal commission ruled that her claim to unbearable pressure could not be substantiated, but that she was a good person nonetheless and did not deserve harsh punishment.[68]

Doubly rejected Emil Holub's incongruously harsh six-month sentence likely stemmed from the fact that he had also "consciously support[ed] the denationalization efforts of the Germans [clause (a), second part]." Holub had encouraged his neighbor to apply for German

[63] "Sto tisíc dokumentů národní zrady nalezeno," *Rudé právo* (17 March 1946), 1.
[64] MV no. B2220-28/11-1946-I/2 (23 December 1946), SÚA, f. MV-NR (B2220), k. 2016; MV no. VIII/C-3426, Státní okresní archiv (SOkA) Kutná Hora, f. ONV-KH, k. 89, sign. III/21c; VK-ONV Kolín (10 October 1946) to MV, SÚA, f. MV-NR (B2220), k. 2016.
[65] TNK no. 32864/46 (3 May 1947), SOkA Lovosice, f. ONV Litoměřice, k. 141.
[66] No. 19 (12 March 1946), SOkA Kutná Hora, f. ONV-KH, kniha č. 31, "Protokoly o schůzích TNK (1945-46)."
[67] TNK no. 14, case no. M17, SOkA Kutná Hora, f. ONV-KH, k. 89, sign. III/21b/c (TNK 1947).
[68] ÚNV Prague TNK no. 53, case no. 256/47, SOkA Kutná Hora, f. ONV-KH, k. 89, sign. III/21b/c (TNK 1947).

citizenship and even declared his daughter to be German.[69] The potential Germanization of Czech children was one of the most feared aspects of the occupation. Thus, it is hardly surprising that a penal commission harshly punished one woman with six months in prison, a 5,000-crown fine, and public censure for having enrolled her daughter in a German school.[70] In a similar case, a mother claimed in defense that she had only wanted her child to learn German. The defendant further argued that a mere year in a German school was not enough time for her daughter to lose her national identity, especially since the child had immediately thereafter taken the entrance examination for a Czech vocational school. Even though the penal commission accepted the validity of this excuse, it nonetheless decided that sending one's child to a German school *ipso facto* offended national honor because everyone knew that such institutions were hotbeds of pro-Nazi and anti-Czech propaganda.[71]

Under clause (h), the national honor directive aimed to punish not only those who permanently crossed over the imaginary boundary between the Czech and German nations, but even those who merely flirted with it. Since native Germans did not technically lose their Czechoslovak citizenship until 2 August 1945, clause (h) effectively punished Czechs for fraternization with a domestic, not a foreign enemy. It criminalized collaboration with Germans *qua* Germans, irrespective of their wartime conduct or even political beliefs. The clause ambiguously punished "social relations," but the national honor directive did not define the concept further. In his explanatory pamphlet, Stach specified that this category "included not only attendance at German theaters, concerts, amusements, [or] hunting and drinking with Germans, but also frequent or regular visits to German families or inviting Germans into one's home."[72] Penal commissions tried Czechs for sending congratulatory notes to Germans, for attending Germans' birthday parties, and for playing cards with them.[73]

The most commonly punished form of "social relations" was likely what the French colorfully termed "*collaboration horizontale.*" In his

---

[69] AMV, 305-583-4, KS-Stb-Praha.

[70] TOK 16/46 (20 March 1946), SÚA, f. ZNV-Pr, sign. TOK, k. 373.

[71] Josef Plzák, "Malý retribuční dekret," *Právní prakse* XI (1947/48), 123.

[72] Stach, *Provinění*, 11.

[73] Plzák, "Malý retribuční dekret," 120–21, 129; Verdict of OS Kutná Hora no. St 66/47 (16 January 1948), SOkA Kutná Hora, f. ONV-KH, k. 90, sign. III/21c.

pamphlet, Fusek urged, "Amorous relations are particularly meant to be apprehended."[74] Even before the Small Decree was issued, authorities in the Moravian town of Frýdek had forced alleged female fraternizers to sweep the streets for a month while wearing signs on their backs stating, "I consorted with German men and am shirking work."[75] Unsurprisingly, Czech women also bore the brunt of the punishment of "amorous" offenses against national honor. Commissions gave harsher penalties to women who, in addition to amorous relations, committed other offenses, for example, "Germanizing" oneself, giving priority to German customers, or, in one case, attending a party to celebrate Franklin D. Roosevelt's death.[76] The Kutná Hora commission ordered six months' imprisonment for a Czech midwife who had "intimate relations" with a German soldier for almost the entire war, sent her daughter to a German school, and hung a picture of Hitler in her apartment.[77] In an example of how indefinite nationality could mix with dishonorable amorous relations, a woman from Roudnice nad Labem received a 10,000-crown fine and public censure for her ties to František Novotný. Novotný had begun the war as a Czech fascist and finished as a German Gestapo informant.[78] In a more notorious case, a Prague honor commission convicted the glamorous Czech film star Adina Mandlová of having maintained "social relations" with a German man. Ironically, he regained Czechoslovak citizenship the very next week thanks to his wartime service to the Czech nation.[79]

Amid the punishment of Czech female fraternizers, some pointed out that Czech men were not being held accountable for their wartime horizontal collaboration. An anonymous letter to Edvard Beneš complained,

And what, Mister President, about our men? After all, they also took up intimate relations with German women. But only when they got to Germany.

---

[74] Fusek, *Provinění*, 30.

[75] "Stýkala jsem se s Němci a štítím se práce," *Lidová správa* I:3 (30 October 45), 10.

[76] Trestní nález no. R14/421/46 (31 May 1946), SOkA Kutná Hora, f. ONV-KH, k. 88, sign. III/21b; Trestní nález, ÚNV Prague no. M/6, TNK no. 32 (18 September 1946), SOkA Kutná Hora, f. ONV-KH, k. 89, sign. III 21b/c (TNK 1947); "Protokoly o schůzích TNK" (1945–46), SOkA Kutná Hora, f. ONV-KH, kniha no. 31, 16; TOK 12/46 (10 April 1946), SÚA, f. ZNV-Pr, sign. TOK, k. 373.

[77] Trestní nález, TNK Kutná Hora no. R14/130/46 (4 January 1946) SOkA Kutná Hora, f. ONV-KH, k. 88, sign. III 21b.

[78] TOK 2044/46 (22 October 1947), SÚA, f. ZNV-Pr, sign. TOK, k. 392.

[79] Mandlová was given time served. Adina Mandlová, *Dneska už se tomu směju* (Toronto: Sixty-Eight Publishers, 1976), 183–84.

In Germany a Czech man wouldn't talk to one of our girls, but when he worked there he socialized with a *German one*, took her to cafés and movie theaters and so on. How many marriages were undermined because the man had a relationship with a German and never went home nor perhaps even wrote. That *isn't investigated*, not to mention punished. On the contrary, [Czech] workers from the Reich were favored when they returned home, it probably occurred to no one to measure men the same. Women always bear everything worse and always unjustly.[80]

In her memoirs Mandlová also noted the sexism that turned a blind eye to Czech men who had labored in the Reich and there fraternized with German women.[81] After the war one such Czech worker, a barber's assistant, pleaded with the authorities to exempt his female German partner from the expulsion. The two had met when he was quartered with her family in Germany. At the end of the war they fled to Bohemia with their three-month-old daughter, who died soon thereafter. In his plea the barber's assistant noted that his predicament was common: "I, like many other good Czech men, made this acquaintance in the belief that I was doing nothing bad." His appeal clearly illustrates a double standard: The threat of punishment for an offense against national honor was so far from his mind that he felt safe presenting his case directly to the Interior Ministry in Prague. Instead of initiating national honor proceedings against him, the local police supported his request and the Interior Ministry approved it.[82]

STANDARDS, PENALTIES, AND CERTIFICATES

The national honor directive left the penal commissions considerable latitude to determine exactly what to punish. The list of nine offenses was prefaced by the word "particularly," implying that other types of national misconduct could be considered. Although a May 1946 Interior Ministry memorandum categorized the list of offenses as "demonstrative," not "exhaustive," Minister Nosek stressed that anything not

[80] Emphasis in original. Anonymous letter to the president, KPR no. R-7678/45 (28 July 1945), Archiv Kanceláře prezidenta republiky (AKPR), f. D-11169/47 (Anonymy), D.
[81] Mandlová, *Dneska už se tomu směju*, 163.
[82] Letter from Josef Miřatský to Interior Ministry, Prague (21 March 1947), Státní oblastní archiv Kutná Hora (SOA-KH), f. ONV-KH, k. 90, s/4-106.

in the directive should not be punished.[83] In their guidebooks for penal commissions, both Fusek and Stach argued for a restrictive, literal interpretation of the national honor directive.[84] Stach adopted the standard of the average citizen, who was neither a valiant resister nor a slavish collaborator:

It is not for each of us to be a hero, but we cannot accept a coward as the measure of everything. When we consider that our nation's overall conduct during the occupation was very honorable and can bear comparison to any other European nation, then we must take the stance of the average citizen towards the violent occupiers as the measure of what was inappropriate and what offended the people's sentiments.[85]

According to the Supreme Administrative Court, "offenses against national honor" had to be judged by local standards. Moreover, to be convicted the defendant had to have undermined *public* morale – comments in a private letter or "between four eyes" (to use a Czech expression) did not suffice. The Court ruled that behavior could not be punished unless it offended locals who learned of the act and were "otherwise personally uninterested" in it.[86] Perhaps appropriately for a beer-loving nation, the tribunals were also instructed to be forgiving in case of inebriation.[87] A Prague penal commission dismissed charges against one man because his fellow workers had declared him to be a good Czech who "enjoyed drinking" but was capable of "rude statements" while intoxicated.[88] Despite these guidelines, each penal commission was free to rule as harshly or leniently as it pleased. In response to complaints about "too much benevolence" on the part of commission members, Interior Ministry officials stated that they could do nothing because such decisions were a matter of "conscience."[89]

---

[83] "Záznam o poradě" (8 May 1946), MV no. B2220-8/5-46-I/2, SÚA, f. MV-NR (B2220), k. 2016; Stach, *Provinění*, 7; MV no. B2220-11/12-1945 (12 Dec. 1945), SÚA, f. MV-NR (B2220), k. 2016; "Provádění dekretu o národní cti," *Lidová správa*, I:8 (1 February 1946), 9–11.

[84] Fusek, *Provinění*, 10–11; Stach, *Provinění*, 7.

[85] Stach, *Provinění*, 7.

[86] Plzák, "Malý retribuční dekret," 119–21; *Lidová správa* I:4 (1 December 1945), 3.

[87] Plzák, "Malý retribuční dekret," 122; Stach, *Provinění*, 8.

[88] ÚNV Prague TNK no. 10, case no. 1511 RVNB/VIII/47, SOkA Kutná Hora, f. ONV-KH, k. 89, sign. III/21b/c (TNK 1947).

[89] "Provádění dekretu o národní cti," *Lidová správa*, I:8 (1 Feb. 1946), 9–11.

The penal commissions sometimes punished collaboration near the end of the war more harshly than that committed in earlier years. One could argue that this perspective was counterintuitive – after all, collaboration was far more demoralizing while the Nazis were riding high than when they were running for their lives. The penal commissions, however, judged behavior by intent and adopted a "should-have-known-better" standard. Marie Kafková had certainly hurt her case when she attended the party to celebrate Franklin D. Roosevelt's death in April 1945. The Kutná Hora penal commission punished two other women for engaging in "dishonorable" activity at the wrong time: One had "amorous relations" with a German soldier from February to May 1945; the other praised the occupation one week before capitulation and then fled with German soldiers on 6 May 1945.[90] The Litoměřice commission punished a man who threatened to denounce a coworker to the German authorities. What apparently most offended the commission members' sensibilities was the date of the threat: 30 June 1944 – "a time when every [politically] conscious Czech must have already known that the end was nigh for the German lordship over the territory of the Czechoslovak republic."[91]

As the cases mentioned above indicate, penal commissions employed a combination of punishments. Sentences that matched time served were common. The appropriately named Rudolf Hrubý (meaning "coarse"), a former police officer, had praised the Nazis, terrorized his subordinates, and socialized with Germans. Most memorably, he had predicted that anyone who could not speak German would soon be using shovels. A penal commission gave Hrubý an eight-month sentence – exactly the amount of time he had been already detained – leaving him free to go.[92] Perhaps such sentences were a way to justify a lengthy imprisonment or to declare guilt without enforcing additional sanctions. Sometimes a sentence was considerably shorter than the time already served by a defendant. One worker who was found guilty of praising the Nazis and their persecution of the Jews and of insulting Beneš and T. G. Masaryk received only one month because of his weak mental

[90] Trestní nález no. R14/25/46 (11 February 1946), no. R14/52/46 (5 February 1946), SOkA Kutná Hora, f. ONV-KH, k. 88, sign. III/21b.
[91] Fr. Zítka, TNK no. 33005/46 (24 April 1947), SOkA Lovosice, f. ONV Litoměřice, k. 141.
[92] No. R14/172/46 (18 October 1946), SOkA Kutná Hora, f. ONV-KH, k. 88, sign. III/21b.

state, even though he had already been in jail for five months.[93] Another defendant was sentenced to two months' imprisonment for her ties to German soldiers, even though she had already been detained for more than four months.[94] The commissions chose to punish many defendants only with "public censure," a penalty that entailed the public announcement of a sentence (for example, posting it on the town hall door or broadcasting it over the radio) for a limited period of time. In these cases, the punishment of "offenses against national honor" functioned as a precursor to the modern "truth commission."

For defendants convicted by penal commissions, their sentences often turned out to be just part of their tribulations. For, along with jail time, a fine, and/or public censure, another onerous "national" penalty loomed – a person guilty of an "offense against national honor" could not acquire a "certificate of national reliability." To be without a certificate was to be outcast and face destitution. In a letter to the president, one woman pleaded, "We are now fighting for our very existence.... My husband can't even get a job. *Because he doesn't have national reliability.* We are in a situation where we stand like beggars at the crossroads.... "[95] Although never convicted of a crime, a citizen without a certificate had essentially been sentenced to a loss of civic honor: He or she was unable to exercise any position of authority in society or to work in any occupation considered vital to the country's health.[96]

The case of Zikmund Hess, a Polish railway worker from Těšín, demonstrates how the withholding of "certificates of national reliability" functioned as a supplementary penalty to the Small Decree. He had been accused of working for the German Railways during the war and of having adopted German nationality. A penal commission convicted him of an offense against national honor, but handed down a moderate penalty, a fine of 2,000 crowns. In retrospect, Hess lamented,

[I] accepted the punishment assuming that when I paid the fine the matter would be settled, that I would finally have peace. Only now am I feeling the

[93] No. R14/733/47 (11 April 1947), SOkA Kutná Hora, f. ONV-KH, k. 88, sign. III/21b.
[94] Trestní nález no. R14/52/46 (5 February 1946), SOkA Kutná Hora, f. ONV-KH, k. 88, sign. III/21b.
[95] Emphasis in original. B. Kozáková to KPR no. P902/46, Archiv Kanceláře prezidenta republiky (AKPR), s. D-11377/47, k. 262(b).
[96] For more on the "loss of civic honor," see the discussion of the Great Decree in Chapter 2.

consequences.... As a result of my punishment I have been released from the service of Č.S.D. [Czechoslovak railways]... [am] without pension [and] for three months I have been without work.

Hess pleaded for a presidential pardon, in his words, "So that I can get back civic rights and a pension for working a full thirty-two years."[97]

These "certificates of national reliability" were actually an unanticipated byproduct of Czechoslovakia's expropriation of its German population. When background checks for "national administrators" – caretakers appointed to run confiscated businesses – proved too laborious, the onus to demonstrate reliability was shifted onto the shoulders of applicants, who were thenceforth required to acquire "certificates of national reliability." According to an official handbook, "Very soon that institution became commonplace and took hold universally."[98] Perhaps the biggest problem with the certificates was that they had, as representatives of the Interior Ministry admitted, "no legal basis!"[99] Not only were there no guidelines for issuing the certificates, it was also unclear when and where such documentation was even necessary.[100] Unsurprisingly, national committees – not known for their judicious and consistent execution of government directives – failed to enforce an extralegal, uncodified sanction to anyone's satisfaction. In October 1945 the Moravian Provincial National Committee commented, "The issuance of a certificate is often refused for reasons that do not pass legal muster... certificates are refused due to personal grudges, animus, prejudice, or for various petty personal interests." Though many individuals were unfairly determined to be "nationally unreliable," apparently other applicants were unjustly approved: "By contrast, there are... cases where such certificates have been issued very benevolently to individuals to whom they could not have and should not have been issued."[101]

Originally, the threshold for acquiring a certificate was higher than that employed by penal commissions to judge "offenses against national

<hr />

[97] KPR no. R05464/47 (17 April 1947), no. R13728/47 (3 October 1947), AKPR, f. D-11377/47, k. 262(b).
[98] Stanislav Šulc, *Národní výbory*, 308–309.
[99] "Provádění dekretu o národní cti," *Lidová správa*, I:8 (1 February 1946), 11.
[100] J. Dubský, ed., *Slovník lidové správy* (Prague, 1947), 296; "Potřeba zákona o národní spolehlivosti," *Lidová správa* I:27 (1 Novomber 1946), 6–7.
[101] Šulc, *Národní výbory*, 309.

honor." Not only could convicted collaborators be denied, ordinary rank-and-file members of fascist groups, whom the commissions could not punish, were also deemed "nationally unreliable." Former members of the banned Agrarian Party, Czechoslovakia's largest prewar political party, who could not prove their wartime patriotism were also ineligible for certificates.[102] Moreover, until cleared by a penal commission, anyone under suspicion of having committed an "offense against national honor" was considered "unreliable." Although the parliament never passed a law governing certificates of national reliability, the Interior Ministry eventually issued a pamphlet so that citizens would no longer face "legal uncertainty."[103] The handbook established a generous standard: "We have (in fact, we must have) trust in anyone who has not yet disappointed us; that is,... anyone who, during the period of heightened danger to the republic, did not waver either as a citizen of the republic, or as a Czech, Slovak, or Slav."[104] By the beginning of 1947 passions had cooled considerably and the Prague Provincial National Committee issued more lenient guidelines for certificates: Unless already convicted or under indictment by a retribution tribunal, every Slav deserved certification. Moreover, anyone who was acquitted or had his or her case dismissed had to be issued a certificate.[105]

"A POWERFUL WEAPON AGAINST THE REACTION"

In March 1946, Gustav Czaban, the secretary of the Communist parliamentary club, appealed to national committee members: "The National Honor Decree is a powerful weapon against the reaction. It is necessary to use this weapon." He called for the honor commissions to punish "not just Hitlerites and out-and-out fascists but also all Czech reactionaries." Thanks to the Small Decree, national committees had several ways to strike against so-called reactionaries. Czaban pointed out one of them when he called for the prosecution of any "lawyer who in defense of a Hitlerite, fascist, traitor or collaborator justifies their crime or disparages our revolution and people's democratic

[102] Šulc, *Národní výbory*, 313; Jaroslav Fusek, *Osvědčení o státní a národní spolehlivosti* (Brno: ZÁŘ, 1946), 8–15, 19–20.
[103] Fusek, *Osvědčení*, 3.
[104] Fusek, *Osvědčení*, 8.
[105] Vyhláška ZNV Prague no. 183/2-1946 (17 January 1947), SOkA Kutná Hora, f. ONV-KH, k. 89, sign. III/21c.

republic."[106] Honor commissions could potentially punish defense lawyers because the Small Decree's jurisdiction actually extended to everyday "collaboration" that occurred *after the war* had ended. Like the People's Courts, the commissions were empowered to try offenses committed during "the period of heightened danger to the republic," which the Great Decree defined as lasting from 21 May 1938 "until a date to be determined by government edict." The government discussed several possible dates for the end of this period and finally settled on 31 December 1946.[107] In other words, honor commissions could still punish "unbecoming behavior, insulting to the national sentiments of the Czech or Slovak people," that occurred more than eighteen months after the end of the war.[108]

Some national committees did not pass up this opportunity to punish postwar offenses. In Kutná Hora, František Pokorný had to endure public censure – the announcement was to be made in two different villages – for having insulted Czechs and been disrespectful to President Beneš during the war and "still in July 1945."[109] In January 1947 a local branch of the Union of Liberated Political Prisoners turned in Alois Tomeš for having committed a postwar offense against national honor. On the night of 20 October 1946, Tomeš had gone drinking in a pub near Litoměřice. Sometime after two in the morning, the heavily inebriated Tomeš unwisely began to antagonize his fellow patrons and the establishment's employees with a tirade about the injustices of the world. A wartime prisoner (and Kapo) in nearby Theresienstadt (Terezín), Tomeš nonetheless praised the concentration camp's former commandant, Heinrich Jöckel, who had recently been hanged by the

---

[106] After February 1948 Czaban, an *alter Kämpfer* Communist from the interwar republic, joined the Justice Ministry. G.C., "Do rázného útoku proti zrádcům a kolaborantům," *Lidová správa*, I:9–10 (1 March 1946), 7–8.

[107] Twenty-one May 1938 was the date of the first Czechoslovak military mobilization against the Nazi threat. Jech, *Dekrety*, I:179, n. 2; Plzák, "Malý retribuční dekret," 127.

[108] Although the guidelines for the "the period of heightened danger to the republic" had been established by the Great Decree, the impact was much greater on the honor commissions than on the People's Courts. Almost all of the crimes enumerated in the Great Decree depended on committing acts "in the service or interest of the enemy," a condition difficult to fulfill once the enemy, Nazi Germany, had ceased to exist. It was, for example, impossible to become a functionary in the Nazi party or to denounce one's neighbor to the Gestapo after the end of the war. The Small Decree, on the other hand, imposed no such limitation.

[109] Trestní nález no. R14/637/46-U.J. (7 February 1947), SOkA Kutná Hora, f. ONV-KH, k. 88, sign. III/21b.

Litoměřice People's Court. Tomeš declared the cemetery in front of the camp to be a "disgrace" and claimed the bodies buried there belonged to "voluntary workers who had accidentally died." The former Kapo added, "Terezín was like a paradise for president Beneš's relatives; they walked around in shorts and played volleyball." Although Tomeš was not tried before retribution ended in May 1947, his case nonetheless demonstrates how penal commissions moved from punishing wartime collaboration to policing postwar speech.[110] Even if few Czechs were ultimately tried for postwar offenses against national honor, the threat of such punishment likely made citizens wary of publicly criticizing the country's leadership and its policies.[111] A group of young intellectuals at the Brno university declared the Small Decree to be the type of law "which punishes the violation of the rulers' interests." The students viewed it as a step on the road to absolutism.[112] Certainly, the punishment of postwar speech crimes supports this interpretation.

While the punishment of postwar offenses may have been a "powerful weapon," the Small Decree ultimately offered national committees a far more effective means to influence the political struggle: disenfranchisement. In its 1945 Košice Program the postwar government had promised to bar "traitors to the nation, fascists, and obvious or masked enemies of the people" from participation in politics and to disenfranchise "all traitors to the nation and helpers of the enemy."[113] The Great Decree, for its part, denied voting rights to convicted persons. As we have seen, however, by the end of 1945 the People's Courts and the penal commissions had only resolved a fraction of the charges before them. On 18 December 1945 Gottwald told the Communist Party Central Committee,

There is yet another great task: to make a voting list law together with the decree on national honor, so that we have the possibility in the villages and the towns ... to preclude compromised collaborators and traitorous elements

---

[110] TNK Zn. 268 (17 October 1949), SOkA Lovosice, f. ONV Litoměřice, k. 141.

[111] As the next chapter discusses, the punishment of postwar offenses may have had a much more important function: deterring Czechs from interfering in the expulsion of the Sudeten Germans.

[112] Emphasized in the original. Vlastislav Chalupa, Ivan Gad'ourek, and Mojmír Povolný, eds., *Tři roky: Přehledy a dokumenty k Československé politice v letech 1945–1948*, 3 vols (Brno, Právnická fakulta Masarykovy univerzity, 1991), I:193.

[113] Jiří Grospič, Jaroslav Chovanec, and Juraj Vysokaj, eds., *Košický vládní program* (Prague: Státní pedagogické nakladatelství, 1977), 128.

from the right to vote. In this regard our organization must use the decree on national honor to strike collaborators.[114]

Two months later Gottwald added that it was not enough to disenfranchise those collaborators who would automatically lose their votes by court order: "Other categories of individuals" should also be kept away from the polls. He predicted, "There will be a tenacious fight about this, but I think we have to wage it."[115] As 1945 turned into 1946, Communist organs, national committees, and branches of the Union of Liberated Political Prisoners advanced demands for the disenfranchisement of suspected collaborators. For example, one youth group declared, "It is unimaginable to us that the achievement of voting rights that has been given to us youth should be shared by people who... betrayed the nation."[116]

At the end of January Nosek received a round of raucous applause from the Provisional National Assembly when he declared, "It is unthinkable that persons who demonstrably transgressed against their homeland and nation could take part in the elections."[117] A People's Party deputy argued that only individuals convicted by People's Courts or by national honor commissions should be prevented from voting. He predicted a wave of false denunciations immediately prior to the elections. Malicious individuals could deny innocents the right to vote out of hatred or political calculation.[118] Despite this prescient warning, on 21 February 1946 parliament passed a strict law governing voting rights. Anyone who had been charged with collaboration was automatically disenfranchised pending the outcome of an investigation or trial. The law also denied the vote to all former ministers of the Protectorate government and members of the thirty-seven fascist and collaborationist groups blacklisted by the national honor directive.[119]

---

[114] Referát s. Gottwalda, ZÚV-KSČ (18 December 1945), SÚA, f. 1, sv. 1, ar.j. 8, str. 12.

[115] Referát s. Gottwalda, ZÚV-KSČ (4 February 1946), SÚA, f. 1, sv. 2, ar.j. 9, str. 7.

[116] Postwar Czechoslovakia lowered the minimum voting age to eighteen years. Svaz české mládeže Praha VII (14 January 1946) to MS (31 January 1946) to MV, SÚA, f. MV-NR (B2220(1)), k. 2016; see also letters from KSČ Červený Kostelec (11 January 1946), SOPV Bolevec (16 December 1945), and ONV Hradec Králové (14 February 1946), SÚA, f. MV-NR (B2220(1)), k. 2016.

[117] V. Nosek, PNS 27 (31 January 1946), 4.

[118] Řehulka, PNS 28 (12 February 1946), 7.

[119] "Osoby jež mají býti zbaveny volebního práva," *Lidová demokracie* (4 March 1946), 1.

In the months before the election the Communist press exhorted party cadres to remove all suspected collaborators from the voting lists. *Lidová správa* declared: "Don't let traitors vote!" Moving far beyond the disenfranchisement law, the journal explained, "On the voting lists there should not be entered a single nationally, economically, politically, culturally, or socially dishonorable person."[120] The National Socialist and People's Party press complained of an "avalanche of false denunciations" intended solely to prevent their supporters from voting.[121] In the Justice Ministry alone, eight officials who had already been cleared by an internal purge committee were informed shortly before the election that the local Prague penal commission was investigating them. After they had been denied the opportunity to vote, their cases were dismissed for lack of evidence.[122] Tigrid claimed that in the twenty-four hours before the polls opened the Communists arranged to have 15,000 warrants mailed.[123] But the accusations flew in various directions. After an inspection of penal commissions, an Interior Ministry official complained that in some areas proceedings had been rushed to return the vote to "influential people."[124] Communist representatives accused their opponents of thinking that collaborators' and profiteers' votes were worth as much as those of partisans and political prisoners – in short, that "reactionary votes don't stink."[125] Such provocative statements raise the suspicion that Communist leaders were preparing an excuse to invalidate the election results if they proved unfavorable to the party. The Communists could claim that they earned the majority of "patriotic" votes from former prisoners and partisans, while the National Socialists won only thanks to the support of "unreliable" elements.[126]

---

[120] J. Dubský, "Zrádci nesmějí rozhodovat o osudu republiky!" *Lidová správa* I:11 (15 March 1946), 1–2; "Nepřipustit zrádce k volbám!" *Lidová správa* I:12 (29 March 1946), 13–14.

[121] Chalupa, *Tři roky*, I:419.

[122] Prokop Drtina, *Na soudu národa: Tři projevy ministra spravedlnosti dr. Prokopa Drtiny o činnosti Mimořádných lidových soudů a Národního soudu* (Prague: Min. Spravedlnosti, 1947), 67–68.

[123] Pavel Tigrid, *Kapesní průvodce inteligentní ženy po vlastním osudu* (Toronto: Sixty-Eight Publishers, 1988), 374.

[124] "Informace pro pana ministra vnitra" (10 June 1946), SÚA, f. MV-NR (B2220(1)), k. 2016.

[125] Chalupa, *Tři roky*, I:272–73.

[126] In early February 1946 Gottwald apparently commented, "Even if it should happen, which is improbable, that we should not gain a favorable result...the working

In the end, the Communist Party scored a stunning victory in the 26 May 1946 election, winning more than 40 percent in the Czech provinces and taking a substantial plurality of the vote statewide. Drtina's National Socialists, despite their high hopes, earned a disappointing 23.6 percent of the Czech vote, while the People's Party (20.2 percent) and the Social Democrats (15.5 percent) fared even worse.[127] The Communists' political competitors retrospectively blamed disenfranchisement for their election debacle.[128] They claimed that machinations by partisan national committees unfairly prevented as many as 250,000 to 300,000 alleged collaborators from casting ballots. Control over the town halls in both Prague and Pilsen may have swung to the Communists as a result. Although claims that disenfranchisement cost the "democratic" parties at least ten parliamentary mandates are probably exaggerated, had a mere three seats (approximately 72,000 votes) changed hands, the Communists and their thus-far obedient Social Democratic allies would have lost their majority in the new Constituent National Assembly.[129] Instead, the Communists maintained their hold over the Interior Ministry and claimed the premiership for party chief Klement Gottwald.

class, the party, and the working people will still have sufficient means, arms, and a method to correct simple mechanical voting, which might be affected by reactionary and saboteur elements." Radomír Luža, "Czechoslovakia between Democracy and Communism," in Victor S. Mamatey and Radomír Luža, eds., *A History of the Czechoslovak Republic, 1918–1948* (Princeton, NJ: Princeton University Press, 1973), 403–404.

[127] The Communists were less successful in Slovakia, where they earned less than one-third of the vote, leaving the Party with a 37.9 percent share statewide. In the new parliament the combined KSČ–KSS controlled 114 of the 300 seats. Together with the Social Democrats and the miniscule Slovak Labor Party, the Marxist left had a slim majority of six members (153 seats). Kaplan, *Nekrvavá revoluce*, 60.

[128] Ota Hora listed eleven reasons for the Communists' victory, including Communist control over the most important ministries, the radio, the biggest news printers, and the country's one union; supporters gained through the distribution of offices and land; the power of the national committees; Soviet troop movements; and the banning of the prewar Agrarian party, many of whose supporters apparently voted in 1946 for the Communists. Ota Hora, *Svědectví o puči* (Toronto: Sixty-Eight Publishers, 1978), 198–206.

[129] Even if the numbers are accurate, there is still no reason to assume that all of those denied the vote would have supported non-Marxist parties. Hubert Ripka, *Czechoslovakia Enslaved: The Story of the Communist Coup d'Etat* (London: Victor Gollancz, 1950), 46–47; Hora, *Svědectví* (1978), 202; Ladislav Feierabend, *Politické vzpomínky*, 3 vols. (Brno: Atlantis, 1994–1996), III:315.

THE NUMBERS

Despite the Communists' impressive political success, party leaders ultimately criticized the honor commissions with nearly as much vigor as they attacked the People's Courts. On 20 January 1946, only weeks after the Interior Ministry had issued the national honor directive, Communist security department chiefs in the Zlín district jointly warned, "If all traitors are not deservedly punished . . . the working people can be expected to fulfill the . . . government program themselves."[130] The next month the Communist parliamentary club sent a resolution to Nosek calling for a radical expansion of the Small Decree. The deputies demanded retribution against Czech policemen who had not participated in "active resistance" or had not aided victims of persecution. Ominously, the resolution also advocated the punishment of lawyers whose defense arguments before People's Courts "in effect amount to the exoneration of criminal acts and disparagement of our revolution and people's democratic republic."[131] The last suggestion, had it been implemented, would have essentially made hollow any right to defense before the courts. At the end of the year Ladislav Kopřiva, the Communist Chairman of the Bohemian Provincial National Committee, expressed his deep dissatisfaction with the implementation of the Small Decree: "In many cases it has been reliably determined that the intention of the penal commission has been to free the defendant at any cost." This was especially true, Kopřiva claimed, when the accused was wealthy or powerful. He concluded: "Whatever [the commissioners] took away from the rich, they added to the sentences of the poor."[132]

From the beginning it was clear that there would be regional differences in the punishment of offenses against national honor. In early 1946 the national committees in Litoměřice, Český Krumlov, and Šumperk estimated that they would only prosecute ten to fifteen, twenty-five, and thirty to forty cases, respectively. After all, Germans could not be punished for most offenses, so in much of the borderlands there was little need for a penal commission at all. By contrast, in Český Těšín and Jihlava, areas with ethnically mixed populations, the national

---

[130] Resoluce krajské konference bezpečnostních referentů-členů KSČ zlínského kraje (20 January 1946) to MV, SÚA, f. MV-NR (B2220), k. 2016.
[131] Klub poslanců KSČ (5 Feb. 1946) to Nosek, SÚA, f. MV-NR (B2220), k. 2016.
[132] "Jak soudí trestní nalézací komise?" Rudé právo (31 December 1946), 1.

committees expected more than 1,000 cases each. In the big cities the numbers were the greatest: In Pilsen more than 2,000 cases were anticipated, in Olomouc 3,500 cases, in Brno 15,000 cases, and in Prague around 60,000 cases. In preparation, on 13 February 1946 the Prague national committee established fifty-two penal commissions and swore in 832 members.[133]

Like the People's Courts, many penal commissions were soon overwhelmed by the sheer number of cases. One national committee complained that members were working extraordinary hours, usually not wrapping up their biweekly sessions until seven to nine at night, and occasionally not until one in the morning. Those were only the deliberations, not the preparations. The committee claimed that it could not solve the problem by creating additional commissions because there were simply not enough qualified individuals in the district.[134] In a May 1946 petition to the parliament, various ministries, and political parties, the Union of Liberated Political Prisoners called for the Small Decree (and its statute of limitations) to be extended by six months because an estimated 110,000 cases remained unresolved. The Union claimed that it had repeatedly received complaints that some national committees were stalling.[135] In October 1946 the Interior Ministry reported that 68,422 cases had been resolved, but another 91,768 remained to be considered. Most of those were in Bohemia, where national honor tribunals had completed only 35 percent of their caseload. In the borderlands, where there were few native Czechs, some national committees had already wrapped up their punishment of offenses against national honor.[136] As with the People's Courts, the backlog of national honor cases justified the extension of the penal commissions' activities until they were finally disbanded on 4 May 1947.

The Interior Ministry never published final results for the Small Decree, but an internal report from 8 August 1947 demonstrates that the

---

[133] Reports from ONV to MV (30 January–19 February 1946), SÚA, f. MV-NR (B2220), k. 2016.
[134] ONV Šluknov (3 December 1946) to MV, SÚA, f. MV-NR (B2220), k. 2016.
[135] SOPV (3 May 1946) to MV, SÚA, f. MV-NR (B2220), k. 2016.
[136] The Ministry also reported that some defendants were missing and approximately 12 percent had been expelled. "Informace pro pana ministra vnitra, *Očista věřejného života*" (October 1946), SÚA, f. MV-NR (B2220(1)), k. 2016, 3–4. For Bohemian figures only, see "Jak je prováděna veřejná očista," *Lidová demokracie* (5 November 1946), 1.

penal commissions ultimately exonerated the vast majority of defendants. The commissions considered 179,896 cases and resolved three-fourths of them. In total, the tribunals found 46,422 defendants guilty and dismissed 88,845 cases. In other words, only one-fourth of the original charges resulted in conviction.[137] Overall, commissions handed out penalties of 3,115 years and fines of 182,524,140 Czechoslovak crowns. Only 21,912 cases ended with a sanction of public censure, indicating that many tribunals were reluctant to resort to this novel means of punishment.[138] Since defendants received a variety of penalties – a prison sentence, a fine, public censure, or any combination of the three (e.g., fine and censure, prison and fine, censure and prison, or all three) – it is impossible to determine the average sentence from these figures. Nonetheless, by comparing the 1947 statistics with earlier results, it is clear that the penal commissions, like the People's Courts, became more lenient as time elapsed. In October 1946 the conviction rate stood at 42.6 percent, but ten months later the final results show a rate of only 34.3 percent.

Results from several districts demonstrate the uneven punishment of offenses against national honor (Table 4). In Klatovy, near the border with Bavaria, only 12.6 percent of the original 1,519 cases resulted in conviction. Fewer than half of the 192 convicted defendants faced imprisonment, 100 had to pay fines averaging 7,095 crowns, and 142 were to submit to public censure. The ninety prison sentences tallied up to 902 weeks, for an average of ten weeks per person. Most interestingly, 506 of the original cases were dismissed because the defendants were missing or had been expelled, leading one to surmise that the Klatovy tribunal investigated local Germans and Germans "of Czech origin" at a higher rate than elsewhere. Of the resolved cases, convictions accounted for 31.8 percent.[139] From January through May 1947 the České Budějovice commission convicted 700 of 2,468 defendants, for a similar rate of 28.4 percent.[140] By contrast, in Benešov, a town southeast of Prague, the national honor tribunal ruled on 423 defendants

---

[137] After the end of retribution on 4 May 1947, district courts inherited 44,629 unresolved cases.

[138] MV č. B-2220-12/8-47-I/2, "Informace pro pana ministra vnitra: výsledek činnosti národních výborů podle dekretu č. 138/45 sb." (18 August 1947), SÚA, f. MV-NR (B2220), k. 2017, sv. 2.

[139] "Stíhání provinění proti národní cti," Věstník ONV Klatovy III:5 (1 June 1947), 2.

[140] Source provided by Jeremy King. Jihočech 45:4 (20 February 1948), 4.

Table 4. *Comparison of National Honor Commission Results*

Commission	Total Cases	Adjudicated	Convicted	Conviction Rate (%)
Benešov[a]		423	77	18.2
Klatovy[b]	1,519	603	192	31.8
Nové Město[c]		714	94	13.2
V. Meziříčí[c]	707	560	80	14.3
Statewide[d]	179,896	135,267	46,422	34.3

[a] "Hlídka referátů ONV," *Věstník ONV Benešov* I:5 (31 May 1947), 5.
[b] "Stíhání provinění proti národní cti," *Věstník ONV Klatovy* III:5 (1 June 1947), 2.
[c] Miroslav Kružík, "Spisy tzv. Malého dekretu v bývalých okresech Nové Město na Moravě a Velké Meziříčí," in Mečislav Borák, ed., *Retribuce v ČSR a národní podoby antisemitismu: Židovská problematika a antisemitismus ve spisech mimořádných lidových soudů a trestních komisí ONV v letech 1945–1948* (Prague: Ústav pro soudobé dějiny Akademie věd České republiky a Slezský ústav Slezského zemského muzea, 2002), 130–31.
[d] MV č B-2220-12/8-47-I/2, "Informace pro pana ministra vnitra: výsledek činnosti národních výborů podle dekretu č. 138/45 sb." (18 August 1947), SÚA, f. MV-NR (B2220), k. 2017, sv. 2.

and penalized only 18.2 percent of them, far below the nationwide average.[141]

The high percentage of acquittals resulted partially from the failure of testimony to hold up under scrutiny. The Klatovy national committee announced that in numerous cases the informer "either completely made the thing up or blew a trifle into a huge bubble which burst once confronted with the evidence."[142] Another national committee, when accused of excessive leniency, reported that numerous charges were based on nothing more than "personal hatred or revenge." Other charges had nothing to do with the retribution laws at all.[143] A Prague penal commission dismissed the case against one woman after it determined that the "entire undertaking... [was] the simple revenge of one individual." Of the forty witnesses called, twenty-nine testified to her good "Czechoslovak" character and her service to the resistance. Eleven spoke against her, but their testimony was mere hearsay – they utilized phrases like: "[according to] public opinion; or I heard [that];

[141] "Hlídka referátů ONV," *Věstník ONV Benešov* I:5 (31 May 1947), 5.
[142] "Všemu občanstvu klatovského okresu," *Věstník Okresního národního výboru v Klatovech* II:1 (January 1946), 1–2.
[143] MV no. B2220-15/5-46 (1 June 1946); ONV Milevsko (8 October 1946) to MV; MV no. B2220-11/10-46-I/2 (15 November 1946), SÚA, f. MV-NR (B2220), k. 2016.

or seeing that it was said around; [or] it's known that; or I know from conversations...."[144]

A June 1946 Interior Ministry report attributed the high acquittal rate to the composition of the honor commissions, in particular, to the practice of choosing one member from each of the four Czech political parties. According to the report, the Communist and the Social Democrat commissioners usually voted to convict, while the representatives from the National Socialist and People's Parties regularly moved to acquit. A plethora of tie votes (two to two) ensued, resulting automatically in defendants' exoneration. Wealthy persons, in particular, had allegedly been freed due to commission deadlocks. To solve this problem and tilt the balance of power toward proponents of harsh retribution, the report recommended the appointment of a fifth judge, a tiebreaker chosen by the local chapter of the Union of Liberated Political Prisoners.[145] In practice, this solution would not necessarily have changed the situation to the Communists' liking. Over time, even former victims of the Nazis apparently grew reluctant to apply the Small Decree to fellow Czechs. An article in a Communist periodical complained that one commission, dominated by members of the Union of Liberated Political Prisoners, had dismissed 180 of the 200 cases it had considered.[146] After their election victory in May 1946, some Communist officials chose a different tack. They changed a commission's entire membership and began even to retry individuals who had already been acquitted. In "Red" Kladno, Communist packing of the tribunals led to a united protest by the other parties. In November 1946, when the local Communists refused to relent, the other three parties' representatives declared a boycott not only of the area's honor commissions, but of its national committees as well.[147]

---

[144] ÚNV Prague TNK no. 35, case no. K/6-921/46, SOkA Kutná Hora, f. ONV-KH, k. 89, sign. III/21b/c (TNK 1947).

[145] "Informace pro pana ministra vnitra" (10 June 1946), SUA, f. MV-NR (B2220), k. 2016.

[146] Jindra Uher, "Trestní, či osvobozující komise dle malého dekretu?" Pochodeň, II:25 (21 June 1946), 1.

[147] "Interpelace no. 138 poslanců Torna a dr. Kácha ministra vnitra o postupu trestních nalézacích komisí" (3 October 1946), Těsnopisecké zprávy Ústavodárného národního shromáždění: Tisk, Archiv Federálního shromáždění; Informace pro pana ministra vnitra" (8 November 1946), SÚA, f. MV-NR (B2220), k. 2016; Bedřich Hostička, "Malý

As with the People's Courts, there are two ways of looking at the final results of the national honor commissions. On the one hand, nearly 90,000 individuals suffered months of uncertainty, were denied the benefit of "certificates of reliability," and were threatened with fines and imprisonment, only to learn that the accusations against them had been deemed groundless. On the other hand, to repeat Vilém Hejl's commentary on the People's Courts, the high number of acquittals also demonstrates the "enduring civic, legal, and human honor of those who dealt with these cases and did not submit to pressure or to the hateful psychosis of revenge."[148] The 34.3 percent rate of conviction, moreover, does not include the results of the Appeals Commissions, which ultimately reduced many sentences and nullified others altogether.[149] As for the 44,629 unresolved national honor cases, we can safely assume that the district courts – which after 4 May 1947 gained jurisdiction over the punishment of offenses against national honor – dismissed charges at a far higher rate than the penal commissions.

THE KING OF COMICS

The prosecution of the Czech "King of Comics," Vlasta Burian, demonstrates both the substantial strengths and ultimate weakness of postwar retribution tribunals. In the 1920s and 1930s Burian was an adored radio and film star who brought laughter to millions of his compatriots. Like many other Czech actors, he continued to perform during the occupation, but for the most part remained apolitical. The one notorious exception was the radio skit "Stars over Baltimore," a viciously anti-Semitic parody of the United States and the Czechoslovak government-in-exile. Aired first on the eve of Pearl Harbor, only weeks

dekret a spravedlnost," *Lidová demokracie* (26 November 1946), 1–2; MV response to interpellation no. 138 (9 January 1947), SÚA, f. MV-NR (B2220), k. 2016.

[148] Vilém Hejl, *Zpráva o organizovaném násilí* (Prague: Univerzum, 1990), 26.

[149] Although there are no known final results for the Appeals Commissions, preliminary statistics indicate that by October 1946 the Prague Provincial National Committee had received 3,256 appeals and the Brno Committee only 822. Of these the Prague commission denied 449 appeals, overtuned 113 guilty verdicts, and reduced penalties in 115 cases. The Brno commission denied forty-four appeals, overturned thirty-seven guilty verdicts, and reduced penalties in seventeen cases. "Informace pro pana ministra vnitra, Očista veřejného života" (Oct. 1946), SÚA, f. MV-NR (B2220(1)), k. 2016; "Urychlíme vnitřní očistu," *Mladá fronta* (5 November 1946), SÚA, f. MZV-VA II, k. 216, j81.

before the Wannsee Conference, the sketch contrasted the starving un-
employed of New York with wealthy Jews, including the allegedly
Semitic Rockefellers. While the "Israelite Boys" provided the mocking
chorus, Burian played an alcoholic Jan Masaryk and slurringly broadcast (mistaking his bottle for a microphone):

Dear colleagues! (hiccup) What should I tell you[?] It's going great for me
here, I have enough money and booze here and I'm looking forward to when
I can return to you with the Jews. Without the Jews I'm totally helpless. I'll
end with the new greeting of the Czechoslovak government in London: Cohen
greets Sarah.

In his defense, Burian argued after the war that he had only performed
one such sketch and did so under compulsion. He had allegedly received
his lines sight unseen, and when he refused to perform them, the occupation authorities threatened to close his theater, an action that would
have endangered the livelihood of his eighty employees.[150]

Both Burian and his supporters later claimed that the comic performed the skit in such a way that made it clear his heart was not in it.
One actor commented, "Rarely did I ever hear something so sad. Nothing that he said was funny. He read the text automatically."[151] Similar
testimony serves as a warning to historians tempted to view transcripts
as irrefutable evidence, but unable to recapture the tone with which an
actor – theatrical, political, or juridical – delivered his lines. However,
Burian's critics pointed out, if his performance was so awful, then why
did the studio rebroadcast "Stars over Baltimore" twice in the following
months? And why did *Aryan Struggle* advertise the radio show ahead
of time and later praise the comic's performance? Chief Editor Novák
enthused,

It's very propitious when not only political forces but also cultural and artistic
workers join in the flow of the Czech nation's new orientation. This is the
best way to demonstrate that behind the new orientation stand all the forces
of the nation. Émigré propaganda ... tries to make the Czech people believe
that behind the new order stand only a few journalist-traitors. And now we
see how even artists of the character of Burian have put their rare artistic

[150] Vladimír Just, *Věc: Vlasta Burian. Rehabilitace krále komiků* (Prague: Rozmluvy, 1993),
59–61.
[151] Just, *Věc: Vlasta Burian*, 61–62.

abilities to use.... After all, they can't just label Burian a "Banner-man" or a "mercenary."

Clearly, collaborationists considered it quite a coup to get Burian. Then again, the comic subsequently avoided similar performances and *Aryan Struggle* soon went from praising the comic to damning him for his "Schweikism" because he had not performed in German films. When the tabloid sent him its anti-Judeo-Bolshevik questionnaire, he ignored it. He risked making antioccupation jokes in his stage performances and was ultimately banned from the Barandov studios.[152]

Based on anonymous denunciations from neighbors and the official accusation of the National Theater Factory Commission, Burian was detained in late May 1945 and held, with a brief one-day interruption, until the following September. When the prosecutor finally examined the charges in October 1945, he determined that the case against the comic did not merit a trial before a People's Court. In particular, the prosecutor ruled that Burian had not performed "Stars over Baltimore" with the intent of supporting the Nazis and therefore there were no grounds to try the King of Comics under Paragraph Three of the Great Decree. Three months after the prosecutor dismissed the case, however, the secret police requested the Burian file. Apparently, higher authorities had taken a special interest in punishing the comic, perhaps because they believed him to be an icon of frivolous bourgeois satire.[153]

Although his case did not merit prosecution before a People's Court, Burian still faced the prospect of punishment for an offense against national honor. On 8 June 1946 the Prague penal commission met in the City Library. The gallery was packed for the comedian's first public performance in two years. The King of Comics stood accused of applying for German citizenship, supporting Nazism, collaborating professionally with the occupiers, and fraternizing socially with Germans more than was necessary. Though Burian's fame likely made him a target of prosecution, it also seems to have afforded him a greater opportunity to present a vigorous defense. Contrary to official regulations, Burian's lawyer actively defended his client and presented evidence that the accusations were based on already disproved rumors. Numerous witnesses were called on the comic's behalf. The commission's Communist

[152] Just, *Věc: Vlasta Burian*, 60–63, 69–75.
[153] Just, *Věc: Vlasta Burian*, 30–32, 43, 78–79, 83, 88–91.

chairman – who with his black eye-patch bore an eerie resemblance to the Hussite military hero Jan Žižka – ended the proceedings by reading letters testifying to Burian's patriotic character from his theater employees and the city's leading soccer club, among other notable supporters of the comedian. After a short break the commission unanimously declared that there was not sufficient evidence to prove that Burian's wartime conduct offended Czech national honor. The crowd greeted the verdict with boisterous applause and Burian completed the performance with a bow to his adoring fans.[154]

It was not, however, to be Burian's final performance before an honor commission. Regardless of the verdict, the secret police initiated further investigation and pushed for a new trial. Meanwhile, *Rudé právo* and likeminded press decried the dismissal and initiated a campaign against the comic's rehabilitation.[155] On the pretext that new evidence had surfaced, at the end of January 1947 a special penal commission voided Burian's acquittal. On 3 May 1947, the day before retribution ended, a new commission with a new chairman reconvened in the City Library to consider the revised case against the comic. This time the commission refused to hear witnesses in his favor and denied his right to consult with counsel. Several key prosecution witnesses whose depositions had been read in the Library later disavowed their testimony. Nonetheless, the proceedings still took six hours before the new commission convicted Burian of "social relations with Germans more than was necessary" and sentenced him to public censure, a fine of 500,000 crowns, and three months in prison. Since he had already been held for longer than that in 1945, Burian was immediately set free.[156] He appealed the conviction, but before the matter could be addressed, the Communist takeover intervened. When the Appeals Commission finally met in October 1948 it merely confirmed the conviction.[157]

Although Burian's fame made the public nature of his case unusual, his experience with the Czech retribution system was not aberrant. Thanks to the heinously anti-Semitic "Stars over Baltimore" skit, the authorities had good cause to arrest the comic as a suspected collaborator.

[154] Just, *Věc: Vlasta Burian*, 91–97; Ivan Černý, *Byl jednou jeden Vlasta... O králi českých komiků* (Prague: Magnet-Press, 1991), 85.
[155] Just, *Věc: Vlasta Burian*, 99–107.
[156] "Potrestání Vlasty Buriana," *Národní osvobození* (3 May 1947), 2; "Vlasta Burian odsouzen," *Lidová demokracie* (4 May 1947), 2.
[157] Just, *Věc: Vlasta Burian*, 121, 228–38.

Like thousands of his compatriots, however, Burian was detained before there was a law under which he could be tried. He waited months in jail before a prosecutor finally investigated the evidence against him and dismissed the charges. In the meantime, the government issued the Small Decree and the comic faced proceedings before a national honor commission. Despite pressure to convict, the commission rejected the charges. But even this second dismissal did not suffice. Political pressure yielded another hearing and a verdict that convicted Burian and gave him a prison term that suspiciously matched the time he had already sat in jail.

CONCLUSION

National honor commissions punished Nazi sympathizers, venal opportunists, and base miscreants who inspired terror and caused great suffering during the occupation. Many defendants, however, had only fallen afoul of Czech society's new rules. Ordinary citizens who never chose to be examples for the nation found themselves held to a standard of conduct they could scarcely have predicted. The case of František Holík, a retired police captain from Litoměřice, illustrates this dilemma. Out of fear that he and his wife would have to leave their home in the newly annexed Sudetenland, he opted for German nationality on 26 October 1938. At the age of sixty-three, Holík probably did not see the point in risking his pension for "national honor" – a concept that would not be defined for another seven years. After all, he was no longer on active police duty; he would not have to participate in any unethical operations or even follow German orders.[158] In the end, his sentence – public censure – was mild, perhaps even appropriate, but as we have seen, formal penalties were often the least of a convict's tribulations. Penal commissions judged Holík and tens of thousands like him to be "dishonorable," while national committees declared them to be "unreliable." They were reduced to second-class citizenship and, put at the mercy of local authorities who all too often followed their own

---

[158] On the grounds that Holík could have moved to the Protectorate and, as matters turned out, would have received his pension there, the Litoměřice national honor commission sentenced him to public censure whereby the guilty verdict was to be posted in the town for one month. TNK no. 16250/46 (12 April 1947), SOkA Lovosice, f. ONV Litoměřice, k. 141.

interests at the expense of individuals and to the detriment of state policy.

In retrospect, it is difficult not to be critical of the Small Decree. Six months after the war ended, the Czechoslovak government defined a new range of transgressions and created a new set of institutions to punish them. At the moment when parliamentary rule, and with it a large measure of legal certainty, was reestablished, the principles *nullum crimen sine lege* and *nulla poene sine lege* were violated once more. In a damning critique of the Small Decree, Peroutka admonished the government,

> Create a law, perhaps revolutionary, even harsh; but from that moment on keep to it, and force others to do so as well; change conditions, but let the people quickly know what is what, so that they can again act with certainty; establish socialism, but then immediately underpin it with laws so steadfast and unwavering, so unaccepting of arbitrariness towards any individual or group...; put people on an miserable foundation, if need be, but let them feel that it really is a foundation.[159]

Several months after inventing "offenses against national honor," the government added to the uncertainty by authorizing the disenfranchisement of suspected collaborators on the flimsiest of pretenses. Thanks to its ability to sow uncertainty, the Small Decree initially represented a victory for those who wanted to push the postwar revolution ever forward. The national honor commissions, however, like the People's Courts, became less and less radical as time progressed. In the face of political pressure, they still dismissed two-thirds of the cases they considered, and the Appeals Commissions further reduced the toll. Critically, the honor commissions, like the People's Courts, wrapped up their operations on 4 May 1947, bringing the Small Decree and the uncertainty it caused to an end.

---

[159] Ferdinand Peroutka, "A přece," *Svobodné noviny* (11 Nov. 1945), 1.

6

RETRIBUTION AND
THE "TRANSFER"

When the munitions dump near Ústí nad Labem exploded on the afternoon of 31 July 1945, Czechs already had an explanation at the ready. Months of propaganda had spread the fear that underground bands of German terrorists operated unchecked throughout the country, sabotaging its reconstruction. The public reflexively concluded that the explosion, which set off a conflagration killing twenty-eight persons and injuring hundreds more, was no accident. In response, crowds of Czechs turned on the Germans remaining in the town. From a bridge across the Elbe rioters threw victims into the river, while on a town square, in the train station, and through the streets, the pogrom spread. Red Army units accompanied by Czechoslovak troops eventually restored order, but by then at least 200 local Germans lay dead.[1] Although the cause of the explosion was never conclusively determined, when the government cabinet met in the wake of the "Ústí catastrophe" the country's Interior Minister, Václav Nosek, left no doubt he believed that German saboteurs were to blame. Several ministers called for the expulsion of "dangerous people" who had played important roles in the Nazi Party and its paramilitary organizations. Communist Party leader Gottwald expressed indifference whether these Nazis would be expelled or jailed. Nosek assured his colleagues, "Instructions for the organized transfer have been issued. Dangerous people, first and foremost, are being

---

[1] Tomáš Staněk, "Co se stalo v Ústí nad Labem 31. července 1945?" *Dějiny a současnost* 2 (1990), 48–51; Karel Kaplan, *Poválečné Československo: Národy a hranice* (Munich: Nár. Politika, 1985), 139–40; Eagle Glassheim, "National Mythologies and Ethnic Cleansing: The Expulsion of Czechoslovak Germans in 1945," *Central European History* 33:4 (2000), 479–82.

transferred."[2] Less than one month after the government had issued the Great Decree, it undercut the commitment that it had made at Košice in April: to "take as its highest responsibility and its moral duty before the Czech and Slovak nations to capture, prosecute, and punish all war criminals." At that time the Czechoslovak leaders had promised to "carry out this task without any delays, without vacillation, and without indulgence for anyone."[3] After the violence in Ústí, the government apparently concluded that the punishment of suspected war criminals was less important than their deportation from the country.

This chapter does not discuss the expulsion of the Sudeten Germans per se – that topic has been well documented and analyzed elsewhere.[4] Nor does it offer an extensive analysis of the prosecution of German defendants, a subject worthy of a book all its own.[5] Rather, this chapter explores the relationship between the so-called Organized Transfer and postwar retribution. The euphemism "Organized Transfer" refers specifically to the systematic expulsion of more than two million indigenous Germans from Czechoslovakia; that is, to their concentration in internment camps and their subsequent deportation to occupied Germany throughout the year 1946. The Transfer and retribution – collective and selective punishment – were clearly linked. Expulsion and prosecution were often seen as alternatives: One Czech newspaper proclaimed, "Sympathy for a German or a traitor does not belong in our dictionary.

[2] Government meeting transcript (3 August 1945), Státní ústřední archiv (SÚA), Prague, f. 100/24 (KG), sv. 137.
[3] Jiří Grospič, Jaroslav Chovanec, and Juraj Vysokaj, eds., Košický vládní program (Prague: Státní pedagogické nakladatelství, 1977), 130–34.
[4] The expulsion of the Sudeten Germans is one of the few topics in Czechoslovak history to have received considerable scholarly attention abroad. For general works, see Detlef Brandes, Der Weg zur Vertreibung 1938–1945: Pläne und Entscheidungen zum 'Transfer' der Deutschen aus der Tschechoslowakei und aus Polen (Munich: R. Oldenbourg Verlag, 2001); Radomír Luža, The Transfer of the Sudeten Germans: A Study of Czech–German Relations, 1933–1962 (New York: New York University Press, 1964); Norman Naimark, Fires of Hatred: Ethnic Cleansing in Twentieth Century Europe (Cambridge, MA: Harvard University Press, 2001); Joseph B. Schechtman, Postwar Population Transfers in Europe, 1945–1955 (Philadelphia: University of Pennsylvania Press, 1962); Tomáš Staněk, Odsun Němců z Československa 1945–1947 (Prague: Naše vojsko, 1991).
[5] In their respective analyses of the Cheb and Ostrava courts, Jiřík and Borák concentrated mainly on the prosecution of Germans, who dominated those courts' dockets. Václav Jiřík, Nedaleko od Norimberku: Z dějin Mimořádného lidového soudu v Chebu v letech 1946 až 1948 (Cheb: Svět křídel, 2000); Mečislav Borák, Spravedlnost podle dekretu: Retribuční soudnictví v ČSR a Mimořádný lidový soud v Ostravě (1945–1948) (Ostrava: Tilia, 1998).

Simply – away with them! Or – punish!"[6] The postwar "national cleansing" commonly lumped treacherous national minorities together with suspected collaborators irrespective of nationality. In the same breath the presidential decree on confiscation declared "Germans, Magyars, traitors and collaborators" to be "unreliable"; their property was to be seized and put under "national administration."[7] Suspected Czech collaborators and Germans awaiting expulsion sometimes found themselves interned in the same camps. Like Germans, indicted Czechs were disenfranchised and often dispossessed; individuals officially charged with retribution crimes could only vote and receive their property back after they had proven their innocence. In sum, the preeminent Czech scholar of the expulsion, Tomáš Staněk, explained, "The course of retribution was connected in many ways to the expatriation [*vysídlení*] of the Germans and to the implementation of civil, material, social, and occupational measures against them (as well as against individuals accused of collaboration)."[8]

The government justified retribution and the Transfer on similar grounds. Both aimed to prevent a recurrence of the destruction of Czechoslovakia by punishing Sudeten Germans and Czecho-Slovak traitors who had allegedly stabbed their own state in the back in the years 1938 and 1939. Both sought a measure of justice for crimes committed during the Nazi occupation. Nonetheless, retribution and the Transfer were based on very different concepts. Whereas retribution entailed trials of selected individuals accused of specific offenses, the Transfer was the collective punishment of an entire national minority. Whereas the punishment of collaborators permitted their eventual release and rehabilitation (at least for those not executed), the expulsion was intended to be irreversible – in Beneš's hauntingly familiar words: It was to be "the final solution to the German question."[9] Most

[6] Staněk, *Odsun Němců*, 213.
[7] Presidential Decree no. 5/1945. Karel Jech and Karel Kaplan, eds., *Dekrety prezidenta republiky, 1940–1945: Dokumenty* (Brno: Ústav pro soudobé dějiny, 1995), I:216.
[8] Tomáš Staněk, *Perzekuce 1945* (Prague: Institut pro středoevropskou kulturu a politiku, 1996), 11. In Czech each of the several different terms employed to refer to the fate of the Sudeten Germans implies a different degree of severity. *Odsun* [transfer] is the most sanitized, followed by *vysídlení* [expatriation, evacuation, or, most accurately, ex-settlement]. *Vyhánění* and *vyhnání* [expelling and expulsion] imply a violent removal.
[9] At the inaugural session of the Czechoslovak Provisional National Assembly on 28 October 1945, Beneš stated, "I call on all of the great Allies from the Second World War...to

importantly, unlike the Transfer, retribution penalized Czechs as well Germans, a fact that had important consequences for the trials' popular support. Despite these differences, retribution and the Transfer were intertwined phenomena that profoundly influenced one other. At first glance, the punishment of individual Nazis and the expulsion of the German minority may have appeared to be compatible programs, but these two goals soon came into conflict. Whereas retribution served to justify and enforce the Transfer, the reverse cannot be claimed. In fact, the Transfer weakened and ultimately undermined postwar retribution.

RETRIBUTION JUSTIFIES THE TRANSFER

By the summer of 1941, at a time when Nazi defeat seemed unlikely, the central Czech resistance organization had already formulated the supporting role that retribution trials could play in the expulsion of Germans from the region. In a message to the government-in-exile in London the underground explained that opinions at home had "radicalized." Czechs demanded not only the reestablishment of the interwar state in its original boundaries, but also the expulsion of its German population. The dispatch conceded, however, that the "international situation" necessitated that "measures against Germans ... be conducted within the framework of the punishment of criminals and traitors and not as national repression."[10] Even after the Allies approved the "orderly transfer of the German population" from Eastern Europe,[11] the Czechoslovak government continued to worry about international reaction to the expulsions. With this concern in mind, on 28 October 1945 President Edvard Beneš told the inaugural session of the Czechoslovak Provisional National Assembly, "When, during the planned trials against our Germans, everything will be told about ... the actual ties of

help us solve this question *definitively*. To put an end to future attempts at some new Munich.... for us the final solution to the German question is simply essential, singularly just, and truly logical." Karel Novotný, ed., *Edvard Beneš: Odsun Němců z Československa: Výbor z pamětí, projevů a dokumentů 1940–1947* (Prague: Dita, 1996), 158.

[10] Jitka Vondrová, ed., *Češi a sudetoněmecká otázka, 1939–1945: Dokumenty* (Prague: Ústav mezinárodních vztahů, 1994), doc. 60, 112–13.

[11] Article XII of the Protocols of the Potsdam Conference (1 August 1945). Jech, *Dekrety*, I:381.

our Germans to Hitler's government, the whole world will see that we are in the right."[12]

In the battle for international public opinion, the greatest postwar trial of them all served as the strongest justification for the most extreme measures. Frequent press reports from the International Military Tribunal (IMT) at Nuremberg reminded the Czech public, as if such a reminder was necessary, of the malice of Nazi Germany.[13] These articles also provided a rationale for the expulsion. The editor-in-chief of the People's Party daily *Lidová demokracie* argued, "The Nuremberg Trial is simultaneously our best defense before the whole world and an explanation why we, like the Poles, do not want, nor even can, continue to live under one roof together with the Germans."[14] No less a figure than Robert Jackson, the chief American prosecutor before the IMT, endorsed this interpretation when, on a visit to Prague, he commented, "After the Nuremberg trial I understand why you are in favor of the transfer of the Germans."[15] According to one Social Democrat, the documents entered into the Nuremberg trial not only justified the decision to expel the Germans; they demonstrated that German capitalism had underpinned fascism and proved the correctness of interwar Czechoslovakia's foreign policy reliance on the combination of a Soviet defense pact and East–West rapprochement. In other words, Czechs must support the nationalization of industry and stick with the Soviet Union.[16]

Trials of individual Germans provided concrete, personified examples of the crimes of which the entire Sudeten population was collectively accused. As Milan Kundera wrote, the "memory of the tribunal" is "the forgetting of everything that is not a crime."[17] In the case of postwar retribution, only Sudeten Germans suspected of war crimes or Nazi

[12] Novotný, *Edvard Beneš*, 158.
[13] See for example: "Dojmy z Norimberku," *Lidová demokracie* (15 February 1946), 1; "Portréty z Norimberku," *Lidová demokracie* (15 February 1946), 6; "Tragédie Lidice před norimberským soudem" *Lidová demokracie* (19 February 1946), 1; "Dokumenty z Norimberku," *Lidová demokracie* (22 February 1946), 1.
[14] Josef Doležal, "Proč s nimi nemůžeme žíti," *Lidová demokracie* (17 February 1946), 1–2.
[15] "Po norimberském procesu chápu," *Rudé právo* (14 April 1946), 1.
[16] After February 1948 the Social Democrat in question, František Tymeš, joined the Communist Party. In 1954 he became a member of the Central Committee. Tymeš, PNS 30 (14 February 1946), 9.
[17] Milan Kundera, *Testaments Betrayed: An Essay in Nine Parts*, trans. by Linda Asher (New York: HarperCollins, 1995), 229; quoted in Robert M. Hayden, "Schindler's Fate," *Slavic Review* 55:4 (winter 1996), 743.

collaboration were put on trial and only their stories were publicized. The prosecution logically selected only that evidence necessary to prove criminal intent. Consequently, the trials reduced the Sudeten German experience to one of hatred, violence, and treachery. Again and again, Czech politicians and journalists stressed that leading Nazis embodied the guilt of the entire German nation. Every prominent trial provided additional proof that the Transfer was not only necessary, it was above all just.

For contemporary Czechs, Karl Hermann Frank was the Sudeten population incarnate. In March 1939 the former Carlsbad bookseller became Nazi State-Secretary (and later the State-Minister) of the Protectorate of Bohemia and Moravia. Though he originally worked in the shadow of Reichs-Protektor Konstantin von Neurath, Frank quickly became known for his advocacy of repression and terror. After Neurath's successor, Heydrich, succumbed to his wounds on 4 June 1942, Frank became the most powerful man in the Protectorate for the remainder of the occupation. After the war Frank was indicted for every single paragraph of the Great Decree, except the one (Paragraph Four) that punished acts committed abroad. The national prosecutor accused him of spying for a foreign power, Nazi Germany, while still a Czechoslovak citizen and of organizing an espionage ring against his own state. As the highest-ranking officer of the Protectorate SS and German police, Frank bore ultimate responsibility for deportations to concentration camps and for sending Czechs to perform forced labor in Germany. He signed orders for numerous death sentences, authorized executions, and instituted martial law. He supervised the repression of Czech students in the fall of 1939 and organized the reign of terror, including the destruction of Lidice, that followed Heydrich's assassination. Under his watch the Nazis expropriated the property of Czech organizations and museums, executed resisters, and deported Jews to certain death.[18]

In preparation for the Frank trial the state issued a 191-page pamphlet of his testimony culled from interrogation reports. Published the month the trial began and sold for thirty-five crowns, the editor introduced the pamphlet to the public as evidence to justify the expulsion. He stated forthrightly that the Germans' treachery predated the rise of

---

[18] Karl Hermann Frank, *Zpověď' K. H. Franka: Podle vlastních výpovědí v době vazby u Krajského soudu trestního na Pankráci* (Prague: Cíl, 1946), 184–91.

Nazism; they had never been loyal citizens of Czechoslovakia, a state that had granted them full civic rights. The editor concluded, "The trial of K. H. Frank, notwithstanding his personal responsibility, cannot be considered a trial of an individual criminal, but a trial of the collective criminality of the German minority in Czechoslovakia."[19] Even those columnists who most vigorously defended the rights of suspected Czech collaborators against police abuses used Frank as a vehicle to condemn the Sudeten Germans as a whole. Bedřich Bobek, who on other occasions argued on behalf of interethnic families, claimed, "That which we judge today – in Pankrác [courthouse] just like in Nuremberg – is the collective guilt of an entire nation." Others argued that the trial illustrated the error of medieval Czech kings who shortsightedly invited German colonists to settle in Bohemia. Regardless of the source, the message was the same: "It is truly a historic trial which for future generations should justify measures so far-reaching as the transfer of the Germans from our lands."[20]

The Frank trial attracted far greater attention than the prosecution of any other German defendant. The attention stemmed in part from the early staging of the event; as time elapsed, public interest noticeably waned. The trial symbolically opened on 15 March 1946, seven years to the day that German troops first entered Prague. Newspaper reports describe waves of spectators streaming from electric trolleys to Pankrác, the hated and feared prison employed by the German authorities to detain and torture Czechs during the occupation. The National Prosecutor, Jaroslav Drábek, later commented, "Entrance was only by ticket, for which there was a real fight."[21] The courtroom itself overflowed, filled not only with a local audience and domestic journalists, but also with foreign correspondents who demonstrated little interest in subsequent Czech trials. Zdeněk Marjanko, who headed the Justice Ministry's department for retribution, and General Bohuslav Ečer, Czechoslovakia's representative to the IMT and chief hunter of war criminals, both attended the opening session. *Lidová demokracie* evoked

---

[19] Frank, *Zpověd'*, 3–5.
[20] Vlastimil Louda, "Co soudí český národ v K. H. Frankovi," *Masarykův lid* XV:10 (1 March 1946), 149; Nosek, *Těsnopisecké zprávy Ústavodárného národního shromáždění Republiky československé* (ÚNS) 17 (24 October 1946), 10; Bedřich Bobek, "≪K. H. Frank≫" *Lidová demokracie* (28 March 1946), 1.
[21] Jaroslav Drábek, *Z časů dobrých a zlých* (Prague: Naše vojsko, 1992), 115.

Figure 6. Karl Hermann Frank before the National Court in Prague. Česka tisková kancelář (Czech Press Agency), 22 March 1946. Reproduced with permission.

the scene, a powerful moment for Czechs who had been accustomed to seeing the defendant in a much different role (Figure 6):

Several minutes before 10:15 A.M. silence settles over the courtroom and the curious faces of all present turn to the doors on the left side of the chamber, from whence K. H. Frank is led between two guards. He sits in the place for the accused.... K. H. Frank is pale. He is dressed in a uniform without distinctions; he has brown laced-up shoes and pants with high cuffs, reminiscent of the former SS-Obergruppenführer K. H. Frank from the time of his doubtful glory.[22]

Paraded before Czechs as a criminal, the Nazi leader could no longer inspire terror; the "former" Frank, the "executioner of the Czech nation," had already perished before his trial even began.

---

[22] "Lidový soud v Praze soudí K. H. Franka za jeho činy," *Lidová demokracie* (23 March 1946), 1.

To obtain maximum effect, state radio broadcast the trial to the public.[23] That the authorities promoted the Frank trial for its propaganda value does not impeach the justness of the verdict. The guilt of the defendant, like that of Goering and Hoess at the trials in Nuremberg and Auschwitz, was never in doubt. As the reigning authority in the Protectorate from the death of Heydrich until the end of the war, he bore ultimate responsibility for the crimes committed by the Nazis. Court evidence convincingly demonstrated his direct complicity in expropriation, deportation, enslavement, and murder. Few could have been surprised on 22 May 1946 when the Prague People's Court sentenced the former State-Minister of the Protectorate of Bohemia and Moravia to death. The final reckoning took place in the Pankrác prison courtyard before an audience of 6,300 spectators, including seven women who had survived the massacre of Lidice.[24]

In the very same courtroom where Frank faced his accusers, on 29 April 1946 the National Court heard opening arguments against five Czech ministers from the wartime Protectorate government.[25] In a radio address to the nation, Justice Minister Drtina revealed that the timing of the two trials was no coincidence: "It has been possible to achieve that German guilt has been judged first through the trial of Frank and only then has come the turn of Czech guilt."[26] With Frank convicted and executed – German dictatorship symbolically beheaded – the people's attention turned next to the Czech leaders who obeyed and implemented the Nazis' orders during the war. Five months later, Heinrich Jöckel, the sadistic commandant of the Theresienstadt prison camp, was executed the day after Interior Minister Nosek declared that the Transfer had been largely completed and the Czechs' age-old battle with the eternal German enemy for control of Bohemia and Moravia had drawn to a final, victorious close. The lessons of the Frank and Jöckel trials were reinforced in the spring of 1947 when, in the prosecution of the Kladno Gestapo, the Prague People's Court relived the June 1942 liquidation of Lidice, the extermination of its entire male population, and deportation

---

[23] Ladislav Drůbek, "Poznatky od mimořádných lidových soudů v Praze a Litoměřicích," SÚA, f. MS (Drtina), k. 2111.

[24] Borák, Spravedlnost podle dekretu, 57.

[25] "The Trial of the Protectorate Government," The Czechoslovak Weekly (19 May 1946), 318.

[26] "Nikoli msta, ale spravedlnost," Svobodné slovo (30 April 1946), SÚA, f. MZV-VA II (j41), k. 208.

of its women and children. On 24 April 1947 the Prague People's Court ordered the execution of six Kladno Gestapo officers. Five days later came the turn of Karel Čurda, the Czech parachutist who had revealed the information that led the Nazis to Heydrich's assassins and thereby set off the chain of events that led to Lidice's destruction.[27] Like the trials of Frank and the Protectorate ministers, in the execution of the Kladno Gestapo and Čurda the Czechoslovak state simultaneously punished the German murderers and their Czech accomplices, whose concurrent deaths evoked the symbiotic nature of their lives.

For Czech leaders, the trial of "Henlein's representatives," – interwar parliamentary deputies and senators from Konrad Henlein's Sudeten German Party [*Sudetendeutsche Partei* (SdP)] – served as the ultimate reminder why the so-called Transfer was necessary and just. In the winter of 1946–1947 the Prague People's Court tried fifteen former SdP representatives, convicted all of them, and sentenced six to death by hanging. In an unforeseen boon to the trial's organizers, one defendant praised the fairness of his Czech defense lawyers and the country's justice system.[28] This statement only confirmed the widely propagated opinion that the Czechs stuck to their principles, even after the horrendous war; the Nazis, it was repeatedly stressed, would hardly have gone to such trouble. Unlike Frank's trial, the prosecution of the SdP leaders primarily concerned treason committed during the fateful year prior to the Nazi occupation of 15 March 1939. The crimes were not those of war; they had been carried out during peacetime, under democratic rule. The defendents could not claim obedience to higher authority or fear of Nazi retribution as mitigating excuses. During the trial the prosecution reviewed the alleged treachery of Czechoslovakia's Germans from its ancient beginnings up through the Munich Pact and beyond. The verdict against the SdP representatives thus formed a closure to the Transfer, if not to centuries of Czech-German coexistence. One Czech newspaper

---

[27] "Rozsudek nad původci zkázy Lidic vynesen," *Lidová demokracie* (25 April 1947), 1; "Zrádní parašutisté popraveni," *Národní osvobození* (30 April 1947), SÚA, f. MZV-VA II (j81), k. 217.

[28] The defendant in question, Gustav Peters, had reason to praise the system: At the opening of the trial the prosecutor changed Peters's proposed sentence from the death penalty to a prison term. Prokop Drtina, *Československo můj osud* (Toronto: Sixty-Eight Publishers, 1982), II:275–76; Sudetendeutscher Rat E. V. München, *Justiz im Dienste der Vergeltung: Erlebnisberichte und Dokumente über die Rechtsprechung der tschechoslowaskischen Außerordentlichen Volksgerichte gegen Deutsche (1945–1948)* (Munich: Universitäts-Buchdruckerei und Verlag Dr. C. Wolf & Sohn, 1962), 25.

summarized the trial: "The just punishment, which the Czech people imposed on the Swastika-ed deputies and senators, is the symbolic conclusion to the final parting of the democratic Czech population from the German parasites.... The day has come when once and for all the 'Sudeten fifth column' has ceased its activity."[29]

Although leading politicians and columnists viewed the SdP trial as a critical juncture in Czech history, both Drtina and National Prosecutor Drábek later lamented a dearth of public interest. In contrast to the Frank trial, by January 1947 the area of the court reserved for the public was at times completely empty.[30] Undeterred, Drtina publicly declared his commitment to ensure that the postwar trials of Germans would not be forgotten:

I myself will see to it that those documents – which demonstrate the Germans' intention to annihilate or, at the very least, deport our nation, and which have been gathered for these [retribution] trials – will be made available in popular and inexpensive publications to all our people.... With no less importance I call on our schools to transmit concrete knowledge of the horrors of the German assault that our generation survived.... And I believe that if we utilize the material about the German war guilt collected by our postwar ... courts, then we will best serve not only the interest of our own nation, but also the securing of a lasting peace.[31]

To that end, the government did print portions of the Frank trial and documents from the Nuremberg Tribunal, but these publications apparently failed to generate much interest on the open market. "Retribution fatigue" seems to have beset the public, as its attention turned from past injustices to present-day problems. One journalist explained with palpable regret, "Our nation is simply looking now to close the door on the painful past that it experienced and for its reading prefers to look to novels, sensational things; it looks for entertainment in light films, just not to have to take stock of ... the years of Nazi dominance."[32]

---

[29] "Konec paté kolony," *Obrana lidu* (16 February 1947), SÚA, f. MZV-VA II (j81), k. 212.

[30] Jaroslav Drábek, "Glosy k procesu s henleinovskými poslanci a senátory," *Dnešek* I:46 (6 February 1947), 728; Prokop Drtina, *Na soudu národa: Tři projevy ministra spravedlnosti dr. Prokopa Drtiny o činnosti Mimořádných lidových soudů a Národního soudu* (Prague: Min. Spravedlnosti, 1947), 15.

[31] Drtina, *Na soudu národa*, 16.

[32] František Bauer, "Velká vina," *Národní Osvobození* 18:37 (13 February 1947), 1. The publications included *Český národ soudí K. H. Franka* (Prague: Ministerstvo informaci, 1947); *Československo a norimberský proces: Hlavní dokumenty norimberského procesu o zločinech nacistů proti Československu* (Prague: Ministerstvo informaci, 1946).

RETRIBUTION ENFORCES THE TRANSFER

In addition to providing examples of Teutonic evil, thereby ideologically reinforcing the will to expel, retribution helped to ensure that few voices would be raised against the Transfer and that few Czechs would sabotage its completion. In the first place, the Great Decree dissuaded Sudeten German antifascist leaders from returning to Czechoslovakia after the war. According to the decree's fourth paragraph, five to ten years' imprisonment were mandated for any "Czechoslovak citizen who... *while abroad* subverted the movement to liberate the Czechoslovak Republic in its pre-Munich constitutional form and unity, or who otherwise consciously harmed the interests of the Czechoslovak Republic."[33] Above all, this paragraph threatened Wenzel Jaksch, the chairman of the German Social Democratic Party, who during the war escaped to Great Britain and there promoted the Sudeten German cause. A proponent of German autonomy within a democratic Czechoslovakia, he challenged the country's 1920 centralist constitution and, for that reason alone, would have fallen afoul of Paragraph Four. In addition, Jaksch argued with Beneš over the latter's plans for the creation of a Czecho-Slovak nation-state and eventually refused to recognize the president's authority. Along with the anti-Beneš, but also anti-fascist, Slovak leader Štefan Osuský, Jaksch never returned to postwar Czechoslovakia.[34] Thus, the Sudeten Germans were denied a strong advocate who could have credibly advanced the position that not all his people were Nazis and that retribution must be individual, not collective.

The Small Decree also helped to enforce the Transfer. The Decree empowered national committees to punish Czechs for "offenses against national honor" with public censure, a one-year prison sentence, a fine up to one million crowns, or any combination of these three penalties. A subsequent Interior Ministry directive specified nine types of offenses that targeted Czechs who had collaborated politically, economically, professionally, and socially with Germans. The Small Decree's significance for the Transfer lay in the national committees' ability to penalize everyday offenses against national honor committed after the war was over. The Great Decree authorized retribution tribunals

---

[33] Italics added. Jech, *Dekrety*, doc. 8, I:169.
[34] Anton Rašla, *L'udové súdy v Československu po II. svetovej vojne ako forma mimoriadneho súdnictva* (Bratislava: SAV, 1969), 80.

to punish acts committed during "the period of heightened danger to the republic," from 21 May 1938 "until a date to be determined by government edict." The government discussed several possible dates for the end to the period and finally settled on 31 December 1946.[35] Although guidelines for the "the period of heightened danger to the republic" actually came from the Great Decree, the impact was considerably greater on the honor commissions than on the People's Courts. Almost all of the crimes enumerated in the Great Decree had to have been committed "in the service or interest of the enemy," a condition difficult to fulfill once the enemy, Nazi Germany, had been defeated. It was impossible to become a functionary in the Nazi party or to denounce one's neighbor to the Gestapo after the end of the war. The Small Decree, by contrast, penalized collaboration with Germans *qua* Germans. And, unlike the Nazi state, after 8 May 1945 Germans continued to exist.

Amid the expulsion of several million Germans, the honor commissions thus obtained the power to punish individual Czechs who continued to fraternize with the declared enemies of their nation. The Communist biweekly for national committee members, *Lidová správa* [*People's Administration*], exhorted party cadres to police their fellow citizens' behavior: "Don't forget that 'social relations' with Germans are also punishable; don't forget that there are still people who not only interact with Germans far more than is necessary, but who even want to marry German women. . . . Apprehend these cases and, as necessary, make an example of them."[36] In February 1946 the national committee in Ústí nad Labem informed the Interior Ministry that it could not estimate the number of expected cases because, "in this district criminal transgressions against the decree on national honor, particularly cases of unapproved contact with Germans, *are still being committed*."[37] Coming from the town that had recently been the site of a murderous anti-German pogrom, the tone of the report was ominous, to say the least.

In March 1946, Gustav Czaban, the secretary of the Communist parliamentary club, urged national committee members to act against

---

35 Vládní nařízení č. 217/1946 Sb., Jech, *Dekrety*, I:179, n. 2.
36 V. Adámek, "Ještě k dekretu o národní cti," *Lidová správa* I:6 (1 January 1946), 8.
37 Italics added. ONV Ústí nad Labem (11 February 46) to MV, SÚA, f. MV-NR (B2220), k. 2017.

contemporaneous collaboration. He argued that the Interior Ministry's instructions were not exhaustive; national committees could and should devise their own guidelines according to necessity. Czaban alleged, for example, that there was no need to get government approval to punish anyone who falsely testified or carelessly signed a "certificate of national reliability" in favor of a German or a collaborator.[38] In response to similar suggestions from various Communist organs, in May 1946 the Interior Ministry issued an amendment to its earlier national honor directive. A new paragraph punished anyone who deceptively vouched for the reliability of someone else.[39] The Ministry thus closed the door on one means by which some Germans had apparently evaded collective sanctions against their conationals.[40]

The ability to punish postwar fraternization with Germans was not an empty threat. On 3 May 1947 an honor tribunal in Litoměřice separately tried and penalized two men for having "maintained amorous relations" with their German female partners after the defeat of the Nazis. The commission issued a two-week jail sentence to Michal Stojko, a veteran of the Czech units that fought with the Allies on the Western Front. In July 1946 his German partner had been expelled, but she illegally returned to the country and took up residence with him. The offense had apparently been exacerbated by the birth of a child. On the same day that the court convicted Stojko, it also sentenced Otto Francl, a former chairman of a postwar national committee, to two weeks and a 1,000-crown fine. His partner had also been deported, but, unlike Stojko, Francl had traveled illegally to join her in occupied Germany.[41] In a third case, another honor commission convicted a "national administrator"[42] for spending the night with two German women a year after the war had ended. His crime apparently consisted of the fact that alcohol had been imbibed and, above all, that he had kissed the

---

[38] G. C., "Do rázného útoku proti zrádcům a kolaborantům," *Lidová správa* I:9–10 (1 March 1946), 7–8.

[39] MV č. B-2220-12/4-46-I/2 (7 May 1946), "Dodatek ke směrnicím ministra vnitra...k provedení dekretu presidenta republiky č. 138/1945 Sb., o trestání některých provinění proti národní cti," SÚA, f. MV-NR (B2220), k. 2018.

[40] Jiřík, *Nedaleko od Norimberku*, 76.

[41] TNK no. 18718/47 (3 May 1947) and no. 19789/47 (3 May 1947), Státní okresní archiv (SOkA) Lovosice, f. ONV Litoměřice, k. 141.

[42] After the war "National Administrators" were appointed to run businesses confiscated from Germans and suspected collaborators.

women.[43] It is probably no coincidence that the three men – a decorated veteran, a national administrator, and a national committee chairman – all had held positions of power or respect within postwar Czech society. Local authorities clearly wanted to send a message that even prominent individuals (and even men) were not permitted to challenge the nationalist segregation of Czechs and Germans. In Stojko's case the commission made this point explicit: "A prison sentence has been assessed because the defendant, as a member of the Czechoslovak foreign army, should have in every respect paid attention to national honor."[44]

In a contemporary polemic inflammatorily titled, "The Devil Speaks German," a leading non-Communist politician pronounced, "We must rap the knuckles of anyone who for any reason would want to favor the Germans in our borderlands."[45] Thanks to its ability to punish postwar acts, the Small Decree was a powerful means to "rap the knuckles" of Czechs who maintained interethnic relationships they had built in the preceding years, including the peaceful decades before 1938. The punishment of offenses against national honor thus stigmatized precisely those Czechs, who, thanks to professional contacts, personal friendships, or intimate relations, might have otherwise intervened to help or defend individual Germans. Instead, these Czechs became potential targets of punishment. It is unknown how many Czechs were prosecuted for maintaining relations with Germans after the war, but we can assume that the threat of retribution dissuaded many from violating the ethnic segregation that ensured the thoroughness of the Transfer. In deterring Czechs from violating newly drawn national boundaries, the Small Decree thus isolated the Germans and thereby facilitated their deportation, just as the Nuremberg Laws and subsequent Nazi polices had criminalized contacts with Jews and thereby paved the way for their extermination. As such, the honor commissions illustrate how auxiliary laws and institutions can provide the conditions necessary for "ethnic cleansing" to occur.

43 Josef Plzák, "Malý retribuční dekret (Dekret pres. rep. č. 138/1945 Sb.) ve světle judikatury Nejvyššího správního soudu," *Právní prakse* XI (1947/48), 129.
44 TNK no. 18718/47 (3 May 1947), SOkA Lovosice, f. ONV Litoměřice, k. 141.
45 Ivan Herben, "Ďábel mluví německy," in *My a Němci: Dějinný úkol strany národně socialistické při vystěhování Němců z Československa* (Prague, 1945), 8.

"GERMANS" ON TRIAL

In a 16 July 1945 radio address marking the promulgation of the Great Decree, Czechoslovak Justice Minister Jaroslav Stránský explained, "Above all else, it's a matter of retribution for German crimes."[46] The final results reflected this commitment as well as the disproportionate German role in administering Nazi rule. According to internal Justice Ministry tabulations, in the first two years after the war the People's Courts sentenced 21,848 defendants, 70.3 percent of whom were of German nationality, to prison terms of varying lengths. An additional 455 Germans and 308 Czechs got life imprisonment. Four hundred sixty-seven Germans and 253 Czechs were sentenced to death.[47] At first glance these figures indicate that Czech provinces' German minority, less than 30 percent of the prewar population, bore the brunt of retribution.

Nationality, however, was not a clear-cut category. In addition to Sudeten Germans and German-speaking citizens of foreign states (primarily Germany and Austria), the Justice Ministry's definition of German nationality encompassed individuals who would have called themselves and were officially considered Czech before 1938, but who adopted German identity and citizenship during the war. When it came to tabulating defendants, the courts normally counted these "renegades" as Germans. Although only a case-by-case examination of each and every trial could establish how many of the "German" defendants were formerly Czech, reports from the first month of trials before the Uherské Hradiště People's Court indicate that a disproportionate number of such "renegades" were prosecuted. Of the first eighteen defendants recorded as having "German nationality," eight had formerly been "Czech." Typical was the case of one defendant who was listed as being of "German nationality," but of "Czech origin."[48]

The courts, like the general population, did not look kindly on so-called Germans of Czech origin. In their final reports to the Justice Ministry, the České Budějovice chief justice and head prosecutor both seized on "national indifference" as an explanation to justify their court's

---

[46] On 6 November 1945 Stránský became a Deputy Chairman of the government and was replaced as Minister of Justice by Prokop Drtina. Jaroslav Stránský, "Národní a lidové soudy," *Právní prakse* IV (1944/46), 189.

[47] "Výsledky retribuce," Vojenský historický archiv (VHA), f. Čepička, sv. 23, aj. 168.

[48] SÚA, f. MS (Org), k. 1930, sv. 1.

exceptional severity.[49] Apparently, the region had spawned many mixed marriages and seen countless cases of prewar "Czechs" who adopted German nationality.[50] The chief justice cited several cases of blood brothers who had been divided by nationality. For example, the brother of a "conscious Czech" who had spent almost the entire war in a concentration camp was punished after the war by the České Budějovice People's Court for his activity in the SS. In another case of two brothers, during the occupation the Nazis executed the "Czech" brother, whereas after the war the České Budějovice People's Court had the "German" brother hanged. The chief justice commented,

Due to the national indifference so common [in] southern Bohemia, . . . [many individuals] of Czech origin declared themselves for German citizenship, were the henchmen and lackeys of Nazism, informers for German authorities and the like, during which they used their local knowledge well.

With severity, made possible by the retribution decree, this court tried once and for all to confront these unhealthy conditions.[51]

The head prosecutor concurred that the České Budějovice court had been exceptionally harsh, especially in the first months. He blamed this development primarily on the "unusually provocative" behavior of local Germans who terrorized the Czech population. He also noted, however, that the Gestapo had found many Czechs willing to act as informers and denouncers.[52]

During the war Czech men who adopted German nationality and received Reich citizenship were immediately liable to be drafted into the Wehrmacht. At the same time, service in the Wehrmacht offered "renegades" German citizenship as a potential reward. Such cases presented the retribution courts with a dilemma. For military treachery Paragraph

[49] Among the twenty-four People's Courts, only the Tábor court issued a higher proportion of capital sentences than the České Budějovice court (approximately 4.6 percent and 4.5 percent of all verdicts, respectively). In absolute numbers, however, the Tábor court sentenced twenty-seven persons to death, while the České Budějovice court sentenced seventy persons to death – a total exceeded only by the People's Courts in the country's two largest cities, Prague and Brno, which handed down 133 and 79 capital sentences, respectively.
[50] For more on the nationality politics of the České Budějovice (Budweis) region, see Jeremy King, *Budweisers into Czechs and Germans: A Local History of Bohemian Politics, 1848–1948* (Princeton, NJ: Princeton University Press, 2002).
[51] "Skončení retribučního soudnictví," přednosta MLS-CB, SÚA, f. MS (Org), k. 1942.
[52] "Skončení," Vedoucí veřejný žálobce (v.v.ž.), MLS-CB, SÚA, f. MS (Org), k. 1942.

One of the Great Decree prescribed exceptionally harsh penalties, ranging from a minimum of twenty years to life imprisonment. In theory, all Czechoslovak citizens who fought for Nazi Germany were liable to be prosecuted for military treachery. In practice, the People's Courts usually did not try veterans of unambiguous German nationality, on the assumption that they had loyally served their true homeland, to which they would be "repatriated" in the Transfer. Germans of "Czech origin," who were not to be expelled even when deprived of citizenship, were a different story. The punishment of "renegades" who fought, or even just tried to fight, for Nazi Germany was sometimes severe. Twenty-two-year-old František Prokop unsuccessfully applied in 1942 to join the German army. In its 30 October 1945 verdict against him, the Kutná Hora People's Court ruled that the fact that the Germans had rejected Prokop's application had no bearing on his guilt because "the accused... did everything in his power, and that would have otherwise sufficed to be conscripted." The court viewed his application as evidence of military treachery according to the 1923 Law for the Protection of the Republic and sentenced him to twenty years in prison, including five years of hard labor and the loss of civic honor forever.[53]

Similar trials elsewhere yielded inconsistent verdicts and led to disagreements over the legality of the punishment. The Czechoslovak General Prosecutor ruled in the spring of 1946 that Czechs who served in the German military and had voluntarily opted for German nationality could be punished according to Paragraph One of the Great Decree. The issue made its way to the country's Supreme Court, which countermanded that military service was not necessarily traitorous. After all, at the moment when a Czech was naturalized as a German, he lost his Czechoslovak citizenship and thenceforth could no longer be guilty of military treachery for service in a foreign army.[54] Despite this ruling, the Great Decree's ban on judicial review prevented convicts like František Prokop from appealing their original verdicts.[55] Meanwhile, some

---

[53] František Prokop was the son of Antonín Prokop, whose case is examined in Chapter 4. F. Prokop verdict (30 Oct. 1945), Státní oblastní archiv (SOA) Prague, f. MLS-KH, Ls 15/45.

[54] "Skončení," v.v.ž. MLS-CR; v.v.ž. MLS-TA; v.v.ž. MLS-PL; v.v.ž. MLS-UH; přednosta MLS-TA; v.v.ž. MLS-HK; přednosta MLS-UH, SÚA, f. MS (Org), k. 1942.

[55] On 12 December 1948, a reconstituted People's Court reduced Prokop's sentence to three and one-half years, all of which he had already served. F. Prokop verdict (12 December 1948), SOA-Prague, f. MLS-KH, Ls 387/48.

retribution courts, operating either out of ignorance or in the belief that they were not subject to the Supreme Court's decision, continued to punish defendants of "Czech origin" for military treachery. The Liberec court convicted three Czechs in April 1947 for having served in an "enemy army."[56]

The Hlučín and Těšín (Teschen) regions presented the People's Courts with another problem. Located in the northeast corner of today's Czech Republic, the Hlučín area, like many others in Central Europe, defies easy categorization. For centuries part of the Bohemian Kingdom, and hence the Habsburg Monarchy, it was taken by Prussia in the 1740 War of the Austrian Succession. After the First World War Czechoslovakia acquired the territory and its heterogeneous population. When Nazi Germany seized the Sudetenland, it annexed the Hlučín region directly to the Reich, whereupon its residents automatically received German citizenship. Confronted by an entire population that had "become" German, the Czechoslovak government decided after the war to overlook the alleged treachery of the Hlučíns and, by and large, reinstate their prewar citizenship. Members of the Nazi party and other fascist organizations, however, remained liable for arrest and punishment. In October 1945 the Hlučín police called for the release of miners who joined the Nazi party to save their jobs. After all, the plea noted, imprisoned miners do not work as well as free ones.[57]

The Ostrava district attorney similarly argued for leniency when it came to the nearby Těšín region, which included many persons of Polish nationality. He insisted that the recent history of the area, where many Slavs had been encouraged to adopt German *Volkslist* status, necessitated a different approach than in the former Protectorate. The district attorney counseled the government to think of the big picture and adopt the "most lenient approach" possible because "in the Těšín region *every* Czech person is needed."[58] As with Czechs who joined the German military, the disagreement over the wartime conduct of the inhabitants of the heterogeneous northeastern corner of the Czech provinces was reflected in the inconsistency of their sentences. After the end of retribution, the Opava head prosecutor recommended that

---

[56] The court, however, only sentenced them to terms of three, six, and twelve months. Lsp 279/1947, 292/1947, 367/1947, SOA Litoměřice, MLS Liberec, Katalog.
[57] SNB Hlučín (23 Oct. 1945) to SZ Opava, SÚA, f. MS (Org), k. 1934.
[58] Italics in original. SZ Ostrava (8 October 1945) to MS, SÚA, f. MS (Org), k. 1934.

presidential clemency be employed to solve these problems "in the interest of the consolidation of conditions in the Hlučín region overall
and securing the Hlučín people for collaboration for the [good of the]
Czechoslovak republic."[59]

Dušan Janák's in-depth study of the Opava People's Court demonstrates that the official postwar determination of nationality masked
the country's heterogeneity. The Justice Ministry figures for the Opava
district, which included the Hlučíns as well as many Poles, indicate that
70.4 percent of the defendants were German, 28.8 percent Czech, and
only 0.7 percent "other," but the Ministry's decision to limit possibilities to only three categories was prejudicial, as was the derogatory label
"other." The claim that fewer than 1 percent of all defendants belonged
to a nationality other than Czech or German is highly suspect in light
of the heterogeneity of the Opava district. In fact, Janák's case-by-case
analysis determined that 15.4 percent of defendants were of a nationality other than Czech or German. Significantly, his total for German
defendants is 66.4 percent, only a fraction less than that of the Justice
Ministry. But his analysis yielded only 17.4 percent Czech defendants,
three-fifths of the amount logged by the Justice Ministry.[60] Apparently,
members of "other" nationalities were entered as Czechs, either on
their own initiative – in the belief that this designation would help their
cases – or by officials intent on minimizing the size of ethnic minority
populations.

Based on Janák's research and evidence from other People's Courts,
we can develop a framework to analyze the problematic nationality figures tabulated by the Justice Ministry: The "Czech" total, it appears,
included other Slavs, while the "German" total included many former
Czechs who had changed their nationality during the war. Rather than
demonstrate the uselessness of the figures tabulated, these problems indicate the contingent nature of national identity – the answer depends on
the circumstances under which the question was asked. Qualifications
aside, the vast differences in the ethnic profiles of average defendants
in different regions permit us to reach some conclusions about the role
that nationality played in retribution.

[59] "Skončení," v.v.ž. MLS-OP; přednosta MLS-OP, SÚA, f. MS (Org), k. 1942.
[60] Dušan Janák, "Činnost Mimořádného lidového soudu Opava v letech 1945–1948"
    Časopis Slezského zemského muzea B43 (1994), 250–52, chart 3, 276.

Table 5. *Percentage of Defendants by Nationality*

Courts	Czechs	Germans	Other Nationalities
Group A	4.1	95.6	0.2
Group B	72.7	25.9	1.4
All courts	39.2	59.6	1.1

For the purpose of illustration let us consider six People's Courts: the three courts with the highest percentage of German defendants (Group A) and the three with the lowest percentage of German defendants (group B) (Table 5). Group A is composed of the People's Courts located in the borderland (Sudetenland) towns of Česká Lípa, Cheb, and Liberec. Group B comprises the courts located in the interior (i.e., former Protectorate) towns of Kutná Hora, Tábor, and Uherské Hradiště. The three courts in Group A tried 4,283 defendants, 95.6 percent of whom were listed as having German nationality. Group B prosecuted 2,817 defendants, only 25.9 percent of whom were recorded as German.[61] As Table 6 illustrates, Group A courts were far more likely to convict a defendant (in approximately 80 percent of all cases compared to 60 percent in Group B), but far less likely to sentence him or her to death. Whereas the three borderlands courts sentenced 37 defendants to death (0.9 percent of all verdicts), the three interior courts handed down 91 capital penalties (3.6 percent) from a far smaller sample. It is clear that of the 467 "Germans" sentenced to death by the People's Courts, the vast majority were not tried in courts in the former Sudetenland. The average borderland defendant also received a substantially shorter sentence than his or her interior counterpart (4.9 years compared to 7.1 years). In sum, borderland (almost entirely German) defendants were convicted at a far higher rate but received significantly lighter sentences on average than their inland (mainly Czech) counterparts.

Considering the indiscriminate Czech hatred for the Germans, it is hardly surprising that the People's Courts convicted German defendants

---

[61] According to the Justice Ministry's nationality tally, the People's Court in Prague belongs in Group B, but the capital city is a case in and of itself and therefore has been left aside. Nonetheless, when added to Group B, the Prague court actually augments the contrasts described. The extremes were Cheb, where 98.3 percent of defendants were recorded as having German nationality, and Tábor, where "Czechs" comprised 76.2 percent of the docket and "Germans" only 22.4 percent. All statistics are my calculations based on Ministry of Justice monthly summaries. SÚA, f. MS (Z.tr.), k. 2076–77; MS (Org.), k. 1930–3.

Table 6. *Percentage of Defendants by Sentence*

Courts	Death	Life	Prison	Convicted[a]	Acquitted	Forwarded[b]	Average Sentence (years)
Group A	0.9	1.7	76.8	1.2	18.5	1.0	4.9
Group B	3.2	2.0	52.6	2.2	30.5	9.4	7.1
All courts	2.1	2.3	60.7	2.3	28.1	4.5	7.3

[a] Defendants convicted but given no penalty according to Paragraph Sixteen of the Great Decree.

[b] Cases forwarded to the Regular Courts because they were either unclear or too complex for the People's Courts to handle in a summary fashion.

at a higher rate than Czech ones. Czech judges were understandably more inclined to grasp the nuances of a fellow Czech's defense (and apparently far more likely to refer his or her case for adjudication by a regular court). German defendants, by contrast, confronted a court already convinced of their nation's collective responsibility for the war.[62] The relatively low acquittal rate resulted, however, from more than mere indifference or reflexive nationalist chauvinism. A collection of personal testimonies of Germans sentenced by the People's Courts retrospectively portrayed the trials as summary justice, where guilt was preordained and quickly determined. Some Germans suspected that their sentences had been set ahead of time by political officials. One reported that he had only learned he would be tried when, on the way back from forced labor one day, he was immediately dispatched to the courtroom. Others recalled that their trials had lasted but a few minutes. Since Germans as a whole had been dispossessed, German defendants could hardly afford to hire their own lawyers. As a result, they were dependent on the luck of receiving a sympathetic and energetic court-appointed lawyer, which, considering the public pressure of the day, was unlikely. Perhaps the greatest problem for many German defendants was overcoming the language barrier. In their testimonies, some former convicts noted that interpreters had been provided and that bilingual judges carried out proceedings

[62] To give one seemingly clear case of injustice, the Cheb court convicted Ondřej (Andreas) Wurdack, a German teacher, even though he had been purged, arrested, and continually harrassed by the Nazis for his antifascist beliefs. To escape persecution Wurdack had joined the SA, but after the war the locals had appointed him mayor because of his antifascist credentials. Although Czechs were willing to testify for him, the court refused to hear witnesses and sentenced him to sixteen months in prison. Jiřík, *Nedaleko od Norimberku*, 183.

in German and Czech. Nonetheless, others recalled that their trials had been conducted entirely in Czech – sometimes only the verdict was read in both languages.[63] Such disadvantageous conditions substantially decreased the opportunity for a German defendant to convince the judges of his or her innocence.

If a higher conviction rate in the borderlands seems logical, the significantly lower average sentence for the "German" courts (Group A) appears counterintuitive. Part of the explanation for the lesser penalties may lie in the particular demographics of the borderlands. Thanks to the relative absence of native Czechs in the wartime Sudetenland, Germans there had less opportunity to harm individual Czechs (or earn their personal hatred). As for crimes against other Germans, the preamble to the Great Decree spoke of the punishment of acts "whose victim was the Czechoslovak people." The People's Courts never reached a satisfactory consensus as to whether the denunciation of a German who had lost (or would lose) his or her Czechoslovak citizenship was punishable. Even when Sudeten Germans had committed serious offenses, the courts sometimes could not prove anything against the defendants since, in the absence of Czechs, "It was a matter of Germans among Germans."[64] When Sudeten Germans stood accused of violent crimes, they were likely to have been committed before the beginning of the war, when Czechs still lived in the borderlands in large numbers. The Cheb People's Court, for example, handed down at least half of its death sentences for treason against Czechoslovakia during the tumultuous weeks surrounding the Munich Pact. The Court sentenced ten Sudeten Germans to death and another sixteen to life imprisonment for their roles in the deadly, but ultimately unsuccessful Freikorps attack on the Habartov (Habesbirk) police station on the evening of 13 September 1938.[65]

The postwar dynamic also contributed to lesser sentences in the former Sudetenland. In the chaos of the first weeks after the war, before the central government belatedly established order, there were far more victims of "wild retribution" in the borderlands than in the interior.

---

[63] The retrospective protests of these defendants, all of whom had been sentenced to long jail terms, mostly for Nazi war crimes and/or membership in the SS and Gestapo, must be taken with a grain of salt. *Justiz im Dienste der Vergeltung*, 8, 23–24. See also Jiřík, *Nedaleko od Norimberku*, 50, 182.

[64] "Skončení," v.v.ž. MLS-CL, SÚA, f. MS (Org), k. 1942.

[65] Jiřík, *Nedaleko od Norimberku*, 415–417, 480, 500.

"Revolutionary people's courts" and vigilantism likely eliminated some of the most hated war criminals, thereby obviating the need for their formal execution later. Moreover, as a result of the disorder, the official People's Courts in the borderlands began operating long after those in the interior.[66] This delay meant, on the one hand, that many suspects suffered additional months of incarceration before prosecutors reviewed and dismissed their cases. On the other hand, in cases that went to trial, the delay was a boon to defendants, who escaped prosecution during the vengeful period immediately following the war. Finally, there was no engaged constituency in the borderlands to complain about lenient sentences.[67] After all, the new Czech migrants to the region did not personally know the defendants and cared little about the fate of individual Germans – as long they left their property behind when they departed.

Keeping all that in mind, the primary cause for the differences in sentencing between borderland and interior courts was likely the collective criminalization of membership. In his speech marking the promulgation of the Great Decree, Stránský stressed, "Not only the leaders' high treason, not only the Gestapoers' atrocities, but the entire merciless mob which helped them on the streets, at meetings and celebrations, must be tried and convicted."[68] The Great Decree ensured that the People's Courts did not limit themselves to the punishment of infamous Nazis like Frank and the SdP parliamentarians. According to Pargraph Two of the Great Decree, all members of paramilitary groups such as the SS, SA, or Freikorps were guilty simply by virtue (or rather by vice) of their membership. In contrast, Pargraph Three stipulated that only leaders, functionaries, and active members of the Nazi Party, SdP, and various Czech fascist organizations were punishable. The government eventually expanded the list of such groups to more than seven dozen organizations and formations including, for example, the Czech Association for Collaboration with Germans, the Anti-Jewish League, the Bund deutscher Osten, and the NS-Volkswolhlfahrt.[69] In London Beneš had originally proposed the criminalization of membership as a clever

---

[66] The last three People's Courts to begin were the borderland courts of Most (30 October 1945), Liberec (28 November 1945), and finally Cheb (February 1946). "Přehled činnosti veřejných žalobců u mimořádných lidových soudů," SÚA, f. MS, k. 1929.

[67] "Skončení," v.v.ž., MLS-CH, SÚA, f. MS (Org), k. 1942, sv. 3, 2.

[68] Stránský, "Národní," 189.

[69] Borák, Spravedlnost podle dekretu, 327–31.

way of getting around his prohibition on separate measures for Czechs and Germans.[70] Because most Nazi and fascist organizations were overwhelmingly or entirely German in nature, punishment of specific groups essentially targeted Germans. The criminalization of entire organizations weakens the claim that retribution, unlike the Transfer, was based on individual, not collective guilt. The Czechoslovak government justified this mass approach as necessary for expedience and defended it as consistent with the practices of the International Military Tribunal at Nuremberg.

Membership charges dominated the docket of borderland People's Courts. Of the 4,049 offenses arraigned before the Opava court, nearly two-thirds (2,678) were charges of membership in a Nazi or fascist organization. Of these, the most common types were Nazi Party [National Sozialistische Deutsche Arbeiter Partei (NSDAP)] or SdP functionaries (929) and SA members (642).[71] In Cheb, defendants were punished most frequently for being active in the SdP and the NSDAP.[72] The Liberec People's Court, for its part, mainly prosecuted an alphabet soup of Nazi organizations: the "NSDAP, SdP, SA, SS, BdM, DAF, NSKK, NSV, NSF, RAD," as well as the Freikorps and the Gestapo.[73] With Nazi membership common in the borderlands and few native Czechs to be victims of more serious crimes, Sudeten Germans were most often tried for Paragraphs Two and Three of the Great Decree. The prosecution of membership was simpler, faster, and more likely to result in a conviction than a trial for a specific criminal act. Guilt was frequently beyond doubt: The prosecutor often had access to a list of an organization's members or even to a defendant's membership card. Whereas conviction was more likely, the penalty was usually less harsh. Sentences for "victimless" offenses like membership tended to be shorter than those for crimes that caused direct harm to individual Czechs, especially when those Czechs (or their next of kin) testified against the

---

[70] "Záznam názorů E. Beneše na trestání válečných zločinců," Jech, *Dekrety*, doc. 8.1, 180.

[71] Janák, "Činnost," 279, chart 10.

[72] Václav Jiřík, "Retribuční realita a Chebsko," in Frank Boldt, ed., *Velké dějiny, malý národ* (Havlíčkův Brod: Český spisovatel, 1995), 211.

[73] Bund deutscher Mädel (BdM), Deutsche Arbeitsfront (DAF), Nationalsozialistisches Kraftfahrkorps (NSKK), Nationalsozialistische Volkswohlfahrt (NSV), Nationalsozialistische Frauenschaft (NSF), Reichsarbeitsdienst (RAD). SOA Litoměřice, Inventory MLS-Liberec, viii.

defendant. Although membership was also a common charge before interior courts, indictments there were move likely to include more serious offenses, for example, denunciation, terrorization, or even torture and murder. Membership may have resulted in a higher rate of conviction, but denunciation and violent crimes earned longer sentences or even execution.

THE TRANSFER UNDERMINES RETRIBUTION

The criminalization of membership may have enabled the state to exclusively target and rapidly convict Germans, but it was a step fraught with unforeseen consequences. As the authorities soon learned, the number of potential defendants was simply overwhelming. The Jihlava chief prosecutor informed the Justice Ministry that most Germans were members of some Nazi organization, while his Opava counterpart estimated participation in certain areas as up to eighty percent.[74] Moreover, many of the accused hardly fit the profile of dangerous criminals. As the chief judge of the Česká Lípa People's Court explained, all the young and healthy local German men had been drafted into the Wehrmacht, leaving only the old and sick behind. Nearly all of those who remained served in some sort of Nazi organization.[75] The punishment of minor offices even reached down to the "Blockleiter," functionaries responsible for the smallest component of the Nazi Party: a "block" composed of forty to sixty households. On 7 September 1945 the Interior Ministry initiated a new wave of arrests when it ordered the detainment of all functionaries of the Nazi party and related organizations, from the level of Blockleiter on up.[76] A Czech police officer called as a court expert testified that some Blockleiter were not even Nazi party members. He explained, "Later on [the party] did not even care so much about reliability because there was a shortage of people. Particularly in villages there was practically no choice of reliable people. So even people who couldn't speak German were appointed."[77]

---

[74] "Skončení," v.v.ž. MLS-OP; v.v.ž. MLS-JH; přednosta MLS-LT, SÚA, f. MS (Org), k. 1942.
[75] "Skončení," v.v.ž., MLS-CL, SÚA, f. MS (Org), k. 1942.
[76] Tomáš Staněk, *Tábory v českých zemích 1945–1948* (Ostrava: Tilia, 1996), 25.
[77] Borák, *Spravedlnost podle dekretu*, 174.

The immense number of cases soon forced the government to abandon its original commitment to judge quickly, if not its determination to rule summarily. By the end of 1945 the twenty-four chief prosecutors reported that a total of 23,049 cases remained on their dockets awaiting a decision whether to proceed to trial. Moreover, they expected another 58,000 cases to be submitted – a figure that turned out to be a gross underestimate. In areas with large German majorities the backlog was enormous: In Litoměřice 8,000 cases were expected, in Opava 5,000, in Cheb 4,000, and in Liberec 3,500.[78] As of 30 June 1946, the prosecutors had resolved 48,383 cases and had another 43,762 remaining. With the exception of the country's largest cities, the biggest caseloads were again in heavily German areas like Cheb, Liberec, and Most, where more than three-fourths of cases remained to be resolved.[79] Despite the original intention to dismantle the *Extraordinary* People's Courts after one year, due to the backlog retribution was extended twice, in July and December 1946, until it was finally brought to a close on 4 May 1947.

Most worrisome for the government, the prosecution of membership began to endanger Czechoslovakia's plans to expel the country's remaining Germans. On 4 March 1946, just six weeks after the Organized Transfer began, the Interior Ministry informed local officials that it had reached the conclusion that the prosecution of all suspects "would in practice make impossible the expatriation and transfer of a preponderant share of those of German nationality." The American occupation authorities in Germany had advised Czechoslovakia that they would only accept "whole" families (defined as spouses, their children younger than eighteen years old, and other dependents incapable of work). Exceptions were to be made only for convicted war criminals serving sentences longer than one year, and for those awaiting trial in the official custody of the court.[80] At the time, however, prison overcrowding had resulted in some 20,000 to 30,000 German suspects being held in internment camps (i.e., not court jails) awaiting trial.[81] The Interior Ministry warned,

---

[78] A few heavily Czech courts also had large backlogs, for example, Uherské Hradiště (4,900) and the country's two largest cities, Prague and Brno (3,500 and 3,850, respectively). Borák, *Spravedlnost podle dekretu*, 340–41.

[79] "Přehled činnosti veřejných žalobců" (11 November 1946), SÚA, f. MS, k. 1929.

[80] Ministry of Interior directive (24 May 1946), SOA-Praha, MLS-PR, Pres. 1.

[81] Prokop Drtina, *O soudcovské nezávislosti, lidovém soudnictví a jiných časových otázkách československé justice* (Prague: Mladá fronta, 1946), 52–53.

If the regulations of the retribution decree were strictly adhered to . . . the Extraordinary People's Courts would be overburdened with such a great number of defendants – whose guilt would consist only of indiscriminate affiliation or even simple membership in certain criminal sections of the NSDAP – that the adjudication of all these cases could not possibly be expected in the foreseeable future. Not to mention that, as a result, an insoluble problem with housing, guarding, and feeding them would arise. According to a rough estimate there would be at least half a million cases of this type. . . . And it cannot be forgotten that to this number of criminals are tied two to three times as many family members. In other words, this would mean that some one to one and a half million individuals could not be transferred, because by November of this year only about one-quarter of all Nazi criminals could be convicted and quartered in prisons and jails.

These facts point to the conclusion that there is no other solution except to adapt the implementation of measures against the Germans to the demands of expediency, and to the prosperity of the republic, and thus give first priority to the demands of expatriation. In other words, to give precedence to [expatriation] before criminal prosecution where it is a question of a mass of war criminals against whom only membership in certain organizations and formations can be charged.[82]

The directive specified that anyone accused only of membership in a fascist or Nazi organization, even in the SA, NSKK (Nationalsozialistisches Kraftfahrkorps), or the Waffen-SS, should be released for expulsion.[83] In other words, membership in many groups was essentially decriminalized, *de facto* if not *de jure*. This exemption did not apply, however, to former members of the SS, SD, or Gestapo, or to anyone who had served as an executioner or concentration camp guard. They, as well as anyone suspected of a specific transgression covered by the Great Decree (e.g., terrorization, denunciation, or murder) were still to be tried before a People's Court. As a defense against anticipated criticism, the directive halfheartedly suggested that Czechoslovakia's failure to prosecute expellees did not mean that they would avoid punishment altogether. Their deportation papers would include notice that they were war criminals.

---

[82] "Odsun Němců," Ministry of Interior directive (4 March 1946), SÚA, f. MV-NR (B2222), k. 2016.
[83] Whereas the Great Decree treated all SS formations the same, the directive drew a distinction between regular, longer-serving SS members and members of the Waffen-SS, in particular those who joined involuntarily. The directive does not specify how active members of the NSDAP or SdP were to be treated, but they evidently belonged in the group to be expelled.

It would then be up to the Allied occupation authorities in Germany to decide whether or not to prosecute.[84]

As the Transfer progressed the central authorities placed an even greater emphasis on expulsion over incarceration. In June 1946 the Justice Ministry requested that each court forward a list of those Germans serving sentences for crimes for which, had they not already been convicted, they would have been deported before trial.[85] Drtina publicly reported that "German transgressors" who had received sentences of less than five years were also included in the Transfer. In his words, this "meant considerable relief for our prison institutions."[86] In July the government went so far as to alter the criminal code to permit the cessation of proceedings and punishment in cases where the defendant was to be extradited, repatriated, or transferred.[87] On 22 January 1947 the Justice Ministry called for a priority on remaining German cases so that the Transfer could be completed. The People's Courts were instructed to inform national committees of any acquittals so that the defendants could be immediately expelled.[88]

For most German defendants, expulsion was probably preferable to imprisonment. If the accused had not already been tried, then his or her release for deportation was merely an administrative matter. Once a German had been sentenced to prison, however, expulsion was likely to be far more difficult.[89] The case of Josef Michelfeit, a former NSDAP Blockleiter, illustrates the odyssey experienced by many Germans convicted of membership crimes. Michelfeit was arrested seventeen days after the end of the war and remained incarcerated until his trial on 4 April 1946. The People's Court in Kutná Hora then sentenced him to five years' imprisonment because, in the words of the verdict, "The accused acted during the occupation like every other ferocious Nazi." Six months after the trial, in October 1946, the District

---

[84] "Odsun Němců," Ministry of Interior directive (4 March 1946), SÚA, f. MV-NR (B2222), k. 2016. This disclaimer was emphasized in the Justice Ministry's similar version of the same directive. "Odsun Němců," Ministry of Justice directive (2 April 1946), SÚA, f. MS (Org), k. 1934.

[85] "Odsun Němců," Ministry of Justice directive (28 June 1946), SOA-Praha, MLS-PR, Pres. 1.

[86] Drtina, O soudcovské nezávislosti, 60.

[87] Law no. 166/46 (19 July 1946), Sbírka zákonů a nařízení Republiky československé (Prague, 1946).

[88] SOA Litoměřice, Inventory MLS-Litoměřice.

[89] Borák, Spravedlnost podle dekretu, 161.

Figure 7. A Transport of Sudeten Germans Leaves Prague. Česká tisková kancelář (Czech Press Agency), 16 May 1946. Reprinted with permission.

National Committee asked for his release so he could be deported. The Justice Ministry approved the request. Despite his relocation to an internment camp one month later and then his subsequent transfer to a second "collection center," Michelfeit did not reach the American zone until the end of May 1947, two years after his arrest.[90] The nationality of a convict or of his or her family often determined whether the authorities permitted his or her deportation. For example, local authorities in the town of Místek answered the court's request for the release of a former Blockleiter: "If he is of Czech origin, he can't be transferred. If he demonstrates German origin, then there is no objection to his transfer."[91] Incarcerated Germans married to Czechs often had

[90] Verdict against J. Michelfeit (4 April 1946), SOA-Prague, f. MLS-Kutná Hora, Ls 117/46.
[91] Borák, *Spravedlnost podle dekretu*, 160.

their petitions for deportation refused because some authorities apparently did not want mixed-marriage families to be broken up.[92] Unlike homogamous Germans, intermarried Germans often had to serve out their prison terms.[93]

So-called German "specialists" were also barred from emigrating, but they generally managed to avoid prison. Facing a shortage of trained workers in the borderlands, the Czechoslovak authorities made exceptions to their commitment to expel the entire German population. In fact, the authorities actually prevented thousands of skilled Germans from leaving the country.[94] As Jiřík noted, however, "for German specialists to be able to stay in Czechoslovakia, it was necessary for them to have a clean retribution record." When, on 29 April 1947, the Cheb People's Court finally got around to trying seven German miners, the judges fully accepted the defendants' suspiciously similar claims that they had joined the Nazi Party and, in one case, the SA under compulsion. The very next day, the Cheb court acquitted eight skilled German porcelain workers, including two SA officers and a former Blockleiter. Two days later four more miners, including two Blockleiter, were exonerated.[95] Suspects from the town of Jáchymov, with its uranium mines firmly in Soviet hands, remained largely beyond the court's purview. Of the few who did face trial, the result was predictable. For example, in February 1947 the Cheb court acquitted Josef Kolitsch, a Jáchymov miner, even though he had been listed as an agent in the SD registry.[96] Once again, expedience had trumped justice, only in these cases economic necessity, not ethnic cleansing, came first.

In its expulsion directive the Interior Ministry warned against releasing "real criminals" who would later have to be extradited by the

---

[92] Other local officials deported intermarried Czechs and their children along with their German spouses. Benjamin Frommer, "Expulsion or Integration: Unmixing Interethnic Marriage in Postwar Czechoslovakia," *East European Politics and Societies* 14:2 (2000), 392–93.

[93] Borák, *Spravedlnost podle dekretu*, 161–63.

[94] Despite the Czechoslovak regime's rhetoric about exceptions for antifascists and its eventual renaturalization of Germans in mixed marriages, skilled workers were by far the largest group of Germans to remain in the country after the main phase of the Transfer. Of the approximately 140,000 Germans still in the country in November 1946 who were not slated for expulsion, more than three-fifths were industrial "experts" (33,537) or members of their families (another 53,103). Luža, *Transfer*, 290; Staněk, *Odsun*, 326.

[95] Jiřík, *Nedaleko od Norimberku*, 277.

[96] Jiřík, *Nedaleko od Norimberku*, 129–30, 228.

Czechoslovak authorities. According to the chief prosecutor in Jihlava, the indiscriminate nature of the Wild Transfer of spring 1945, when local Germans had been brutally chased en masse across the border into Austria, had already enabled thousands of serious offenders to escape justice.[97] After the Interior Ministry directive, national committees and the police expelled indicted Germans without the approval, and occasionally even without the knowledge, of the People's Courts. Sometimes judges and prosecutors only learned of a defendant's expulsion when he or she failed to appear at trial. For example, a prosecutor in Opava requested that one German be handed over to the court two days after he had been expatriated.[98] In Ostrava dozens of SA members and even several SS officers were expelled before trial. Some releases were later regretted: after he had been expelled, František Wallek, a former SS guard at the Mathausen concentration camp, was tried in absentia by the Ostrava People's Court.[99] Despite the general belief that "Henlein's representatives" were guilty of high treason, at least five SdP deputies and senators, significant ones at that, were expelled.[100] The discharge of convicted Germans was to be limited to minor sentences, but more serious cases were involved. For example, on 10 October 1946 Vilém Voigt – who had been sentenced by the Liberec People's Court the previous January to ten years for membership in the SdP, NSDAP, and SA – was released from prison and "transferred," having served only a fraction of his term.[101] The priority on the Transfer also undermined subsequent efforts to extradite war criminals. Although by January 1947 the Interior Ministry had brought 470 German suspects back to Czechoslovakia for trial, it refused many others because it feared "we would have to support them at our own cost and then set them free again."[102]

By spring 1947 a total of 14,879 cases had been dismissed for the expulsion of Sudeten Germans or the repatriation of citizens of other states.[103] Statistics from the Opava court demonstrate the detrimental effect of the Transfer on retribution. Of the 978 German suspects expelled, the majority (534) had never even been prosecuted.

---

[97] "Skončení," v.v.ž. MLS-JH, SÚA, f. MS (Org), k. 1942, 2.
[98] Janák, "Činnost," 257.
[99] Borák, *Spravedlnost podle dekretu*, 159.
[100] Drábek, "Glosy," 728.
[101] SOA Litoměřice, f. MLS-Liberec, Ls 7/1945.
[102] Staněk, *Odsun Němců*, 256.
[103] Drtina, *Na soudu národa*, 11.

Only forty-nine had served their entire sentences before being deported.[104] The Ostrava court, for its part, indicted 382 individuals who were later "transferred" to Germany. One hundred and forty cases were dismissed before the main trial and another thirty-eight were prosecuted *in absentia* because the defendant had already been expelled. A mere twenty-five of the 198 defendants who were convicted actually sat out their entire sentences.[105] Although the Great Decree established the mandatory minimum sentence for any crime at five years, as of 16 June 1948 little more than half (7,965 of an original 15,360) of the Germans convicted remained in Czech prisons. By the end of 1948 Czechoslovakia had released 3,183 Germans from incarceration.[106] Finally, in 1956 Czechoslovakia deported an additional 1,437 German convicts, including many prisoners serving life sentences.[107]

For Germans accused of membership crimes the Interior Ministry directive made a trial's date a primary factor in determining its outcome.[108] Until the directive the People's Courts sentenced numerous defendants to long jail terms solely on the basis of membership in a Nazi or fascist organization. Afterward such cases were often dismissed. The greatest differences occurred in the treatment of SA membership. Simple membership in the SA was originally prosecuted along with the SS according to Paragraph Two of the Great Decree, which mandated a minimum of five years' imprisonment. According to the March 1946 Interior Ministry directive, however, SA membership when accompanied by no other infraction was grounds for dismissal and expulsion. As a result, many SA members languished in prisons and labor battalions while their former comrades escaped trial altogether. This inequality was exacerbated by the Nuremberg Tribunal's ruling that, unlike the SS, the SA was not a criminal organization. It is thus not surprising that of the 219 cases

[104] Janák, "Činnost," 283, charts 16 and 17.
[105] Borák, *Spravedlnost podle dekretu*, 158–59.
[106] "Výsledky retribuce," VHA, f. Čepička, sv. 23, aj. 168.
[107] The mass release was part of a warming of relations with West Germany. In 1961 Generals Richard Schmidt and Rudolf Toussaint were released from prison and deported from the country. At the time they claimed that 100 Germans remained in prisons and work battalions in Czechoslovakia. Tomáš Staněk, *Německá menšina v Českých zemích 1948–1989* (Prague, 1993), 469; Borák, *Spravedlnost podle dekretu*, 160; *Justiz im Dienste*, 7.
[108] "Přehled činnosti veřejných žalobců" (11 November 1946), SÚA, f. MS, k. 1929.

before the Opava court in which SA membership was the only charge, only 136 were even tried and only sixty-two resulted in jail terms.[109]

The Transfer especially undermined the courts by depriving them of witnesses who were expelled before they had the opportunity to testify. This was particularly problematic in those areas where few Czechs had lived during the occupation. Once local Germans had been deported, there was no one left who had been an eye-witness to the Nazis' crimes.[110] German victims of Nazism, who had initially greeted the opportunity to turn in and testify against their oppressors, became increasingly reluctant to participate in the People's Courts as the hopelessness of their nation's future in Czechoslovakia became abundantly clear. When German antifascists opted for voluntary emigration, borderland courts lost perhaps their most valuable source of evidence.[111] The dearth of witnesses was further exacerbated by the decision to expel minor collaborators, who could then no longer testify against their superiors. The chief justice of the Litoměřice court commented, "For that reason numerous grave (capital) cases ended with the acquittal of the accused."[112]

After the main phase of the Transfer drew to a close, the release of suspected "war criminals" earned bitter condemnation. In the final parliamentary debate on retribution, one speaker argued,

The insufficiency of the retribution decree can be found in the fact that it measured Czechs the same as Germans, even though the Germans were the main criminals.... The injustice of punishment was exacerbated particularly by the transfer of the Germans, nearly one-third of whom essentially escaped punishment.... [That] turned retributive justice completely on its head.[113]

The prosecutors themselves complained that government policy had been unfair and inconsistent. The Znojmo prosecutor remarked, "as

---

[109] Where serving as a functionary in the NSDAP and SdP was the only charge, of the 367 indicted, only 189 were tried, and of these, 108 were sentenced to jail terms. Janák, Činnost," 261–63.

[110] "Skončení," v.v.ž. MLS-LT; přednosta, MLS-OP; přednosta MLS-LT, SÚA, f. MS (Org), k. 1942.

[111] Jiřík, *Nedaleko od Norimberku*, 52, 161, 182, 196, 221.

[112] "Skončení," přednosta MLS-LT, SÚA, f. MS (Org), k. 1942.

[113] Rozehnal, ÚNS 56 (10 June 1947), 16.

a result of the transfer of the Germans the Extraordinary People's Courts became more or less tribunals for those of Czech nationality. In other words, the real collaborators escaped punishment while only their collaborators remained here for judgment."[114] His colleague in Uherské Hradiště added, "This in turn aroused the incorrect impression that Czechs... had been treated more harshly than the Germans themselves."[115] In response to such criticism, Drtina admitted that many Germans had escaped justice. He nonetheless defended the government's actions, arguing that "the state interest in the transfer [of German suspects] and the transfer of their families was greater than its interest in their punishment."[116]

In the end, judges and prosecutors singled out the punishment of minor functionaries as one of the greatest failures of retribution. The Litoměřice chief justice complained that membership cases "reduced the People's Courts to the level of police courts."[117] The Opava head prosecutor argued that minor functionaries should have never been tried in the first place.[118] The government's response to the problem only made matters worse. The chief justice in Česká Lípa harshly criticized the crafters of the Great Decree:

After all, it must have been obvious from the beginning that the prosecution of all members of organizations according to §2 of the retribution decree and all of the most minor functionaries in the [Nazi] party would cause problems in housing, feeding, and guarding. After all, it must have been known that the possibility of transfer would be time-limited. And, considering the known fact that practically all Germans were either voluntary or involuntary members of Nazi organizations, it was imperative from the outset to count on the fact that there would be tens of thousands of Germans here after the completion of their sentences.

If these realities had been taken into account, the embarrassing experience – that a particular act was prosecuted as a crime and punished with hard time of a minimum of five years, then later the transfer was given priority over punishment and then, when the transfer was temporary halted, was again

---

[114] "Skončení," v.v.ž. MLS-ZN, SÚA, f. MS (Org), k. 1942.
[115] "Skončení," v.v.ž. MLS-ÚH, SÚA, f. MS (Org), k. 1942.
[116] Drtina justified the decision by the "international situation" and by the claim that prison sentences would not have rehabilitated the Germans anyway. Drtina, *Na soudu národa*, 48.
[117] "Skončení," přednosta MLS-LT, SÚA, f. MS (Org), k. 1942.
[118] "Skončení," v.v.ž. MLS-OP, SÚA, f. MS (Org), k. 1942.

prosecuted – would not have occurred. Only chance, when a particular case came up, was decisive in determining how it would be disposed of.

The judge further commented that as a result of such "vacillation" not only did Germans doubt the fairness of Czechoslovak justice, but the people's judges themselves "understood it with great difficulty and unfavorably criticized it."[119]

By undermining the courts, the expulsion of indicted Sudeten Germans inadvertently led to more lenient judgment of Czechs. While throughout 1946 the jails were progressively emptied of Germans slated for expulsion, Czechs remained incarcerated awaiting trial. Even after the March 1946 directive they could still be prosecuted for those paragraphs from which the expellees had been exempted. As the typical defendant became less "German" and more "Czech," the public desire to prosecute waned and dissatisfaction with abuses and delays mounted. The courts apparently became reluctant to incarcerate Czechs for crimes that Germans had "gotten away with" thanks to the Transfer. The chief prosecutor in Olomouc reported that the people's judges there refused to punish intermarried individuals for lesser crimes. Not only would punishment have been unfair, it would have harmed "Czech" families.[120] The Cheb chief justice reported that people's judges repeatedly invoked mitigating circumstances contrary to the provisions of the law and often handed down penalties well below the mandated minimum sentences. In their defense they argued that they were not the first to disregard the Great Decree. After all, "an ordinary directive from one ministry violated the law and absolved from punishment criminals who should have been rightly prosecuted and convicted according to the clear sense of the decree."[121]

It is a basic principle of "transitional justice" that the more time elapses, the less willing are the courts and the public to punish adherents of a previous regime, be they politicians, generals, or everyday collaborators. In their final reports to the Justice Ministry, the one thing that almost every judge and prosecutor agreed on was that there was an inverse relationship between the passage of time and the severity of the courts. Although it is impossible to isolate the Transfer as the direct

[119] "Skončení," přednosta MLS-CL, SÚA, f. MS (Org), k. 1942.
[120] "Skončení," v.v.ž. MLS-OL, SÚA, f. MS (Org), k. 1942.
[121] "Skončení," přednosta MLS-CH, SÚA, f. MS (Org), k. 1942.

cause of increased leniency, the Interior Ministry order likely accelerated an already existing trend. On 24 October 1946 Nosek declared that the main phase of the Organized Transfer had been successfully completed.[122] If we divide the postwar trials into two groups, those before and after 1 November 1946, we see a clear relationship between the proportion of Czech defendants and the rate of acquittal. Prior to that date some sixty-four percent of the defendants were recorded as having German nationality; afterward the number drops to fifty-three percent. Before November 1946 only twenty percent of trials ended in an acquittal. Afterward the number jumps to a striking forty-two percent.[123]

In addition to accelerating a trend toward leniency, the completion of the main phase of the Organized Transfer brought an end to the contemporaneous prosecution of collaboration. Originally the Interior Ministry had proposed to end the "period of heightened danger to the republic" on 31 December 1945, "in light of the progressive consolidation of conditions."[124] In January 1946, however, the government put this proposal aside on the grounds that the continued presence of large numbers of Germans in the country meant that a serious threat to the state arguably still remained. Not until the last days of October 1946, the moment when Nosek announced the successful completion of the Organized Transfer, did the Interior Ministry forward another proposal to end the "period of heightened danger." The new proposal clearly showed that the continuing presence of the Sudeten Germans had been a critical justification for the period's extension. The conclusion of the Transfer, the report argued, would remove "one of the main causes of danger to the republic."[125] The Office of the Government Presidium seconded this recommendation:

It is now possible to consider the state of heightened danger to the republic as overcome, especially because [via] the completion of the Organized Transfer of the Germans, whose last transports will leave the state's territory

---

[122] Kaplan, *Poválečné Československo*, 152–53.

[123] These figures do not include trials initiated by People's Courts but subsequently transferred to regular criminal courts before a verdict was reached. Statistics are my calculations based on Justice Ministry monthly summaries. SÚA, f. MS (Z.tr.), k. 2076–77; MS (Org.), k. 1930–33.

[124] "Referát ÚPV" k č.j. 20.654-III-1663/45 (2 Jan. 1946), SÚA, f. ÚPV-běžná spis., k. 810, sign. 801/56.

[125] "Informace pro pana ministra vnitra: Očista veřejného života," SÚA, f. MV-NR (B2220(1)), k. 2016, 4–5.

by ... 28 October 1946, the republic will do away with that element, forever inimical to [it], and thus achieve the internal security of the republic.[126]

In January 1946 ongoing deportations justified an extension of the "period of heightened danger to the republic," but later that year the completion of the Organized Transfer permitted its abrogation. Had large numbers of Germans remained in the country, radicals could have extended the period indefinitely on the grounds that a significant internal enemy persisted. From the perspective of power politics, thus, the completion of the main phase of the expulsion played against the Communists, who arguably profited from the legal uncertainty that the "period of heightened danger to the republic" created.

CONCLUSION

The so-called Transfer of the Sudeten Germans has been widely criticized as "collective punishment" that indiscriminately persecuted many who bore no responsibility for the crimes of the Nazis. In this respect, retribution can be considered an appropriate response to the problem of wartime collaboration. Despite their shortcomings, the People's Courts tried individuals for specific offenses according to established procedure and, moreover, provided an opportunity for defense. Many of those convicted were guilty of heinous atrocities committed in the name of the Third Reich. As has been described here, however, the Great Decree was not limited to particular offenses, but also criminalized entire organizations. This collective aspect of retribution mandated mass arrests of "members" and "functionaries," forced courts to expedite trials, and, ultimately, caused great inequalities in judgment. Thus, the conflict between retribution and the Transfer, analyzed in this chapter, was also a conflict within retribution itself, between the individual punishment of specific perpetrators and the blacklisting of entire groups. Even without the Interior Ministry directive prioritizing expulsion before prosecution, the criminalization of Nazi and fascist organizations caused great incoherence and dissatisfaction. One of the lessons postwar Czechoslovak retribution can offer future attempts to carry out "transitional justice" is that justice can only be individual – lists of names are no basis

[126] MV no. A-1149-23/10-1946-I/1 (24 Oct. 1946), SÚA, f. ÚPV-běžná spis., k. 810, sign. 801/56.

for fair punishment. Perhaps if this lesson had been learned, the pitfalls of post-Communist Czechoslovakia's "Lustration" [Lustrace] program could have been avoided.

When the Czechoslovak government chose to deport indicted and convicted Germans, it undermined the country's commitment to exact just retribution for wartime crimes. Even before this decision, however, the prosecution of tens of thousands of "ordinary" Nazis hampered efforts to punish more serious war criminals. Although the criminalization of membership in certain formations, for example, the SS, may have been justified (as it was by the IMT), trials of simple Nazi functionaries, especially the Blockleiter, were counterproductive. Samuel Huntington argued that for transitional justice to be successful, it must be swift and limited. He advised "democratizers" to "prosecute the leaders of the authoritarian regime promptly . . . while making clear that you will not prosecute middle- and lower-ranking officials."[127] Although Huntington referred mainly to regimes whose crimes pale in comparison to the horrors unleashed by the Nazis, his analysis still resonates in the context of postwar Europe. This is especially true of his warning that with time "popular support and indignation necessary to make justice a political reality fade."[128] The Czechoslovak government's decision to prosecute membership crimes meant that postwar retribution was lengthy and laborious. As the People's Courts dragged on well beyond their original mandate, the will to prosecute waned and public dissatisfaction grew. In the end, both the criminalization of membership and the expulsion of German defendants contributed to the common perception that postwar Czech retribution was uneven, incomplete, and, all too often, unjust.

---

[127] Samuel P. Huntington, *The Third Wave: Democratization in the Late Twentieth Century* (Norman: University of Oklahoma Press, 1991), 231.
[128] Huntington, *The Third Wave*, 228.

7

THE NATIONAL COURT

In March 1945, when representatives of the Beneš government-in-exile entered into negotiations with the Czechoslovak Communists in Moscow, there was virtually no disagreement over the nature of post-war retribution. The Communist leaders accepted the decree drafted in London and the others agreed to the creation of a new institution, a "National Court," to try the most prominent domestic collaborators. At Košice the following month, the new government pledged that the National Court would try the leaders of fascist organizations, "treacherous journalists," "traitors from the ranks of banking, industrial and agrarian magnates," and all the members of the Protectorate government from 14 March 1939 until the end of the war.[1] First mentioned in the Košice Program and later codified in Presidential Decree no. 17/1945, the Prague National Court ultimately tried eighty-three Czech men, convicted sixty-five of them, and sentenced eighteen to death.[2] The executions of pro-Nazi journalists and fascist leaders caused relatively little controversy, but the trials of nonfascist politicians and industrial magnates proved to be far more complicated. In the end, the one National Court generated more debate and dissension than the twenty-four People's Courts combined.

Communist leaders initially expressed great hopes for postwar retribution. Addressing a gathering of party functionaries in early April 1945, Klement Gottwald proclaimed, "[A] tool, which we have today

---

[1] Jiří Grospič, Jaroslav Chovanec, and Juraj Vysokaj, eds., *Košický vládní program* (Prague: Státní pedagogické nakladatelství, 1977), 131–32.
[2] The National Court did not try any female defendants. "Činnost Národního soudu v Praze," *Svobodné noviny* (8 May 1947), Státní ústřední archiv (SÚA), Prague, f. MZV-VA II, (j41), k. 213.

in the fight for leadership of the nation, is the struggle against traitors and collaborators – that is, against the physical leaders of the compromised ... Czech bourgeoisie. ... With this weapon we can strike our enemy directly, physically."[3] With the Košice Program's commitment to prosecute "traitors from the ranks of banking, industrial and agrarian magnates," the National Court may have appeared to be the weapon of choice for the punishment of bourgeois leaders, but it failed to live up to Gottwald's expectations. Far from propagating the Communists' rigidly severe view of collaboration, the Court frequently adopted the home front's more forgiving understanding of wartime behavior. Ultimately, Communist leaders were reduced to griping that the National Court treated prominent Czechs more benevolently than the People's Courts did ordinary defendants, a complaint not entirely without merit.

THE ESTABLISHMENT OF THE NATIONAL COURT

Presidential Decree no. 17 of 19 June 1945 (Appendix 2) established a National Court to render political and moral judgment upon the country's leaders who had been "duty-bound to serve as a patriotic example to their fellow citizens." Aside from its prominence, the National Court differed from the twenty-four People's Courts in several important ways. First, the National Court's judicial panel included two more people's judges, for a total of six, plus one professional judge. The people's judges were to "be proven patriots, especially those persons who have distinguished themselves in the resistance either at home or abroad, or who were the victims of enemy persecution or treachery." Unlike the People's Courts, where the four lay judgeships could be parceled out evenly among the four Czech political parties, the presence of six lay judges on the National Court meant that two parties would be overrepresented and two underrepresented. Second, the National Court also differed in that there was no limit to the length of a trial, a provision that allowed both the prosecution and the defense a greater opportunity to present arguments in detail. Third, in cases where criminal culpability was doubtful, the state could opt to use the National Court as an honor tribunal – a sort of supreme national honor commission – empowered to give civil sanctions to any defendant who had acted "in a manner

---

[3] SÚA, f. 1 (ZÚV KSČ), sv. 1, aj. 1, str. 14.

unbecoming to [a] loyal and brave Czechoslovak citizen."[4] Most importantly, the Prague National Court only tried defendants of Czech nationality.

Despite these differences, National Court defendants were prosecuted according to the offenses outlined in the Great Decree, from military treachery to denunciation. The same grounds for mitigating circumstances also applied. Like the People's Courts, the National Court was designed to be a summary tribunal – neither the prosecution nor the defense could appeal the judges' ruling, and death sentences had to be carried out within a maximum three hours. Ultimately, National Court judges also ruled like People's Court judges: Different judicial panels measured defendants by different standards, politics interfered in some deliberations, and the panels' verdicts became progressively more lenient as time elapsed.

Decree no. 17 explicitly empowered the National Court to try former State-President Emil Hácha and the ministers of his governments during the Second Republic and the Protectorate. These governments were not, however, declared criminal in and of themselves; to be liable for prosecution a minister had to have committed a crime according to the Great Decree. Other candidates for the National Court included leaders of various collaborationist groups, including the Banner movement, the Czech League against Bolshevism, and the National Union of Employees, the monolithic wartime workers' organization. The list ended with "journalists, who propagandistically served the invader government in the daily press," and individuals who, due to the significance of their political, administrative, or economic position, were "duty-bound to serve as a patriotic example to their fellow citizens."

The National Court was not established until 2 October 1945; its first people's judges were not sworn in until 12 December.[5] Off to a late start, the Court immediately faced a setback when its first chief justice, Ferdinand Richter, suddenly resigned. Resistance groups and the government had approved the selection of the judge, but soon after Prokop Drtina became Justice Minister he was presented with a letter,

---

[4] *Sbírka zákonů a nařízení Republiky československé* (Prague, 1946), č. 17/1945 Sb.
[5] "Spravedlnost je nástrojem mravního pokroku lidstva," *Národní osvobození* (13 December 1945), SÚA, f. MZV-VA II (j81), k. 215; Mečislav Borák, *Spravedlnost podle dekretu: Retribuční soudnictví v ČSR a Mimořádný lidový soud v Ostravě (1945–1948)* (Ostrava: Tilia, 1998), 60.

sent by Richter to Adolf Hitler, in which the future National Court chief justice had pleaded with the Fuehrer for mercy. Despite Richter's wartime resistance and imprisonment, Drtina later explained, someone thus compromised did not have the moral authority to preside in judgment over collaborators. In Richter's place, the Justice Minister appointed František Tomsa, the chairman of the Prague Criminal Court.[6] Hardly an auspicious beginning, one that foreshadowed the problems the National Court soon faced evaluating the ambiguities of collaboration among the Czech elite.

The patriotism of the anointed National Court chief prosecutor was beyond reproach, but soon he, too, became a target of criticism. František Tržický, a former judge, district attorney, and chairman of the organization of Social Democratic judges, had been arrested by the Nazis in 1943, sentenced to prison, and not freed until 5 May 1945.[7] Despite his patriotic pedigree, Tržický did not take long to stir up controversy. In December 1945 he recommended that the government approve the release of several defendants pending their trials. Not only did the cabinet ministers reject the proposal, but Vilém Široký even suggested that Tržický be dismissed. Joining the Slovak Communist leader, Fierlinger, Gottwald, Kopecký, and even Hubert Ripka, the National Socialist Minister of Foreign Trade, questioned the prosecutor's judgment.[8] This was merely the opening salvo in a debate to which the government returned time and time again. In an attempt to share responsibility for controversial trials, and thereby evade blame for their outcome, Drtina repeatedly turned to his fellow ministers to decide which defendants to call before the National Court. With the support of Tržický, the Justice Minister and his allies argued for the dismissal of unwinnable cases, while the Communists and their allies invariably pushed for prosecution at all costs. Some of the most contentious and vitriolic government debates of the immediate postwar period revolved around which retribution cases to dismiss and which to pursue.

[6] In 1948 Richter joined the Communist Party and became chairman of the National Assembly. Prokop Drtina, *Československo můj osud* (Toronto: Sixty-Eight Publishers, 1982), II:123–24.

[7] "Národní soud ustaven," *Právo lidu* (3 Oct. 1945), SÚA, f. MZV-VA II (j41), k. 208.

[8] Transcript of the eighteenth meeting of the second government (21 December 1945), SÚA, f. 100/24 (KG), sign. 1494, sv. 139, 43.

Six months after the promulgation of the National Court decree, the new institution still had not tried its first case. Thousands of ordinary Czechs and Germans had been convicted by People's Courts, more than 100 sentenced to death and hanged, but the most prominent Czech collaborators had yet to take the stand. Unsurprisingly, the press soon began to complain. One newspaper proclaimed, "France has already tried Pétain and Laval, Norway Quisling;... other states are hounding their traitors before courts. Even Hungary. Only here are the minnows hunted and nothing is done with the big fish."[9] In his memoirs, Drtina ascribed the delay to Richter's resignation, but others, including Tržický, blamed the Interior Ministry for failing to prepare cases in time.[10] The inability, or the likely unwillingness, of the Interior Ministry to forward material to prosecutors in a timely fashion plagued the National Court throughout its existence. By maintaining control over defendants and evidence until the last possible moment, the ministry's Communist bosses could monopolize information about the occupation and employ it to intimidate and manipulate political opponents and allies alike. As with the People's Courts, however, there was a price to be paid for such practices: The prosecution often did not have the time to adequately prepare its case.

On the eve of the first National Court trial, Drtina proclaimed the beginning of "the reckoning with weaklings, defeatists, traitors, quislings, betrayers, freeloaders and parasites." To do so was nothing more than self-defense, he argued, necessary for the health of the nation: "In a time of danger no viable nation can allow its members to jump out of line with impunity and thus disrupt national solidarity and discipline. Evil would come to any nation which permitted that."[11] *The Weekly Bulletin*, Czechoslovakia's magazine aimed at a foreign, English-speaking audience, claimed that retribution would be a "warning to future generations." The trials would amass documentary evidence that would educate Czechs and all Europe about the failures of the 1930s.[12] For

---

[9] "Kdy konečně půjdou velezrádci před Národní soud?" *Právo Lidu* (14 November 1945), SÚA, f. MZV-VA II (j41), k. 208.

[10] Drtina, *Československo*, II:125; National Prosecutor (16 February 1946) to MS, SÚA, f. MS (Drtina), k. 2111.

[11] Drtina, *Československo*, II:207.

[12] "The National Court," *The Weekly Bulletin* (20 January 1946), 41; "Spravedlnost je nástrojem mravního pokroku lidstva," *Národní osvobození* (13 December 1945), SÚA, f. MZV-VA II (j41), k. 208.

the postwar Czech leaders there was one more goal for the trials: political legitimacy.

GENERALS, FASCISTS,
AND "JOURNALISTIC PROSTITUTES"

Despite the fanfare accompanying the opening of the National Court, the public did not express much interest in the first defendants' fates.[13] The three former generals who stood before the National Court on 15 January 1946 were apparently neither the most despised nor the most admired collaborators. Generals Otto Bláha, Robert Rychtrmoc, and Gustav Mohapl all had distinguished prewar records, but during the occupation they had organized the Union of Czech Veterans [Český svaz válečníků] to gather together soldiers who had fought for Austria–Hungary during the First World War. Using this organization, the three men had attempted to enlist Czech military support, including troops, for the Nazi war effort. As a Gestapo agent, Bláha had also denounced Czech army officers and members of the Union, including a former chairman who consequently perished. The National Court sentenced Bláha and Rychtrmoc to death and refused their final request to be shot instead of hanged.[14] In the end, the defendants caused more controversy dead than they did alive. When their corpses were burned at the national crematorium, the outraged Communist press claimed that the cremation defiled sacred ground and posthumously honored the executed men. In a bizarre argument, members of the government debated at some length whether retribution could apply to one's remains or whether punishment ended with death.[15] This unexpected controversy over the allegedly favorable treatment of defendants who had been executed foreshadowed what lay in store when the National Court issued more lenient sentences.

Aside from the executions of Bláha, Rychtrmoc, and a fellow general, František Bartoš,[16] the remainder of the National Court's eighteen

---

[13] Drtina, *Československo*, II:126.

[14] Traditionally, military officers view execution by firing squad as a more honorable death. "The National Court," *The Weekly Bulletin* (20 January 1946), 41–42; "The First Verdict of the Czech National Court in Prague," *The Weekly Bulletin* (27 January 1946), 52–53.

[15] Second government, twenty-seventh meeting (1 February 1946), SÚA, f. 100/24 (KG), sign. 1494, sv. 139, 7–9.

[16] Another general, Alois Podhajský, died in prison awaiting trial. Jan Obručník, a general in the Protectorate's Government Militia, the 7,000-troop force permitted by the Nazis,

death sentences was handed down exclusively to fascist leaders and "activist" newspaper editors. In fact, four group trials alone accounted for all of the other executions. First, in spring 1946 the National Court tried seven former leaders of Banner, the most powerful Czech fascist movement. The following spring, it was the turn of eight former leaders of Kuratorium, the organization Emanuel Moravec established during the occupation to indoctrinate Czech youth in the benefits of Nazism. In March and April of 1947 the National Court also held two group trials of a total of nine "activist" journalists, Czech editors who had written pro-Nazi articles and directed their newspapers to support the occupation and the German war effort.

The Banner movement leaders went on trial before the National Court in May 1946. Despite the movement's limited numbers – it had at most 13,000 members[17] – it played a pernicious role in post-Munich Czechoslovakia. Banner started, like other radical right movements in the region, as a hypernationalist admirer of Mussolini's brand of fascism, but its anti-German ideology did not prevent leading members from fostering links with SdP leader Konrad Henlein. After Munich the group became especially active, and vociferously demanded a "final solution to the Jewish question" in the Czech provinces. In the month before the Nazi takeover, Banner members bombed synagogues and committed other violent acts against Jews. Josef Rys-Rozsévač, the movement's leader, called the Second Republic a "Jew-mason government" and accused it of democratic tendencies.[18] The Beran government finally lost its patience and ordered the arrest of Banner's leaders for sedition, but they were released on the eve of the Nazi invasion. Twice, in March 1939 and August 1940, Banner members attempted to seize power, but their calls for the Protectorate government to resign were heeded neither by Hácha nor by the Germans, who preferred the stewardship of

attempted suicide and was later sentenced to life. The National Court sentenced two other former Czech generals, Václav Kuneš and Libor Vítěz, to life and four years in prison, respectively. The former head of the Government Militia, General Jaroslav Eminger, was acquitted by the National Court in its capacity as a national honor tribunal. Borák, *Spravedlnost podle dekretu*, 65.

[17] Vojtech Mastny, *The Czechs under Nazi Rule: The Failure of National Resistance* (New York: Columbia University Press, 1971), 157; Tomáš Pasák, *Český fašismus (1922–1945) a kolaborace (1939–1945)* (Prague: Práh, 1999), 199; Detlef Brandes, *Die Tschechen unter deutschem Protektorat*, 2 vols. (Munich: R. Oldenbourg, 1969, 1975), I:102.

[18] J. Rys-Rozsévač et al., verdict (27 June 1946), SÚA, f. NS, TNs 7/46, 12.

conservative Czechs.[19] Even the Nazis eventually grew tired of the Ban-nermen's antics, especially their criticism of Moravec for his supposedly opportunistic collaboration. In 1942 Karel Hermann Frank banned the movement's newspaper, ordered the deportation of several hundred of its members to work in Germany, and interned its leaders in Dachau.[20] Despite these failures, throughout the occupation the prospect of a Banner-led government remained a threat that the Nazis repeatedly wielded to intimidate more moderate Czech leaders. Unsurprisingly, the National Court trial of the universally despised Banner leaders ended on 27 June 1946 with the conviction of all seven defendants, prison sentences for three and death penalties for four, including one *in absentia*.[21] A year later, the Kuratorium trial resulted in eight convictions, including four death sentences, two *in absentia*, the other two commuted to life in prison.[22]

In January 1946 a Communist parliamentary deputy expressed his dismay that the courts had not yet punished the "journalistic prostitutes."[23] Perhaps no National Court defendants were more hated than the editors who had written pro-Nazi articles throughout the occupation. On 28 February, *Zemědělské noviny* [*Agrarian News*] welcomed the first National Court trial of an "activist" editor, Václav Crha, with the words, "Finally we have lived to see it. All of us honorable Czechs who never betrayed."[24] After a three-day trial the National Court sentenced Crha to life imprisonment and the loss of all his property. When his trial was not soon followed by the prosecution of other "activists," *Rudé právo* demanded, in the name of nation, the chance to

---

[19] Mastny, *The Czechs under Nazi Rule*, 57–59, 158.

[20] Pasák, *Český fašismus*, 303, 343–48.

[21] Josef Rys-Rozsévač, Josef Burda, and Jaroslav Čermák were executed; Otakar Polívka was sentenced to death *in absentia*; Jindřich Thun-Hohenstein was sentenced to life imprisonment; and Václav Cyphella and Jindřich Streibl to were sentenced to twenty and eight years of hard labor, respectively. "Činnost Národního soudu v Praze," *Svobodné noviny* (8 May 1947), SÚA, f. MZV-VA II, (j41), k. 213.

[22] The sentences were as follows: Eduard Chalupa and Jan Svoboda, death commuted to life imprisonment; Josef Victorin, life; Karel Žalud, twenty-five years; Jiří Málek, ten years; Václav Krigar, six years; Jaroslav Krigar, four years; Karel Mihalíček and František Teuner, death *in absentia*. (Teuner was subsequently caught and had his sentence commuted.) Borák, *Spravedlnost podle dekretu*, 65; "Činnost Národního soudu v Praze," *Svobodné noviny* (8 May 1947), SÚA, f. MZV-VA II, (j41), k. 213.

[23] Kliment, PNS 24 (23 January 1946), 15.

[24] "První zrádný šéfredaktor před soudem," *Zemědělské noviny* (28 February 1945), SÚA, f. MZV-VA II (j81), k. 216.

"justly settle . . . accounts with all those revolting names which appeared on the pages of the Protectorate newspapers." The Communist flagship alleged that certain "circles" were delaying the journalists' trials in order to prevent them from naming their coconspirators who might then also be prosecuted.[25] The two group trials of nationally prominent "activist journalists" did not take place until March and April 1947, but there is no evidence that their prosecution was held up for political reasons. Although time may have benefited some of them, especially Jan Křemen, who had his death sentence commuted to life in prison, these men faced insurmountable evidence: numerous articles signed with their names. In Drtina's words, "Their prosecution was accordingly a straightforward and uninteresting matter."[26]

The pernicious activity of Rudolf Novák, the editor-in-chief of *Aryan Struggle*, should be familiar to the reader from Chapter 4.[27] According to the court's estimate, he wrote or signed 556 pro-Nazi and anti-Semitic articles during the war. Novák regularly exploited the tabloid's well-known Gestapo connections to extort advertisements, articles, or even just bribes from Czechs.[28] His attacks in *Aryan Struggle* contributed to the persecution of numerous prominent Czechs – above all, Jews and

---

[25] "Hlemýždí tempo v souzení zrádných novinářů," *Rudé právo* (28 August 1946), SÚA, f. MZV-VA II (j81), k. 216.

[26] Drtina, *Československo*, II:278.

[27] Like many other Czech fascists, Novák had a patriotic pedigree, which included working during the First World War to organize Czech deserters in Italy to fight Austria–Hungary. Novák returned to Prague a captain and a hero of the national liberation struggle, and was put in charge of the weekly *Czechoslovak Legionary*. After failing to gain a parliamentary seat in 1920, Novák turned to business. Like his future subordinate Václav Píša, he was soon sentenced to imprisonment for embezzlement and fraud. Somehow he managed to regain his footing and rejoin the journalistic profession, albeit only as a reporter for a factory newspaper, a job he lost when he extracted bribes in exchange for suppressing unfavorable stories. During the occupation he quickly moved up in the world, thanks to his relationship with an SD officer, who procured for Novák the directorship of a publishing house and a salary of several thousand crowns a month. In his new sinecure Novák investigated the "Aryan" background and politics of his employees and turned the company into a publisher of pro-Nazi books. Plucked from relative obscurity, on 1 March 1941 Novák was appointed editor-in-chief of *Aryan Struggle*. R. Novák verdict (26 March 1947), SÚA, f. NS, TNs 6/47, 5–10.

[28] Novák threatened to expose businesses that refused to advertise in *Aryan Struggle*. He also devised a plan to force intellectuals, who he believed to be weak-kneed wafflers, to denounce Bolshevism. He sent a letter requesting that prominent individuals express their agreement with the anti-Bolshevist struggle and included the warning that those who failed to respond would soon find their names printed in the weekly. In exchange for bribes Novák also permitted some of his targets to "correct" articles written about them. R. Novák verdict (26 March 1947), SÚA, f. NS, TNs 6/47, 21, 27–28.

intermarried Gentiles. His victims included Oldřich Nový, the leading romantic hero of Czech interwar film, E. F. Burián, a prominent Communist intellectual, and Olga Drtinová-Löwenbachová, the sister of the future Justice Minister. Novák went out of his way to persecute her, inquiring personally at her home and place of work whether she was in fact related to Prokop Drtina. Thanks to Novák's efforts, which included several vicious attacks in *Aryan Struggle*, Drtinová-Löwenbachová was eventually arrested by the Germans.[29] For good reason, Drtina considered Novák to be a "disgusting" and "repulsive character."[30]

As Novák's conviction indicates, often the National Court did not view an editor's collaborationist writings to be his greatest crime. Like Novák, Vladimír Krychtálek went out of his way to harm the families of Czech émigré leaders. The editor publicly and repeatedly asked why the Germans had not arrested them. Karel Werner, another "activist," denounced one of Czechoslovakia's leading interwar feminists, Senator Františka Plamínková, who was subsequently arrested and killed. Emanuel Vajtauer worked for the SD, and Jaromil Kožíšek delivered important documents to the Gestapo. On 5 May 1945 Alois Kříž allegedly fired into the crowd trying to defend Czechoslovak Radio against the Germans.[31] In all, the National Court tried twenty-one journalists and sentenced seven of them, including Novák, to death.[32]

Not all editors, however, were doomed. In one of the first indications of the National Court's independence, on 20 July 1946 Rudolf Halík received a sentence below the mandatory minimum. As the editor of the *Venkov [Countryside]* newspaper, the Court determined, he had written nine articles with "hazardously activist content," six of which had been published after Heydrich's assassination. Nonetheless, the judges

---

[29] The trial considered sixty-seven cases where *Aryan Struggle* articles led directly to the arrest and interrogation of the victims named. R. Novák verdict (26 March 1947), SÚA, f. NS, TNs 6/47, 25–28.

[30] Drtina, *Československo*, II:280.

[31] Vojtěch Dolejší, *Noviny a novináři: Z poznámek a vzpomínek* (Prague: Nakladatelství politické literatury, 1963), 404; Borák, *Spravedlnost podle dekretu*, 67.

[32] In addition to Novák, the National Court gave capital sentences to Antonín Kožíšek, Vladimír Krychtálek, Jaroslav Křemen, Alois Kříž, Emanuel Vajtauer, and Karel Werner. In April 1947 the National Court also met once in Brno to try the "Moravian activist" editors Jaroslav Pelíšek, Leopold Zeman, and Jan Hloužek, who, in contrast to their colleagues from Prague, received relatively lenient sentences ranging from one and a half to three years in prison. Borák, *Spravedlnost podle dekretu*, 68l; Dolejší, *Noviny*, 402; "Činnost Národního soudu v Praze," *Svobodné noviny* (8 May 1947), SÚA, f. MZV-VA II, (j41), k. 213.

accepted Halík's defense that he had written due to fear of reprisal from, among others, Krychtálek; that he had not forced any of his subordinates to write pro-Nazi articles; and that he had thrown out the most offensively collaborationist columns sent to him from above. In the defendant's favor, the judges cited his "weak" character, his outspoken belief in Nazi defeat, his behavior as a good Czech in private, his financial support of persecuted individuals, and, most importantly, his service to the resistance – from 1943 onward Halík provided regular reports to the government-in-exile about the state of affairs in the Protectorate. Based on Paragraph Sixteen, the National Court sentenced Halík to eighteen months in prison, fourteen of which he had already served. Regardless of the actual merits of the defendant's case – and one might question the judges' determination that Halík did not "subjectively" seek to undermine Czech resistance – the trial's outcome demonstrated that even collaborationist editors had the opportunity to persuade the National Court.[33]

THE LAST ACT OF EMIL HÁCHA

Unlike the trials of fascist leaders and activist journalists, the prosecution of Protectorate government ministers presented the postwar regime with a dilemma. While men like *Aryan Struggle* editor Novák and Banner leader Rys-Rozsévač remained a separate breed, isolated and despised, members of the Protectorate government could not be dismissed as renegades – they belonged to the prewar Czech elite and retained the sympathy, if not support, of a large portion of the population throughout the occupation. Whereas fascists' and activists' crimes earned universal opprobrium and their deaths widespread approval, the trials of political leaders promised to be contentious and had the potential to divide the Czech nation. The most controversial candidate for prosecution was undoubtedly Emil Hácha, the 73 year-old former State-President of the Protectorate of Bohemia and Moravia. Nine days after the war ended, George F. Kennan sent a memorandum to the U.S. State Department in which he argued that Hácha was neither a Nazi nor a traitor. As the

---

[33] R. Halík verdict (20 July 1946), TNs 9/46, SÚA, f. MS (VI/19), k. 1245. The Communists' dissatisfaction with the original verdict was demonstrated when, after the 1948 coup, the editor was retried, convicted, and sentenced to ten years in prison. "R. Halík dostal deset let," *Svobodné slovo* (19 May 1948), SÚA, f. MZV-VA II (j81), k. 218.

last American representative in Prague, Kennan had personal experience of Czech collaboration (though his special insight was limited to the events of 1938 and 1939). Laying out arguments similar to those later used by National Court defendants, he explained that the endurance of Hácha in an unenviable position helped to protect the Czech people from the horrors of direct Nazi rule. In Kennan's opinion,

Certainly Hácha and his assistants did indeed render lip service to a German domination of Europe. But as every Czech knows who was in Czechoslovakia during the German occupation, they were not Quislings. They were not seeking self-advancement. They sponsored no Czech fascist party and even succeeded in breaking up those that were started by other people. Their main motive, however misguided, was loyalty to their people; and their purpose in doing what they did was clearly to preserve some elements of cohesion and of national recognition for a people who, they felt, were in vital danger of complete dispersal and destruction.

Kennan concluded that if Hácha were executed, he "could regard such drastic punishment only as an act of internal political revenge, and not one of justice."[34]

Contrary to Kennan's assessment, the postwar government ministers, irrespective of party affiliation, believed in Hácha's guilt. They disagreed, however, on the political utility of prosecuting the elderly statesman. By 13 June 1945, when the government met to discuss Hácha's fate, he was extremely ill and being held in a prison hospital. Stránský argued that the former president's poor health was probably a blessing because the "only end to a criminal trial of Hácha could be his defense." The Justice Minister added that public opinion was divided. The government's was, too: the Communists and Social Democrats favored a trial, even if it had to be conducted *in absentia*, while the National Socialists and Populists hoped to avoid the spectacle altogether.[35] Hácha generously saved the government the trouble – two weeks later he passed away, settling the question of his trial once and for all.

---

[34] Kennan, Moscow, telegram to the Secretary of State, Washington, D.C. (17 May 1945), Department of State, Decimal file 860f, General Records, Record Group 59, National Archives, Washington, D.C., *Records of the U.S. Department of State Relating to the Internal Affairs of Czechoslovakia, 1945–1949* (Wilmington, DE: Scholarly Resources, 1986), film 860f.00/5-1745.

[35] Transcript of the twenty-ninth meeting of the first government, SÚA, f. 100/24 (KG), sign. 1494, sv. 137, 8–9.

In the government meeting Stránský argued that trials of other Protectorate ministers would provide ample opportunity to discuss and assess Hácha's conduct during the war. But it was not only the former State-President's behavior that needed explication. The trials, the Justice Minister added, would also present the opportunity "to properly explain the scope of the contacts which existed for a specific period between the [London exiles] and members of the Protectorate government."[36] Despite later condemnation, at first the exiles were generally sympathetic to Hácha's compromises and secretly corresponded with Alois Eliáš, the Protectorate Prime Minister. After the German invasion of March 1939, both Beneš and Jan Masaryk asked the Protectorate ministers to remain in government for the good of the Czech people.[37] An April 1941 message from the London government to the Czech underground expressed Beneš's belief that Hácha was an "honorable person" and relayed the president-in-exile's comment, "If our people throw manure on Hácha, they're throwing it on themselves."[38]

After Germany's June 1941 invasion of the Soviet Union, Beneš distanced himself from earlier contacts and warned the Protectorate government ministers to be prepared to resign if the Germans demanded that they compromise themselves. At that fateful moment the president looked appreciatively back on the preceding years, "One day our collaboration [spolupráce] up till now will be a beautiful page in our [nation's] history."[39] Only the assassination of Heydrich, the execution of Eliáš, and the massacre of Lidice brought about a final break. When Hácha denounced Beneš in a radio address, calling him "enemy number one of the Czech nation," the government-in-exile responded by declaring the Protectorate ministers traitors.[40] Many, if not most, of the National Court charges against the Protectorate ministers, however, revolved around the period before this final break. In preparation for the trials, Beneš penned a justification of his relations with the Protectorate government.

---

[36] Transcript of the twenty-ninth meeting of the first government SÚA, f. 100/24 (KG), sign. 1494, sv. 137, 8–9.

[37] Brandes, Die Tschechen, I:48.

[38] Archiv Kanceláře prezidenta republiky (AKPR), dok. J. Smutného, O-3201/61, č. VI/106 (15 April 1941).

[39] "Zpráva domů," AKPR, dok. J. Smutného, O-3201/61, č. VII/92 (24 June 1941).

[40] Brandes, Die Tschechen, I:235; Libuše Otáhalová and Milada Červinková, eds., Dokumenty z historie československé politiky 1939–1943, 2 vols. (Prague: Academia, 1966), doc. 234, I:285.

He sent it to then-Justice Minister Stránský on the condition that the potentially embarrassing document be produced only if absolutely necessary.[41] In fact, defendants mainly steered clear of the issue, keeping to the unwritten rules of postwar debate, even when their own lives were at risk. Nonetheless, Beneš remained susceptible to blackmail, a weapon others may not have forsaken.

THE TRIAL OF THE PROTECTORATE GOVERNMENT

On 29 April 1946 the curtain opened on what one Czech newspaper called "the greatest political trial in our history." Five men stood in the dock: former premier of the Protectorate government, Jaroslav Krejčí; former Minister of Interior, Richard Bienert; former Minister of Railroads, Jindřich Kamenický; former Minister of Finance, Josef Kalfus; and former Ministerof Agriculture and Forestry, Adolf Hrubý (Figure 8). The prosecutor indicted them for "supporting the fascist and Nazi movement through the press, over the radio and at public gatherings; of praising and defending the enemy government on the republic's territory and the individual illegal acts of the occupation leadership." The defendants were further accused of facilitating the German occupation of 1939, of organizing forced labor, and of assisting in the theft of Czechoslovak wealth.[42]

From the very beginning the trial was hampered by the absence of stars: The most despised Czech collaborator, Education Minister Emanuel Moravec, wisely committed suicide at the end of the war; the proappeasement, prewar Foreign Minister, Ferdinand Chvalkovský, perished in a bombing raid on Berlin in February 1945; and former State-President Hácha died in prison in June. As a result, the supporting cast had to carry the show, but had great difficulty playing the role assigned to them as the main villains or masterminds of the wartime debacle. Despite their prominent positions, for most of the occupation the five defendants were little more than high-ranking bureaucrats. Nonetheless,

---

[41] The letter became Drtina's charge when he replaced Stránský. Beneš later betrayed the two ministers' trust by mentioning his testament to Fierlinger, who in turn revealed it to the rest of the government. Drtina, according to his memoirs, found himself attacked for keeping such an important document secret, claimed the decision was his own, and thus shielded the Czechoslovak President. Drtina, *Československo*, II:222–26.

[42] "Protektorátní vláda před soudem," *Svobodné noviny* (30 April 1946), SÚA, f. MZV-VA II (j41), k. 208.

Figure 8. The Protectorate Government Ministers on Parade in Pankrác Prison. Česká tisková kancelář (Czech Press Agency), 27 June 1945. Reproduced with permission.

in light of Beneš's "theory of continuity," the postwar Czech leaders be-lieved that the conviction of the Protectorate ministers was necessary to demonstrate that the occupation had been illegal and, consequently, that the postwar regime was the legitimate and direct successor to the First Republic. In a radio address on the eve of the trial, Drtina un-abashedly explained, "For domestic and international political reasons, the trial of the entire system of the so-called Protectorate government [is] necessary . . . to the state continuity of the Czechoslovak Republic."[43]

For their part, Communist Party leaders saw the prosecution of the Protectorate ministers as an opportunity to fulfill Gottwald's mission to "cut so many limbs away from the bourgeoisie that only its trunk will remain."[44] *Rudé právo* explained to its readers the meaning of the trial: "The accusation . . . is the indictment of a whole class of financial,

[43] "Nikoli msta, ale spravedlnost," Svobodné *slovo* (30 April 1946), SÚA, MZV-VA II (j41), k. 208
[44] SÚA, f. 1 (ZÚV KSČ), sv. 1, aj. 1, str. 14.

industrial, and agroindustrial magnates who betrayed the nation."[45] The day after the trial began, the newspaper insisted, "None of them must be allowed to escape justice.... The harshest punishment must strike those ministers...of Hitler, Himmler, [and] Heydrich."[46] The Communists' view was supported, or perhaps encouraged, by the Soviet Deputy Ambassador, who informed Drtina that "the activity and even the mere existence of [the Protectorate] government [must] be clearly branded as treachery." Moscow, the diplomat explained, desired this declaration to be "concretely" demonstrated by death sentences, at least three of them.[47] Throughout the trial, Rudé právo prepared the public for a lynching. In April it declared, "Traitors to the nation don't feel guilty!" In May, it explained "The Nation fought – the Protectorate Traitors went with the Germans." In June, it asserted, "The Germans needed the Protectorate government to cover their crimes." Finally, in July, the newspaper proclaimed, "The Nation expects a just verdict against its traitors...The Danger to the Nation always came from the wealthy classes."[48] The Ministry of Information, headed by strident Communist Václav Kopecký, contributed to this one-sided coverage by suspending the daily radio broadcast of the trial just before the defense summed up its case.[49]

Although the non-Communist ministers agreed that the defendants were guilty, they were not nearly as bloodthirsty as their Communist colleagues. Perhaps their moderation stemmed from a realization that the government was not in a particularly strong position to judge just how Czechs should have conducted themselves during the occupation. With the exception of two ministers who had been interned in concentration camps, the rest of the Czechs in the cabinet, including those in charge of the most important ministries, had weathered the war in either London or Moscow. Despite repeated promises to the contrary, the returning government-in-exile had marginalized the leaders of the Protectorate underground. The National Court, thanks to the presence of people's judges chosen primarily from the domestic resistance and

[45] "Gestapo doporučilo protektorátní ministry," Rudé právo (30 April 1946), SÚA, f. MZV-VA II (j41), k. 208.
[46] "Gestapo doporučilo," Rudé právo (30 April 1946), SÚA, f. MZV-VA II (j41), k. 208.
[47] Drtina, Československo, II:189–91.
[48] Rudé právo (29 April, 11 May, 19 June, 4 July 1946), SÚA, f. MZV-VA II (j41), k. 209–12.
[49] "Katharse," Svobodné slovo (2 August 1946), 1.

survivors of Nazi imprisonment, could, however, claim to represent the home front's experience and opinion. On the eve of the trial Drtina made this very point by defensively lecturing the public, "None [of the judges] belongs to the so-called foreign resistance and thus they are fully legitimated [*legitimování*] to know exactly what was possible here during the war and what was not."[50] The six people's judges and the professional chief justice had all endured the Nazi occupation, some of them in concentration camps. In other words, Drtina insinuated, the verdict would represent the unimpeachable will of the home front, not the mere wishes of the regime.

Despite Drtina's disclaimer, the charge of "victor's justice" hung over the trial. In a barely concealed swipe at the exiles, one of the accused testified, "If I had been clever, I would have left the country too."[51] It was not just the defendants who questioned the government's view of wartime collaboration. Early in the trial the editors of the Social Democratic daily *Právo lidu* noted that they had received numerous letters defending the five ministers and accusing the court of not hearing witnesses in the defendants' favor. The editors also remarked that similar appeals were being regularly received by the chief justice, prosecutor, and people's judges.[52] In the most visible display of public support for the defendants, on 28 June 1946 a crowd in front of the courthouse demanded that the judges and state radio give more attention to defense speeches.[53] Even more authoritative sources questioned the basis of the trial. An article in *Lidová demokracie*, the official organ of the People's Party, argued,

The National Court must come to terms with the fact that the *entire nation* and all its classes were given the *possibility to refuse* any sort of collaboration with the Germans. If the nation in its entirety did not seize this possibility and instead craftily chose the wait-and-see path, it is necessary to look for the causes in the desperate apathy, forlornness, and geographical and physical isolation [that prevailed] after the Munich Pact, and not in intentional treachery.[54]

[50] "Nikoli msta, ale spravedlnost," *Svobodné slovo* (30 April 1946), SÚA, MZV-VA II (j41), k. 208.
[51] Statement by R. Bienert. Verdict, SÚA, f. NS, Ns 10/46, 6.
[52] *Právo lidu* (22 May 1946), f. MZV-VA II, j41, k. 210.
[53] Dušan Tomášek and Robert Kvaček, *Obžalována je vláda* (Prague: Themis, 1999), 171.
[54] Emphasis in original. "Na vahách spravedlnosti," *Lidová demokracie* (14 July 1946), 1–2.

Although the cabinet unanimously denounced the article, the non-Communist ministers used public opinion as an excuse to argue for leniency. Drtina drew his colleagues' attention to the numerous letters he had received from "distinguished individuals" who warned the government against being out of step with the people. He added that even the workers seemed to be in favor of leniency.[55]

Although the government had originally agreed to press for three death penalties (for Krejčí, Bienert, and Hrubý), after six weeks of testimony, much of it favorable to the defendants, the prosecutor demanded capital punishment only in two cases (Krejčí and Hrubý).[56] In mid-July, Drtina informed the government that even the prosecutor's reduced demand was unlikely to be met. Apparently the necessary majority of the seven judges (the professional judge and six people's judges: two Communists, one National Socialist, one Social Democrat, and two members of the People's Party) could not agree on the death penalty in a single case. Gottwald stated that there was no need to worry about the Communist judges: "I know ... quite well that they will represent the opinion of our party." As a solution to the deadlock, he suggested, "The simplest route is for each party to instruct its members [of the court], to guarantee that they will actually proceed according to its political opinion."[57] In response to such meddling, the National Court's chief justice tendered his resignation, but the government refused the gesture.[58]

Two days later Drtina told his colleagues that his prediction had been accurate – there would be no death sentences. He claimed that he personally preferred there to be one capital sentence, but added, "It is, however, a question of whether it is possible to achieve this without us bringing about ... a moral and political shock to our public." To Drtina's remark, "We are all from the foreign emigration," Gottwald angrily retorted. "Believe that our assessment [of public opinion] is more

[55] Transcript of the meeting of the government presidium (15 July 1946), reprinted in Karel Kaplan, *Dva retribuční procesy: Komentované dokumenty (1946–1947)* (Prague: Ústav pro soudobé dějiny, 1992), doc. 4, 46–47.

[56] The prosecutor proposed the death sentence for Hrubý and Krejčí, but argued that Bienert should only received a prison sentence thanks to the testimony of witnesses who claimed that he had helped them during the war. *Svobodné noviny*, (27 June 1946), SÚA, MZV-VA II (j41), k. 211.

[57] Presidium meeting transcript (15 July 1946), Kaplan, *Dva retribuční procesy*, doc. 4, 49–51.

[58] Presidium meeting transcript (17 July 1946), Kaplan, *Dva retribuční procesy*, doc. 5, 59.

correct – the elections demonstrated that."[59] Gottwald's reference to the May 26 election, in which the Communist Party won an impressive 40 percent plurality of the Czech vote, failed to persuade the other parties to lean on "their" people's judges to approve at least two death sentences. Drtina, nonetheless, did agree to postpone the verdict's promulgation in the hope that some new incriminating evidence might be found. On 30 July he informed the government that no additional material had been discovered: The verdict would have to be announced. Kopecký warned that an "unfavorable reaction" should be expected.[60] In fact, as Central Committee Presidium records reveal, the Communist leaders had already planned the "unfavorable reaction" two weeks in advance.[61]

On 31 July 1946, under the guard of 300 policemen, the National Court announced its verdict (Figure 9): Hrubý, life in prison; Krejčí, twenty-five years; Kamenický, ten years; Bienert, three years; Kalfus, guilty, but absolved of punishment thanks to his financial support for the resistance.[62] That evening the Justice Ministry received a report from Ostrava that "the verdict against the Protectorate government has brought about a spontaneous wave of indignation among the workers... who see [it] as an expression of solidarity on the part of the National Court with the defendants."[63] The next day a delegation of miners from nearby "Red" Kladno paid a visit to the Justice Ministry to demand an explanation for the court's lenient decision. On 2 August Drtina informed the government that his Ministry had already received 110 letters and telegrams decrying the verdict. Of these forty-eight had been sent by factory councils and another forty-eight by Communist organs.[64] Over the next several weeks angry letters and petitions deluged government ministries: In the Czech State Central Archive three

---

[59] Presidium meeting transcript (17 July 1946), Kaplan, *Dva retribuční procesy*, doc. 5, 61.

[60] Presidium meeting transcript (30 July 1946), Kaplan, *Dva retribuční procesy*, doc. 6, 63.

[61] The Communist Party presidium resolved that no action be taken before the verdict, but that local party organs "be entrusted with preparations by which, in the case of the declaration of a lenient verdict against the Protectorate government, a massive protest campaign can be launched." "Zápis 42. schůze předsednictva ÚV KSČ" (17 July 1946), SÚA, f. 02/1, sv. 1, aj. 42.

[62] Presidium meeting transcript (30 July 1946), Kaplan, *Dva retribuční procesy*, doc. 6, 63; J. Krejčí et al., Verdict (31 July 1946), SÚA, f. NS, Ns 10/46, 1–3.

[63] SÚA, f. MS, k. 2108.

[64] Government meeting transcript (2 August 1946), Kaplan, *Dva retribuční procesy*, doc. 7, 66.

Figure 9. The Verdict against the Protectorate Government. Česká tisková kancelář (Czech Press Agency), 31 July 1946. Reproduced with permission.

cartons are filled only with protests received by the Ministry of Justice.[65] *Rudé právo* trumpeted a "wave of anger against the National Court verdict" and gave prominent daily coverage to those factories, resistance organizations, and Communist organs that denounced the verdict and demanded a retrial.[66]

From the very beginning the protest campaign had its flaws. As the non-Communist press pointed out, the resolutions seemed to be coming exclusively from one segment of society and particularly from one party.[67] The Ministry of Justice's second count of letters and telegrams confirmed this trend: Of the 318 protests received, 139 came from Communist Party organs and another 134 from Communist-dominated

[65] SÚA, f. MS, k. 2108–2110.
[66] "Vlna rozhorčení proti rozsudku Národního soudu," *Rudé právo* (1 August 1946), 1.
[67] *Svobodné slovo* (6 August 1946), SÚA, f. MZV-VA II (j41), k. 212; government meeting transcript (2 August 1946), Kaplan, *Dva retribuční procesy*, doc. 7, 67.

factory councils.[68] Moreover, the Justice Ministry also received letters that supported the verdict, disowned the protests, and even denounced the harshness of the sentences.[69] The righteous anger of the Kladno miners was contradicted by several letters to the Justice Ministry, one of which explained to Drtina, "Terror reigns here in the mines, just like in the factories. Whoever does not go with the Communists...is a reactionary. It's not true that we don't agree with the National Court's verdict...but we keep silent.... You see, we have families, and that keeps a fellow in check."[70] Most of one major industrial plant's workforce, which supposedly protested against the verdict, was actually on vacation at the time.[71] Both the National Socialist and the Social Democratic Party learned from their regional organizations that neither their memberships nor the general public was particularly concerned about the verdict. Karel Kaplan commented that some Social Democratic leaders characterized the protests as little more than "a political comedy that only serves the reaction."[72] Not only was the protest movement limited to a particular segment of the population, the resolutions tended to undermine their own legitimacy. Their content was suspiciously similar, a few arrived before the verdict was announced, and one was even written on the back side of a request for such a protest.[73]

In the first government meeting after the verdict the National Socialist ministers immediately challenged the authenticity of the protest movement. Drtina wondered aloud, "Whether it is not... Rudé právo's writing which has resulted in these protests coming from those particular circles and establishments." In the absence of Gottwald, Kopecký spoke for the Communists. He wished that "the nation were even angrier, although the anger is in any event enormous." He duplicitously denied that the Communists had incited the protests – they were, "in fact, exhorting the workers not to demonstrate and especially not to stop work in the factories." Kopecký argued, in line with Rudé právo, that

---

[68] Drtina, Československo, II:195.

[69] SÚA, f. MS (Drtina), k. 2112.

[70] Letter (5 August 1946) to MS, SÚA, f. MS (Drtina), k. 2112.

[71] Government meeting transcript (2 August 1946), Kaplan, Dva retribuční procesy, doc. 7, 68.

[72] Kaplan, Dva retribuční procesy, 14.

[73] Jan Stránský, Těsnopisecké zprávy Ústavodárného národního shromáždění Republiky československé (ÚNS) 57 (11 June 1947), 24.

the government should establish a new court that would retry the Protectorate ministers based on undetermined "new facts." Failing that, the government must at least denounce the verdict. Only then, he claimed, could "calm be guaranteed."[74]

Though Drtina initially resisted any official statement, four days later the Communists successfully pressured the government to voice its dissent openly. In a public resolution the government stated that it "understood [the protests] as declarations of loyalty and devotion to the republic." Moreover, the verdict represented neither the government's opinion nor its will, which had been expressed by the prosecutor's indictment.[75] In his memoirs Drtina recalled his "sense of satisfied relief" that he had achieved a "concession" on the part of the Communists – an opinion he appears to have held at the time since he immediately left Prague on vacation.[76] Although Kopecký had abandoned his call for a retrial, the final declaration contained some curious wording: The verdict was described as "legally valid *today*."[77]

Drtina's satisfaction proved premature. On 10 August 1946 the Czech National Council [Česká národní rada] "unanimously" denounced the verdict and called for a public demonstration to be held on Prague's Old Town Square to demand a retrial.[78] The announcement was a bit of a surprise. The resistance group had essentially ceased functioning over a year before. After leading the May 1945 Prague Uprising against the Nazis, the National Council had run afoul of the Soviets, who had accused it of having negotiated with the German forces.[79] Since the Communists had played the leading role in marginalizing the Council's leaders, *Rudé právo*'s championing of the group in August 1946 was, to say the least, somewhat inconsistent – a charge the National Socialist press did not fail to make.[80] The "unanimity" of the National

---

[74] Government meeting transcript (2 August 1946), Kaplan, *Dva retribuční procesy*, doc. 7, 70–73.

[75] Government meeting transcript (6 August 1946), Kaplan, *Dva retribuční procesy*, doc. 9, 92.

[76] Drtina, *Československo*, II:196–97.

[77] Italics added. Government meeting transcript (6 August 1946), Kaplan, *Dva retribuční procesy*, doc. 9, 92.

[78] "Česká národní rada svolává...," *Národní osvobození* (11 August 1946), 1.

[79] Kaplan, *Dva retribuční procesy*, 14, n. 15.

[80] "Lid věří jen osvědčeným vlastencům," *Svobodné slovo* (20 August 1946), SÚA, f. MZV-VA II (j41), k. 212.

Council was particularly suspect in light of the organization's multiparty character.

At the next government meeting Gottwald used the Czech National Council's resolution as a pretext to reopen the question of the verdict's validity. After disingenuously stating that he had learned of the organization's protest from the newspapers, the premier assured his colleagues that the National Council would meet later that day to approve a one-week postponement of the demonstration. He then suggested that the Ministries of Interior and Justice each prepare a report on the possibility of a retrial. In response to Stránský's objection that a retrial would make it impossible in the future to convince anyone to adjudicate retribution cases, Gottwald assured his colleagues that they "could still find judges who will demonstrate the will of the people and cast judgment upon Hitler's ministers." Gottwald heightened the pressure on the others by suggesting that "some parties in the National Front had not [even] wanted the members of the Protectorate Government to be tried."[81] This accusation echoed Moscow *Pravda*'s claim, featured that very morning in *Rudé právo*, that "the defendants had found a protector in the persons of some members of the current government."[82]

The Communists' attacks did not pass unchallenged. Stepping gingerly over the agreed line not to criticize the Soviet Union, *Svobodné slovo* threatened that if *Rudé právo* would not let up, it would print Communist speeches from 1940 – when "the war against Hitler and Hitlerism was still an imperialist war."[83] The National Socialist newspaper attempted to expose, or even provoke, divisions among the Communists. Under the headline "Moral Crisis in the Communist Party Continues," it questioned why the Communist press and the Communist cochairman of the National Council were agitating against the government, headed by the Communist Gottwald. It suggested that the "Communist ministers do not have enough influence over their own party's press."[84] On the day of the demonstration, *Svobodné slovo* compared the methods of the protest's organizers to those of the Nazis. It revealed

---

[81] Government meeting transcript (14 August 1946), Kaplan, *Dva retribuční procesy*, doc. 10, 103–104.
[82] "Sovětský tisk o rozsudku...," *Rudé právo* (14 August 1946), 1.
[83] "Lid věří...," *Svobodné slovo* (20 August 1946), SÚA, f. MZV-VA II (j41), k. 212.
[84] "Mravní krise...," *Svobodné slovo* (22 August 1946), SÚA, f. MZV-VA II (j41), k. 212.

that in two factories employees had been told that they would have to work an additional two hours that afternoon and then would march, or perhaps be marched, to the demonstration.[85]

The Czech National Council demonstration proved to be the storm before the calm. The tendentious coverage of the daily papers, several of which ignored the event altogether, makes an accurate assessment of participation near impossible. It is worth noting, however, that Rudé právo's maximal estimate of 50,000 people was barely one-fourth of the number the Communists claimed to have summoned to a party rally earlier in the week.[86] Moreover, Albert Pražák, the Council's highly respected Social Democratic cochairman, failed to appear at the demonstration, allegedly due to health reasons.[87] Add to that the absence of the vice chairmen from National Socialist and People's Parties, and Svobodné slovo's characterization of the gathering as a "Communist demonstration" seems quite apt.[88] Although Rudé právo gave the event banner coverage the next morning, within two days the Communist flagship had demoted the protest movement from the front page to the inside flap. By 30 August the reaction to the verdict, which had merited raging headlines for weeks, had completely disappeared from the pages of Rudé právo.[89] Almost exactly one month to the day after it had begun, the protest campaign had been inexplicably abandoned.

Although public protests had ceased, the Protectorate trial continued to preoccupy the government. Its last meeting in August was the most heated to date, as the Communist ministers turned to threats as a means to achieve their goal. If changes were not made to the retribution laws, they argued, popular unrest could not be avoided. They also employed the threat of another protest campaign to prevent the release of one indicted defendant, whose poor health made a trial unlikely anytime soon.[90] Kopecký outrageously warned his fellow ministers, "The

[85] "Jak je režírován nástup k demonstraci," Svobodné slovo (23 August 1946), SÚA, f. MZV-VA II (j41), k. 212.
[86] Rudé právo (20, 24 August 1946).
[87] "Pro mravní...," Národní osvobození (24 August 1946), 1.
[88] "Přinese čistka komunistům úlevu?" Svobodné slovo (24 August 1946).
[89] Rudé právo (25–31 August, September 1946). At the August 27 government meeting not a single minister so much as referred to the Czech National Council demonstration. Government meeting transcript (27 August 1946), Kaplan, Dva retribuční procesy, doc. 11, 107–12.
[90] Faced with concerted opposition, Drtina agreed to keep the defendant in question, Otakar Kruliš-Randa, in custody, but only for "political reasons." The government even refused

members of the other parties ought to be grateful to the Communist Party that conditions here have not arisen like those in Poland and Yugoslavia; that here we maintain even the principles of formal democracy and legality." He ominously added, "We just want to keep abiding by them."[91] In the face of the Communist offensive, the government could only agree on the formation of a inter-ministerial commission with two goals: to consider contradictory proposals from the Ministries of Interior and Justice regarding the possibility of a retrial of the Protectorate ministers and subsequently to propose amendments to the retribution laws. When an early September meeting between representatives of the two ministries failed to result in a compromise, the government agreed to form yet another commission. In contrast to August, now Gottwald asked his colleagues not to inform the public of their decision.[92]

Two months later, when the ministers met to discuss the commission's conclusions, a compromise was finally reached: In exchange for several changes to the Great Decree, the government established an unbreachable date, 4 May 1947, to end the retribution courts.[93] While in legal terms the changes to the Great Decree were substantive, in practice their effect was predictably minimal. Though it became harder to consider mitigating circumstances (Paragraph Sixteen) and easier to retry cases, the ultimate decision on such matters was left to the courts, which were handing out increasingly lenient sentences irrespective of the law's stipulations. As shown in previous chapters, the trend toward leniency and more frequent use of Paragraph Sixteen accelerated after the fall of 1946. It is hard to imagine how the Communist Party could publicly trumpet such legalistic tinkering as an achievement commensurate with the energy exerted in the protest campaign.

Perhaps the mystery of the protest campaign's demise can be explained by reports received by the Communist leadership. In preparation for its late September meeting, the Central Committee instructed local

to endorse moving the accused to a hospital, preferring instead merely to note that it was aware of Drtina's decision. When the case finally came to trial, Kruliš-Randa was acquitted. Transcript of the twenty-third of the third government (24 September 1946), SÚA, f. 100/24 (KG), sign. 1494, sv. 141, 27–32.

[91] Government meeting transcript (27 August 1946), Kaplan, *Dva retribuční procesy*, doc. 11, 110.

[92] "Novelisace retribučního dekretu...," SÚA, f. MS, k. 1928; Government meeting transcript (10 September 1946), Kaplan, *Dva retribuční procesy*, doc. 12, 121.

[93] Third government, forty-second meeting (25 November 1946), SÚA, f. 100/24 (f. K. Gottwalda), k. 142.

party officials to summarize the mood of the membership and the general public concerning, among other issues, the "Response to the verdict against the Protectorate government."[94] Though many reports adopted the sycophantic approach one might expect, nearly half of the more than 100 responses were critical of the leadership's decisions. Local officials commented that the verdict had not only damaged the Party in the public's eyes, the protests had demoralized the rank and file. The Prague XVI district reported,

The verdict against the Protectorate Government... has brought about [among workers] psychological depression and significantly shaken trust in the government, particularly in our party, since the working people consider the verdict a political defeat for the Party.... From the time when the verdict was announced, increasing activity by functionaries of the other parties has been apparent.

The failure of the protest movement was most striking in light of the Party's recent electoral victory. The Zlín secretariat reported, "Among the people and also among our comrades there is a lot of talk that in this matter [retribution] we are losing influence and that the Party, even though it has 40% of the votes, cannot manage to use them sufficiently." To the Prague IX secretariat the entire campaign appeared useless: "The verdict against the Protectorate Government has left certain doubts about the strength of our party.... The campaign against the verdict either... should not have been initiated or we should had led it to its completion."

More seriously, the failure of the protests caused local leaders to worry about the commitment of party members and the future of mass demonstrations. Only the most "mature" cadres, the Prague XVI secretariat noted, even understood the party's position as it was elaborated in *Rudé právo*. The Pelhřimov district reported,

Even though the entire staff of a factory approves a resolution, they are in the majority convinced that it is useless; without direction from the Party even Communists would not do it.... the failure of this action has caused the workers to be aware of, and the majority even to exaggerate, obstacles

[94] The following responses are from secretariat reports to the Central Committee, SÚA, f. 1 (ZÚV-KSČ), sv. 2, aj. 13, str. 360–71.

and adversaries;...[They] don't even want to believe in the success of the Two-Year Plan.

The secretariat of Prague VIII – which, according to *Rudé právo*, had protested as late as 29 August[95] – nonetheless criticized the party's tactics: "Workers, if they are called upon, take part in every action where success is expected. In this case it...was hopeless." The central Prague organization warned that the protests' lack of closure could, "in future actions of the party, awaken the impression among the masses that they demonstrate uselessly and waste their strength and time." The Litovel district (near Olomouc) even reported, "70% of the inhabitants agree that the verdict against the Protectorate government should be valid and that the whole matter with the cleansing be finally finished."[96] Despite, or perhaps because of, the reports' critical tone, the Central Committee ignored the Protectorate trial verdict at its late September meeting. One member, however, summarized what may have been the prevailing view: "The demonstration on Old Town Square was a disappointment to us."[97]

POLITICAL JUSTICE

When Gottwald argued for a change in the Great Decree to "prevent a similar scandal in the future," he was likely thinking of the upcoming trial of Rudolf Beran, Czechoslovakia's premier in the fateful days from December 1938 to the Nazi occupation of March 1939.[98] Perhaps more than any other National Court trial, the prosecution of Beran was "political justice." As the former leader of the banned Agrarian Party, Beran's conviction was necessary to justify the decision to purge postwar Czechoslovak politics of conservatives. A longstanding opponent of Edvard Beneš – Beran had originally tried to prevent the president's election in 1935 – he had few if any friends in the postwar political order. The Communists, for their part, blamed the Agrarian leader for banning their party during the Second Republic. Well in advance of

---

[95] *Rudé právo* (29 August 1946), 2.
[96] SÚA, f. 1 (ZÚV-KSČ), sv. 2, aj. 13, str. 360–71.
[97] SÚA, f. 1 (ZÚV-KSČ), sv. 2, aj. 13, str. 20.
[98] Third government, forty-second meeting (25 November 1946), 13, SÚA, f. 100/24 (KG), aj. 1949, sv. 142.

Beran's trial the left-wing press categorically declared him to be a high traitor, guilty of undermining the nation's will to oppose Nazi Germany and, ultimately, of delivering it to foreign occupation and bondage. Article after article explained his betrayal and prepared the public for his conviction. A publication, *Rudolf Beran: Documents of Treachery*, was even released in his dishonor.[99]

The events of March 1939, when Nazi Germany destroyed the Second Czechoslovak Republic and created the Protectorate of Bohemia and Moravia, were a major focal point of the prosecution. Beran could not, after all, be charged with committing any serious crimes after April 1939, when he lost his position as premier and retreated into private life, only to be arrested in June 1941, tried by a Berlin court, and imprisoned for two years.[100] If Beneš's connections to the Protectorate ministers raised doubts about their prosecution, then the trial of Beran and his associates was a massive exercise in hypocrisy. Before September 1938 Czechoslovakia had heavily fortified borders, an impressive modern army prepared to fight, and the unified support of at least its Czech and Slovak population. The Munich Pact left the Second Republic leaders with a divided, indefensible rump state that had no hope of resisting the German invasion. Comparisons between September 1938 and March 1939 were inevitable and potentially unfavorable to Beneš, but apparently, the president "did not see the danger which threatened him from the political trials that would revolve around Munich."[101]

In the end, the National Court threw out almost all of the prosecution's case against Beran, rejecting more than a dozen charges in the process, but gave the defendant a lengthy sentence on two of the more inconsequential counts. He was found guilty of welcoming German leaders to Prague Castle on 16 March 1939 and of selling military materiel to Germany prior to the occupation.[102] Otherwise, the lengthy

---

99 "Beranovo přiznání k velezradě," *Rudé právo* (23 May 1946); "Beran – muž Mnichova," *Práce* (23 May 1946); "Jak Beran pomáhal Hitlerovi obsadit České země," *Rudé právo* (19 May 1946), SÚA, f. MZV-VA II (j41), k. 210.
100 On 25 June 1942 a German People's Court convicted Beran of high treason and sentenced him to ten years. Beran verdict (21 April 1947), SÚA, f. NS, TNs 1/47, 71.
101 Ladislav Feierabend, *Politické vzpomínky*, 3 vols. (Brno: Atlantis, 1994–1996), III:234.
102 Beran verdict (21 April 1947), SÚA, f. NS, TNs 1/47, 120, 127. Of course, no one mentioned that the Soviet Union was flagrantly guilty of having committed the same crime – arming Nazi Germany – *after* the outbreak of the war.

verdict was primarily devoted to refuting the remainder of the indict-ment, not only for its lack of supporting evidence, but even more for its senseless deductions. The Court rejected the prosecution's assertion that Beran favored totalitarianism and instead affirmed his "democratic disposition" and his contributions to the Czech resistance.[103] In re-sponse to the charge that he was anti-Communist, the judges ruled,

The circumstance that the defendant Rudolf Beran was an opponent of Com-munism and the USSR . . . cannot in and of itself be a reason for the defendant to be ruled guilty . . . , for divergence in political conviction and other worldly opinions, the same as in, for example, religion, cannot in a democratic state be grounds for criminal responsibility.[104]

The judges even exonerated Beran for the banning of the Communist Party, a decision they ruled necessary for the good of the country and accepted as such by the Communists at the time.[105] If a person can be exonerated in a conviction, then the verdict mainly cleared Beran while condemning him to prison for twenty years – the rest of his life. Although the Court saw multiple grounds for the use of Paragraph Sixteen, it de-cided not to lessen Beran's sentence because he was a "very experienced politician . . . whose conduct and behavior should [have been] an exam-ple to the nation."[106] One cannot avoid the suspicion that the judges felt obligated to convict Beran, but registered nonetheless their protest against the indictment. Like the prosecution of the comedian Vlasta Burian, the trial of Beran illustrates both the existence and limits of judicial independence in contemporary Czechoslovakia.

The role of political revenge in trials of Agrarian leaders was even more clearly demonstrated by the government's decision to prosecute František Machník and Ferdinand Klindera. According to the indict-ment the pair's guilt, like that of other Agrarian politicians, consisted of procollaboration speeches made before the events of March 1939.[107]

---

[103] Beran verdict (21 April 1947), SÚA, f. NS, TNs 1/47, 81, 84.
[104] Beran verdict (21 April 1947), SÚA, f. NS, TNs 1/47, 217.
[105] Beran verdict (21 April 1947), SÚA, f. NS, TNs 1/47, 210–12.
[106] Beran verdict (21 April 1947), SÚA, f. NS, TNs 1/47, 133.
[107] During the occupation a German court had sentenced Machník to death, but like Beran his request for mercy, in which he plaintively described his years of pro-German activity, was recovered after the war and used by the Interior Ministry to prepare the case against him. Transcript of the sixty-fourth meeting of the third government (18 February 1947, SÚA, f. 100/24 (KG), s. 1494, sv. 143.

When Drtina proposed dropping charges against the two men, neither of whom had been active during the occupation, his Communist colleagues reacted with outrage. The fact that Machník had been sentenced to death by the Nazis, spent 120 days in irons, and survived a death march was apparently not sufficient to clear his name. Kopecký denigrated him as just another Agrarian politician, an opponent of Communism and the Soviet Union, who advanced the interests of rich landowners to the detriment of poor farmers. According to Kopecký, the Agrarian party deserved punishment for its activities as far back as 1933.[108] Under Communist pressure, the National Court finally tried Machník and Klindera, but only for offenses against national honor, and acquitted the former Agrarian leaders on all counts.

If the Communists led the charge against Agrarian leaders, then the National Socialists apparently pushed for the harsh punishment of Josef Kliment, Hácha's political secretary. A conservative from the interwar period, Kliment had argued for a corporatist state, a theme he took up in a 19 March 1939 article that analyzed the Protectorate positively as a renewal of the Holy Roman Empire. The strongest charge against the defendant rested on his acceptance in 1943 of an award in memory of Reinhard Heydrich.[109] The day before Kliment's trial began, the National Socialist flagship, *Svobodné slovo*, condemned Hácha and proclaimed that his "ghost" now stood before the court. On the day of the verdict another National Socialist newspaper, *Svobodný zítřek* [*Free Tomorrow*], declared in an editorial,

If this time we exceptionally violate our principle not to write about wartime guilt, which at the moment is being deliberated, so as not to influence the people's judges, we do so... only because we see a real danger.... There is no avoiding it: the people's judges must now decide, whether this man who accepted the Heydrich Award... was in the right.... Every single member of the people's tribunal must be aware that he is making a decision about this question.

Kliment later claimed that the author of this editorial was none other than Prokop Drtina. Czech scholar Michal Musil argued that the National Socialists seized upon the trial as an opportunity to prove their

[108] Transcript of the sixty-fourth meeting of the third government (18 February 1947, SÚA, f. 100/24 (KG), s. 1494, sv. 143, 33–36.
[109] Michal Musil, "Příběh Háchova politického sekretáře: Josef Kliment před Národním soudem roku 1947," *Soudobé dějiny* 4 (1995), 533–35.

toughness against collaborators.[110] In the end, the National Court sentenced Kliment to life in prison.

Despite the lengthy sentencing of Beran and Kliment, Kopecký's claim – that a "lenient" Protectorate trial verdict might prevent the execution of other wartime political leaders – proved to be an understatement.[111] In addition to the five men tried in 1946, nine other Czech Protectorate ministers had survived the war. Of the others, only four were ever brought to trial and only one of them was convicted, and even he was absolved of punishment.[112] (Figure 10) The one conviction demonstrated that the National Court had clearly rejected the exiles' belief that the Protectorate government was a criminal organization. Josef Ježek, who had preceded Bienert as Protectorate Minister of Interior, was acquitted of the more serious charge of treachery and convicted only of "supporting Nazism and fascism" – for which he was given no sentence. In its verdict, the Court adopted the home-front's forgiving view of wartime behavior: "The defendant, like many other Czechs, be they people in leading political positions, ministers,... industrialists or labor leaders, had to feign loyalty to the Germans in order to conceal their own activities, directed against the Germans."[113]

ECONOMIC COLLABORATION

The National Court's verdict in the Ježek case illustrates its rejection of the Communists' demands to punish the so-called bourgeoisie for its alleged support of Nazism. Contrary to Gottwald's claim in Košice, the Great Decree was a fairly blunt weapon for punishing economic offenses. Three paragraphs (Eight through Ten) covered "Crimes against Property," but these concerned acts committed against property of the state, a business, or another person. None of the paragraphs addressed

---

[110] Musil, "Příběh," 541–42.

[111] Government meeting transcript (2 August 1946), Kaplan, *Dva retribuční procesy*, doc. 7, 72.

[112] Prokop Drtina, *Na soudu národa: Tři projevy ministra spravedlnosti dr. Prokopa Drtiny o činnosti Mimořádných lidových soudů a Národního soudu* (Prague: Min. Spravedlnosti, 1947), 23. With the support of a majority of the government Drtina successfully argued against prosecuting the others. He repeatedly stressed that it would be detrimental to the government and the Court to try defendants when there was no reasonable chance of success. Presidium meeting transcript (17 January 1946), Kaplan, *Dva retribuční procesy*, doc. 13, 123–6; seventy-second meeting (secret part) of the third government (25 March 1947), SÚA, f. 83, aj. 300.

[113] J. Ježek verdict (28 January 1947), 41, SÚA, f. NS, TNs 16/46.

Figure 10. Lawyer: "I did what I could, but you won't escape the noose." Convict: "Then why the devil don't you prove that I'm a Protectorate Minister. I'd be freed immediately." *Mladá fronta*, 28 January 1947. Reprinted with permission.

the problem of economic collaboration with one's own legitimate possessions. Anyone who forcibly acquired property during the war could be punished, but to convict someone who directed his own factory to aid the Nazi war effort was a far more difficult task. Such economic support could only be prosecuted as supporting and propagating Nazism (Paragraph Three), a charge normally applied to far less opaque infractions. As was clearly illustrated at the Nuremberg International Military Tribunal (e.g., in the Hjalmar Schacht case) and in retribution trials in other European countries, economic collaboration is an extraordinarily difficult charge to prove. In occupied Europe there was often a very fine line between earning a living and working for the enemy.[114]

In the spring of 1947 Communist ministers tried to force a trial of the wartime directors of the Bat'a factory in Zlín. At stake was more than just the punishment of a few men who may have aided the Nazis. The Bat'a shoe company, a symbol of national pride, represented a form of paternalistic capitalism that undermined the image of a cruel bourgeoisie intent on exploiting the working class. Under the leadership of company founder, Tomáš Bat'a, the firm built affordable housing and offered generous social benefits to its workers, while expanding sales to much of the world. Gottwald explained to his fellow government ministers,

It is necessary to show the nation…how the captains of industry behaved themselves.…We must destroy the legend which that unfortunate brother of Tomáš Bat'a created for himself.…It is high time that the nation and especially people in Zlín were shown who Jan Bat'a was. A certain aura still endures around the Bat'a family there.[115]

The "unfortunate brother," Jan Antonín Bat'a, technically still the owner of the company, could have made an excellent poster-boy for the collaborationist bourgeoisie – he had allegedly promoted a scheme to "resettle" the Czech nation to Patagonia in South America – but the government could not lay its hands on him. He had fled during the Second

---

[114] For evidentiary reasons, economic collaborators were tried late in France and received far lighter treatment than former journalists. Like their Czechoslovak comrades, French Communists accused the courts of being lenient toward economic collaborators. Peter Novick, *The Resistance versus Vichy: The Purge of Collaborators in Liberated France* (New York: Columbia University Press, 1968), 162.

[115] Third government, sixty-eighth meeting (4 March 1947), 32; SÚA, f. 100/24 (KG), sign. 1494, sv. 143.

World War and ended up eventually in Brazil, which refused to extradite him. In addition to wrangling over whether Jan Bat'a should be tried *in absentia*, the government repeatedly discussed the possibilities of trying other managers of the Bat'a firm. The National Prosecutor had indicted four senior company officials (Hynek Bat'a, Dominik Čipera, František Malota, and Hugo Vavrečka), but believed that the prospects for conviction of them were slim. Drtina defended this view: "Conditions at the Bat'a factories were so complicated and mixed-up that there is a serious danger here that criminal proceedings will end in acquittal." To that, Education Minister Zdeněk Nejedlý responded, "It's not a matter simply of individual company functionaries, but of the entire system of the firm itself."[116] Despite their protests, the Communists and their allies were overruled in a series of votes on 4 March 1947: A slim majority of ministers voted not to prosecute Malota, Vavrečka, or Hynek Bat'a.

Only Čipera went on trial – not primarily as the former General Director of Bat'a, but as Minister of Public Works in the Beran and Protectorate governments. He was joined in the dock not by a member of the Bat'a family, but by Jan Kapras, former Protectorate Minister of Education, a man who had nothing to do with the Bat'a firm. The prosecutor indicted Čipera on a litany of charges associated with his tenure at the company.[117] The National Court examined the claims that Čipera had "supported and propagated fascism and Nazism" and came to a simple conclusion: He was innocent on all counts. More importantly, the Court used the trial as an opportunity to clear the name of the Bat'a company altogether. In the words of the verdict, "The Bat'a firm . . . , it is true, did not avoid the necessity of working for the German defense forces, but neither did any other company in the occupied Czech lands."[118] The court went so far as to view Čipera as a positive representative of his social class. One witness testified that

[116] Third government, sixty-eighth meeting (4 March 1947), 40; SÚA, f. 100/24 (KG), sign. 1494, sv. 143.
[117] The prosecution accused Čipera of producing war materials for the Wehrmacht, seeking profit through military production, strengthening German control over the Bat'a company, introducing the "Aryan salute" into the firm, mandating employee contributions to the German Red Cross and Winterhilfe program, overseeing company and local newspapers that praised the Nazis, allowing the factory's radio to be abused for fascist purposes, and delivering prooccupation addresses. Verdict against D. Čipera and J. Kapras (2 May 1947), TNs 11/47, SUA, f. MS (VI/19), k. 1241.
[118] Čipera and Kapras verdict, TNs 11/47, 58.

Čipera had not joined the League against Bolshevism during the war because he "did not want to create the impression that the so-called 'bourgeoisie' was 'anti-communist.'" The court concluded, "He was therefore aware that if he joined the League, he would cast a shadow on the entire stratum of the nation to which he belonged."[119] Gottwald sarcastically commented that prosecution of Čipera seemed more like an awards ceremony than a trial.[120]

In order to nationalize Jan Bat'a's property – a desire the government ministers openly discussed among themselves – a kangaroo court trial of the Czech industrialist was hastily arranged. Since he resided in Brazil, the proceedings had to take place *in absentia*. In fact, as Nosek futilely explained to his colleagues, the trial itself was superfluous because the Interior Ministry could seize his property anyway, on the grounds of the indictment alone. Stránský recommended stopping proceedings for the very same reason. Bat'a could only have regained his property if he was formally acquitted by a court, a chance the émigré was unlikely to take. Nonetheless, Gottwald insisted on a trial so that a Bat'a could be convicted for the "moral–political" consequences.[121] Ultimately, the National Court sentenced Jan Antonín Bat'a *in absentia* to a meaningless fifteen years in prison and the very significant loss of all his property.

Union leaders fared as well as industrial bosses. Evžen Erban and Jindřich Jungmann never faced any charges for their roles in the monolithic wartime workers' organization, the National Union of Employees [Národní odborová ústředna zaměstnanecká (NOÚZ)]. Like many lesser-known collaborators, the two union bosses found salvation in political affiliation: Both Erban and Jungmann assumed leading positions in the monolithic postwar workers' organization, the Central Council of Unions [Ústřední rada odborů (ÚRO)], and even gained seats in the parliament, the former for the Social Democrats, the latter for the Communists. Three others, Václav Stočes, Arnošt Hais, and František Kolář, represented the organization before the National Court.

---

[119] Čipera and Kapras verdict, TNs 11/47, 124.

[120] Transcript of the eighty-first meeting of the third government (25 April 1947), 40, SÚA, f. 100/24 (KG), aj. 1494, sv. 144.

[121] A complication was introduced into the case by Tomáš Bat'a, Jr., the son of the company's founder. He had served in the Allied armies during the war and returned to claim that the family's property belonged to him and not his uncle, in which case it could not be confiscated. Transcript of the eighty-first meeting of the third government (25 April 1947), 38–46, SÚA, f. 100/24 (KG), aj. 1494, sv. 144.

In addition to repeatedly encouraging workers to denounce, Hais had publicly condemned Heydrich's assassins and defended the Nazis' destruction of Lidice. The former union leader had visited occupied Soviet territory as part of a workers' delegation and thereafter called the Nazi regime there a great improvement on the Bolsheviks.[122] Despite these and other charges, the National Court decided that the union leader's acts did not fulfill the subjective conditions for collaboration and acquitted Hais along with his two codefendants. While publicly praising the Nazis, Hais had also been an active member of the Social Democratic resistance and a delegate to the overall underground umbrella organization. Moreover, the leaders of the underground as well as workers in the union had asked Hais to stay in NOÚZ to help cover his resistance work. At his postwar trial numerous witnesses who were beyond reproach testified to Hais's good character, anti-Nazi sentiment, and even pro-Soviet beliefs. They expressed their faith in the union leader and stressed how he had suffered at the Nazis' hands. For the Germans had soon tired of his double game and in 1942 imprisoned Hais for the remainder of the war. Czech scholar Dalibor Státník summarized, "[Hais's] life story . . . demonstrates the ambiguity and problematic nature of involvement in the underground movement camouflaged by activist work (or vice-versa?) under the conditions of Nazi occupation."[123]

The acquittal of Hais and his codefendants did achieve one thing: thereafter the Communists' political competitors could also complain about the National Court's leniency. Unlike other disputes, the National Socialists did not keep this one within the confines of cabinet meetings. *Svobodné slovo* argued that the trial exposed a double standard because there were no protests when the NOÚZ leaders employed the same defense as the Protectorate ministers. The newspaper explained the quiescence as a ploy "to alchemically cover up the reality that ÚRO is in fact the heir to NOÚZ, from which it inherited not only its organizational apparatus, but many, many leading officials."[124] In his memoirs Drtina decried the "double-facedness" of the Communists for their failure to

---

[122] Transcript of the seventy-second meeting of the third government, secret session (25 March 1947), 7–16, SÚA, f. 83, aj. 300.

[123] Dalibor Státník, "Mezi odbojem a kolaborací: Případ Arno Haise," *Soudobé dějiny* 8:4 (2000), 692.

[124] "NOÚZ a ÚRO," *Svobodné slovo* (27 April 1947), SÚA, f. MZV-VA II (j41), k. 213.

protest the whitewashing of the union bosses' guilt.[125] Following on the Minister's assessment, historians have condemned the acquittals as Communist-inspired hypocrisy. Vilém Hejl, for example, wrote, "The NOÚZ organization was too useful for the KSČ to want to shock it or upset it by adherence to some sort of 'abstract' justice."[126]

A different picture, however, emerges from the transcript of the secret session of the 25 March 1947 government meeting. Despite Drtina's later insistence that Jungmann deserved punishment, in the cabinet meeting the Justice Minister recommended the prosecution of only two union bosses, Stočes and Kolář. Even then, he downplayed their collaborationist speeches and spoke at length about the good that they had done for the Czech people. Drtina also proposed dropping the charges against Hais because he had been in prison and a concentration camp since 1942. The Communists Nosek and Gottwald, by contrast, pushed for the prosecution of all four, including Hais and Jungmann, on the grounds that their prooccupation speeches alone sufficed to merit a trial. By a slim majority of one, on the second try the government approved prosecution of Hais – against Drtina's will.[127] In the end the Communist ministers alone voted to indict Jungmann.[128]

The Communists' intransigence could be chalked up to an unwillingness to be charged with inconsistency or to the confidence that the rest of the ministers, led by fellow-traveler Fierlinger, would vote against prosecution anyway. It seems unlikely, however, that the Communists sought to protect Hais, a man who been expelled from the party in 1930 and had repeatedly condemned Bolshevism and the Soviet Union during

---

[125] Drtina, *Československo*, II:281.

[126] Vilém Hejl, *Zpráva o organizovaném násilí* (Prague: Univerzum, 1990), 44.

[127] Transcript of the seventy-second meeting of the third government, secret session (25 March 1947), 7–16, SÚA, f. 83, aj. 300.

[128] František Jungmann, a former Communist turned Social Democrat, found his strongest defenders in his new party. *Právo lidu*, the official organ of the Social Democrats, publicly defended NOÚZ as a patriotic organization that had protected Czech interests. Zdeněk Fierlinger, the Social Democratic leader, acknowledged that NOÚZ had its faults, but maintained that it had concealed substantial underground activity. He accused the National Socialists of using the trial to persecute the Social Democrats for "foolish political competition." Although Fierlinger's outburst may have been coordinated with the Communists, Jungmann found no open support from his erstwhile comrades, who, unlike the National Socialist ministers, pressed for his prosecution. Transcript of the eighty-second meeting of the third government, secret session (29 April 1947), 20–29, SÚA, f. 83, aj. 304; "NOÚZ před Národní soud," *Právo lidu* (16 April 1947); "NOÚZ a retribuce," *Svobodné slovo* (29 April 1947), SÚA, f. MZV-VA II (j41), k. 213.

the war. Gottwald and his comrades may have sought a trial of NOÚZ leaders either to gain an exculpatory verdict against the union bosses or to discredit the Social Democrats, to facilitate the Communist takeover of organized labor. If the Communists were duplicitous, however, that does not alter the fact that Drtina and the National Socialists, despite their public and postmortem protests, argued in private at the time against prosecution. The Communists, by contrast, maintained a consistent line that demanded trials for all prominent collaborators, including union bosses. Despite Drtina's later claims, *Rudé právo*'s coverage of the NOÚZ trial was remarkable not because the newspaper failed to criticize the verdict, but because it failed to mention the defendants' acquittals altogether. On 24 April 1947 *Rudé právo* featured a typically tendentious headline: "The Public Activity of NOÚZ Served the Occupiers in All Facets." Citing the Communist head of the postwar national union (ÚRO), Antonín Zápotocký, the article stressed the importance of debunking revisionist attempts to make NOÚZ into a patriotic organization. He explained that the Nazis would not have maintained the union if it had not served their interests. Far from protecting the working class, Zápotocký claimed, NOÚZ had actually harmed it.[129] After this grand, polemical beginning, however, *Rudé právo*'s coverage of the trial became minimal, consisting of brief bulletins of a purely factual nature, until on 30 April the newspaper mentioned the trial for the last time.

The silence of *Rudé právo* could be considered smug satisfaction, especially when compared to its vociferous reaction to earlier National Court verdicts. The striking absence of any reaction to the NOÚZ verdict, however, was no anomaly. Despite boisterous arguments within the confines of government meetings, the Communist Party's rhetoric against the retribution courts rapidly waned in the final weeks of their operations. When, on Drtina's recommendation, President Beneš commuted the death sentences of several National Court defendants, the decision was met with silence – a surprising development, especially considering the earlier controversy over the cremation of Bláha and Rychtrmoc.[130] Not only did *Rudé právo* ignore the verdict against the

---

[129] "Veřejná činnost NOÚZ sloužila ve všech směrech okupantům," *Rudé právo* (24 April 1947), 3.

[130] The way the commutations came about was disturbingly haphazard. For some unexplained reason, Drtina decided after the second group trial of activist journalists that the

union bosses, the Communist flagship also neglected to report on the acquittal of Čipera, a man whom it had recently lambasted on page one as a Nazi henchman.[131] Even the astonishingly lenient sentence of two years – all but a few days of which had already been served – given to Rudolf Gajda, the father of the Czech fascist movement and inveterate enemy of the Communists, failed to elicit more than a three-sentence bulletin in *Rudé právo*.[132] The executions of the infamous betrayer of the Czech parachutists, Karel Čurda, the butcher of the Theresienstadt ghetto, Karl Rahm, and the son of Emanuel Moravec, Igor, all merited only brief announcements on inside pages. After nearly two years of bombastic rhetoric, *Rudé právo* greeted the last days of the retribution courts with a whimper, not a bang.

COLLABORATION REVISITED

As Gottwald's "sharp weapon" speech revealed, from the very beginning partisan politics shaped the Communist leadership's approach to retribution. The Communist press regularly declared defendants guilty

time had finally come to try out his power to recommend commutation to the president. After ruling out several defendants, including the hated Novák, the Justice Minister settled on Jaroslav Křemen, and the president immediately granted the defendant clemency. To Drtina's surprise there was no public reaction. Even *Rudé právo* covered his decision in a factual manner. In his memoirs Drtina noted, "After that experience I regretted that I had not proposed Kříž and Kožíšek for mercy as well." Soon thereafter the president also granted mercy to Eduard Chalupa and Jan Svoboda, two defendants from the Kuratorium trial. Drtina, *Československo*, II:278–81; "Krychtálek, Křemen, Werner a Vajtauer odsouzení k trestu smrt," *Rudé právo* (23 April 1947), 1.

[131] "Pravá tvář Dominika Čipery," *Rudé právo* (26 April 1947), 1.

[132] Gajda (1892–1948), born Rudolf Geidl in Montenegro, deserted the Habsburg Army during the First World War and eventually joined the Czechoslovak Legion, an auxiliary force of former prisoners of war that Russia established to support its military against the Central Powers. When Bolshevik Russia withdrew from the war, the Legion attempted to reach the Western front via an odyssey across the vast expanses of Siberia to the port of Vladivostock. After Czechoslovak units guarding the trans-Siberian railroad became enmeshed in the Russian Civil War, Gajda, by then raised to the rank of general, enthusiastically promoted severe reprisals against the Reds. In the interwar republic, he repeatedly boasted, "I, alone among Czech generals, established summary courts and ordered the hanging of numerous Bolsheviks," including the brother of Soviet Foreign Commissar Maxsim Litvinov. In 1926 *Rudé právo* warned, "Thanks to his Siberian adventure, Gajda is a marked man." Twenty years later, however, the Communist Party proved incapable of ensuring a harsh sentence against the fascist leader. Tomáš Pasák, *Český fašismus (1922–1945) a kolaborace (1939–1945)* (Prague: Práh, 1999), 76–77, 83, 117; "Gajda a Dominik dva roky žaláře," *Rudé právo* (6 May 1945), 1.

before their trials even began. In many cases *Rudé právo* either mocked the defense – statements by the accused were preceded by the word "supposedly" – or simply labeled the defendant a "collaborator" or "traitor."[133] The Party's leaders, as we have seen, tried to instruct their people's judges and were angered when their colleagues in government did not do so as well. Nevertheless, the Communist critique of retribution, especially the claim that "small fish" were punished more harshly than big ones, was not all political bluster. At the root of the conflict was a disagreement over the definition of "collaboration." The Communists, Gottwald explained, held a different opinion than their colleagues in government:

Here stand against each other two basic concepts that fundamentally differ. The Justice Minister and his friends maintain that if a certain defendant is not himself responsible for a concrete criminal act, that if he did not kill anyone with his own hands and did not himself denounce someone to the Gestapo, then he cannot be prosecuted. They overlook that these people exhorted others to denounce....

In contrast, the premier and his friends start from the viewpoint that the accused committed criminal acts, that they are guilty for their participation and activities in responsible positions and, therefore, that they should be tried.[134]

Despite the duplicity of many Communist criticisms of retribution, Gottwald's complaint was not baseless. The National Court frequently did not hold prominent Czech defendants accountable for their encouragement of denunciation, even though their words legitimated the work of informants throughout the country.

The acquittal of Jan Kapras illustrates the double standard that rankled the Communists. A member of the Czechoslovak delegation to the Paris Peace Conference, Kapras had been a professor of legal history at Charles University, and an active player in Prague city government

---

[133] *Rudé právo* defended this approach in the controversy over Velíšková – when the judge attacked the newspaper for calling her a "denouncer" prior to the verdict – on the grounds that such a legalistic interpretation would mean that even Beran could not be called a "collaborator" prior to his conviction. "Povede státní zastupitelstvo...," *Rudé právo* (2 February 1947), 3.

[134] Transcript of the seventy-second meeting of the third government, secret session (25 March 1947), 10–11, SÚA, f. 83, aj. 300.

before he became Protectorate Minister of Education.[135] On 30 October 1941, a month after Heydrich initiated a terror campaign, Kapras delivered a speech in Prague to a large hall filled with secondary school teachers and pupils. The actual audience was far greater: The press reprinted the speech and Kapras instructed schools to display copies of it in the classrooms of older students. Before the assembled audience he began,

Principals and students! I have gathered you in this wholly extraordinary way because the matter concerned is of such extraordinarily national importance that it cannot abide delay.... [I]n several districts of Bohemia and Moravia the Reich Protector has declared martial law. The cause was...that some hotheads and an array of people seduced by foreign agitation have prepared resistance against the Reich.... No state, not even in peacetime, can allow itself to abide similar conduct, less so the great German empire today fighting its grand struggle for a new social, economic, and political order in Europe.... Such behavior, whether committed by Czechs or Jews, is therefore punished according to martial law with death by shooting or hanging. These people, who some of you probably view as martyrs, have damaged our national interests in this very difficult time, because they do not understand what is going on around them. The victorious great German empire, destroying on one side anti-cultural Bolshevism and on the other side Western plutocracy, is building this new Europe on new strong foundations. The question is whether or not the Czech nation will take part in this building of a new Europe and utilize all the advantages that will flow from it to our nation.

That much alone sufficed to fulfill the objective conditions for the "support" of the occupation authorities according to Paragraph Three of the Great Decree. Kapras continued,

The vast majority of members of the teaching corps and of pupils in our high schools and vocational schools calmly, undisturbedly, and reasonably fulfill their scholastic responsibilities and do not allow any agitation to divert them. Still there are some hotheads among you who, seduced by foreign agitation, carelessly think that they are heroes if they gather behind closed doors, write anonymous threatening and abusive notes, prepare and distribute fliers, meet secretly at night, deface walls, or listen to foreign radio. Be aware that these childish, silly pranks and these illegal acts cannot hurt the Reich, but they can hurt our nation, and that can lead it into great danger and cause

---

[135] Drtina described Kapras as his favorite Czech history professor. František Kolář et al., *Politická elita meziválečného Československa 1918–1938: Kdo byl kdo* (Prague: Pražská edice, 1998), 122; Drtina, *Československo*, II:281.

it immense damage.... The Reich Protector told me recently that the patience of the German authorities is exhausted and as a punishment the permanent closure of all Czech secondary schools and vocational schools in Bohemia and Moravia has been prepared. Let us clearly realize the seriousness of this moment; let us realize what the loss of all secondary and vocational schools would mean for our nation.

Clearly, Kapras sought to make the teachers and students understand that his goal was the preservation of Czech secondary education. Perhaps that goal alone merited passive accommodation to Nazi rule. But the Protectorate Minister of Education not only warned the audience against resistance, he called on them to actively participate in repressing others. He proclaimed,

Whoever does not allow himself to be further advised, whoever still thinks that he must follow the refugee Beneš gang and their Jewish comrades, he should realize that he will be crushed by the Reich. For the good of the nation your task will now be to mercilessly wipe out from your ranks and *hand over for justifiable punishment* those teachers and students, who after this day still cannot be reached by my and your warnings. I therefore emphatically lay on your hearts that you yourselves guard your schools against all those who thus threaten their existence.... I, therefore, expect from you, teachers and students,... unconditional loyalty to the Reich as the foundation of a new social, economic, and state order in Europe.[136]

In plain language the Protectorate Minister of Education called on teachers and students to police their own schools and denounce anyone who acted against the Nazis.

In his defense Kapras claimed that he had tried to edit the already written text he received from Frank, but that the German censors in turn undid his attempts to moderate it. Kapras also claimed that, through conversations with teachers and students, he made sure that "it was clear to all present that it was a speech dictated to [me] by the Germans." The most effective defense, however, was Kapras's argument that he had warned the students to save them from severe reprisals and their schools from closure. The evidence, in particular a letter from Frank to Kapras threatening the schools' closure and proposing that the Education Minister make a public address, supported the defendant's claims. In the end, the National Court acknowledged that Kapras's speech

[136] Italics added. Čipera and Kapras verdict, TNs 11/47, 35–37.

fulfilled the objective conditions for collaboration, but then decided that subjective grounds for conviction, especially the criminal intent to support the occupation, were lacking. In their decision to acquit the former Education Minister, the judges even cited his heroism, claiming that he had sacrificed his own good name for the sake of preserving Czech education.[137]

Granting the difficult situation faced by Kapras and the work he may have done to help the Czech underground, he had nonetheless encouraged the students to denounce one other. While most of his audience may have known that the Kapras was playing a double game, what about the child who accepted the Education Minister's words at face value? In Chapter 4, we saw that a student who denounced his history teacher was sentenced after the war to fifteen years in prison. Unlike *Aryan Struggle* editor Václav Píša or Banner chief Josef Rys-Rozsévač, Kapras was a respected Czech educator, a longstanding member of the Academy of Sciences and former parliamentary representative.[138] His words held far greater weight than those of despised traitors and fascists. Like Kapras, Arnošt Hais had encouraged denunciation, and, like the professor, the union leader found a sympathetic hearing after the war. Drtina argued, "The National Prosecutor maintains that although [Hais] exhorted the members of NOÚZ in the press and at public places to denounce, this was simply a general appeal."[139] Despite their roles as Czech leaders who had been "duty-bound to serve as a patriotic example to their fellow citizens," to quote the National Court decree, neither Kapras nor Hais was ultimately held accountable for his encouragement of denunciation.

In Kapras's case the National Court ruled that his address to the students, though objectively collaborationist, did not fulfill the subjective grounds for collaboration. In other trials judges also accepted the substance of the prosecution's case as fact, only to discard it on the grounds that criminal intent was lacking. Subjectivity was, however, in the eye

---

[137] Čipera and Kapras verdict, TNs 11/47, 35–39.

[138] Václav Píša was not unaware of the consequences of his actions, but he, too, found legitimacy in the words of respected Czech leaders. In his forlorn defense, the *Aryan Struggle* editor testified, "In writing those articles, in their collection and solicitation, I followed the slogan of National Solidarity – that anyone who associates with Jews is an outcast of the nation." Státní oblastní archiv (SOA) Praha, MLS-KH, Ls 646/46, 377.

[139] Transcript of the seventy-second meeting of the third government, secret session (25 March 1947), 7–16, SÚA, f. 83, aj. 300.

of the beholder. The National Court saw the necessary criminal intent in Beran's 16 March 1939 "welcoming" address, but found it lacking in Kapras's 1941 speech, although the former was far vaguer than the latter.[140] Once subjective guilt was differentiated from objective guilt, the defense had a better opportunity to prove its case. In addition to claims of ignorance and poor memory – which both proved ineffective strategies – defendants rallied a number of arguments in their defense. First, defendants argued that if they had resigned, the Nazis would have replaced them with fascists from the ranks of groups like the Banner movement. Either the Czechs would have suffered a domestic, fascist regime or direct rule by the Germans. Second, defendants claimed that any time they had acted in a manner that appeared to support Nazi rule, they had done so only due to coercion. Third, they argued that their apparent collaboration was nothing more than a cover for the resistance activity they carried out behind the scenes.

The most common defense was the argument that collaboration had prevented a greater evil.[141] Noncompliance would either have invited severe reprisals against civilians or led to the defendant's replacement by an out-and-out fascist, for example, a member of the Banner movement or even a German. Before the National Court Kapras successfully argued that if he had refused to make his collaborationist speech, Frank would have closed Czech secondary schools. While this claim was certainly plausible – Czech universities had already been shut down – if the Nazis had wanted to terminate Czech secondary education and deport teenagers for work elsewhere, then any pretext, including the resistance activity already cited by Kapras, would have sufficed. In fact, several months after his speech, Kapras was replaced by Emanuel Moravec, but Czech secondary schools remained open throughout the war. In other words, Kapras's speech did not save his position and even under Moravec, the most pro-Nazi Czech leader, the secondary schools were not in jeopardy. In fact, the Germans rarely turned to groups like Banner to fill prominent positions in occupied lands. In the Protectorate, as

[140] Beran verdict (21 April 1947), SÚA, f. NS, TNs 1/47, 127.
[141] Both Tigrid and Feierabend repeated this argument in their analyses of the postwar period. Tigrid praised the defense of the Protectorate ministers, who allegedly proved "that by remaining in government they saved the people from even worse persecution." For Feierabend, his former colleagues in the Protectorate government, especially Hácha, had sacrificed themselves for the good of the nation. Tigrid, *Kapesní průvodce*, 381; Feierabend, *Politické vzpomínky*, III:260.

elsewhere in Europe, Nazi leaders preferred traditional conservative elites to local fascists, and usually employed the latter merely to frighten the former into compliance. István Deák explained, "Characteristically, the Germans did not put their trust in these fanatics, exploiting them primarily as agents and for propaganda purposes. In the eyes of Hitler and his associates, National Socialism was not for export; whenever they could, the Germans entrusted the leadership of defeated or allied countries to conservative anti-communists."[142] Hitler and his associates not only mistrusted "national roads to fascism," they also understood that domestic conservatives, even reluctant ones, could elicit a higher degree of obeisance from the population than could despised radicals from the extreme right.

Even when the judges concluded that the Nazis would not have retaliated if the defendant had refused to comply, they sometimes admitted the defendant's unjustified fear as exculpatory evidence. After Heydrich's assassination, Čipera praised the former Nazi chieftain in a public speech, an act which the court viewed as objective support for the occupation, but again found subjective proof lacking. Although the court noted that no Czech leader was ever punished for refusing to give a similar speech, it nonetheless accepted that the defendant could have feared execution and therefore absolved him of responsibility.[143] In the trial of Josef Drachovský, the National Court ridiculed his defense but then accepted its subjective basis. On 23 January 1944 Drachovský became chairman of the Czech League against Bolshevism, the organization created by the Nazis to express the Czechs' alleged rejection of the defense pact that Beneš had signed with Stalin the previous month. At a time when the Red Army was in full advance, the long-term risks of accepting the Nazis' offer were clear. In his defense the former university professor claimed that he had assumed the position because he feared what might happen to him if he refused. Witness testimony revealed, however, that Drachovský was actually the Germans' third choice for the chairmanship. Although the previous two nominees had refused the offer on the grounds of overwork, illness, and advanced age, neither suffered any consequences. The court also found no evidence to support Drachovský's claim that he joined to protect his role as a leader

---

[142] István Deák, "Resistance, Collaboration, and Retribution during World War II and its Aftermath," *The Hungarian Quarterly* 35:134 (1994), 67.
[143] Čipera and Kapras verdict, TNs 11/47, 90–92.

of the Czech underground. Nonetheless, the judges concluded that the defendant's mistaken belief that he was a head of the resistance led him to assume that he must accept the position so as not to jeopardize the underground by bringing himself under suspicion. Although he really faced no danger, this "cowardly man," to quote the verdict, actually believed that a serious threat existed. Therefore, from the subjective perspective his guilty intent was not proven and the National Court sentenced him to only eight months in prison. Because he had already served nine months in pretrial detention, Drachovský was immediately released.[144] If nothing else, the sentence demonstrated that the Communist Party could not even deliver a harsh verdict against the former chairman of the Czech League against Bolshevism.

CONCLUSION

Strange as it may appear in hindsight, little more than a year before the February 1948 Communist coup d'état the conduct of the National Court, and especially the government's refusal to overturn the verdict against the Protectorate government ministers, had given reason to hope for a democratic future for Czechoslovakia. Ferdinand Peroutka, the most respected contemporary Czech journalist, exulted, "The year 1946 decided whether the Czechoslovak state will be totalitarian or democratic." Greeting the New Year, while reflecting on the old, he wrote,

If we look back, we must recognize those summer days, when the Communist Party began to mobilize the masses against the Protectorate government verdict, as the greatest crisis of the past year.... At that moment, it was a greater matter than whether the verdict was just – in these questions there will always be some disagreement between the exiles and the majority of those who remained at home during the war. It was a matter...of whether we will maintain the laws which we ourselves just issued; or whether...we will arrive at a state of affairs where it will be possible to annul the validity of any law whatsoever because against it we organize a mob of people. It was like standing on the edge of precipice and staring into the chasm: no

[144] The former professor also delivered a speech after Heydrich's assassination to representatives from forty-two cultural institutions and corporations in which he expressed sadness over the Nazi leader's death and exhorted the audience to collaborate for the good of the Reich. In 1944 the Germans arrested and imprisoned Drachovský for the remainder of the war. J. Drachovský verdict (5 April 1946), TNs 4/46, SÚA, f. MS (VI/19), k. 1236; Josef Tomeš and Alena Léblová, eds., *Československý biografický slovník* (Prague: Academia, 1992), 117.

one could know where it would all end, if that critical attempt to break the law had succeeded, if above the law had been placed some sort of unclear, shapeless principle of the will of a section of the people, hurriedly called by the megaphone to the street. It was a crisis, but in the end justice emerged arguably stronger.... At that time it was decided that our trials will be trials and not political lynchings."[145]

Peroutka's encomium to 1946 points to the paradox of the struggle over the Protectorate trial verdict. The retribution courts, revolutionary organs that violated some of the most fundamental principles of Western jurisprudence, became the issue upon which believers in the rule of law successfully made their stand. In government meetings Drtina immediately cast the controversy in such terms: "It is a question of the existence of our legal order ... and its further development."[146] The other parties rejected the Communist opinion that "the National Court is dependent on the people – it is their spokesman."[147] Even the Social Democrats refused to accept such an elastic approach to justice. Echoing Peroutka, the party's official organ insisted, "we cannot very well step all over the revolutionary laws which we ourselves enacted."[148] During the controversy over the Protectorate government trial, the non-Communist parties rallied in defense of judicial independence and thereby strengthened the shaky foundations of Czechoslovak democracy.

The National Court's stubborn independence both surprised and unnerved Communist leaders. In 1946, after activist editor Rudolf Halík received a sentence of only eighteen months in prison, the Communist Party's Legal Council sent the Central Committee a report on the "Deficiencies of the National Court." The Halík trial, among others, the Council claimed, had clearly demonstrated that court officials favored defendants. Prosecutors who supported the establishment of a new "people's democratic" order were apparently few and far between. Compounding the problem, the Communists' own people's judges, hand picked by the Party, had allegedly failed to perform their duties. They were reluctant to contradict the professional jurist who chaired the court for fear of betraying their own ignorance of the retribution laws'

---

[145] Ferdinand Peroutka, "Chvála roku 1946," *Dnešek* I:41, 642.
[146] Government meeting transcript (2 August 1946), Kaplan, *Dva retribuční procesy*, doc. 7, 69.
[147] Government meeting transcript (2 August 1946), Kaplan, *Dva retribuční procesy*, doc. 7, 71.
[148] *Právo lidu* (23 August 1946), SÚA, f. MZV-VA II (j41), k. 212.

intricacies. Worst of all, the report continued, "As a rule they form the greatest part of their judgment *only during the trial itself.*" The Legal Council recommended "informative schooling" as a way to overcome this deficiency. The report despondently concluded, "The National Court has not fulfilled its mission."[149]

---

[149] Italics added. "Nedostatky Národního soudu," SÚA, f. 29 (Právní výbor), sign. 80.

8

THE ROAD TO FEBRUARY
AND BEYOND

On 3 May 1947, in a speech to the Union of Liberated Political Prisoners, President Beneš welcomed the end of the People's Courts: "I did not expect that the retribution law would be applied to such a degree and altogether relatively well, without greater political conflicts. I expected many more injustices and I expected many more mistakes."[1] In revealing his fears, the Czechoslovak President expressed a sentiment shared by many of his compatriots: relief. With the end of retribution, retroactive and summary justice was curtailed and Czechs took a significant step down the road back to legal certainty. In his speech Beneš also proposed that the time had come to correct the errors and compensate for the abuses of retribution. When the trials were revisited, however, it was not as he had foreseen. Retribution's end on 4 May 1947 proved to be only a pause. One month after the February 1948 coup, the parliament, purged of the Communists' political opponents, voted to reinstate the People's Courts and empowered them to retry cases already decided. After years of outspoken criticism the Communists finally achieved the opportunity to prosecute collaborators as they saw fit. Though the new regime purged the judiciary and wreaked vengeance upon individuals who had dared to stand in the way of the Interior Ministry and the police in preceding years, even in a one-party state retribution proved to be a cumbersome and unwelcome task.

[1] Speech to Prague SOPV, reported by ČTK (3 March 1947), Státní ústřední archiv (SÚA), Prague, f. MS, k. 2113; "President o ukončení retribučního řízení," *Lidová demokracie* (4 May 1947), 1.

JUDGING RETRIBUTION

Two weeks before the People's Courts tried their last cases, the Communist Party had already articulated its final assessment of postwar Czech retribution. In *Rudé právo*'s featured editorial, Antonín Gregor categorically declared that the Košice Program's commitment to punish Czech collaborators had not been fulfilled. He warned that the public knew who had prevented the punishment of wealthy traitors. The "national cleansing," Gregor ominously concluded, was a "still unfinished chapter."[2] Although retribution had seen its fair share of critics, the official nature of this commentary, coming as it did from the chairman of the parliament's Legal Committee, spurred Drtina to demand that the Communists issue a statement of support for the Justice Ministry. Instead, the party's ministers openly accused Drtina of sheltering collaborators. Kopecký declared retribution to be "the most embarrassing chapter" of the country's postwar transformation; Gottwald called retribution a total disaster.[3] On 7 May 1947 *Rudé právo* seconded the prediction Gregor had made a fortnight earlier. In its lead editorial the Communist mouthpiece warned, "The cleansing is not over."[4]

In contrast to *Rudé právo*, most of the Czech press welcomed the end of retribution with qualified satisfaction and unmitigated relief. In *Lidová demokracie* one columnist noted the injustices perpetrated in the hunt for collaborators, but still praised the Czechs for having the courage and resolve to try themselves.[5] In its lead editorial *Mladá fronta* defended retribution against the charge that innocents had suffered injustices while criminals had escaped punishment. The daily argued that the severity of the courts at the beginning reflected the popular will, as did the leniency toward the end. Surprisingly, the editorial – featured in the newspaper that had printed some of the most vehement and tendentious attacks on indicted collaborators – noted that biased reporting often had the opposite effect of that intended. Ultimately, *Mladá fronta* concluded, "We must admit that the carrying out of retribution was

---

[2] Antonín Gregor, "Lidové soudy končí," *Rudé právo* (25 April 1947), 2.
[3] Third government, eighty-first meeting (25 April 1947), 48–55, SÚA, f. 100/24 (KG), aj. 1494, sv. 144.
[4] "Zásada očisty platí nadále," *Rudé právo* (7 May 1947), 2.
[5] "Národ byl osvobozen," *Lidová demokracie* (4 May 1947), SÚA, f. MZV-VA II (j81), k. 217.

a great and praiseworthy act for the cleansing of the nation."[6] Many articles expressed simple relief that the onerous task of retribution had been completed. In the Social Democratic weekly one editorial commented, "The majority of us will surely agree that it is already high time for the end [of the People's Courts]." In the weekly of the People's Party, Bedřich Bobek urged, "The nation now deserves to be granted a moment to catch its breath." The National Socialist weekly expressed the same sentiments in four simple words: "Finally it has come."[7]

From abroad *The New York Times* proclaimed, "Good News from Prague." Claiming that "democracy [had] won a round," the American newspaper noted that Czechoslovakia was the first East European country to end retribution trials and return to normal judicial procedures.[8] In fact, the Czechs had concluded retribution earlier than West European countries as well. The U.S. Ambassador to Czechoslovakia, Laurence Steinhardt, similarly observed,

The political effect of the termination of the National and People's Courts is the removal of one means of intimidation of the general public by revolutionary elements. While the sentences imposed by these courts were in general more just and reasonable than had been expected, nevertheless, there was a deep-seated fear on the part of the people of being brought to trial before these courts. It was also normal for persons imprisoned for political reasons to wait many months in jail before being arraigned and tried. The normal system of professional justice has now been restored, which requires all arrested persons to be arraigned and brought to trial promptly.... This is expected to reduce the general feeling of apprehension and timidity on the part of the general public, since all who were in Czechoslovakia during the war are vulnerable, to a greater or lesser degree, to charges of collaboration. The end of the "revolutionary" system of justice may well result in greater freedom of speech and press.[9]

[6] "'Omyly' lidového soudu," *Mladá fronta* (7 May 1947), SÚA, f. MZV-VA II (j81), k. 217.
[7] Jiří Veltruský, "Očista, která nebyla ještě provedena," *Cíl* III:19 (23 May 1947), 292; "Bedřich Bobek, "Konec retribuce," *Obzory* III:18 (3 May 1947), 233; "Konec," *Svobodný zítřek* III:19 (8 May, 1947), 1.
[8] "Good News from Prague," *The New York Times* (7 May 1947), 26.
[9] Steinhardt, U.S. Embassy in Prague, to the Secretary of State, Washington, D.C. (5 May 1947), Department of State, Deciminal file 860f, General Records, Record Group 59, National Archives, Washington, D.C., *Records of the U.S. Department of State Relating to the Internal Affairs of Czechoslovakia, 1945–1949* (Wilmington, DE: Scholarly Resources, 1986), film 860f.041/5-547.

The end of retribution meant an end to trials without appeals. It meant an end to the constant drum of death sentences, followed by summary executions. It meant that judges and prosecutors, who had devoted countless hours to a thankless task, could return to the regular responsibilities they had long neglected. Above all, it meant a return to legal certainty for Czechs who had finally rid themselves of a prime reason to fear arbitrary arrest and indefinite detention. After 4 May 1947 the 2,345 retribution cases that remained to be tried became the responsibility of regular criminal courts, where ordinary procedural rules prevailed. In the next eleven months the District Courts convicted another 270 indicted collaborators and sentenced only one defendant to death.[10]

The greater openness for which Steinhardt hoped was already palpable from the beginning of 1947. Perhaps not coincidentally, the end of the "period of heightened danger to the republic" (on 31 December 1946) had been followed not only by a vigorous Communist campaign against "profiteers," but also by a new willingness to confront the violent "excesses" of postwar Czechoslovakia. With retribution drawing to a close, focus increasingly shifted from the crimes of the wartime period to those committed after liberation. National and regional newspapers ran numerous exposés of brutality committed against alleged collaborators.[11] After the end of retribution, the Social Democratic weekly printed a call for a second cleansing, to purify the nation of those who had robbed, beaten, and killed innocents in the months after liberation. The article warned that a failure to prosecute would haunt the country:

For precisely all the bestialities that the Hitlerites committed are a cautionary illustration of the end towards which is headed a regime that loosens the bridle of uncontrolled revenge.... The twisted Gestapoism, which by chance broke

[10] Borák and Kaplan claim that the regular courts handed down 270 verdicts, but the Justice Ministry's count shows 270 convictions from an unmentioned number of total verdicts. "Výsledky retribuce," Vojenský historický archiv (VHA), f. Čepička, sv. 23, aj. 168; Karel Kaplan, *Dva retribuční procesy: Komentované dokumenty (1946–1947)* (Prague: Ústav pro soudobé dějiny, 1992), 34; Mečislav Borák, *Spravedlnost podle dekretu: Retribuční soudnictví v ČSR a Mimořádný lidový soud v Ostravě (1945–1948)* (Ostrava: Tilia, 1998), 75.

[11] For example, Michal Mareš, "Proč jsem nepsal?" *Dnešek* I:44 (23 January 1947), 698–99; "Demokracie nebo nacismus," *Kutnohorský kraj*: III:11–16 (14 March–18 April 1947), 1; "Ve jménu lidskosti," *Kutnohorský kraj*: III:24 (13 June 1947), 1–2; "A ještě Kolín," *Kutnohorský kraj*: III:26 (27 June 1947), 1–2; "Těm, kdož hrozí revolucí," *Kutnohorský kraj*: III:31/32 (15 August 1947), 1–2; "Čáslavští gestapáčci," *Kutnohorský kraj*: III:33–34 (22–29 August 1947), 1–2.

through to public view in the Čadek-Volf case, is proof that the impunity thus far for the bestialities committed in the first days [after liberation] is already bearing its fruit.

While not challenging the Transfer itself, the article even called for the investigation of crimes committed against Germans.[12] For that very purpose parliament established an investigative commission, which in September 1947 unearthed what remained of the 763 victims of a massacre committed two years earlier near the town of Postoloprty.[13] Parliamentary deputies, led by Ota Hora, submitted interpolations pressing the Interior Ministry to probe so-called "excesses," including those committed at the notorious Kolín camp.[14] The process of coming to terms with the "revolutionary justice" of 1945 had begun.

The new willingness to confront the country's shortcomings was strikingly evident when it came time for parliament to discuss the results of postwar retribution. Following Drtina's summary report about the Czech People's Courts and the Prague National Court, the Czechoslovak National Assembly held its longest debate since the war.[15] On 10 June 1947 speaker after speaker took the podium until finally, after two in the morning, the session was suspended for the night, only to recommence with full intensity the next day. Representing the People's Party, Alois Rozehnal set the tone for the debate when he pronounced retribution to be little more than "victor's justice." He declared,

The stance of the Czechoslovak People's Party on retribution is given by the worldwide Christian opinion that renounces the principle, an eye for eye, a tooth for a tooth. Just as it renounces the death penalty, for it stands on the position that man does not give man life and therefore has no right to take it from him.... Against retribution we put forward prevention.... Against revenge we put forward eternal justice.[16]

Of the more than two dozen speeches, one had greater gravity than the others. Seven hours into the first day's deliberations, Vojta Beneš, the Czechoslovak president's older brother, took the podium. On behalf of

---

[12] Jiří Veltruský, "Očista, která nebyla ještě provedena," *Cíl* III:19 (23 May 1947), 292–94.

[13] Tomáš Staněk, *Perzekuce 1945* (Prague: Institut pro středoevropskou kulturu a politiku, 1996), 109–13.

[14] Ota Hora, *Svědectví o puči* (Toronto: Sixty-Eight Publishers, 1978), 261–69.

[15] Prokop Drtina, *Československo můj osud* (Toronto: Sixty-Eight Publishers, 1982), II:311.

[16] Rozehnal, 56 *Těsnopisecké zprávy Ústavodárného národního shromáždění Republiky československé* (ÚNS) (10 June 1947), 15.

the Social Democratic Party – or at least one wing of it – Vojta Beneš defended individuals convicted by the National Court and declared that "not even collaborators were all from the same wood." In the end, he left no doubt that he believed retribution had gone too far: "We have excessively propagated the guilt of collaboration." He called for a review of questionable cases and for the use of presidential clemency, if not an amnesty, to make amends for the "wrongs" of retribution.[17]

In addition to criticizing retribution, Rozehnal also accused the Communists of sheltering collaborators. He provocatively explained, "It was not an expression of heroism and courage in the May days of 1945 to pin on the lapel of one's coat a star, which served many not just as a party symbol, but mainly as a protective shield against pursuant justice." Outraged Communist deputies responded that Rozehnal's speech was "the sharpest and most clearly formulated of all attacks on our retribution thus far" and "the greatest insult to members of the Communist Party that has been delivered in this assembly." Gregor accused Rozehnal of attempting to defend treachery and traitors. Another Communist deputy warned that the parliamentary debate had revealed who favored just retribution and who protected collaborators. Speaking on behalf of his party, Gregor ended his speech by repeating his ominous prediction: "We know that the cleansing is not over."[18] Although such threats may have appeared empty at the time, in private Interior Minister Václav Nosek assured the Communist Party Central Committee that the opportunity to finish retribution properly would some day arrive:

We know that retribution did not fulfill everything that our people expected in their just anger against traitors and collaborators; we know, however, that even the proletarian revolution in Russia did not immediately reckon with all its overt and hidden enemies . . . , but that even after twenty years . . . it had to punish a traitorous field marshal and some generals. Though I don't want only to make a mechanical comparison, I want to express the conviction that our traitors, those freed today, will in the end one day get their deserved retribution.[19]

[17] V. Beneš, 56 ÚNS (10 June 1947), 61–70.
[18] Rozehnal, 56 ÚNS (10 June 1947), 13; Kokeš, 56 ÚNS (10 June 1947), 56; Šling, 57 ÚNS (11 June 1947) 36; Gregor, 56 ÚNS (10 June 1947), 20, 22, 28.
[19] ÚV-KSČ meeting (5 June 1947), SÚA, f. 1 (ZÚV-KSČ), sv. 3, aj. 15, str. 127–28.

That day would have to await the coup. In the meantime the Communist Party's parliamentary faction joined retribution's other critics and unanimously voted to approve Drtina's report.[20] Czech retribution had officially come to an end.

FROM BRATISLAVA TO PRAGUE

In an addendum to his report, Ambassador Steinhardt informed the State Department that, in fact, the "normal system of professional justice" had not yet been restored throughout the entire country: The Slovak People's Courts planned to continue prosecuting alleged collaborators until 31 December 1947.[21] From the beginning, Slovak retribution was administered separately under different legal statutes. Drtina did not disguise his relief that he bore no responsibility for the thorny problem of punishing collaborators who had lived in a state formally allied with Nazi Germany.[22] Reflecting this ambiguous wartime experience, Slovak retribution proved more lenient than its Czech counterpart. Slovak People's Courts – which included not only the Bratislava National Court and Regional People's Courts, but also Local People's Courts, the equivalent of the Czech national honor tribunals – tried 20,561 defendants prior to 31 December 1947 and convicted only 8,059 of them.[23] If we add together the results of the Czech National Court, People's Courts, and national honor tribunals, we arrive at a total of more than 168,000 persons tried and approximately 69,000 convicted. While the prewar population of the Czech provinces exceeded that of Slovakia by a factor of three, the number of collaborators punished by Czech retribution was more than eight times greater. The total of executed defendants in the Czech provinces (686) exceeded that in Slovakia (twenty-seven) by a factor of twenty-five.

Although Slovak People's Courts convicted fewer defendants, both absolutely and proportionally, than their Czech counterparts, the Communist Party leadership nonetheless had reason to be satisfied with

---

[20] Drtina, *Československo*, II:316–17.
[21] Steinhardt, U.S. Embassy in Prague, to the Secretary of State, Washington, D.C. (15 May 1947), *Records of the U.S. Department of State*, film 860f.041/5-1547.
[22] Drtina, *Československo*, II:272.
[23] "22.278 súdených, 8.962 odsúdených," *L'ud* (6 February 1949), SÚA, f. MZV-VA II, k. 218.

the political consequences of Slovak retribution. From the beginning, charges of collaboration divided Czech and Slovak non-Communists. At the first meeting of the Provisional National Assembly on 28 October 1945, Drtina and the National Socialists led Czech representatives in refusing admission to Petr Zat'ko, a deputy appointed by the Slovak Democratic Party.[24] They objected to Zat'ko because, as a member of the Slovak parliament, he had voted for Slovak independence in March 1939. From 1940 onward, however, he had also been an active and important member of the resistance against the Tiso regime. In the end, a People's Court acquitted Zat'ko, but his thwarted attempt to join the postwar parliament confirmed, on the one hand, the Czech opinion that Slovaks refused to confront their wartime past, and, on the other, the Slovak suspicion that Czechs employed the charge of collaboration as a tool of national oppression. The Democratic Party's stunning victory in the 1946 elections – when it won sixty-two percent of the vote in Slovakia – represented perhaps the greatest setback to the Communist Party during the brief postwar republic. Rather than exploit the Democrats' victory, the National Socialists – blinded by their advocacy of centralism and their belief that fascism still posed a danger to Slovakia – joined the Communists and acceded to an evisceration of Slovak autonomy. Meanwhile, the Communists intensified their attacks on the Democratic Party, repeatedly accusing it of being a haven for collaborators and traitors.[25]

The trial of Jozef Tiso, the priest who had ruled wartime Slovakia, played a critical role in the exacerbation of tensions. Slovak historian Michal Barnovský wrote, "It was not a matter just of reckoning with the past – the condemnation of Jozef Tiso, his policies, and [his] state – but also about discrediting and weakening the Democratic Party."[26] After a ten-week trial, on 15 April 1947 the National Court in Bratislava sentenced the former Slovak president to death. When the Slovak National Council's Board of Commissioners deadlocked over whether

---

[24] Drtina, *Československo*, II:104–105.
[25] Vlastislav Chalupa, Ivan Gad'ourek, and Mojmír Povolný, eds., *Tři roky: Přehledy a dokumenty k Československé politice v letech 1945–1948*, 3 vols (Brno: Právnická fakulta Masarykovy univerzity, 1991), II:22–23.
[26] Michal Barnovský, *Na ceste k monopolu moci: Mocenskopolitické zápasy na Slovensku v rokoch 1945–1948* (Bratislava: Archa, 1993), 123.

to recommend the commutation of Tiso's sentence to life imprisonment, the Czechoslovak government cabinet voted to have him executed, over the objections of the Slovak Democrats. Communist General Secretary Rudolf Slánský declared the hanging a "victory" for the Party.[27] The political significance of the Tiso trial lay not so much in the damage it caused to the Democrats – despite Communist hopes, the party remained intact and continued to claim the support of most Slovaks. Nonetheless, the controversy over Tiso's execution isolated the Democratic Party from its Czech allies and furthered the mutual mistrust that crippled the anti-Communist forces.[28]

The Communist attack on the Democratic Party entered a new phase on 16 September 1947, when the Interior Ministry announced the discovery of an "anti-state conspiracy" in Slovakia. The evidence supposedly pointed to the existence of a network of fascist traitors within the Democratic Party, including two of its parliamentary deputies. When the two men were placed under arrest, they immediately called on parliament to strip them of their immunity so that they could be placed in court custody. As with similar plots in the Czech provinces, Kaplan explained, "As soon as the whole matter was transferred into the hands of the judicial organs, the fabrication began to collapse." The accused disavowed their testimony and claimed that it had been originally extracted through police brutality.[29] Another conspiracy was traced to the personal secretary of Jan Ursíny, a Deputy Chairman of the Czechoslovak government and a former leader of the Slovak non-Communist resistance. When his secretary was arrested, Ursíny was forced to resign. After a mass demonstration by the Slovak trade union called for a purge of collaborators, Gustáv Husák, the Communist chairman of the Slovak Board of Commissioners, illegally dismissed the Board without the approval of a majority of its members, who were from the Democratic Party. The subsequent crisis, punctuated by a mass strike, was only resolved when representatives from two small Slovak parties were

[27] Slánský exulted, "We pushed through the government the refusal of Tiso's request for clemency and Tiso was hanged." Zasedání ÚV KSČ (4–5.6.47), SÚA, f. 1, sv. 3, aj. 15, 34.

[28] For more on the Tiso trial and its political context (and subtext), see Brad Abrams, "The Politics of Retribution: The Trial of Josef Tiso," *East European Politics and Societies* 10:2 (spring 1996), 255–92.

[29] Karel Kaplan, *Nekrvavá revoluce* (Prague: Mladá fronta Archiv, 1993), 94–95.

added to the Board. The Democratic Party had lost its majority – the Bratislava putsch, a "dress rehearsal" for events in Prague three months later, had succeeded.[30]

Six days before the unveiling of the Slovak "conspiracy," a mysterious package marked "perfume" arrived at the Justice Ministry addressed to Drtina. Similar boxes had been sent to the Foreign Minister, Jan Masaryk, and the Deputy Premier from the National Socialist Party, Petr Zenkl. All three packages contained explosives. Thanks to the amateurish manner in which the bombs had been prepared, they were detected and disarmed.[31] The Communist leadership immediately declared the entire affair to be a "provocation" manufactured by the National Socialists themselves. The Interior Ministry carried out a half-hearted investigation that produced a suspect of dubious authenticity. The matter might have ended there if Vladimír Krajina, General Secretary of the National Socialist Party, had not followed a confidential tip to the carpentry of a Communist Party member in the village of Krčman near Olomouc. When court officials took up the case, "The Security [corps] not only lost the monopoly over the investigation, the case started to turn back against it."[32] Under interrogation the carpenter and his wife confessed to their role in the assassination attempt and implicated other members of their party. As during the Holubová–Velíšková trial, the security police unsuccessfully attempted to thwart the investigation's new direction. Under the supervision of Zdeněk Marjanko, the Justice Ministry official formerly in charge of retribution, district attorney František Doležal charged the carpenter, his wife, and their Communist coconspirators for preparing the assassination attempt

---

[30] Radomír Luža, "Czechoslovakia between Democracy and Communism," in Victor S. Mamatey and Radomír Luža, eds., *A History of the Czechoslovak Republic, 1918–1948* (Princeton, NJ: Princeton University Press, 1973), 411.

[31] Karel Kaplan noted that the circumstances surrounding the bombing plot had yet to be clearly elucidated. The appearance of the packages (the tripwire for the explosives was apparently visible from the outside) makes it doubtful that the actual intent was to kill the ministers, especially since they did not usually handle their own mail. Kaplan also noted that it is unlikely that the small cell of Communists from Krčman were acting on their own initiative. He suspected that Olomouc party functionaries and former partisans, possibly spurred by Soviet agents, aimed to heightened tensions and thereby precipitate a crisis. Another motive may have been to justify putting the non-Communist ministers under police guard for their own "protection." Karel Kaplan, *Pět kapitol o Únoru* (Brno: Doplněk, 1997), 120 n. 83, 124.

[32] Kaplan, *Pět kapitol*, 120.

and for storing a considerable cache of arms.[33] The trail soon led to a Communist parliamentary deputy, Jaroslav-Jura Sosnar, and from him it pointed toward Alexej Čepička, Chairman of the Communist Regional Committee in Olomouc and the newly appointed Minister of Domestic Trade. Before parliament, on 21 January 1948 Drtina accused the Interior Ministry of obstructing the investigation of the bombing attempt. The Justice Minister further announced the Olomouc court's request for parliament to strip Sosnar of his immunity so that he could be prosecuted for the illegal possession of weapons and for armed conspiracy.[34]

By themselves the courts could only embarrass the Communist Party, but this threat loomed larger as the country approached elections scheduled for May 1948. National Socialist Hubert Ripka later claimed that the investigation of the bombing attempts "precipitated the coup d'état: the Communists had no better way of freeing themselves from all checks than by putting an end to the independence of the courts."[35] But it was the National Socialists and their allies in the People's and Democratic Parties, not the Communists, who initiated the governmental crisis of February 1948. On 13 February Drtina delivered an update on the investigation of another conspiracy apparently manufactured by the security police. Like earlier plots, this one – which claimed to have uncovered a National Socialist espionage ring in the service of Western powers – foundered when suspects fell into the hands of investigative judges.[36] The security forces, Drtina told the government, refused to hand over their operatives to court custody. Amid a heated debate, a Social Democratic minister announced that a half-dozen police chiefs

---

[33] In another indication of how the tail often wagged the Communist dog, the party leadership was apparently unaware of the stored arms. In a letter written in 1957, Sosnar, the local party chief, claimed that he had received the weapons from the Red Army. Although he was supposed to turn the arms over to the police (which were under Communist control), Sosnar and his fellow comrades chose to keep some of the weapons for the imminent "class struggle." Kaplan, *Pět kapitol*, 122.

[34] Hubert Ripka, *Czechoslovakia Enslaved: The Story of the Communist Coup d'Etat* (London: Victor Gollancz, 1950), 162–69; Josef Korbel, *The Communist Subversion of Czechoslovakia, 1938–1948: The Failure of Coexistence* (Princeton, NJ: Princeton University Press, 1959), 191–94.

[35] Ripka, *Czechoslovakia Enslaved*, 169. See also Vladimír Krajina, *Vysoká hra: Vzpomínky* (Prague: Eva, 1994), 190.

[36] Kaplan, *Nekrvavá revoluce*, 132.

in Prague had been dismissed.[37] Aware that a purge of the few remaining independent officers was underway, ministers from all of the non-Communist parties banded together to demand the establishment of a commission to examine the police. Over the Communists' vehement opposition, the government cabinet, including the Social Democrats, then voted to order Nosek – who was absent due to "illness" – to reinstate the police chiefs. When the government reconvened four days later, however, Nosek was still absent and Gottwald refused to comment on the status of the earlier resolutions.[38]

Confronted with outright disobedience of a government resolution and a general sense that matters were reaching the boiling point, on 20 February 1948 twelve ministers from the National Socialist, People's, and Slovak Democratic Parties tendered their resignations. They expected President Beneš either to name a new government or to refuse their resignations. They had failed, however, to assure the support of the President or even a majority of the twenty-six ministers, including Foreign Minister Jan Masaryk and the Social Democrats, who stayed in their posts. The Communist Party did not await Beneš's decision. A mass demonstration on Old Town Square, presided over by Klement Gottwald, was merely the most visible manifestation of various measures intended to immobilize the non-Communist parties and pressure the President to accept their resignations. Around the capital city and the country, special police units seized control of radio, telegraph, and the railroads. Armed "factory militia" appeared, ostensibly to ensure order. Paper manufacturers refused to deliver newsprint to non-Communist presses. "Action committees" of trusted Communists and fellow-travelers organized themselves within ministries, state offices, factories, and even national committees. In the midst of all this, Drtina telephoned an urgent message to the Castle:

Mr. President, what has been happening in the city since this morning is no longer a political crisis, it is a revolution, a putsch. The Ministry of Justice is occupied by the political police.... [Department Chief] Dr. Marianko [sic] has been arrested and so have the commander, the chief physician, and other high

[37] Various sources claim that from eight to thirteen police officers were dismissed. Barnovský, *Na ceste*, 235.
[38] Kaplan, *Nekrvavá revoluce*, 149–52.

officers from the Pankrác Penitentiary. The main post office [has been] seized, and I was refused entrance into the building of the Ministry of Justice.[39]

Drtina called on Beneš to intercede, but the President did not heed the Justice Minister's plea; in fact, he did not even grant Drtina an audience. After a general strike of 2.5 million workers, on 25 February 1948 Beneš accepted the resignations of the non-Communist ministers and permitted Gottwald to replace them.[40] The "February Coup" was over; the Communists had won.

RETRIBUTION RETURNS

On 20 February 1948, the first day of the government crisis, *Rudé právo* explained the ministers' resignations as an attempt to infect the security police with the "spirit of Drtina's justice." The newspaper also used the occasion to accuse the Justice Minister and his fellow National Socialists again of intervening on behalf of collaborators and so-called profiteers.[41] Since at least the previous fall, attacks on the Justice Ministry had been a formal component of the Communists' plans to seize power. At a 17 October 1947 meeting a dozen senior Party officials had resolved to "expose Drtina as the enemy of people's democracy, the violator of the legal code, and the protector of collaborators and traitors."[42] After months of attacks on his character Drtina could not have doubted what awaited him if the Communists achieved victory. In January Gottwald had even warned him, "Drtina, you will meet with a bad end."[43] After Beneš accepted the ministers' resignations, Drtina attempted to commit suicide, but failed, first when his revolver jammed,

---

[39] Edward Taborsky, *President Edvard Benes: Between East and West, 1938–1948* (Stanford, CA.: Hoover Institute Press, 1981), 283–84, n. 22.

[40] The Communist Party leaders threatened to call rallies to demand Beneš's resignation as well. Soviet Foreign Minister Vladimir Zorin suggested that Gottwald make use of Red Army troops, but the Czechoslovak Communist leader uncharacteristically declined Moscow's advice. Kaplan, *Nekrvavá revoluce*, 157–68.

[41] "Štvou proti SNB, protože stíhá," *Rudé právo* (20 February 1948), 1.

[42] Gregor, the author of the blistering critique of retribution the previous spring, assumed the task of assembling materials that could be used against the Justice Ministry in the upcoming parliamentary debate about the budget and in the daily press. "Zápis č. 28 ze schůze org. sekretariátu ÚV KSČ" (17 Oct. 1947), SÚA, f. 02/3, sv. 1, ar.j. 28.

[43] Korbel, *Communist Subversion*, 193. See similar comments in Jaroslav Drábek, *Z časů dobrých a zlých* (Prague: Naše vojsko, 1992), 135; Ripka, *Czechoslovakia Enslaved*, 169.

and then when he survived a jump from a third-floor window. The former Justice Minister was rushed to a city hospital and put under police guard.[44]

While Drtina lay physically broken in a hospital bed, the new regime carried out a purge that transformed the country's political, administrative, and judicial systems. In all, more than 28,000 persons, including 145 judges, were dismissed from their posts.[45] In the Kutná Hora district, for example, the victims included five judges, a prison chief, the former Security Officer for the Local National Committee, and a court stenographer. The former chief justice of the Kutná Hora People's Court was also pensioned off.[46] The new regime immediately returned to the September 1947 bombing attempt on the three ministers. Sosnar was freed and all charges against him were dropped. Instead, the men who had conducted the investigations of the Communist deputy and his coconspirators were arrested. After months of interrogation Marjanko perished in police custody.[47] Former district attorney Doležal languished in prison for five years before he was even tried. In what a Czech encyclopedia termed his "last manly act," President Beneš intervened to save Krajina, who was released from detention and soon fled the country. In May 1948 the Justice Ministry announced that the bombing had been a National Socialist conspiracy, led by Krajina, intent on defaming the Communist Party. In August Krajina was sentenced *in absentia* to twenty-five years' imprisonment.[48] Despite a vociferous *ad hominem* campaign against Drtina, which made him out to be the greatest

---

[44] Drtina, *Československo*, II:641–45.

[45] Two-thirds of the victims of the purges were socially demoted to menial labor. On national committees, the membership of the Social Democratic, National Socialist, and Populist Parties dropped from forty-nine percent to a mere five percent. In June the Social Democratic Party was eliminated by absorption into the Communist Party. Karel Kaplan, *Political Persecution in Czechoslovakia, 1948–1972* (Munich: Projekt, 1983), 8.

[46] "Seznamy postižených únorovou očistou," (14 January 1949), Státní okresní archiv Kutná Hora (SOkA-KH), f. ONV-KH, k. 79, sign. III/21a (1948).

[47] Secret police interrogation records reveal that the former Justice Ministry official survived at least until October 1948. Vilém Hejl, *Zpráva o organizovaném násilí* (Prague: Univerzum, 1990), 55–56; Marjanko protocol (12 October 1948), Archiv Ministerstva vnitra (AMV) Prague, ZV-26MV, Prokop Drtina Podsvazek č. 1, list 7.

[48] Fourth government, meeting three (12 March 1948), SÚA, f. 100/24 (KG), aj. 1494, sv. 147; Ripka, *Czechoslovakia Enslaved*, 170–71; Kaplan, *Nekrvavá revoluce*, 247; Kaplan, *Pět kapitol*, 124 n. 91; Milan Churáň et al., *Kdo byl kdo v našich dějinách ve 20. století* (Prague: Libri, 1994), 283; Josef Tomeš and Alena Léblová, eds., *Československý biografický slovník* (Prague: Academia, 1992), 355–56.

villain of the pre-February period, the former Justice Minister was not publicly humiliated in a show trial like several of his former comrades in the National Socialist Party. For some reason the new regime did not believe he would make a good defendant. Perhaps it was his injured legs, which could only arouse sympathy, or perhaps the regime did not believe its propaganda had sufficiently sullied Drtina's reputation. Instead, after five years of interrogation, in December 1953 a secret court finally sentenced the former Justice Minister to fifteen years in prison.[49]

At the beginning of March 1948 the new masters of the Justice Ministry announced that they had found proof that Drtina had protected traitors from just retribution. In the Ministry there was allegedly an extensive catalogue detailing thousands of cases where National Socialist leaders had intervened on behalf of collaborators.[50] On its front page *Rudé právo* offered its readers two images: one of the suddenly infamous catalogue and another of protest letters from workers that the former Justice Minister had allegedly discarded. A "new spirit," the article promised, had entered the Justice Ministry now that Drtina, "who persecuted resistance workers," had been replaced by Alexej Čepička. For non-Communists Čepička's possible involvement in September's bombing attack on Drtina, Masaryk, and Zenkl hardly qualified him for the job of Justice Minister. *Rudé právo*, in contrast, expected great things from the new minister. The newspaper described Čepička's arrival, his immediate "airing out of every corner" in the Justice Ministry, and his new clock, which showed the correct time – "the time of people's democracy." There was another item of note in the minister's office: On his desk lay a draft of a new retribution law.[51]

---

[49] A presidential amnesty released the former Justice Minister in May 1960. In September 1969 the Czechoslovak Supreme Court annulled the secret conviction, but a prosecutorial appeal soon led to that decision being overturned. Drtina was reconvicted for having prepared "the counterrevolutionary putsch" of February 1948 and sentenced to six years (which he had already served). Prokop Drtina passed away in 1980. Drtina, *Československo*, II:641–66.

[50] In a government meeting Čepička claimed that there were actually two catalogues: a regular one and an "express" one containing letters from National Socialist and Populist officials. Only the latter were positively resolved. Fourth government, meeting three (12 March 1948), SÚA, f. 100/24 (KG), aj. 1494, sv. 147.

[51] "Několikatisícová kartotéka," *Rudé právo* (4 March 1948), 1; "Nový duch v bývalém Drtinově království," *Rudé právo* (5 March 1948), 1.

Little more than a week after the coup, an interministerial meeting was held to discuss a revision of the Great Decree. The next day the government took up the matter, and by the end of March both the purged parliament and a cowed President Beneš had approved the reestablishment of the People's Courts. The law authorized judges to retry cases that had already been decided in the period before February 1948. Defendants who had been acquitted or had received "lenient" sentences were liable once again to be prosecuted for wartime collaboration. The revised law also permitted retrials in cases where the defendant had received an excessive sentence.[52] Otherwise, the most substantive change made to the Great Decree was to reduce the number of people's judges to two per court panel for new cases. With political pluralism at an end, there was no longer a need for a representative of each of the four political parties. Now people's judges were to be drawn equally from among former partisans and political prisoners.[53] The government officially promulgated the new retribution law (no. 33/1948) on 2 April 1948 together with a revision of the Small Decree (Law no. 34/1948), reestablishing the national honor commissions. Unlike the pre-February decrees, the revised retribution laws applied to the entire state of Czechoslovakia.[54] Dualistic retribution had come to an end.

Not all Communists leaders welcomed the renewal of retribution uncritically. Deputy Premier Antonín Zápotocký warned his comrades, "We shouldn't forget that three years have already elapsed since the end of the war, that today people look at war criminals differently from back then, leaving aside the fact that today it would be a question of Czech defendants and not Germans."[55] In response to such concerns, Čepička justified the new law to his government colleagues on several grounds. With an eye to the past, he stated that pre-February retribution

[52] "Záznam ze schůze práv. výboru ÚNS" (23 March 1948), MV no. B2220–24/3–1948-I/2 ú.p., SÚA, f. MV-NR (B2220), k. 2018; "Zápis o pracovní poradě" (15 March 1948), VHA, f. Čepička, sv. 20, aj. 137, 10.

[53] Retrials were required to take place before four people's judges. "Revize retribuce i podle malého dekretu?" *Rudé právo* (4 March 1948), 1.

[54] Čepička prepared two draft laws, one for the whole state and one just for the Czech provinces. The government voted for the unitary version. Fourth government, meeting three (12 March 1948), SÚA, f. 100/24, aj. 1494, sv. 147, str. 100–105.

[55] Fourth government, meeting three (12 March 1948), SÚA, f. 100/24, aj. 1494, sv. 147, str. 102–103.

had failed to fulfill the Košice Program and that justice demanded re-trials. With an eye to the future, the new Justice Minister argued that retrials were necessary to disarm reactionaries who remained free. As a clinching argument, Čepička alleged that the people demanded retribution.[56] Although this claim is dubious, communist leaders may well have responded to pressure from below. Back in 1946, amid the Protectorate trial fiasco, one Party secretariat warned the Central Committee, "Before the [May] elections we told the people at campaign meetings . . . that after the elections – after our victory – everything would change and all would be deservedly punished. That's why we can't disappoint the people in this respect."[57] That was after the Party had only won a plurality in elections; now it had gained unchallenged control of the state. Although we may be tempted to view the renewal of retribution as a devious plan, it is entirely possible that the Communist leaders may have felt boxed in by their own pre-February rhetoric. After three years of vocal complaints and empty promises, facing pressure from radical party members and organizations like the Union of Liberated Political Prisoners, the government may have seen little alternative but to restart trials. The state's half-hearted approach to retribution in 1948 seems to support this interpretation.

In an attempt to balance potential public unease with actual partisan demands, a high-ranking Justice Ministry official instructed prosecutors that the revision of retribution cases aimed to be "selective," not "universal."[58] A Ministry directive instructed "action committees" to suggest cases that had "upset" the local populace. Communist Party secretariats could then veto the prosecution of certain defendants if a trial was not deemed "politically appropriate." The selection process was to be guided by the principle that "in all cases the social standing of the perpetrator will be taken into account."[59] People's Courts did revisit select controversial cases from the pre-February period. Leopold Pospíšil, the non-Communist resistance leader who had been acquitted in 1946, was now convicted *in absentia* and sentenced to twenty-five years in

---

[56] Fourth government, meeting three (12 March 1948), SÚA, f. 100/24, aj. 1494, sv. 147, str. 99–100.

[57] OS Turnov, SÚA, f. 01 (ÚV KSČ), sv. 2, a.j. 13, l. 458.

[58] "Zápis o pracovní poradě" (15 March 1948), VHA, f. Čepička, sv. 20, aj. 137, 38.

[59] "Zásady o dalším postupu v retribučním řízení," VHA, f. Čepička, sv. 23, aj. 168, 19–22; SÚA, f. 29, aj. 96, 10–13.

prison.[60] In a case of local note, the Kutná Hora People's Court retried a former judge, Ludvík Urban, who had originally been sentenced to two years in a labor battalion. The 1948 verdict added another four years to his penalty, but by then, Urban, like Pospíšil, had wisely made himself scarce.[61]

Individuals who had stood up the police before February 1948 found themselves the targets of retribution courts. The new regime used a trumped-up charge of Paragraph Twenty (aiding and abetting a collaborator) to convict Michal Mareš, one of the greatest critics of postwar "excesses." In November 1948 a People's Court ignored the testimony of witnesses in favor of the irrepressible journalist and sentenced him to seven years in prison.[62] The renewal of retribution also served to punish the fortune-teller Marie Kaňková for her courageous exposure of police brutality in the February 1947 trial of Anna Velíšková and Zdenka Holubová.[63] On 17 December 1948 a reconstituted People's Court overturned the original verdict and acquitted Holubová because, according to *Rudé právo*, "It was shown that all the previous testimony of the witnesses was not based on the truth."[64] The primary focus of the retrial was not Holubová, however, nor even the original charge that she had denounced her husband to the Gestapo. Instead, the judges concentrated on exonerating the police of any wrongdoing in their pursuit of the case. Fourteen men testified that officers had not brutally beaten Kaňková or Velíšková in October 1945 and that the women's confessions had been "spontaneous." As for Kaňková's horrendous wounds, the verdict perversely alleged that she had suffered from nothing more than a "female malady" which had resulted in "uterine bleeding."[65] On

---

[60] "Olomoucký advokát Pospíšil odsouzen," *Národní osvobození* (26 October 1948), SÚA, f. MZV-VA II (j81), k. 218.

[61] As of April 1952 the former judge remained at large; in all likelihood he was no longer in the country. L. Urban, Státní oblastní archiv (SOA) Praha, f. MLS Kutná Hora, Ls 337/46, Ls 289/48.

[62] Mareš served the entire sentence in some of the country's worst prisons. In 1991, twenty years after the journalist's death, the Czechoslovak Supreme Court voided the 1948 verdict. Michal Mareš, *Ze vzpomínek anarchisty, reportéra a válečného zločince* (Prague: Prostor, 1999), 21–23.

[63] See Chapter 3 for more on the Holubová–Velíšková case.

[64] "Náprava zločinu Drtinovy justice," *Rudé právo* (21 December 1948), 2.

[65] Verdict (20 December 1948) against Zd. Holubová, SOA-Praha, MLS-PR, Ls 1033/48, 43–44.

the very last day of the year, the Prague People's Court wrapped up the case by convicting the fortune-teller for allegedly having induced the concierge Velíšková to denounce Holubová's husband. In the judges' new opinion, Kaňková was the instigator and therefore deserved the harsher penalty: ten years spent in a prison labor battalion. Velíšková, by contrast, received a sentence of five years.[66]

Perhaps no case so well demonstrates the new spirit of Čepička's justice than the prosecution of two judges from the Kutná Hora region. In December 1946 Jan Schödlbauer had earned the enmity of local radicals by acquitting František Čapek, the technical director of a chocolate factory, on charges of collaboration with the Germans. In April 1948 a local branch of the Union of Liberated Political Prisoners greeted the renewal of retribution by proposing Schödlbauer as a candidate for prosecution.[67] Nine days later the authorities charged Schödlbauer and another judge, Jiří Komers, with aiding and abetting a collaborator in violation of Paragraph Twenty of the retribution decree.[68] According to the prosecution, Komers had improperly intervened with Schödlbauer on behalf of his acquaintance, Čapek. The brief, error-filled indictment incorrectly described Schödlbauer as the chairman of the Czechoslovak National People's Court in Kolín and the People's Court in Kutná Hora. In fact, the so-called National People's Court never existed and Čapek had been actually tried by the regular Regional Court.[69] In the twisted logic of Stalinist justice, the prosecution argued that Čapek's 1948 emigration retrospectively incriminated the two judges: "Through his flight František Čapek proved his guilt from the occupation period and thus also proved that Dr. Komers aided him to get his acquittal."[70] The Prague People's Court even accepted the 1948 rigged retrial and conviction of Čapek *in absentia* as proof that the two judges must have ignored facts in 1946. In the face of such "evidence," the court convicted

[66] Verdict (20 December 1948) against Velíšková and Kaňková, SOA-Praha, MLS-PR, Ls 1089/48, 13–14.
[67] "Návrh na zahajení trestního řízení," SOPVP Kutná Hora (15 April 1948) to OAV-KH, SOkA-KH, ONV-KH, k. 79, sign. III/21b.
[68] Trestní oznámení Tk XXIX 3027/48 (11 September 1948), SOA-Praha, MLS-PR, Ls 941/48, 1.
[69] Indictment MLS-PR no. Lst 26.421/48 (20 October 1948), SOA-Praha, MLS-PR, Ls 941/48, 112–113.
[70] Trestní oznámení Tk XXIX 3027/48 (11 September 1948), SOA-Praha, MLS-PR, Ls 941/48, 7.

Schödlbauer and Komers and sentenced them to prison terms of two and a half and three years, respectively.[71]

Despite this obvious injustice, the trial also demonstrated that the country's legal culture had not yet been fully debased. Witnesses still spoke courageously in defense of Schödelbauer and Komers. Balancing out one disgruntled former employee, other court officials insisted that both men were exemplary, conscientious, and fair, and that their conduct in the Čapek case had been by the book. Two active judges who had participated in the original Čapek case openly defended their former colleagues even though such testimony clearly put their livelihoods at risk. Most impressive was the Jewish witness Mahler, who praised Komers for saving his life. During the occupation the judge had intentionally stalled Mahler's divorce from a Gentile woman (who had left him) and thereby delayed his deportation to Theresienstadt. As a result, Mahler had been sent to the ghetto late enough in the war to avoid transfer to, and certain death in Auschwitz. Another witness, the Gentile widow of a Jewish man, testified that Komers had faithfully hidden their family's valuables and had contributed to parcels sent to her husband in a concentration camp.[72] Although the prosecutor surely tried to find some blameful wartime conduct, the 1948 indictment did not even attempt to tie the two judges to the Nazis. In fact, the verdict invoked Paragraph Sixteen to give Komers less than the mandatory sentence because, as chairman of the Kolín revolutionary national committee in spring 1945, he had "saved... many Czech lives" and had even been arrested by the Gestapo.[73] That a man like Komers should have been convicted for collaboration painfully illustrates the abyss into which Czech justice had fallen by October 1948.[74]

---

[71] Verdict Ls 941/48 (27 October 1948), SOA-Praha, MLS-PR, Ls 941/48, 141–43.

[72] Transcript of "Hlavní přelíčení" Ls XIII 941/48 (27 October 1948), SOA-Praha, MLS-PR, Ls 941/48, 124–126, 129–130.

[73] Verdict Ls 941/48 (27 October 1948), SOA-Praha, MLS-PR, Ls 941/48, 143.

[74] After serving his entire term, Komers was forced to work as a manual laborer on the railroads. Komers apparently died in 1963, but Schödlbauer lived long enough to gain rehabilitation. In January 1969 the Kolín District Court finally heard his appeal and acquitted Schödlbauer on all charges. Jiří Komers (14 March 1956) to the President, KPR no. 105359/56, SOA-Praha, MLS-PR, Ls 941/48, 165–67; "Protokol sepsaný u okresní prokuratory v Kutné Hoře dne 4.3.1965," SOA-Praha, MLS-PR, Ls 941/48; Rozsudek 2T 195/68 Kolín Okresní soud (24 January 1969), SOA-Praha, MLS-PR, Ls 941/48.

Nonetheless, not all of the 1948 trials were political. The restored People's Courts also punished war criminals who had managed to evade justice in the preceding years. In May 1948 the Bratislava People's Court executed Dieter Wisliceny, Adolf Eichmann's deputy, who had played a central role in the Holocaust of Slovak and Hungarian Jewry.[75] Four months later the Litoměřice People's Court sentenced to death and executed three former guards from the Theresienstadt prison and ghetto.[76] The courts also made amends for unduly severe verdicts, for example, in the case of František Prokop. In 1945 the Kutná Hora People's Court harshly punished Prokop for his unsuccessful attempt to join the German army. In 1948 the judges reduced his sentence from twenty years' imprisonment to three and one-half years, all of which he had already served.[77] Other retrials merely confirmed the original verdict. Bohumila Lerchová, for example, had been acquitted in February 1947 of denouncing a man during the occupation for illegally riding a motorcycle. In August 1948, a People's Court acquitted Lerchová again when the victim could not identify her handwriting on the denunciation note.[78] Not every new case, moreover, led to a conviction. On 17 June 1948 the Kutná Hora People's Court acquitted Anna Czeřowská of denouncing her neighbors because it determined that the case, like so many others tried before the February coup, was based on nothing more than personal animosity between landlord and tenant.[79]

Although parliament also passed a new version of the Small Decree, the regime soon ensured that few Czechs would be punished by the restored national honor commissions. On the occasion of his ascension to the Czechoslovak presidency in June 1948, Klement Gottwald

---

[75] Katarína Hradská, *Prípad Wisliceny: Nacistickí poradcovia a židovská otázka na Slovensku* (Bratislava: Academic Electronic Press, 1999), 80–82.

[76] "Terezínský kat před soudem lidu," *Práce* (17 September 1948); "Smrt terezínskému Burianovi," *Svobodné slovo* (23 September 1948); "Terezínský dozorce Neubauer popraven," *Obrana lidu* (29 September 1948), SÚA, f. MZV-VA II (j81), k. 218.

[77] The Justice Ministry instructed prosecutors to forward cases where a Czech defendant only faced charges of serving in the German military to the appropriate national committee for punishment as an offense against national honor. SOA-Prague, f. MLS-KH, Ls 387/48; "Zásady o dalším postupu v retribučním řízení," VHA, f. Čepička, sv. 20, aj. 137, 10; see also SÚA, f. 29, aj. 96.

[78] In 1947 the Kutná Hora People's Court convicted Lerchová's husband and sentenced him to eight years' imprisonment for the denunciation. After her second acquittal, Lerchová was sentenced to public censure by a national honor commission. Bohumila Lerchová, SOA-Prague, MLS-KH, Ls 613/46 and Ls 142/48.

[79] Anna Czeřowská, SOA-Prague, MLS-KH, Ls 44/48.

declared an amnesty covering misdemeanors, including offenses against national honor, as long as they had not yet been adjudicated.[80] Because the amnesty covered all sentences of one year or less and all fines not greater than 100,000 crowns, it effectively robbed the Small Decree of its punitive power. Consequently, the Interior Ministry recommended that national committees restrict prosecution only to those cases where a fine in excess of 100,000 crowns might be assessed or "where the consequences of conviction themselves without regard to the size of the penalty [were] particularly significant."[81] One national committee informed the Interior Ministry that since no large fines were expected, it had concluded that there was no need to even reexamine a single national honor case.[82] The Benešov commission did not hold its first session until 1 November 1948 and only sentenced fourteen persons to a total of twelve months and ten days in prison. The fines handed down, however, were considerable: 388,000 crowns in all.[83] The purged Kutná Hora commission reported that it had assessed penalties of twenty-eight months and ten days of imprisonment, plus 192,000 crowns in fines. Entirely new cases, however, only accounted for 10,000 crowns in fines; apparently no additional defendants were imprisoned.[84]

Unlike the People's Courts and the national honor tribunals, the National Court was not reestablished after the February coup. Perhaps mindful of the August 1946 protest campaign fiasco, Gottwald immediately rejected Čepička's proposal to retry the Protectorate government ministers. The Communist leader cavalierly dismissed the idea: "that's not so important."[85] Aside from two former editors, Rudolf Halík and Jaroslav Pelíšek, the Justice Ministry made little effort to pursue those

[80] MV no. B-2223–23/6–1948-I/2 (24 June 1948), *Věstník Ministerstva vnitra* (1948), no. 132, 248–51; fifth government, second meeting (18 June 1948), SÚA, f. 100/24 (KG), sign. 1494, sv. 149.
[81] MV no. B2220-13/10-1948-I/2 (15 Oct. 1948) to ZNV/ONV/ÚNV, SÚA, f. MV-NR (B2220), k. 2018.
[82] Copy of "Zápis jednání TNK ONV Olomouc-venkov" (23 July 1948), SÚA, f. MV-NR (B2220), k. 2016.
[83] "Referát bezpečnostní a dopravní," *Věstník ONV Benešov* II:8 (30 Dec. 1948), 7.
[84] ONV no. 26106/48 (27 November 1948), SOkA-KH, f. ONV-KH, k. 89, sing. III 21b/c (TNK 1948).
[85] Fourth government, meeting three (12 March 1948), SÚA, f. 100/24, aj. 1494, sv. 147, str. 103.

National Court cases that had allegedly outraged the public in previous years.[86] Others, however, seized the initiative. In May 1948 a Brno prosecutor proposed retrying Dominik Čipera and František Malota as representatives of the Bat'a firm. At roughly the same time the chief prosecutor of the Prague People's Court suggested retrying the leaders of National Solidarity: Josef Nebeský, Jan Fousek, and Tomáš Krejčí.[87] For half a year the Justice Ministry did not react, until in November it became aware of a thorny legal predicament. The Prague prosecutor had not only proposed a retrial of the National Solidarity leaders; he had actually initiated proceedings against them, thereby voiding the original verdicts – legally, it was as if the three had never been convicted. Faced with this untenable situation, the Justice Ministry insisted that it was necessary to retry the three men.[88] In December 1948 Nebeský and Fousek were each sentenced to twelve years in prison, and Krejčí, who was prosecuted *in absentia*, to twenty-five years.[89] Malota was acquitted, while Čipera, who had fled abroad and thus also had to be tried *in absentia*, received a fifteen-year sentence.[90]

Despite all the heated rhetoric prior to February 1948, retribution claimed far fewer victims after the coup than before. The frequency of acquittals in the first month of post-February retribution prompted Karel Klos, a high-ranking official in the newly revamped Justice Ministry, to recommend that prosecutors withdraw some indictments. Moreover, he admonished prosecutors not to allow their actions to

---

[86] In May 1948 the activist editor Rudolf Halík, who had been sentenced to eighteen months in 1946, received a penalty of the loss of his civic rights for life, the confiscation of all his property, and ten years' imprisonment. MLS-PR 1948, SÚA, f. MS (Varia), k. 1652; "Rudolf Halík dostal deset let," *Svobodné slovo* (19 May 1948), SÚA, f. MZV-VA II (j81), k. 218.

[87] Originally, Fousek and Krejčí had been convicted but received no penalty; Čipera and Nebeský had been acquitted; and Malota's case had never gone to trial. ZSZ Brno (3 May 1948); Vedoucí veřejný žálobce (v.v.ž.), MLS-PR (28 May 1948), SÚA, f. MS (IV/19), k. 1241.

[88] Kabinet MS (11 November 1948) to Sekr. ÚV Kádrové komise, SÚA, f. MS (IV/19), k. 1241.

[89] "Rozsudek nad bývalými agrárními předáky," *Rudé právo* (22 December 1948), 1; "Znovu před lidový soud," *Svobodné slovo* (2 December 1948), SÚA, f. MZV-VA II (j81), k. 218.

[90] Together with Čipera and Malota, the People's Court tried Hugo Vavrečka, a former newspaper editor and Bat'a official. The court convicted Vavrečka *in absentia* – he was in a hospital at the time – and sentenced him to three years' imprisonment. "Bývalí Bat'ovi ředitelé odsouzeni," *Lidové noviny* (23 Dec. 1948), SÚA, f. MZV-VA II (j81), k. 218.

appear as personal revenge for events prior to the coup. Most importantly, he stressed,

It is necessary also to take into consideration the political consequences of carrying out the renewal of retribution. For this reason it is necessary to proceed especially circumspectly where there is a capital case. Especially with individuals of Czech and Slovak nationality, it is not desirable for the death penalty to be proposed.[91]

Mindful of potential threats to the new regime's grip on power, Klos even suggested that capital trials of German defendants be postponed until after the Sokol athletic movement held its rally in July.[92] By the end of 1948, the Czech and Slovak People's Courts together sentenced a total of thirty-one defendants to death, only nine of whom were listed as "Czech or Slovak."[93]

The regime never published final results for post-February retribution, but in his 22 December 1948 address to the Czechoslovak parliament Čepička claimed that the new People's Courts had reexamined approximately 15,000 cases. Based on his research, Borák counted a total of 4,761 cases tried in the Czech provinces in 1948.[94] An internal tally by the Justice Ministry shows that Czech People's Courts convicted only 2,384 defendants between 2 April and 31 December 1948.[95] When

[91] "Provádění revise retribučního soudnictví," MS no. 36900/48-III/5 (26 April 1948), SÚA, f. MS (Org), k. 1942.
[92] As the largest independent Czech organization, Sokol [Falcon] was a thorn in the side of the Communists, who feared it might become a center of opposition to the regime. In a display of dissatisfaction with the new regime, during the July rally many Sokol members turned the back of their heads to Gottwald, while others praised Beneš, Tito, and even the United States. In response, the police arrested 237 persons and the regime initiated a massive purge of the Sokol ranks. Kaplan, *Nekrvavá revoluce*, 190–91; Karel Kaplan, *Poslední rok prezidenta: Edvard Beneš v roce 1948* (Brno: Doplněk, 1994), 71.
[93] "Výsledky retribuce," VHA, f. Čepička, sv. 23, aj. 168.
[94] Alexej Čepička, *Zlidovění soudnictví* (Prague: Min. informací a osvěty, 1949), 21; Mečislav Borák, "Spisy mimořádných lidových soudů z let 1945–1948 v českých archivech a možnostech zkoumání židovské problematiky," in Mečislav Borák, ed., *Retribuce v ČSR a národní podoby antisemitismu: Židovská problematika a antisemitismus ve spisech mimořádných lidových soudů a trestních komisí ONV v letech 1945–1948* (Prague, 2002), 55.
[95] In 1948 Czech People's Courts convicted 2,384 persons and sentenced twenty of them to death. Slovak People's Courts convicted 903 defendants and sentenced eleven of them to death. "Výsledky retribuce," VHA, f. Čepička, sv. 23, aj. 168.

we combine the last two figures we find that under Čepička's watch retribution judges actually issued acquittals at a substantially higher rate than under Drtina: In 1948 Czech courts apparently convicted barely fifty percent of all defendants. Even that total included a considerable number of cases prosecuted *in absentia*, a practice that became common after the coup. Although the conviction rate appears suspiciously low, it may simply reflect the fact that, after the completion of the Transfer, most defendants in 1948 were Czech. Despite the fanfare accompanying the return of retribution after February, the press, by now uniform in its coverage, devoted little space to coverage of the trials. The government had even less to say. Borák commented, "The Communist regime... did not like to publicize statistical data that did not directly speak in its favor. Such were the data about the reestablishment of retribution."[96]

Although the 1948 results do not seem all that impressive, the renewal of retribution may have still provided the regime a valuable tool with which to consolidate power. At a time when Communist leaders found some radical policies premature, retribution offered an opportunity to employ old institutions to achieve new goals. To turn a phrase, the regime poured new wine into old bottles. Although the Czech People's Courts took only nineteen or twenty lives in 1948, this figure actually represented at least eighty percent of the convicts legally executed in the Czech provinces in that fateful year.[97] Retrials were a way to settle scores against people like Mareš, Kaňková, and judges Komers and Schödelbauer. Most importantly, renewed retribution was a bridge between the old, allegedly "bourgeois," justice and the new, Communist one. On 25 October 1948 the regime established a new institution, the State Court, to punish alleged enemies of the new order. In a speech marking the occasion Čepička stressed that there was a clear link between the missions of the old and the new courts: "The core of anti-state activity... is being recruited primarily from the ranks of estate-owners, industrialists, wealthy farmers, large merchants,

---

[96] Borák, *Spravedlnost podle dekretu*, 79.
[97] "Zemřeli ve věznících a tresty smrti 1948–1956," *Seznamy*, Dokumenty o perzekuci a odporu, part 1 (Prague: Ústav pro soudobé dějiny, 1992), 73–80; Otakar Liška et al., *Vykonané tresty smrti Československo 1918–1989* (Prague: Úřad dokumentace a vyšetřování zločinů komunismu, 2000), 154–99.

collaborators, profiteers and traitors who had already betrayed during the occupation."[98]

If anyone mistakenly believed that the second and final dismantling of the Extraordinary People's Courts on 31 December 1948 meant a relaxation in the expansion of the police state, an article in *Lidová správa* put this vain hope to rest. In Stalinist terms, the author explained,

The completion of retribution will not mean the conclusion of the struggle against elements inimical to people's democracy. On the contrary! The completion of retribution means that our courts, completing the struggle against past forms of bourgeois sabotage and treachery, will aim fully at the destruction of today's ... growing forms of bourgeois reaction.[99]

Unlike in May 1947, the end of retribution in December 1948 did not represent a return to normalcy. It meant a further deterioration in legal certainty. After all, despite the broad, class-based interpretation of "collaboration" that predominated in 1948, retribution was still ostensibly limited to crimes committed during the "period of heightened danger to the republic," which had ended on 31 December 1946. Neither the State Court nor the new Law for the Protection of the People's Democratic Republic suffered such temporal bounds on its jurisdiction. Together, the new treason law and the new court, the U.S. Chargé d'Affaires informed his superiors in Washington, represented the "end [of] personal liberty in Czechoslovakia."[100]

CONCLUSION

There was more than a grain of truth in Nosek's apologetic assertion at the November 1947 Central Committee meeting: "We would have been finished earlier with reactionary conspirators and their allies, if only they hadn't been shielded by their buddies [*kumpáni*] in the judicial organs."[101] Burdened with the onerous task of retribution, Czechoslovakia's judicial system proved to be one of the strongest links in the democratic chain. From the Holubová–Velíšková trial to the exposure of the bombing plot, the courts repeatedly shed light on the murky

---

[98] "Slavnostní zahájení činnosti Státního soudu," *Rudé právo* (26 October 1948), 2.
[99] A. Dressler, "Poslední fáze retribuce," *Lidová správa* III:17 (1 September 1948), 261–63.
[100] Penfield, U.S. Embassy in Prague, to the Secretary of State, Washington, D.C. (27 November 1948), *Records of the U.S. Department of State*, film 860f.044/11-2748.
[101] SÚA, f. 1 (ZÚV-KSČ), sv. 3, aj. 15, str. 145.

world of the Interior Ministry. But National Socialist leader Ripka was only half right when he claimed, "the Ministry of Justice allowed us to a certain extent to apply the brakes to the arbitrary procedures of the Communists."[102] Prosecutors and judges could limit the damage caused by the police and security forces, but the courts were largely reactive. If the Justice Ministry acted as a "brake," then it only slowed down the Communists – neither Drtina nor his subordinates proved capable of stopping them. Ironically, the application of this "brake" was one of the primary factors that led to the ministers' resignations in February 1948 and the Communist seizure of power. Ultimately, during the coup the courts and the Justice Ministry proved powerless against the police and the Interior Ministry.

Nonetheless, the Communists' difficulties with retribution in 1948 illustrate a fascinating and unexplored aspect of the post-February regime. Émigrés typically portrayed the coup as the division between light and darkness, while Communist scholars saw "Victorious February" as a decisive break between the old and the new. The inconsistent record of the People's Courts in 1948, however, hints at enduring legacies of legal culture that stalled the communist transformation (or *Gleichschaltung*) of justice and society. The regime's reluctance to employ the death penalty illustrates that its leaders were not entirely confident of their seemingly unshakeable grip on power. Only in the early autumn, after the crackdown on the Sokol movement, amid the intensification of the Cold War, did the new form of Czechoslovak justice become apparent. It is probably no coincidence that the trials of Mareš, Kaňková, and the two Kutná Hora judges all took place after the establishment of the State Court and the passage of a new sedition law in October 1948. As in the period between May 1945 and February 1948, after the coup retribution played a complex and contradictory role in the Communist consolidation of power. On the one hand, prosecutors continued to dismiss the overwhelming majority of cases and the courts still acquitted defendants in large numbers. On the other hand, revamped retribution offered the country's rulers an acceptable tool with which to maintain pressure on their political opponents as the regime prepared the ground for a new wave of repression in the autumn of 1948.

---

[102] Ripka, *Czechoslovakia Enslaved*, 148–49.

CONCLUSION

Summing up parliament's June 1947 debate – during which deputies criticized the retribution courts both for their severity and their leniency; for their class bias toward the bourgeoisie and their partisan bias toward the working class; for their failure to punish more Germans and their failure to punish more Czechs – Vojta Beneš concluded that all the contradictory criticism made "clear that we did not have just retribution."[1] Czechs were not alone in their dissatisfaction. In France, as Peter Novick wrote, "Frenchmen who agree[d] on nothing else . . . joined in denouncing the purge, although, to be sure, for very different reasons." Some found retribution to be too mild, others considered it too severe.[2] In subsequent decades scholars and political leaders have perpetuated the view that postwar retribution throughout Europe was petty, partisan, and, ultimately, a failure. In response to such charges, Martin Conway argued,

The improvised and imperfect nature of postwar justice should not be used – as has become increasingly fashionable in recent years – to discredit the entire project of prosecution of crimes committed during the war years. Amidst the inevitable examples of miscarriages of justice and of inconsistencies in the judgments and sentences passed, it is important to bear in mind that the prosecutions also represented an attempt to pursue those responsible for manifold forms of suffering and to do so in a manner which reasserted principles of justice and liberty.[3]

[1] V. Beneš, *Těsnopisecké zprávy Ústavodárného národního shromáždění Republiky československé* 56 (10 June 1947), 70.
[2] Peter Novick, *The Resistance versus Vichy: The Purge of Collaborators in Liberated France* (New York: Columbia University Press, 1968), 188.
[3] Martin Conway, "Justice in Postwar Belgium: Popular Passions and Political Realities," *Cahiers d'Histoire du Temps Présent* 2 (1997), 7.

Even in the Western democracies of today, built on decades of peace and prosperity, verdicts repeatedly fail to please large portions of the general public. Police occasionally manufacture evidence, prosecutors sometimes ignore exculpatory testimony, defense counsel for indigent defendants is often subpar, and judges and jurors are not immune to personal prejudice. Even under the best of circumstances, miscarriages of justice are all too frequent.

The aftermath of the Second World War was not the best of circumstances. Throughout occupied Europe the crimes of the Nazis created a groundswell of support for swift and brutal vengeance, and many vigilantes did not await the establishment of courts. The wartime debasement of public institutions, through their participation in the administration of foreign rule and the brutal oppression of dissent, hampered their reconstruction after liberation. Above all, Nazi occupation and its attendant horrors discredited liberal ("bourgeois") democracy as a form of government and radicalized the population. Extreme solutions were sought for a range of problems, from political instability to social inequality.[4] In the context of the times, today's academic and policy debates over the merits of "transitional justice" seem oddly out of place. Although the construction of a democratic society founded on the rule of law may best be furthered by drawing a thick line between the present and the past, that possibility was not considered by countries emerging from years of German occupation. The unprecedented brutality of the Nazis' crimes and the sheer number of their victims created universal agreement that the perpetrators of inhuman acts had to be brought to justice. If war criminals were not to be shot outright, as various Allied leaders suggested, then they would have to be tried.[5] For formerly occupied Europe retribution was not a question of "whether," but of "how" and "how much." The Czech answer, as we have seen, was far-reaching and extraordinarily punitive.

If the conditions for impartial justice were not ideal in postwar Europe, then in the Czech case several critical factors further

---

[4] Jan T. Gross, "Themes for a Social History of War Experience and Collaboration," in István Deák, Jan T. Gross, and Tony Judt, eds., *The Politics of Retribution in Europe: World War II and Its Aftermath* (Princeton, NJ: Princeton University Press, 2000), 22–23.

[5] Gary Jonathan Bass, *Stay the Hand of Vengeance: The Politics of War Crimes Tribunals* (Princeton, NJ: Princeton University Press, 2000), 181.

complicated the task of retribution. The Czechoslovak government's primary goal of expelling the country's national minorities created an atmosphere in which a significant portion of the population was effectively placed beyond the rule of law. The expectation that Germans would furnish the vast majority of defendants before the People's Courts was a prime reason why the London Czechs did not concern themselves excessively with the Great Decree's shortcomings. The vigilantism of spring 1945 resulted in large part from the decision to permit violence in order to magnify the expected "Wild Transfer." The criminalization of membership overwhelmed the courts and the subsequent directive to deport suspected war criminals undermined their legitimacy. In the wave of anti-German hysteria, promoted by leaders across the political spectrum, journalists and judges who protested the treatment of suspected collaborators faced threats to their own existence. That justice was a partisan battleground was hardly the fault of the courts – after all, in postwar Czechoslovakia every sphere of society, including athletic and youth organizations, became political. If anything, because the courts resisted external pressure longer than most other institutions, they remained politically contested until February 1948 and perhaps even after.

Weighed down by the legacy of the Nazi occupation, infected by the poisoned atmosphere of the Transfer, and confronted by the incessant pressures of postwar politics, the People's Courts were straitjacketed by the legal regulations adopted by the Czechoslovak government-in-exile. The Great Decree's flaws did not lie in its retroactivity – the unforeseen nature of the Nazis' crimes made *ex post facto* law necessary for justice to be done. Nor should the introduction of "people's judges" bear the prime responsibility for arbitrary judgments and inconsistent verdicts. From the outset, the greatest injustices of postwar Czech retribution were imbedded within the very process thanks to the ban on appeals that prevented judicial review, which could have ironed out differences in sentencing. The combination of the ban on appeals and the regulation that executions had to be carried out within a maximum three hours led to nothing short of "judicial murder." Although the majority of death sentences were given to war criminals, many from the Gestapo and SS, there is little doubt that the summary nature of the verdicts resulted in the execution of innocents.

The flaws of the Great Decree were compounded by additional sanctions introduced after the war. The Small Decree, with its invention of "offenses against national honor," represented a serious erosion of legal certainty. Six months after the occupation ended, Czechs suddenly learned that they could be punished with up to a year in prison for conduct that had theretofore been entirely legal. When parliament acceded to the Communist demand to disenfranchise all suspected collaborators, the other parties gave the national committees carte blanche to deprive whomever they chose of the right to vote. If Czechs could still be held accountable for offenses against national honor committed before 31 December 1946, then they could not be prosecuted for any violent acts perpetrated against Germans or suspected collaborators prior to 28 October 1945. The impunity law (no. 115/46) prevented the courts from punishing policemen guilty of gross violations of human rights and thereby left these men in positions of authority, free to intimidate the general public. The repeated failure to confront police brutality helped to undermine the rule of law in Czechoslovakia.

The responsibility for the failures of Czech retribution was a shared one. As Gottwald's speech at Košice revealed, from the outset Communist leaders viewed the prosecution of collaborators as an instrument for the attainment of power. They repeatedly pressured their colleagues in government to adopt radical measures that favored the expansion of retribution and the erosion of civil rights. Meanwhile, Communist operatives subverted the police and manufactured plots to discredit the Party's political competitors. But Gottwald and his comrades did not write the Great Decree; they did not introduce the concept of summary justice. Pressure certainly came to bear on the non-Communists, but they were in agreement on the broad outlines of nearly every step adopted by the government. If Stránský initially opposed the Small Decree, he and his allies still desired a law to legalize the mass arrests of the previous spring. Although Drtina evidently disapproved of Law no. 115/46, he originally proposed an amnesty – the difference between the two was a question of degree, not of kind. Nor can retribution's flaws be laid at the feet of Stalin. In light of the Soviet domination of postwar East-Central Europe, the reader cannot have failed to notice how small a role Moscow seems to have played in Czech retribution, despite Czechoslovakia's increasing relegation to the eastern side of the descending Iron

Curtain. Especially after the Red Army departed the country in December 1945, the available archival records show barely any trace of Soviet interference, while the courts' verdicts, particularly those of the National Court, demonstrate the judiciary's frequent refusal to rule as the Communists desired. Future research may demonstrate otherwise, but for now it is the Czechs alone who must bear responsibility for both the successes and failures of postwar Czech retribution.

Beneš was right in May 1947 when he told the Union of Liberated Political Prisoners that retribution could have been far worse, but this welcome result was no thanks to him. After all, it was Beneš, the self-proclaimed "dictator" of the government-in-exile,[6] who instructed his subordinates in London to write a retribution law that criminalized membership in large organizations, eliminated most grounds for mitigating circumstances, and, above all, permitted no appeals. Back in the country, Beneš could have refused to sign the Small Decree – to do so he would merely have had to delay for twenty-four hours. As president he had the power to commute death sentences to imprisonment, but he did so only in the rarest of cases, and only on recommendation of the Justice Ministry and government. Finally, in March 1948, despite his expression of relief only ten months earlier, Beneš approved the reintroduction of retribution courts.

Only the professional conduct of prosecutors and judges, and the gradual coalescence of a majority within the government and throughout the country against attempts to pervert retribution, prevented more "injustices" and "mistakes." Of course, many prosecutors and judges did not resist political pressure or their own personal urge for vengeance. Many others rapidly adapted themselves to the new order after February 1948. Nonetheless, of all the institutions in postwar Czechoslovakia, the courts proved to be the most reliable protectors of individual rights, even when it came to punishment for wartime collaboration. Burdened by the Nazi legacy, inadequate laws, and poisoned politics, Czech prosecutors, judges, and people's judges executed the task entrusted to them, according the legal regulations provided, within the time allotted. With the hindsight of more than half a century, it is easy to point to numerous cases of injustice, but the fact that many abused retribution

[6] Zbyněk Zeman and Antonín Klimek, *The Life of Edvard Beneš: Czechoslovakia in Peace and War* (Oxford: Clarendon Press, 1997), 230.

for personal and partisan gain should not obscure the efforts of many others to seek legitimate redress for the horrors perpetrated during the Nazi occupation of Bohemia, Moravia, and Silesia. Despite its undeniable shortcomings, postwar Czech retribution represented a serious and thorough attempt to face the crimes of the past, including those committed by the Czechs themselves.

APPENDIX I
THE GREAT DECREE
(NO. 16/1945)

Decree of the President of the Republic of 19 June 1945, concerning the punishment of Nazi criminals, traitors and their accomplices, and concerning the Extraordinary People's Courts

The shocking crimes committed by the Nazis and their treasonous accomplices in Czechoslovakia call for stern justice. The oppression of the homeland and the murder, enslavement, robbery, and humiliation to which the Czechoslovak people were subjected, and all of the extreme German barbarities, in which, regrettably, traitorous Czechoslovak citizens also took part (including some who abused their high office, mandate, or rank), must be punished without delay in order to eradicate completely the Nazi and fascist evil. Upon the proposal of the government, I therefore decree:

CHAPTER I
CRIMES AGAINST THE STATE
§ 1

Whoever, during the period of heightened danger to the Republic (§18), committed any of the following crimes on the territory of the Republic or outside of it in violation of the Law for the Protection of the Republic of 19 March 1923, No. 50 Coll., will be punished:

Conspiring against the republic is punishable by death (§1); Anyone involved in the preparation of conspiracies (§2), threatening the security of the Republic (§3), treason (§4, no. 1), the betrayal of state secrets (§5, no. 1), military treason (§6, nos. 1, 2, and 3), or violence against constitutional authorities (§10, no. 1) will be sentenced to a term of imprisonment of twenty years to life, and in particularly aggravating circumstances, to death.

§2

Whoever, during the period of heightened danger to the Republic (§18), was a member of the following organizations: Die Schutzstaffeln der Nationalsozialistischen Deutschen Arbeiterpartei (SS), the Freiwillige Schutzstaffeln (FS), or of the Rodobrany, Szabadcsapatoku, or other organizations of a similar nature not listed here, will be sentenced to a term of imprisonment of five to twenty years, and in particularly aggravating circumstances, to a term of imprisonment of twenty years to life, provided he did not commit a crime carrying a greater sentence.

§3

(1) Whoever, during the period of heightened danger to the Republic (§18), promoted or supported the fascist or Nazi movement, or whoever during that period endorsed or defended enemy rule over the territory of the Republic or individual illegal acts of the occupying military command and administration and authorities under them in print, over the radio, in film or theater, or at public meetings, will be sentenced to a term of imprisonment of five to twenty years, provided he did not commit a crime carrying a greater sentence; if he committed such a crime with the intent of subverting the moral, national, or state consciousness of the Czechoslovak people, and especially Czechoslovak youth, he will be sentenced to a term of imprisonment of ten to twenty years, and in particularly aggravating circumstances, to a term of imprisonment of twenty years to life, or to death.

(2) Whoever, during the same period, was a functionary or officer in the Nationalsozialistische Deutsche Arbeiterpartei (NSDAP), or the Sudetendeutsche Partei (SdP), or in Banner, the Hlinka or Svatopluk Guards, or in other fascist organizations of a similar nature, will be sentenced to a term of imprisonment of five to twenty years, provided he did not commit a crime carrying a greater sentence.

§ 4

A Czechoslovak citizen who, during the period of heightened danger to the Republic (§18), while abroad subverted the movement to liberate the Czechoslovak Republic in its pre-Munich constitutional form and unity, or who otherwise consciously harmed the interests of the Czechoslovak Republic, and especially whoever jeopardized the safety of its citizens working for the liberation of the Republic from within, will be sentenced to a term of imprisonment of five to twenty years, provided he did commit a crime carrying a greater sentence.

CRIMES AGAINST PERSONS
§ 5

(1) Whoever, during the period of heightened danger to the Republic (§18), committed the following crimes in the service or in the interest of Germany, its allies, a movement hostile to the Republic, or its [the movement's] organizations or members:

a) as defined by the Criminal Code of 27 May 1852, no. 117 of the imperial law code (i.l.c.), the crimes of public violence by human trafficking (§90), public violence by the enslavement of a human being (§95), murder (§§134 and 137), manslaughter (§§140 and 141), and grievous bodily harm (§156),

b) as defined by the Criminal Code Article V/1878, the crimes of murder (§278), voluntary manslaughter (§279), grievous bodily harm resulting in death (§§406 and 307), and the kidnapping of children (§317),

shall be sentenced to death.

(2) Whoever, during the same period, under the same circumstances and with the same purpose, committed the following crimes:

a) as defined by the Criminal Code of 27 May 1852, no. 117 i.l.c., the crimes of public violence through the unlawful restriction of the personal freedom of a human being (§93), public violence through extortion (§98), public violence through dangerous threats (§99), and grievous bodily harm (§§152 and 155),

b) as defined by the Criminal Code Article V/1878, the crime of the unlawful restriction of the personal freedom of a human being (§§323, 324, and 325), grievous bodily harm (§301), and extortion (§§350 and 353), shall be sentenced to a term of imprisonment of ten to twenty years.

§6

(1) Whoever, during the period of heightened danger to the Republic (§18), ordered the performance of forced or mandatory labor for the benefit of the war effort of Germany or its allies, or whoever participated in the issuing and execution of such orders, shall be sentenced to a term of imprisonment of five to twenty years, provided he did not commit a crime carrying a greater sentence.

(2) If, through the issuance of such an order, an inhabitant of the Republic was forced to work abroad, or in circumstances or places that posed a danger to his life or health, the culprit shall be sentenced, without regard to the purpose of the work, to a term of imprisonment of ten to twenty years.

§7

(1) Whoever, acting alone or in cooperation with others, during the period of heightened danger to the Republic (§18), in the service or interest of Germany, its allies, a movement hostile to the Republic, or its [the movement's] organizations or members, was responsible for the loss of liberty of an inhabitant of the Republic without further consequences, shall be sentenced to a term of imprisonment of five to twenty years. If the culprit was responsible for the loss of liberty of a greater number of inhabitants of the Republic, the court may impose a prison sentence of twenty years to life, and in particularly aggravating circumstances, the penalty of death.

(2) Whoever, in the same period, under the same circumstances, for the same purpose and in the same manner was responsible for grievous bodily harm to an inhabitant of the Republic without permanent injury (section 3), shall be sentenced to a term of imprisonment of ten to twenty years, and in particularly aggravating circumstances of twenty years to life. If a larger number of persons was thereby affected, the court may impose the penalty of death.

(3) Whoever, in the same period, under the same circumstances, for the same purpose and in the same manner, caused the death or

deportation of an inhabitant of the Republic, or grievous bodily harm to an inhabitant, with the consequences specified in §156 of the Criminal Code no. 117/1852 i.l.c. and §§306 and 307 of the Criminal Code Article V/1878, through a court decree, verdict, order, or other administrative decision of any kind, shall be punished for his crime by the penalty of death.

CRIMES AGAINST PROPERTY
§8

(1) Whoever, during the period of heightened danger to the Republic (§18), committed the following crimes in the service or in the interest of Germany, its allies, a movement hostile to the Republic, or its [the movement's] organizations or members:

a) as defined by the Criminal Code of 27 May 1852 no. 117 i.l.c., the crime of public violence through the willful damage of another's property (§85), with the consequences in accordance with §86, section 2; arson (§166), under the circumstances and with the consequences defined by §167, letter a); robbery (§190), under the circumstances and with the consequences defined by §195,

b) as defined by the Criminal Code Article V/1878, the crimes of arson (§424) and robbery (§§344 and 345), under the circumstances and with the consequences defined in §349, section 1, point 2 and section 2,

shall be sentenced to death.

(2) Whoever, in the same period, under the same circumstances, for the same purpose and in the same manner, committed the following crimes:

a) as defined by the Criminal Code of 27 May 1852 no. 117 i.l.c., the crime of public violence through breaking and entering into another's real estate (§83); of public violence through willful damage to another's property (§§85, 86 section 1); arson (§166) under the circumstances and with the consequences defined in §167, letters b) through g); larceny (§§171 through 180); embezzlement (§§181 through 183); complicity in larceny or embezzlement (§§185 and 186); robbery (§190), under the circumstances and with the consequences defined in §§191 through 194; complicity in robbery (§196); fraud (§§197 through 201, 203);

b) as defined by the Criminal Code Article V/1878, the crime of private nuisance (§§330 and 331); the misdemeanor of damage to another's property (§§418 and 420), which under the circumstances of section 1 of this paragraph is defined as a criminal offense; arson (§§422 and 423); larceny (§§333 and 341), provided that the act is not punishable under section 1, letter b) of this paragraph; complicity (§370); fraud (§379, as amended by §50 of the amendment to the criminal code), under the circumstances defined in §383, section 2, with the exception of §382, shall be sentenced to imprisonment for a term of ten to twenty years, and in especially aggravating circumstances, by imprisonment for a term of twenty years to life.

§9

Whoever, acting alone or in cooperation with others during the period of heightened danger to the Republic (§18), in the service or in the interest of Germany, its allies, a movement hostile to the Republic, or its [the movement's] organizations or members, caused the total or partial dispossession of the assets of the Czechoslovak state or its legal entities or natural persons in contradiction of the laws of the Republic through a court decree, verdict, order, or other administrative decision of any kind, or through the enforcement of a verdict, order, or administrative decision, will be sentenced to imprisonment for a term of ten to twenty years, and in especially aggravating circumstances, to imprisonment for a term of twenty years to life, provided he did not commit a crime carrying a greater sentence.

§10

Whoever, during the period of heightened danger to the Republic (§18), exploited the distress caused by national, political, or racial persecution to enrich himself at the expense of the state, its legal entities or natural persons, shall be sentenced to imprisonment for a term of five to ten years, provided he did not commit a crime carrying a greater sentence.

DENUNCIATION
§ 11

Whoever, during the period of heightened danger to the Republic (§ 18), in the service or interest of the enemy, or by exploiting the situation created by the enemy occupation, denounced another for some real or invented activity, shall be sentenced to imprisonment for a term of five to ten years. If, however, the denouncer caused the loss of liberty of a Czechoslovak citizen through his denunciation, he shall be sentenced to imprisonment for a term of ten to twenty years. If the denunciation resulted, either directly or indirectly, in the loss of freedom of a larger number of persons or in grievous harm to health, he shall be sentenced to imprisonment for life, and if his denunciation resulted in someone's death, he shall be punished by a sentence of death.

GENERAL PROVISIONS
§ 12

Any foreigner who committed the crime set forth in § 1 or any of the crimes set forth in §§ 4 through 9 while abroad is liable to punishment under this decree if he committed these crimes against a Czechoslovak citizen or against Czechoslovak property, whether public or private.

§ 13

(1) The behavior (conduct, acts, actions) punishable under the terms of this decree shall not be exonerated by the fact that it was ordered or permitted by the provisions of a law other than that of Czechoslovakia, or by authorities established by a state power other than that of Czechoslovakia, nor are such actions excused by the fact that the perpetrator considered such invalid provisions to be justified.

(2) Nor shall the perpetrator be exonerated by the fact that he performed his official duties if he acted with especial zeal, exceeding thus significantly the normal scope of his duties, or if he acted with the intent of aiding the war effort of the Germans (their allies), harming or thwarting the war effort of Czechoslovakia (its allies), or if he acted out of other manifestly reprehensible motives.

(3) Irresistible coercion resulting from a superior's order shall not absolve from guilt anyone who voluntarily became a member of an organization that required its members to carry out every order, even if illegal.

§14

If the court convicts a person for a criminal offense mentioned in this decree, and does not waive the sentence (§16, section 2), it shall concurrently pronounce:

a) that the convicted shall lose his civic honor, for a specified period of time or in perpetuity (§15);
b) that the convicted shall serve part or all of his prison sentence in special forced labor units, which shall be established by a special law;
c) that all or part of his possessions shall be forfeited to the state.

§15

The loss of civic honor entails:

1. the permanent forfeiture of decorations, orders, and honorary distinctions, positions in public service, ranks and offices, university degrees, as well as the forfeiture of retirement and living allowance benefits, charitable remunerations, and all other remunerations from public funds;
2. for noncommissioned officers, degradation, and for officers, cashierment;
3. forfeiture of the capacity to obtain, exercise, or regain the rights set forth in numbers 1 and 2, as well as the rights associated with the lost ranks;
4. the forfeiture of the right to vote, to be elected or appointed to public office, or to vote on public matters;
5. the forfeiture of the legal capacity to hold a position in associations (clubs or other such groups);
6. the forfeiture of the legal capacity to be the owner, publisher, or editor, or to participate in any way in the publication or editing

of a periodical publication, or to publish or issue nonperiodical publications;

7. the forfeiture of the legal capacity to give public lectures or addresses;
8. the forfeiture of the legal capacity to work in educational or artistic institutions or enterprises;
9. the forfeiture of the legal capacity to be an employer or coemployer;
10. the forfeiture of the legal capacity to practice the free professions;
11. the forfeiture of the legal capacity to be a member of the board of directors (administrative board) of a corporation or partnership;
12. the forfeiture of the legal capacity to act as the executive of a private enterprise.

Whoever violates the prohibitions set forth in this paragraph will be punished for this offense by an ordinary court to a jail term of one week to three months.

§ 16

(1) A sentence of imprisonment cannot be reduced below the minimum penalty nor replaced with a more lenient type of punishment.

(2) The court may reduce the sentence below the minimum penalty and replace it with a more lenient type of punishment, in cases deserving particular consideration it may abstain from imposing a sentence in the verdict, if it is generally known or can be proven without delay that the accused acted with the intent to benefit the Czech or Slovak nations or the Czechoslovak Republic or its allies, or some other general interest, or if he later rendered outstanding service toward the liberation of the republic from the enemy power, or if he attempted to rectify or minimize the evil caused by the enemy, and remained steadfast after his return to the path of duty. This provision cannot, however, be applied in cases in which the damage caused by the perpetrator disproportionately outweighs the general good that he pursued.

§ 17

The criminal offenses punishable under this decree and the execution of the sentence shall be subject to no statute of limitations.

§18

The period of heightened danger to the Republic is defined as the period from 21 May 1938 until a date to be determined by government edict.

§19

The criminal offenses punishable under this decree shall always be considered especially heinous, as defined by §1, section 1 of the law on state imprisonment of 16 June 1931, No. 123 Coll.

§20

Aiding and abetting the criminal offenses punishable under this decree shall be punished according to the current criminal code, with the following modifications:

1. in the case of crimes against the government, aiding and abetting shall be punished the same as the crime itself;
2. in the case of these crimes, aiding and abetting by the harboring of intimates (§39, no. 4 of Law no. 50/1923 Coll. on the Protection of the Republic) is punishable as a criminal offense and is punishable by a term of imprisonment from one to ten years, but if the crime itself is punishable by death according to this decree, [then it is punishable] by a term of imprisonment from five to twenty years;
3. for all other crimes, aiding and abetting shall be punished by imprisonment:
   a) from ten to twenty years, if this decree itself imposes for the crime the death penalty or a prison term of more than twenty years,
   b) from one to ten years, if this decree itself imposes for this crime a lesser punishment.

CHAPTER II
THE EXTRAORDINARY PEOPLE'S COURTS
§21

(1) The Extraordinary People's Courts are authorized to adjudicate all criminal offenses punishable under this decree, if the persons listed in §2 and §3, section 2, are held criminally accountable for them

as perpetrators, coperpetrators, conspirators, participants, or accessories; if other persons are held criminally responsible for these crimes, the Extraordinary People's Courts will adjudge them if a public prosecutor (§24) moves to institute proceedings against them before the Extraordinary People's Court.

(2) The local competence of the Extraordinary People's Courts shall be determined by the codes of criminal procedure in force on the territory of the Republic.

THE COMPOSITION AND SEAT OF THE EXTRAORDINARY PEOPLE'S COURTS
§22

(1) The Extraordinary People's Court exercises its authority in a five-member senate composed of a chairman, who must be a judge by profession (a civil or military judge) and four people's judges.

(2) On the recommendation of the government the President of the Republic shall name the chairmen of the Extraordinary People's Courts, their deputies, and the professional judges (section 1) from a list of persons drawn up for this purpose by the District National Committees. The government will appoint the people's judges from different lists drawn up by the District National Committees.

(3) The chairman of the Extraordinary People's Court or his deputy is charged with establishing the necessary number of senates with substitutes from the persons named in section 2.

(4) The Extraordinary People's Courts shall be established in the seats of the Regional Courts; each senate of the Extraordinary People's Court may also convene, however, in any location within the judicial district if the need should arise. The Local National Committee in the seat of the Regional Court shall appoint the executioners with the required number of assistants.

(5) A government edict shall establish the oath that the people's judges will swear and the compensation for expenses and lost income they are due.

§23

When voting, the people's judges shall vote first, in order from the oldest to the youngest.

THE PUBLIC PROSECUTOR
§24

(1) The public prosecutors shall be appointed by the government or, on its authorization, by the Minister of Justice for a set period of time, for certain cases, or for the entire period of the court's activity, from among public prosecutors or other persons who hold a doctorate in law or who have passed three state law examinations, or at the very least the state judiciary examination, as long as they are on the lists prepared for that purpose by the District National Committees.

(2) The public prosecutors of the Extraordinary People's Courts are subordinated to the Minister of Justice.

PROCEEDINGS BEFORE THE EXTRAORDINARY PEOPLE'S COURTS
§25

(1) The proceedings of the Extraordinary People's Courts shall follow the principles of proceedings under martial law, in the modification set forth in §§26 through 31 of this decree. In places where the decree refers to the provisions of ordinary procedure, the provisions of the criminal code in force shall be used.

(2) An acquittal by the Extraordinary People's Court does not preclude prosecution before the competent ordinary court, or before the state court in accordance with Law no. 68/1935 Coll., or before the regional court competent to judge military treason in according to law no. 130/1936 Coll., and government edict no. 238/1937 Coll. This court will adjudicate the case anew (*de novo*) in ordinary proceedings, in which the substantial legal provisions of this decree (§§1 through 20) shall apply, as if the accused had been brought before an ordinary court in the first place (§21). The motion to proceed against the accused in this fashion must be made by the latest within three months of the acquittal.

§26

(1) The proceedings before the Extraordinary People's Court shall be initiated by a motion by the public prosecutor (§24). Pregnant

women shall not be brought before the court during the term of their pregnancy.

(2) The entire proceeding against any individual shall be conducted, whenever possible, without interruption, from beginning to end before the Extraordinary People's Court. The proceedings against any one individual must not last longer than three days. This time period commences at the moment when the accused is brought before the court.

(3) If the People's Court is unable to reach a verdict within the three-day period, the case shall be forwarded to the competent ordinary court (§23, section 2). In this case, it will also decide whether the accused shall remain in pretrial custody.

(4) If the accused does not appear or cannot appear before the court for whatever reason, the public prosecutor can move to try the accused *in absentia*. In such a case the court must appoint counsel for the accused *ex officio*.

§27

The proceedings before the Extraordinary People's Court shall be oral and public. The accused has the right to choose his own counsel or to request court-appointed counsel if he is indigent. If the accused does not exercise this right, the court shall appoint counsel *ex officio*. Both the accused and the court may entrust the defense to a person who is not registered in the list of defense attorneys, but who holds a doctorate in law or has passed three state law examinations, or at the very least the state judiciary examination.

§28

(1) The main trial before the Extraordinary People's Court shall commence after the matter has been called and the public prosecutor has stated the general facts of the case and has laid out the specific criminal charges against the accused. The interrogation of the accused and the introduction of evidence shall be governed by the provisions of the code of criminal procedure. The records of the interrogation of accomplices and witnesses and the opinions of expert witnesses

may be read whenever the chairman of the senate deems them to be expedient.

(2) As a rule, the proceedings shall be limited to the act or acts for which the accused was brought before the Extraordinary People's Court. Acts that are not punishable under this decree are not to be taken into consideration. If they are prosecuted at a later time in proceedings before the Extraordinary People's Court, or before a ordinary court, a state court, or a regional court, competent to adjudicate military treason, the sentence of a prison term already pronounced by the Extraordinary People's Court shall be taken into account in determining the sentence.

(3) The proceedings before the Extraordinary People's Court must not be delayed by the determination of claims for compensation for damages caused by the criminal offense.

(4) The discovery of accomplices shall not be neglected, but the pronouncement and execution of the verdict should not be delayed thereby.

(5) Following the conclusion of the preliminary [attendant] proceedings, the public prosecutor shall evaluate the results and make his final motion. The chairman will then allow the accused and his counsel to argue the case for the defense. If the public prosecutor responds to their arguments, the accused and his counsel have the right to the last word.

§29

(1) Thereafter the court determines the verdict in closed deliberations, governed by the appropriate provisions of ordinary procedure, unless this decree provides otherwise.

(2) If a guilty verdict for a crime upon which this decree imposes the death penalty is supported by only three votes, or if the court comes to the conclusion that the circumstances of the case are such that the death penalty would be disproportionately severe, the court may impose a prison term of twenty years to life and, under the conditions set forth in §16, section 2, may use that provision as well.

(3) The verdict will be announced immediately in open court.

§30

The proceedings before the Extraordinary People's Court shall be recorded in accordance with ordinary procedure. This transcript shall be signed by all members of the senate and by the court clerk.

§31

(1) Against the verdict of the Extraordinary People's Courts there are no means of legal redress. Appeals for clemency will not have a dilatory effect regardless of who files them.

(2) As a rule, the death penalty is to be carried out within two hours of the pronouncement of the verdict. At the express request of the condemned, the time limit may be extended for an additional hour. If the accused was tried *in absentia*, the death penalty is to be carried out within twenty-four hours of the apprehension of the condemned.

(3) The Extraordinary People's Court may also rule that the death penalty is to be carried out in public. Such a decision should be rendered in particular in cases in which the savage nature of the crime, the degenerate character of the perpetrator, the number of his crimes, or his rank call for the public execution of the verdict. To ensure the public nature of the execution, in such a case the court may extend the two hour time-limit, but not beyond twenty-four hours.

TEMPORARY AND FINAL PROVISIONS
§32

(1) The provisions of the law of 3 May 1934, no. 91 Coll., concerning the imposition of the death penalty and on life sentences, is not valid for criminal acts punishable under this decree.

(2) The provisions of the law of 11 March 1931, No. 48 Coll., concerning criminal jurisdiction over youthful offenders, shall remain in force.

§33

This decree shall become effective on the day of its publication and for one year thereafter, unless it is modified or amended, or the period of its effectiveness shortened or extended, by the appropriate legislative institutions.

§34

All members of the government are charged with the execution of this decree.

Signed:

Dr. Beneš
Fierlinger

David	Laušman
Gottwald	Ďuriš
Široký	Dr. Pietor
Dr. Šrámek	gen. Hasal
Ursíny	Hála
gen. Svoboda	Dr. Šoltész
Dr. Ripka	Dr. Procházka
Nosek	Majer
Dr. Šrobár	Dr. Clementis
Dr. Nejedlý	also for Minister Masaryk
Dr. Stránský	gen. Dr. Ferejnčík
Kopecký	Lichner

APPENDIX 2
THE NATIONAL COURT
DECREE (NO. 17/1945)

Decree of the President of the Republic of 19 June 1945 on the National Court

Upon the proposal of the government, I decree:

§ 1

(1) A National Court shall be established in Prague.
(2) The National Court shall function as a criminal court and as an honor court.

§ 2

If the state president of the so-called Protectorate, the members of the so-called Protectorate government, the members of the central command of Banner, the members of the Board for Youth Education, the committee members and functionaries of the Czech League against Bolshevism, the chief functionaries of the National Union of Employees and the Agriculture and Forestry Trade Union, journalists who served the government of invaders by disseminating propaganda in the daily press, or any other persons who, by virtue of their prominent positions in politics, their high office, high commanding function, or important position in economic life, were duty-bound to serve as a patriotic example to their fellow citizens, have committed criminal offenses as defined by the Decree of the President of the Republic of 19 June 1945, no. 16 Coll., on the punishment of Nazi criminals, traitors, and their accomplices and on the Extraordinary People's Courts (in another retribution decree), they shall be judged by the National Court in its capacity as a criminal court.

§ 3

The National Court is bound by the substantive provisions of the retribution decree.

§ 4

The persons specified in §2 will be adjudged by the National Court in its capacity as an honor court, even if they did not commit any crimes, but acted after 21 May 1938 in a manner unbecoming to loyal and brave Czechoslovak citizens.

§ 5

(1) Whoever is found guilty according to the preceding paragraph will be stripped by declaration of the National Court of active and passive electoral rights to representative bodies, of the right to call public meetings or participate in them, to join political associations or organizations, and to publish, write for, or edit political periodicals or other political publications.

(2) The violation of any of these prohibitions is punishable by an ordinary court as a misdemeanor carrying a sentence of three to six months in prison.

§ 6

(1) The National Court shall deliberate in seven-member senates, which shall be constituted by the president of the National Court.

(2) The president of the National Court, his two deputies, and the chairmen of the senates must be judges by profession. They shall be appointed by the President of the Republic based on the nominations of the government. The associate justices of the National Court shall be appointed by the government based on nominations by the

Minister of Justice from lists compiled by the Provincial National Committees. The associate judges of the National Court shall be proven patriots, especially those persons who have distinguished themselves in the resistance either at home or abroad, or who were the victims of enemy persecution or treachery.

§7

(1) Based on the nomination of the Minister of Justice, the government shall select from among the ranks of legal professionals a public prosecutor (National Prosecutor) for the National Court, along with the appropriate number of deputies.

(2) The National Prosecutor and his deputies are subordinate to the Ministry of Justice.

(3) The National Prosecutor shall determine which of the persons designated in §§2 and 4 should be judged by the National Court, and for which crimes or acts. Such a designation annuls the jurisdiction of the Extraordinary People's Courts and ordinary courts.

§8

(1) The general provisions of the criminal code shall remain in force for proceedings before the National Court, unless this decree specifies otherwise.

(2) The proceedings against offenders defined by this decree will commence without delay and shall proceed as quickly as possible.

(3) Regular police investigations shall not take place. Investigations of the case shall be limited to matters of fundamental importance. They will be carried out by the National Prosecutor, who may ask the courts and law enforcement agencies to perform individual operations.

(4) Upon completion of the investigation, the National Prosecutor will submit a written indictment for criminal acts, or a written charge based on §4. Objections to this are inadmissable.

(5) The indictment or charges must also indicate the positive facts that constitute the basis of the indictment or charges.

§9

In the case of charges relating to acts described in §2, the National Prosecutor will decide whether to hold the accused in custody, basing his decision on the provisions in §§175 and 180 of the Criminal Law Code.

§10

(1) The accused has the right to choose a counsel for the defense or to request that the court appoint him one, if he is indigent. If the accused does not make use of his right, the court shall appoint a defense counsel *ex officio*.

(2) The counsel for the defense must be a person who has earned a doctorate in law or at least has passed three state law examinations, or at the very least the state judiciary examination.

§11

(1) The indictment or the charges, as the case may be, shall be delivered to the accused directly with a subpoena to appear at the main trial proceedings, the date of which shall be set at least eight days from the date of delivery of the subpoena.

(2) If the accused does not appear or cannot appear before the court for whatever reason, the National Prosecutor may move to try the accused *in absentia*. In such a case the court must appoint a defense counsel *ex officio*.

§12

(1) The main trial before the National Court shall commence after the matter has been called and the general facts have been established through the reading of the indictment or charges, as the case may be (§8). The examination of the accused and the introduction of evidence shall follow the provisions of the code of criminal procedure. The activity of the court and of both sides shall be limited to the acts for which the accused has been brought before the National

Court. The discovery of accomplices shall not be neglected, but the pronouncement and execution of the verdict should not be delayed thereby.

(2) The main trial proceedings before the National Court are public and oral. The records of the interrogation of accomplices and witnesses as well as the opinion of expert witnesses may be read whenever the presiding judge deems it expedient.

(3) Following the conclusion of the preliminary [attendant] proceedings, the national prosecutor shall evaluate the results and make his final motion. The chairman will then permit the accused and his defense counsel to argue their case. If the National Prosecutor responds to the defense arguments, the accused and his counsel have the right to the last word.

§ 13

(1) Thereafter the court determines the verdict in closed deliberations, governed by the appropriate provisions of the ordinary code of criminal procedure, unless this decree provides otherwise.

(2) When voting, the associate judges shall vote first in order from oldest to youngest.

(3) If a guilty verdict for a crime upon which the death penalty is imposed is supported by fewer than five votes, or if the court comes to the conclusion that the circumstances of the case are such that the death penalty would be disproportionately severe, the court may impose a prison term of twenty years to life and, under the conditions set forth in §16, section 2, of the retribution decree, may use the provisions contained in it.

(4) The verdict will be announced immediately in open court.

§ 14

The proceedings shall be recorded in accordance with ordinary procedure. This transcript shall be signed by all members of the senate and by the court clerk.

§ 15

Against the verdict of the National Court there are no means of legal redress.

§16

(1) Appeals for clemency will not have a dilatory effect regardless of who files them.

(2) As a rule, the death penalty is to be carried out within two hours of the pronouncement of the verdict. At the express request of the condemned, the time limit may be extended for an additional hour. If the accused was tried *in absentia*, the death penalty shall be carried out within twenty-four hours of the apprehension of the condemned.

(3) The National Court may rule that the death penalty is to be carried out in public. Such a decision should be rendered in particular in cases in which the savage nature of the crime, the degenerate character of the perpetrator, the number of his crimes, or his rank call for the public execution of the verdict. To ensure the public nature of the execution, in such a case the court may extend the two-hour time limit, but not beyond twenty-four hours.

§17

The provisions of the law of 3 May 1934, no. 91 Coll., concerning the imposition of the death penalty and of life sentences, is not valid for sentencing under this decree.

§18

The provisions of this decree shall become effective on the day of its publication and for one year thereafter, unless it is modified or amended, or the period of its effectiveness shortened or extended, by the appropriate legislative institutions.

§19

All members of the government are charged with the execution of this decree.

Signed:

> Dr. Beneš
> Fierlinger

David
Gottwald
Široký
Dr. Šrámek
Ursíny
gen. Svoboda
Dr. Ripka
Nosek
Dr. Šrobár
Dr. Nejedlý
Dr. Stránský
Kopecký

Laušman
Ďuriš
Dr. Pietor
gen. Hasal
Hála
Dr. Šoltész
Dr. Procházka
Majer
Dr. Clementis
  also for Minister Masaryk
gen. Dr. Ferejnčík
Lichner

APPENDIX 3
THE SMALL DECREE
(NO. 138/1945)

Decree of the President of the Republic of 27 October 1945, no. 138 Coll., on the punishment of some offenses against national honor

Upon the proposal of the government, I decree:

§1

(1) Whoever, during the period of heightened danger to the Republic (§18 of the Decree of the President of the Republic of 19 June 1945, no. 16 Coll., on the punishment of Nazi criminals, traitors and their accomplices and on the Extraordinary People's Courts), undermined public morale by unbecoming behavior insulting to the national sentiments of the Czech or Slovak people, will be punished – if the act is not a criminal offense punishable by the courts – by District National Committees with up to one year in prison, a fine of up to 1,000,000 Czechoslovak crowns, or public censure, or with two or three of these punishments.

(2) If a fine is imposed, an alternate sentence of imprisonment for up to one year, depending on the severity of the offense, should be imposed if the fine cannot be recovered. If a term of imprisonment was imposed along with the fine, the term of imprisonment and the alternate punishment of prison time together must not exceed a period of one year.

(3) Directives issued in this matter by the Minister of the Interior are binding on the national committees.

§ 2

The period of time during which the perpetrator was held in custody shall be considered time served of the sentence of imprisonment (Constitutional Decree of the President of the Republic of 27 October 1945, no. 137 Coll., on the detention of persons considered politically unreliable during the revolutionary period).

§ 3

The acts punishable under § 1 are subject to a six-month statute of limitations. The period of limitation shall begin on the day on which the act was committed; in the case of acts committed prior to this decree coming into effect, the period of limitation shall begin on the day this decree takes effect.

§ 4

This decree comes into effect on the day of its pronouncement and is valid in the lands of Bohemia and Moravia-Silesia; it shall be executed by the Minister of the Interior.

Signed:

> Dr. Beneš
> Nosek
> Fierlinger

SELECTED BIBLIOGRAPHY

ARCHIVES

Archiv Kanceláře prezidenta republiky (AKPR)
 D-11169/47 (anonymy)
 D-11377/47 (prominut.)
 f. J. Smutného
 Londýnský archiv (LA)
Archiv Ministerstva vnitra (AMV), Prague, Czech Republic
Columbia University Rare Books and Manuscripts Library, New York,
 Jaromír Smutný collection
Slovenský národný archiv (SNA), Bratislava, Slovakia
Státní oblastní archiv (SOA), Litoměřice, Czech Republic
 Mimořádný lidový soud (MLS) Liberec
 Mimořádný lidový soud (MLS) Litoměřice
Státní oblastní archiv (SOA), Prague, Czech Republic
 Mimořádný lidový soud (MLS) Kutná Hora
 Mimořádný lidový soud (MLS) Prague
Státní oblastní archiv (SOA), Zámrsk, Czech Republic
Státní okresní archiv (SOkA), Hradec Králové, Czech Republic
Státní okresní archiv (SOkA), Kutná Hora, Czech Republic
 Okresní národní výbor (ONV) Čáslav
 Okresní národní výbor (ONV) Kutná Hora
Státní okresní archiv (SOkA), Lovosice, Czech Republic
 Okresní národní výbor (ONV) Litoměřice
Státní ústřední archiv (SÚA), Prague, Czech Republic
 Ministerstvo spravedlnosti (MS)
 Ministerstvo spravedlnosti-Londýn (MS-L)
 Ministerstvo vnitra – Nová registratura (MV-NR)
 Ministerstvo zahraničních věcí – Výstřižkový archiv (MZV-VA II)
 Národní soud (NS)
 Úřad předsednictva vlády-běžná spisovna (ÚPV-běž.)
 Zemský národní výbor (ZNV-Pr)
 f. 1 (ZÚV KSČ)
 f. 02/1 (KSČ Presidium)

f. 29 (Právnická komise KSČ)
f. 83 (tajné schůze Presidia vlády)
f. 100/24 (K. Gottwald)
Ústav pro soudobé dějiny (ÚSD), Prague, Czech Republic
Vladimír Krajina, memoirs.
Vojenský historický archiv (VHA), Prague, Czech Republic
f. Alexeje Čepičky
Zemský archiv (ZA), Opava, Czech Republic

CONTEMPORARY PERIODICALS

Árijský boj (Aryan Struggle)
Čechoslovák (Czechoslovak)
Cíl (Goal)
Dnešek (Today)
Kutnohorský kraj (Kutná Hora Country)
Lidová demokracie (People's Democracy)
Lidová správa (People's Administration)
Lidové noviny (People's News)
Masarykův lid (Masaryk's People)
Mladá fronta (Young Front)
Národní osvobození (National Liberation)
Obrana lidu (Defense of the People)
Obzory (Horizons)
Právní praxe (Legal Praxis)
Právo lidu (Right of the People)
Rudé právo (Red Right)
Svobodné Československo (Free Czechoslovakia)
Svobodné noviny (Free News)
Svobodné slovo (Free Word)
Svobodný zítřek (Free Tomorrow)
Těsnopisecké zprávy Prozatímního národního shromáždění Republiky českoslo-venské (Stenographic Records of the Provisional National Assembly of the Czechoslovak Republic)
Těsnopisecké zprávy Ústavodárného národního shromáždění Republiky českoslo-venské (Stenographic Records of the Constitutive National Assembly of the Czechoslovak Republic)
Věstník Ministerstva vnitra (Bulletin of the Ministry of Interior)
Věstník Okresního národního výboru Benešov (Bulletin of the Benešov ONV)
Věstník Okresního národního výboru v Klatovech (Bulletin of the Klatovy ONV)
The Weekly Bulletin
Zemědělské noviny (Agrarian News)

SELECTED CONTEMPORARY PUBLICATIONS, MEMOIRS, AND PUBLISHED DOCUMENTS

Baarová, Lída. *Útěky* (Toronto: Sixty-Eight Publishers, 1983).
———. *Život sladké hořkosti* (Ostrava: Sfinga, 1991).

Bareš, Gustav, ed. *Na soud lidu s válečnými zločinci a zrádci!* (Prague: Svoboda, 1945).

———, ed. *Rozhlasový projev předsedy vlády Zdeňka Fierlingera k dekretu o lidových soudech* (Prague: Svoboda, 1945).

Beneš, Edvard. *Demokracie dnes a zítra*, part 2 (London: Kruh přátel československé knihy, péčí "Čechoslovák," 1941).

———. *Šest let exilu a druhé světové války: Řeči, projevy a dokumenty z r. 1938–45* (Prague: Orbis, 1946).

———. *Světová krise, kontinuita práva o nové právo revoluční* (Prague: V. Linhart, 1946).

———. *Paměti: Od Mnichova k nové válce a k novému vítězství* (Prague: Orbis, 1947).

———. *Edvard Beneš: Odsun Němců: Výbor z pamětí a projevů doplněný edičními přilohami*, ed. by Věra Olivová (Prague: Společnost Edvarda Beneše, 1995).

———. *Edvard Beneš: Odsun Němců z Československa: Výbor z pamětí, projevů a dokumentů 1940–1947*, ed. by Karel Novotný (Prague: Dita, 1996).

———. *Edvard Beneš: Vzkazy do vlasti*, ed. by Jiří Šolc (Prague: Historický ústav AVČR, 1996).

Bude odsouzen zrádce J. A. Baťa? Sbírka dokladů o kolaborantské činnosti bývalého majitele závodů Baťa a. s., brazilského občana J. A. Baťa (Zlín: Baťa, Národní podnik, 1947).

Čepička, Alexej. *Zlidovění soudnictví* (Prague: Min. informací a osvěty, 1949).

Černý, Václav. *Paměti.* 3 vols (Brno: Atlantis, 1992).

Československo a Norimberský proces: Hlavní dokumenty norimberského procesu o zločinech nacistů proti Československu (Prague: Ministerstvo informací, 1946).

Chalupa, Vlastislav, Ivan Gad'ourek, and Mojmír Povolný, eds. *Tři roky: Přehledy a dokumenty k Československé politice v letech 1945–1948.* 3 vols. (Brno: Právnická fakulta Masarykova univerzita, 1991).

Diamond, William. *Czechoslovakia between East and West* (London: Stevens and Sons, 1947).

Drábek, Jaroslav. *Z časů dobrých a zlých* (Prague: Naše vojsko, 1992).

Drtina, Prokop. *A nyní promluví Pavel Svatý. . . . Londýnské rozhlasové epištoly z let 1940–1945* (Prague: Vladimír Zikeš, 1945).

———. *O soudcovské nezávislosti, lidovém soudnictví a jiných časových otázkách československé justice* (Prague: Mladá fronta, 1946).

———. *Na soudu národa: Tři projevy ministra spravedlnosti dr. Prokopa Drtiny o činnosti Mimořádných lidových soudů a Národního soudu* (Prague: Ministerstvo spravedlnosti, 1947).

———. *Právo v pojetí a díle presidenta dr. Edvarda Beneše* (Prague: Československý Kompas, 1947).

———. *Československo můj osud.* 3 vols. (Toronto: Sixty-Eight Publishers, 1982).

Duba, Josef. "Národní bezpečnost." In Josef Duba and Jaroslav Mildorf, eds., *Národní bezpečnost a národní očista* (Pilsen: ÚV KSČ, 1947), 5–22.

Dubský, Josef, Jaromír Mencl, and Miroslav Cihlář, eds. *Slovník lidové správy: Rukověť pro funkcionáře národních výborů* (Brno: Rovnost, 1947).

Grant Duff, Shiela, et al. *Czechoslovakia: Six Studies in Reconstruction* (London: The Fabian Society and George Allen & Unwin, c. 1946).

Ečer, Bohuslav. *Jak jsem je stíhal*, ed. by Edvard Cenek (Prague: Naše vojsko, 1946).

Feierabend, Ladislav. *Politické vzpomínky*. 3 vols. (Brno: Atlantis, 1994–1996).

Fierlinger, Zdeněk. *Ve službách ČSR: Paměti z druhého zahraničního odboje.* Vol. 1 (Prague: Dělnické nakladatelství, 1947).

———. *Ve službách ČSR: Paměti z druhého zahraničního odboje*, Vol. 2 (Prague: Svoboda, 1948).

Frank, Karl Hermann. *Zpověď K. H. Franka: Podle vlastních výpovědí v době vazby u Krajského soudu trestního na Pankráci* (Prague: Cíl, 1946).

———. *Český národ soudí K. H. Franka* (Prague: Ministerstvo informaci, 1947).

Fusek, Jaroslav. *Osvědčení o státní a národní spolehlivosti* (Brno: ZÁŘ, 1946).

———. *Provinění proti národní cti* (Prague: V. Linhart, 1946).

———. *Organisace a činnost ONV* (Prague: Ministerstvo Vnitra, 1947).

———. *Organizace a působnost MNV* (Prague: Ministerstvo Vnitra, 1947).

Gottwald, Klement. *O politice Komunistické strany Československa v dnešní situaci* (Prague: ÚV KSČ, 1945).

———. *O úloze bezpečnostního aparátu*, ed. by Vlastislav Kroupa (Prague: Naše vojsko, 1975).

Grňa, Josef. *Sedm roků na domácí frontě* (Brno: Blok, 1968).

Grospič, Jiří, Jaroslav Chovanec, and Juraj Vysokaj, eds. *Košický vládní program* (Prague: Státní pedagogické nakladatelsvtí, 1977).

Herben, Ivan. "Ďábel mluví německy." In *My a Němci: Dějinný úkol strany národně socialistické při vystěhování Němců z Československa* (Prague: Československa strana národně socialistická, 1945).

Hindus, Maurice. *The Bright Passage* (New York: Doubleday, 1947).

Hora, Ota. *Svědectví o puči* (Toronto: Sixty-Eight Publishers, 1978).

Hůrský, Josef. *Zjišťování národnosti: Úvod do problému odnárodnění* (Prague: Československý ústav zahraniční, 1947).

Jacoby, Gerhard. *Racial State: The German Nationalities Policy in the Protectorate of Bohemia and Moravia* (New York: Institute of Jewish Affairs of the AJC and WJC, 1944).

Jech, Karel, and Karel Kaplan, eds. *Dekrety prezidenta republiky 1940–1945: Dokumenty*. 2 vols. (Brno: Ústav pro soudobé dějiny AV ČR, 1995).

Jech, Karel, ed. "Dodatky k edici dokumentů Dekrety prezidenta republiky 1940–1945," unpublished manuscript.

Kaplan, Karel, ed. *Dva retribuční procesy: Komentované dokumenty (1946–1947)* (Prague: Ústav pro soudobé dějiny ČSAV, 1992).

———. *ČSR a SSSR: Dokumenty mezivládních jednání, 1945–1948* (Brno: Doplněk, 1997).

Kennan, George F. *From Prague after Munich: Diplomatic Papers, 1938–1940* (Princeton, NJ: Princeton University Press, 1968).

Klimeš, Miloš, ed. *Cesta ke Květnu: Vznik lidové demokracie v Československu* (Prague: Československá akademie věd, 1965).

Kopecký, Václav. *ČSR a KSČ: Pamětní výpisy k historii Československé republiky a k boji KSČ za socialistické Československo* (Prague: Státní nakladatelství politické literatury, 1960).

Krajina, Vladimír. *Vysoká hra: Vzpomínky* (Prague: Eva, 1994).

Král, Václav. *Pravda o okupaci* (Prague: Naše vojsko, 1962).

———. *Cestou k Únoru: Dokumenty* (Prague: Svobodné slovo, 1963).

Laštovička, Bohumil. *V Londýně za války: Zápasy o novou ČSR 1939–1945* (Prague: Svoboda, 1978).

Liška, Otakar, et al. *Vykonané tresty smrti Československo 1918–1989* (Prague: Úřad dokumentace a vyšetřování zločinů komunismu, 2000).

Mandlová, Adina. *Dneska už se tomu směju* (Toronto: Sixty-Eight Publishers, 1976).

Matějka, Dobroslav, ed. *Právní aspekty odsunu sudetských Němců* (Prague: Ústav mezinárodních vztahů, 1995).

Mildorf, Jaroslav. "Trestání zrádců, kolaborantů a šmelinářů." In Josef Duba and Jaroslav Mildorf, eds., *Národní bezpečnost a národní očista* (Pilsen: ÚV KSČ, 1947), 23–30.

Mucha, Josef, and Karel Petrželka. *O některých současných problémech národnostně smíšených manželství* (Prague: Svoboda, 1946).

Otáhalová, Libuše, and Milada Červinková, eds. *Dokumenty z historie československé politiky 1939–1943.* 2 vols. (Prague: Academia, 1966).

Peroutka, Ferdinand. *Ferdinand Peroutka: Deníky, dopisy, vzpomínky* (Prague: Lidové noviny, 1995).

Plzák, Josef. "Malý retribuční dekret (Dekret pres. rep. č. 138/1945 Sb.) ve světle judikatury Nejvyššího správního soudu," *Právní prakse* 11 (1947/48) 113–31.

Polák, Ervín. *Čísla mluví o voličích a o národních výborech* (Prague: Státní tiskárna, 1947).

Program první československé vlády národní fronty Čechů a Slováků přijatý 5. dubna 1945 v Košicích (Prague: Rudé právo, 1955).

Ripka, Hubert. *Le Coup de Prague: Une Révolution préfabriquée* (Paris: Librairie Plon, 1949).

———. *Czechoslovakia Enslaved: The Story of the Communist Coup d'Etat* (London: Victor Gollancz, 1950).

Sbírka zákonů a nařízení republiky Československa, Vols. 1945–1948 (Prague: Státní tiskárna, 1945–1949).

Sbírka dekretů presidenta republiky: Souhrn všech dekretů, jež byly vydány. (Brno: Zemského výkonného výboru čs. strany národně socialistické [Melantrich], c. 1945).

Schieder, Theodor, ed. *The Expulsion of the German Population from Czechoslovakia: A selection and Translation from Dokumentation der Vertreibung der Deutschen aus Ost-Mittel Europa, Band IV, 1 und IV, 2,* trans. by G. H. de Sausmarez et al. (Bonn: Federal Ministry for Expellees, Refugees, and War Victims, 1960).

Šebestík, Josef, and Zdeněk Lukeš, eds. *Přehled předpisů o Němcích a osobách považovaných za Němce* (Prague: Státní tiskárna, 1946).

Šedivý, Karel. *Why We Want to Transfer the Germans* (Prague: Orbis, 1946).

Sobota, Emil. *Co to byl protektorát* (Prague: Kvasnička a Hampl, 1946).

Sokol, Rudolf, and Marta Sokolová, ed. *Rukověť pro národní výbory v zemi České a Moravoslezské pro rok 1947* (Prague: Státní tiskárna, 1947).

Stach, Jindřich. *Provinění proti národní cti* (Brno: ZÁŘ, 1946).

Štafl, Adolf. *Národní výbory: Místní, okresní, ústřední, zemské a Ústřední národní výbor Hlavního města Prahy* (Prague: V. Linhart, 1947).

Statistická příručka Československé republiky (Prague: Státní úřad statistický, 1948).

Stransky, Jan. *East Wind over Prague* (New York: Random House, 1951).

Sudetendeutscher Rat E. V. München. *Justiz im Dienste der Vergeltung: Erlebnisberichte und Dokumente über die Rechtsprechung der tschechoslowaskischen Ausserordentlichen Volksgerichte gegen Deutsche (1945–1948)* (Munich: Dr. C. Wolf & Sohn, 1962).

Šulc, Stanislav. *Národní výbor: Vývoj, právní základy, poslání, práce* (Brno: ZÁŘ, 1946).

Taborsky, Edward. *Czechoslovak Democracy at Work* (London: George Allen & Unwin, 1945).

———. *President Edvard Benes: Between East and West, 1938–1948* (Stanford, CA: Hoover Institute Press, 1981).

Turnwald, W. K., ed. *Documents on the Expulsion of the Sudeten Germans*. (Munich: Dr. C. Wolf & Son, 1953).

U.S. Department of State. *Records of the U.S. Department of State Relating to the Internal Affairs of Czechoslovakia, 1945–1949*. Decimal file 860f, General Records, Record Group 59, National Archives, Washington, D.C. (Wilmington, DE: Scholarly Resources, 1986).

Vartíková, Marta, ed. *Komunistická strana Slovenska: Dokumenty z konferencií a plén 1944–1948* (Bratislava: Pravda, 1971).

Verner, Vladimír. *Státní občanství a domovské právo Republiky československé* (Prague: V. Tomsa, 1947).

Veselý, Zdeněk, ed. *Sborník dokumentů a materiálů k studiu nejnovějších dějin Československa*. Vol. I (1945–1948) (Prague: Státní pedagogické nakladatelství, 1986).

Vondrová, Jitka. *Češi a sudetoněmecká otázka 1939–1945: Dokumenty* (Prague: Ústav mezinárodních vztahů, 1994).

Wechsberg, Joseph. *Homecoming* (New York: Alfred A. Knopf, 1946).

"Zemřeli ve věznicích a tresty smrti 1948–1956." *Seznamy*, Dokumenty o perzekuci a odporu, part 1 (Prague: Ústav pro soudobé dějiny, 1992).

Zieris, Karel F. "The New Czech Press." In *Newspapers and Newspapermen in Czechoslovakia* (Prague: Union of Czech Journalists, 1947), 30–37.

———. *Nové základy českého periodického tisku* (Prague: Orbis, 1947).

INDEX

INDEX

INDEX

INDEX

Studies in the Social and Cultural History of Modern Warfare

Titles in the series: